The Masterworks of Monet

The Masterworks of
MONET

Douglas Mannering

Colour Library Direct

CLD 21249
This edition was printed in 1999 for
Colour Library Direct
Godalming Business Centre,
Woolsack Way,
Godalming,
Surrey GU7 1XW

This edition first published in Great Britian in 1997
by Parragon
13 Whiteladies Road,
Clifton, Bristol BS8 1PB

Reprinted in 1998

ISBN 1-84100-001-9

Editor: Linda Doeser
Design Director: Robert Mathias Publishing Workshop
Designer: Helen Mathias
Picture research: Charlotte Deane
Special thanks go to Joanna Hartley of the Bridgeman Art Library, London
for her invaluable help

Contents

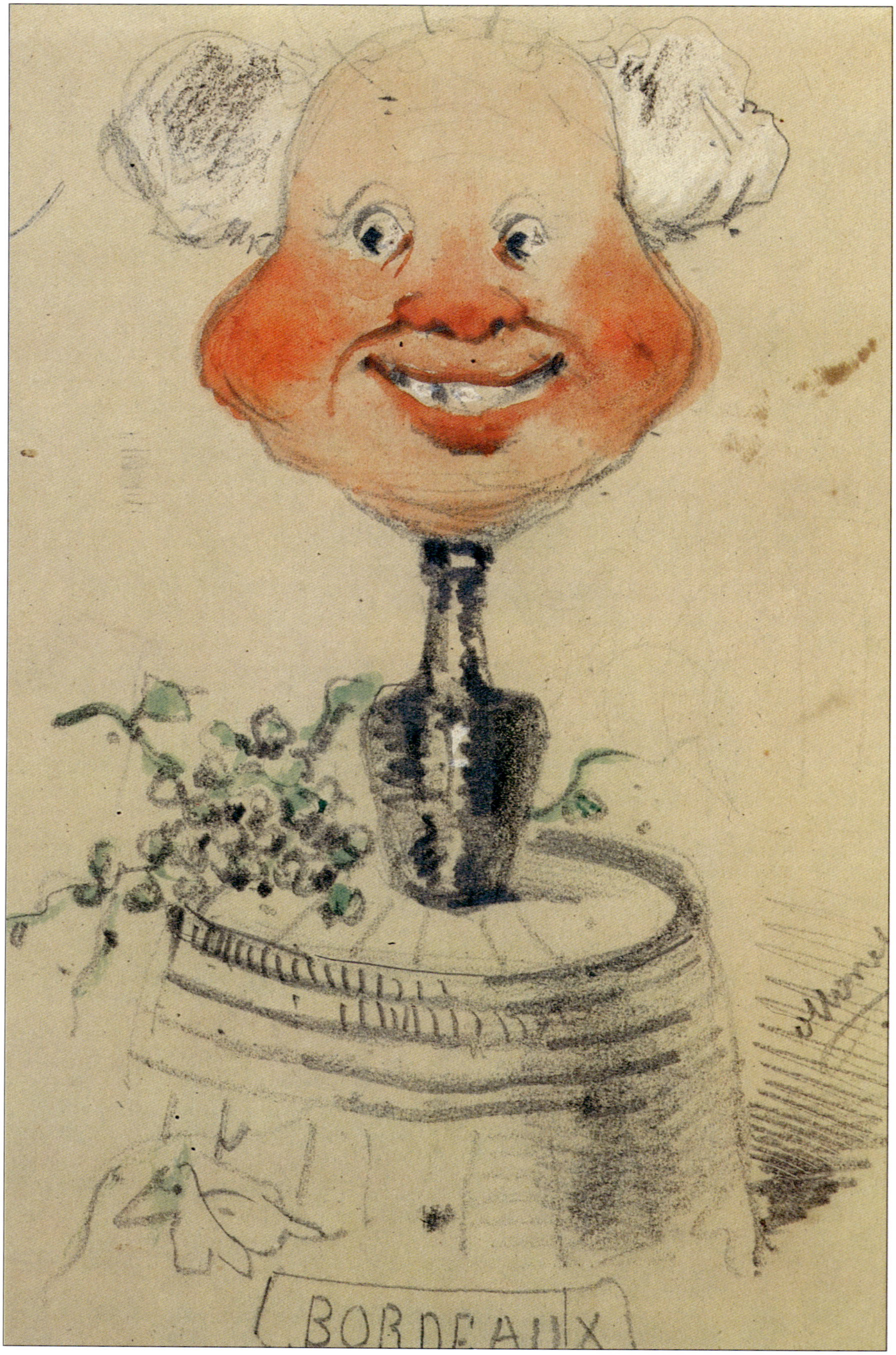
BORDEAUX

CHAPTER ONE

The Young Monet

NINETEENTH-CENTURY FRENCH PAINTING was transformed by a small group of artists who became known – at first in mockery – as the Impressionists. Once abused as incompetent daubs, their canvases are now universally admired for their brilliant, joyful celebration of the world about them. Among the notable achievements of Impressionism was its revelation of the dazzling possibilities of landscape painting, especially when it was practised by an artist prepared to set up an easel in the open air and work freely and spontaneously to capture the fugitive moods of nature. Of all the Impressionists, Claude Monet was the most dedicated to recording the impression of the moment. For most of his long life he travelled indefatigably, seeking new settings and effects; his 2,000 completed paintings, light-saturated, vibrantly coloured and intensely atmospheric, make up an unrivalled achievement. However, Monet's story is far from being a tale of unbroken triumphs for, like most of his fellow Impressionists, he achieved worldly success only after decades of poverty and struggle.

Oscar-Claude Monet was born in Paris, at 45 Rue Lafitte, on 14

LEFT:
Caricature
MUSÉE MARMOTTAN, PARIS

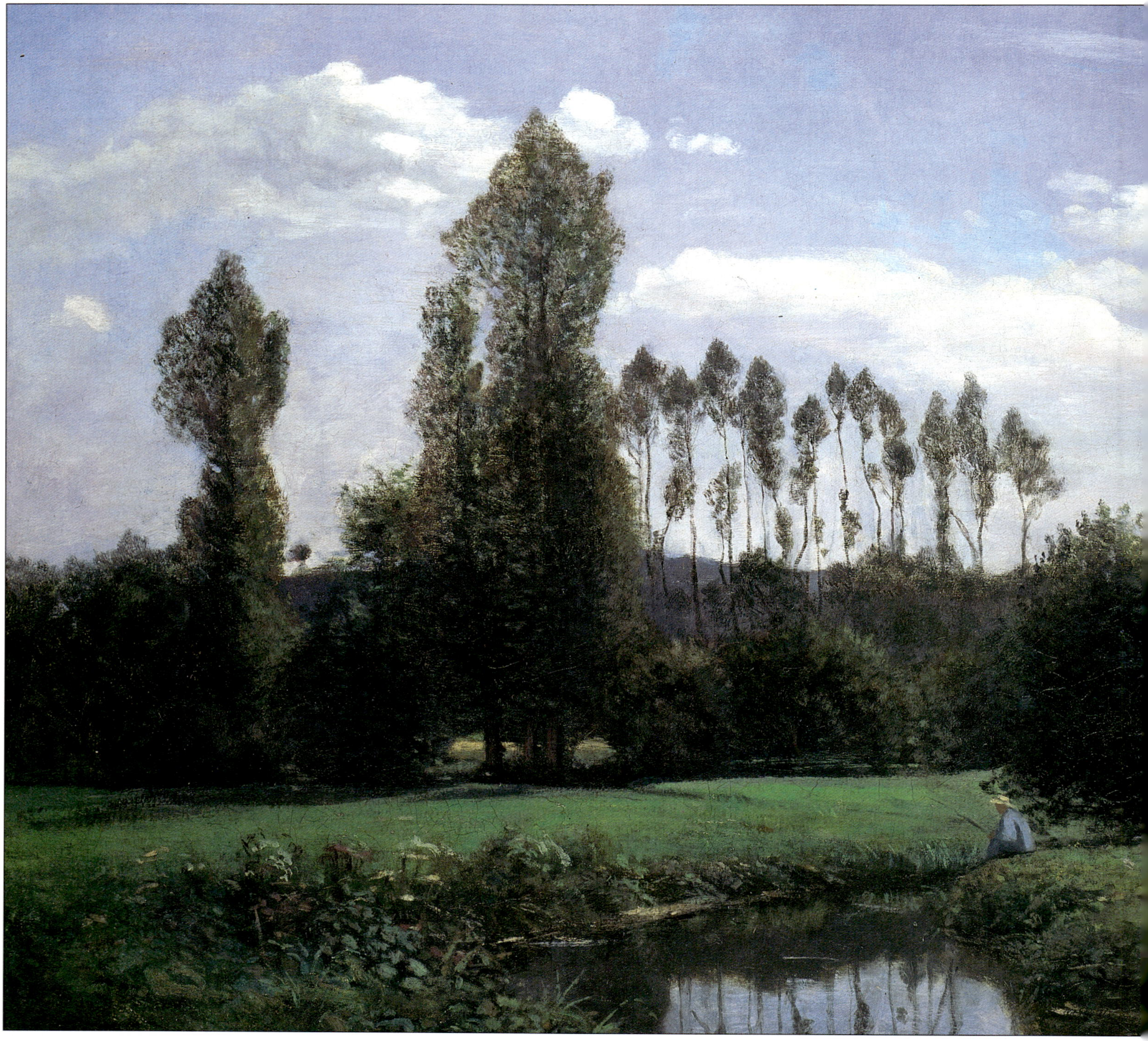

November, 1840. But his family left the capital before he was five years old, and Monet was never destined to become a true Parisian. His father, Adolphe Monet, went into partnership with his brother-in-law, a wholesale grocer and ship's chandler, at Le Havre in Normandy, where the Monets settled. Oscar, as his parents preferred to call him, grew up in Le Havre, a bustling port at the mouth of the River Seine; the sea, the river and the surrounding Norman countryside were always to be among the great passions of his life and art.

Even during his boyhood, Monet preferred tramping in the open air to working indoors – especially when indoors meant the schoolroom. If his later reminiscences are to be believed, he was an inveterate truant who rarely completed the journey between home and class. Whether this was so, Monet certainly left the Collège Communal as soon as possible – at 16 – without sitting a single examination. As he evidently had no intention of joining the family business, it looks as though Monet was already developing a notably headstrong, rebellious personality.

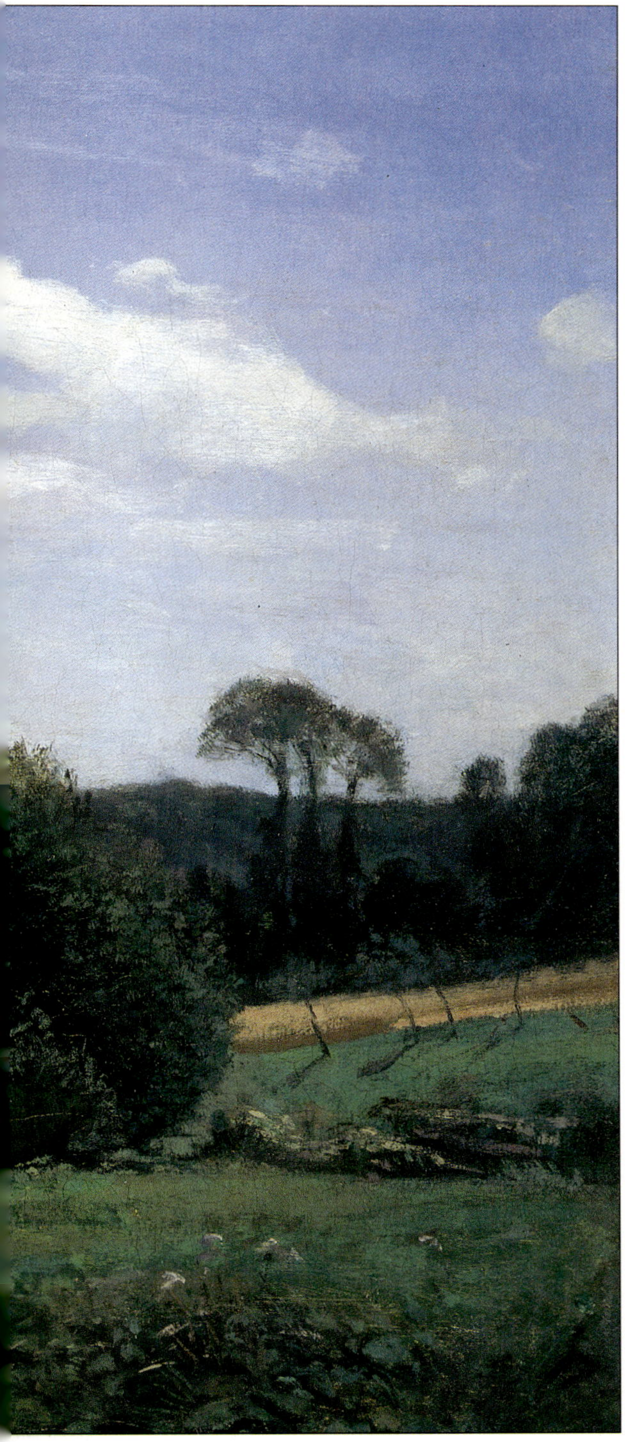

ABOVE:
Landscape at Rouelles (1858)
PRIVATE COLLECTION

Early Success

His artistic talent was also becoming apparent, although it took an unexpected direction at first. If Monet learned anything from his drawing master at school, Jacques-François Ochard, he never acknowledged the debt. During his years of fame he was anxious to portray himself as a self-created genius in the Romantic tradition, with no debts to the past or banal growing pains. Nevertheless, albums of competent drawings have come to light which show that Monet, like most young artists, began by imitating received models before starting to find his own way. Then, as a teenager, he became not a conventional artist but a highly proficient caricaturist, basing his early efforts on magazine pictures and then turning his pen on his teachers, his family and friends and well-known local figures. Using the cartoonist's time-honoured tricks, he gave his victims large heads set on shrunken bodies and emphasized distinctive features, such as mighty noses, wild eyebrows and luxuriant growths of side-whisker.

The results were impressive enough to make him a minor celebrity in Le Havre, where Monet found clients willing to pay him ten or 20 francs a time for a portrait. Later, characteristically dramatizing the past, he declared that 'If I had carried on, I should have been a millionaire by now!'. It was certainly ironic that Monet, the great master of colour, received his first commissions because he was so good at drawing and that, at 17, he had more gratifying commercial successes than he was to enjoy again until he was a middle-aged man.

Some drawings by the celebrated 'O. Monet' were displayed in the window of Gravier's, a shop in Le Havre that sold artists'

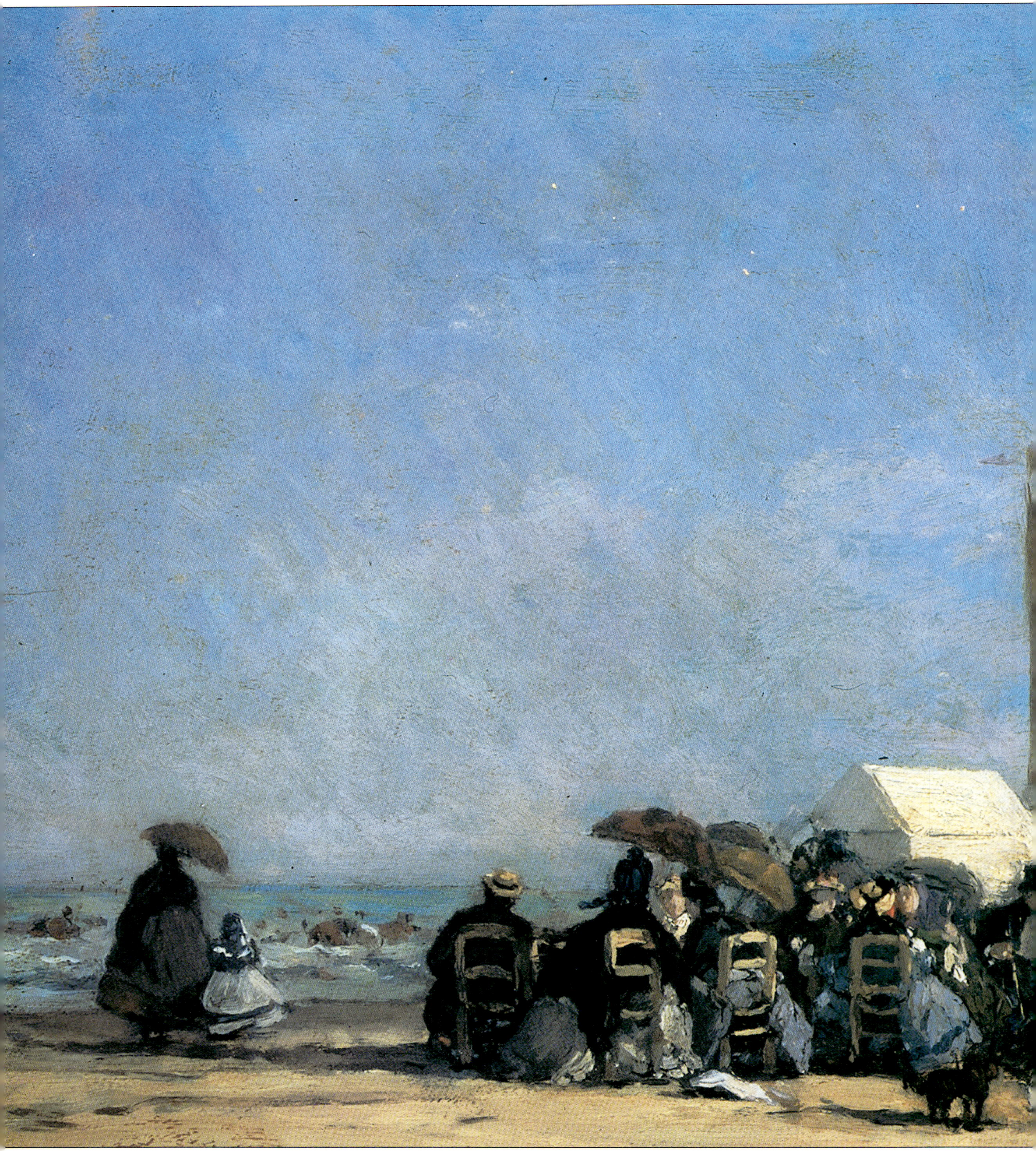

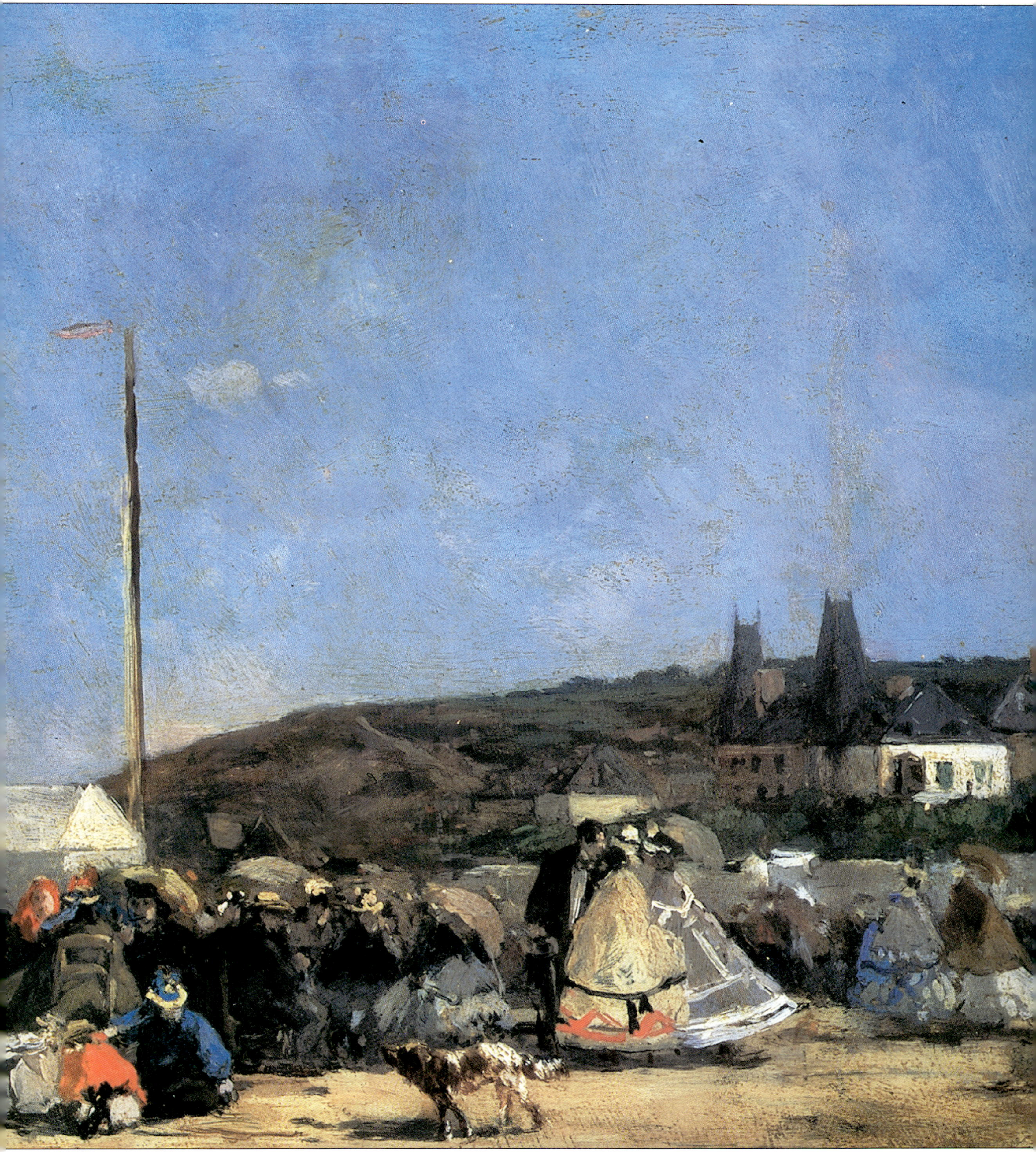

PREVIOUS PAGES 10-11:
The Beach at Trouville (1864)
Eugène Boudin
MUSÉE D'ORSAY, PARIS

materials and offered a picture framing service. The teenager's works shared the space with landscapes by a local artist in his early thirties, Eugène Boudin (1824–98), and nothing could have been more natural than an encounter between the two men and the development of a friendship based on mutual interests. However, Monet actually avoided Boudin for as long as he could, since he shared the general low opinion of the older artist's paintings. Even after they had been introduced by Gravier and had found each other personally congenial, Monet took a good deal of persuading before he would venture to work side by side with Boudin.

Boudin's eccentricity was to believe that paintings done directly from nature had a vitality and freshness that could never be achieved by the conventional method, which was to work up an elaborate composition in the studio. A few recognized artists, such as Camille Corot (1796–1875) and Charles-François Daubigny (1817–78), shared Boudin's outlook to some degree, but it was a view slow to find favour with the art establishment or the general public.

The notion of painting outdoors was of recent vintage, since it had only been made possible in the 1840s by the development of portable tubes of paint. Even so, it was regarded as a dubious notion, for there was felt to be something ungentlemanly – too reminiscent of manual work – in clumping around the countryside, weighed down with easel, canvas, palette, brushes and paints. (Even half a century later, the British Impressionist Wilson Steer passed himself off in hotels as a respectable person by concealing his equipment in a capacious cricket bag.) In mid-nineteenth-century France, under the authoritarian Second Empire, the landscapist might even be seen as politically suspect. The Imperial Superintendent of Fine Arts, Count Emilien Nieuwerkerke, distrusted the intentions of even 'respectable' landscapists such as Corot and Daubigny, announcing loftily that 'This is the painting of democrats, of people who don't change their linen and want to put themselves above men of the world. This art displeases and disquiets me.'

Monet's prejudices were soon overcome, and during the summer of 1858, working alongside Boudin, he produced his first *plein-air* (open air) landscapes. One of these was the charming *Landscape at Rouelles* (pages 8-9), a painting of precocious assurance and skill that was shown in late summer at the Le Havre municipal exhibition. Beside Monet's later works it looks quite conventional, but its brightness and sense of enjoyment were already rather unusual by the standards of the time.

RIGHT:
Alfred Sisley and his Wife (c.1868)
Pierre-Auguste Renoir
WALLRAF-RICHARTZ MUSEUM, COLOGNE

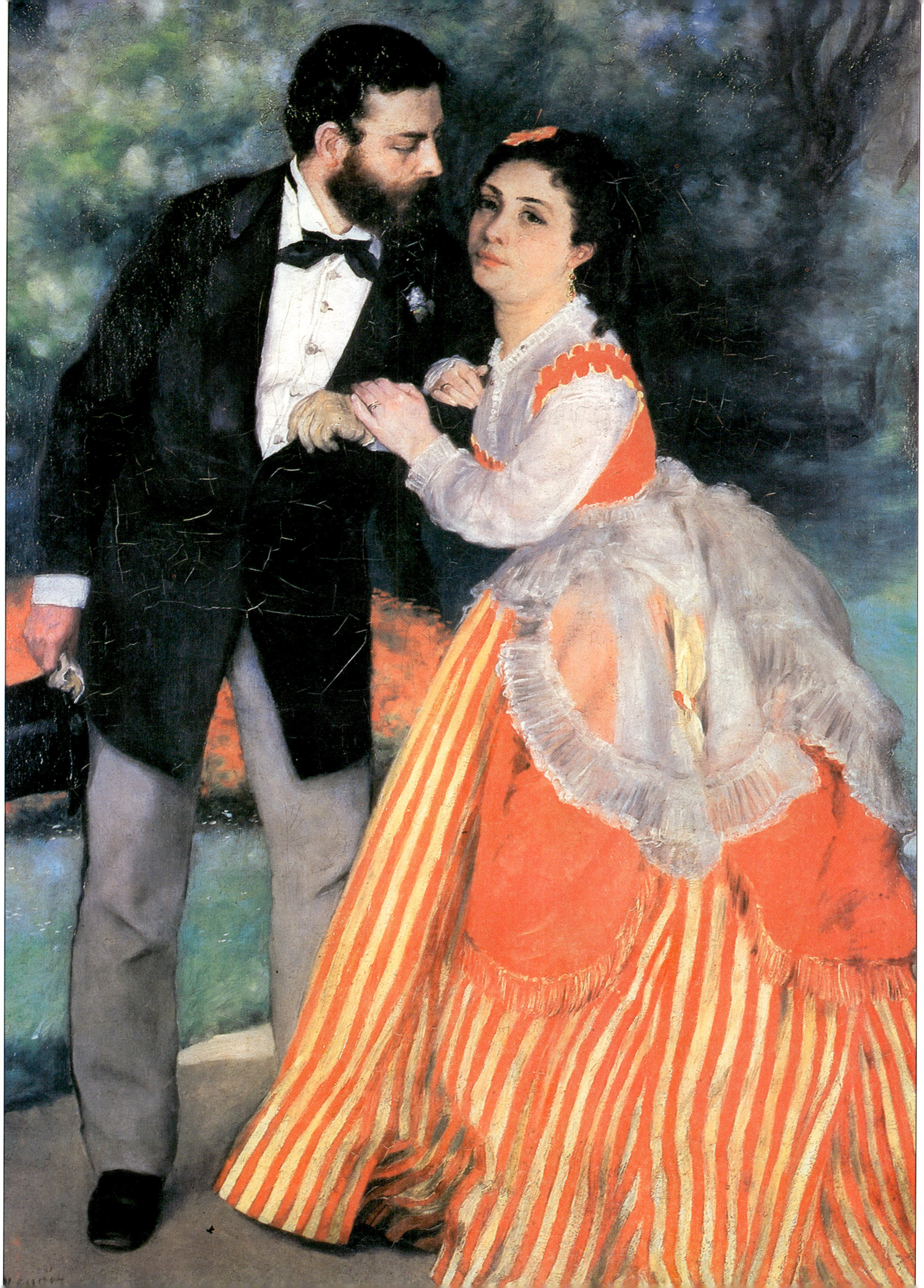

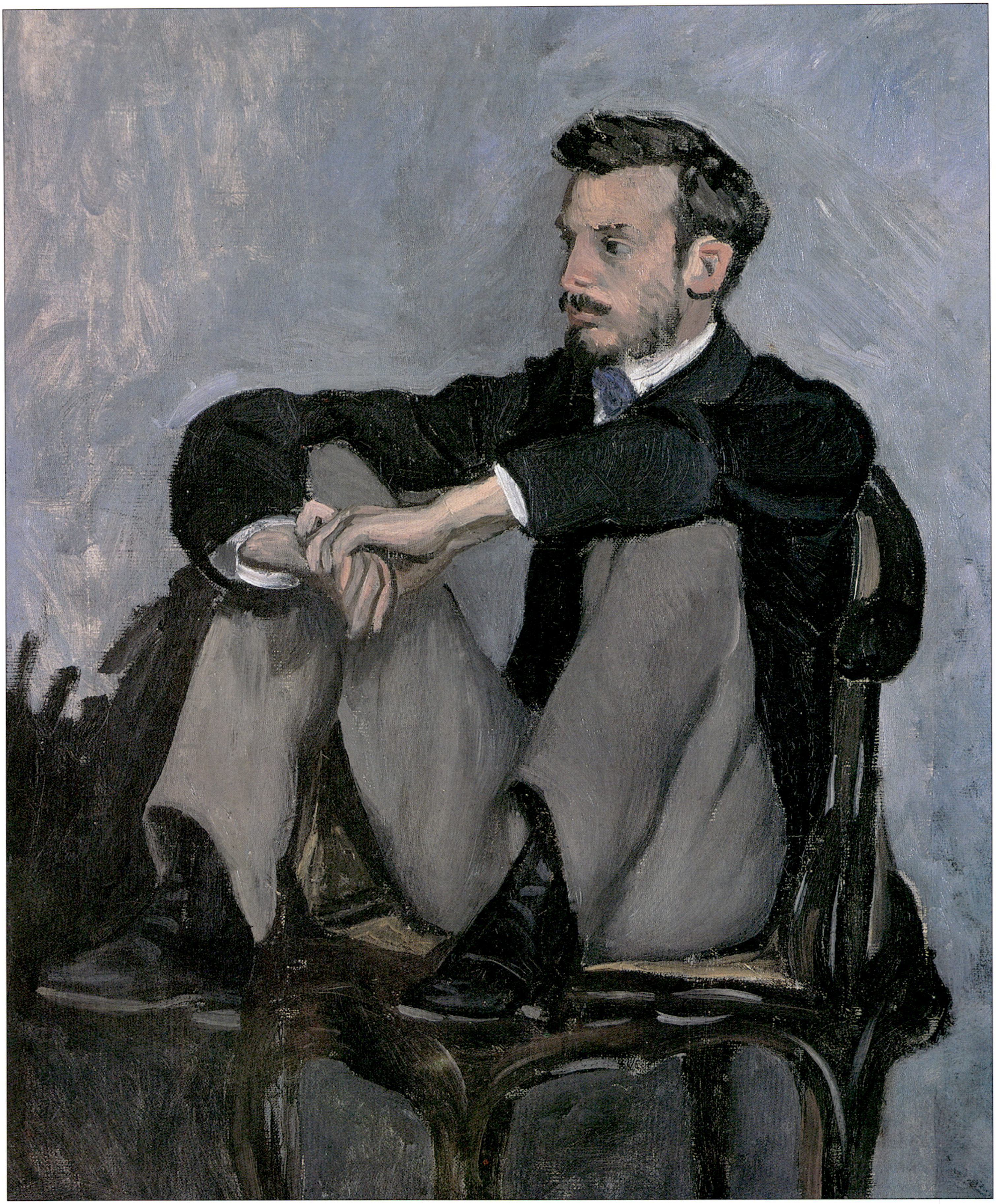

Monet's conversion was permanent: painting out of doors in all weathers became so central to Monet's art that the importance of his early friendship with Boudin can hardly be overstated: 'Gradually my eyes were opened,' he later declared, 'and I understood nature'. Ironically, Boudin himself was torn between his impulse to paint landscapes and seascapes, and a conviction that art should be socially relevant. At his best, in a painting such as *Beach at Trouville* (pages 10-11), he managed to combine the two in a particularly charming fashion.

Monet was also struck by the high seriousness with which Boudin approached his art; perhaps for the first time, the young man realized that painting might be more than a hobby or a profitable sideline. Within a few months, Monet's family was informed that he had found his vocation.

A Trip to Paris

The news seems to have been received calmly enough. Monet's mother was dead and his father had no particular sympathy with art or artists. However, he had an ally in his aunt Marie-Jeanne Lecadre, Adolphe Monet's sister and the widow of his partner; herself an enthusiastic amateur artist, she allowed Monet to use her attic as a studio and proved to be a generous provider of art materials and much-needed funds. She may not have had much difficulty in persuading her brother that this was an opportunity to place the unpromising Claude in a career for which he had at least a modicum of talent.

Adolphe agreed to let Monet go ahead, but he was unable or unwilling to finance him. Instead, he applied to the municipality on his son's behalf, requesting a study grant. The application was refused on the rather odd grounds that Monet was unlikely to be weaned away for long from his profitable trade in caricatures and portraits. Evidently the local authority could not believe that a young man who was capable of making good money would turn to the 'more serious but less rewarding' study of art.

Pending a second application, Monet was allowed to spend some time in Paris laying the foundations of his career. Boudin and Marie-Jeanne Lecadre gave him introductions to a leading Parisian master, Constant Troyon. Although Troyon was a landscapist with considerable breadth of sympathies (he had encouraged Boudin's independent efforts), the advice he gave to Monet was well-meaning but conventional: to work in a studio under the

LEFT:
Portrait of Auguste Renoir (1867)
Frédéric Bazille
MUSÉE D'ORSAY, PARIS

RIGHT:
Farmyard in Normandy
(c.1864)
MUSÉE D'ORSAY, PARIS

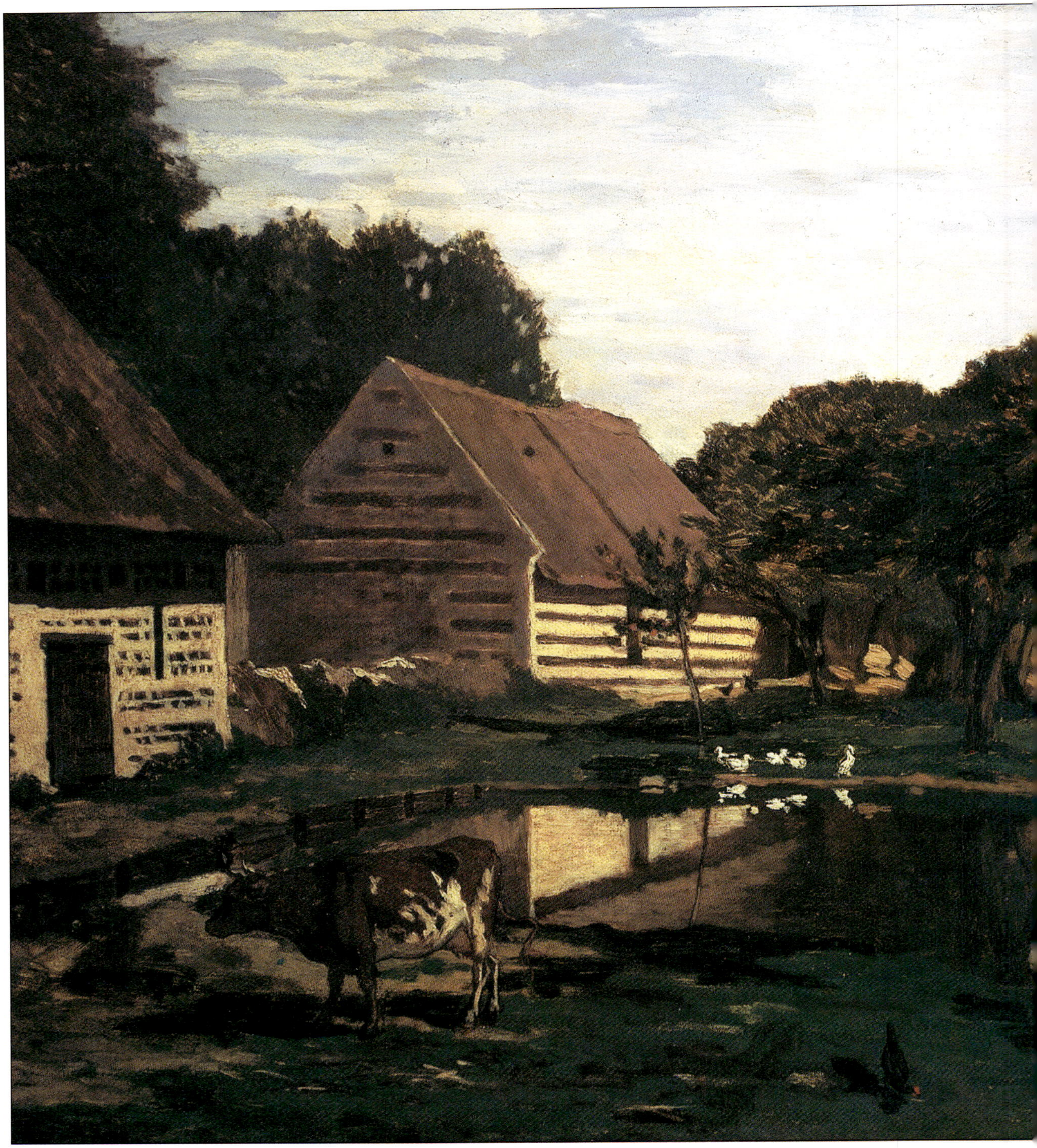

tutelage of a recognized master, to study drawing and to copy the masterpieces in the capital's magnificent museum, the Louvre.

Predictably, Monet took little notice of Troyon's words of wisdom. Like many a young provincial in Paris, he was besotted by the glamour of the capital, delighting in the city's bohemian café life and the bustle of the great boulevards, which were still being laid down in the 1850s. He later claimed to regret spending so much time at the Brasserie des Martyrs, a smoke-filled café-bar much

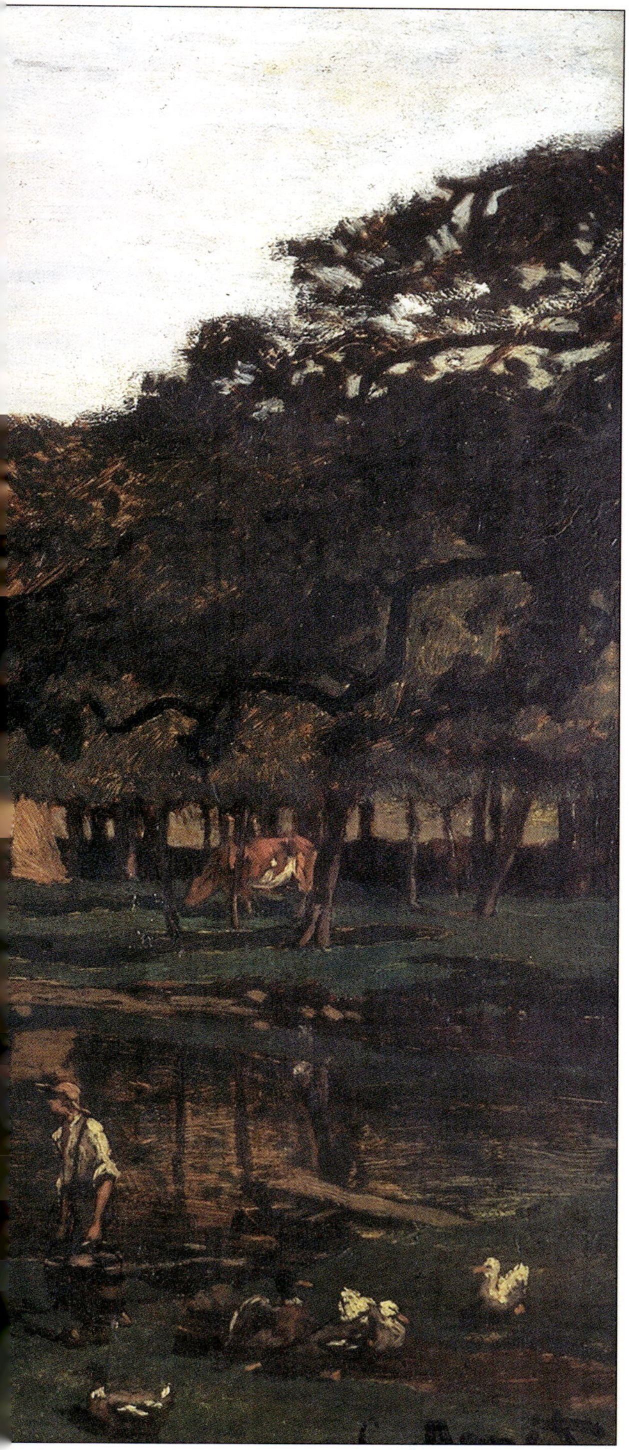

patronized by writers and artists; its dominant figure, the realist painter Gustave Courbet, would later become one of Monet's friends, but during this period he was away – ironically, in Normandy, where he met Boudin.

Monet did find time to visit the Salon – the official show of contemporary art, held in May at the Palais d'Industrie – where his enthusiasm was almost exclusively reserved for the works of Corot, Daubigny, Troyon and other landscapists. Since landscape painting was regarded at this time as a minor art, Monet's responses were obviously genuine, revealing that his preference for truth to nature was already well established. Implicitly, by omission, he rejected as worthless the fashionably grandiose paintings inspired by history and mythology that were regarded by the general public as great art.

During his months in Paris, Monet did go to work in a studio, but not one in which a master undertook to supervise and correct pupils. He enrolled at the Académie Suisse, an unprepossessing building on the Quai des Orfèvres where generations of rebellious artists before and after Monet found a congenial atmosphere in which to work – or play – at being artists. Its title was deceptive, for it was, in fact, a 'free' studio, open to any would-be artist on payment of a small fee and providing no more than a live model and space in which to work. Perhaps Adolphe Monet, like other parents both before and afterwards, felt reassured when he was told that his son was to be seen regularly at an 'academy'.

At the Suisse, Monet became friendly with a fellow student, Camille Pissarro (1830–1903), who had quitted his birthplace in the Danish West Indies to make a career as a painter in France. Designating himself a follower of Corot, he was, although ten years older than Monet, still slowly finding his way. Pissarro was to become Monet's comrade-in-arms as one of the founding figures of Impressionism, but during this period the friendship was short-lived, lapsing for some years when the younger man left Paris early in 1861 and seemingly renounced the art of painting for the art of war.

Algerian Interlude

This abrupt change of direction was not entirely voluntary. Every Frenchman was liable to be conscripted into the army, but in practice only a minority of young men in any particular 'year' were summoned to serve. The choice was made by lot and Monet was one of the unlucky ones whose number came up. However, middle-class people

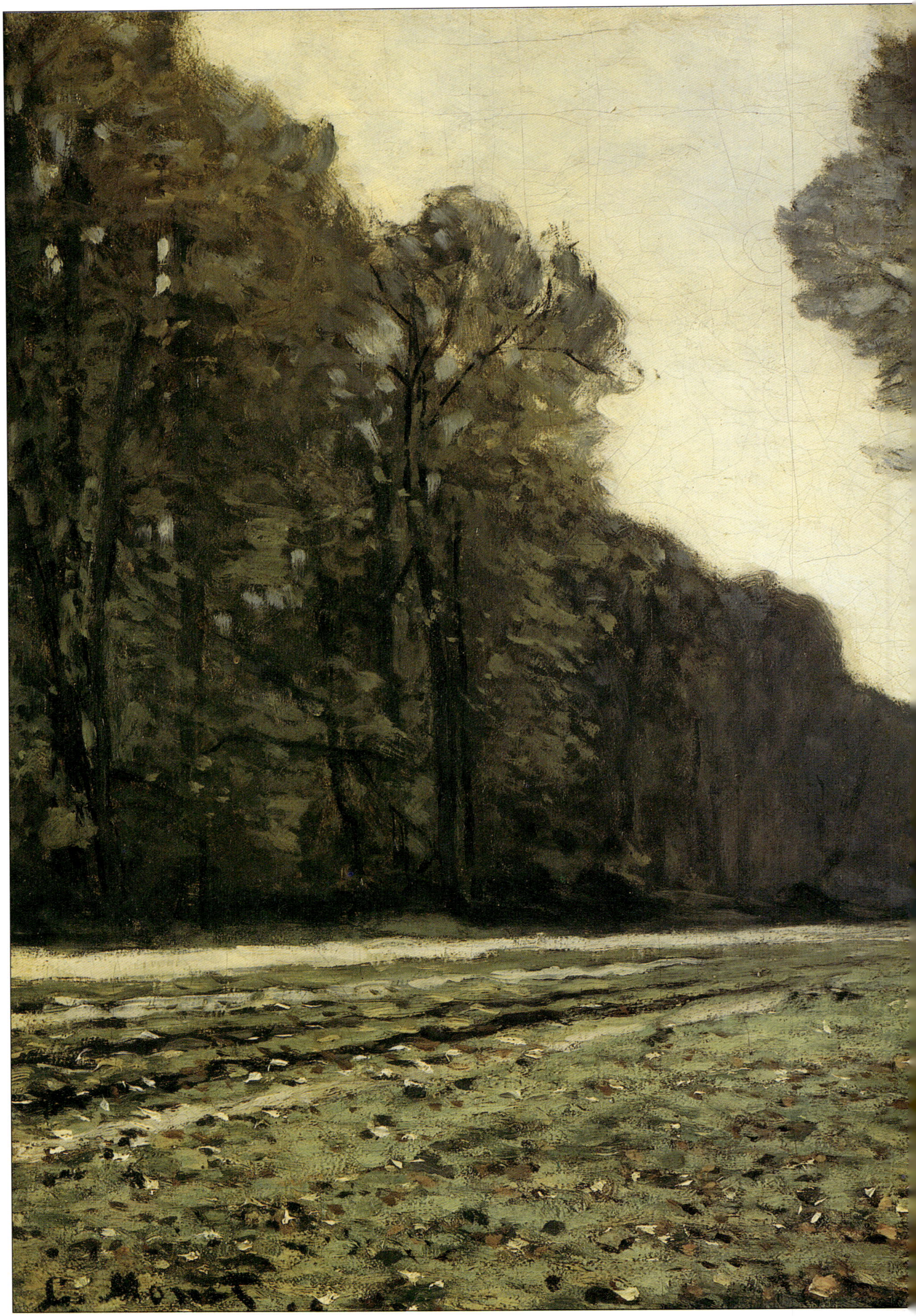

RIGHT: **The Road to Chailly** (1865)
MUSÉE D'ORSAY, PARIS

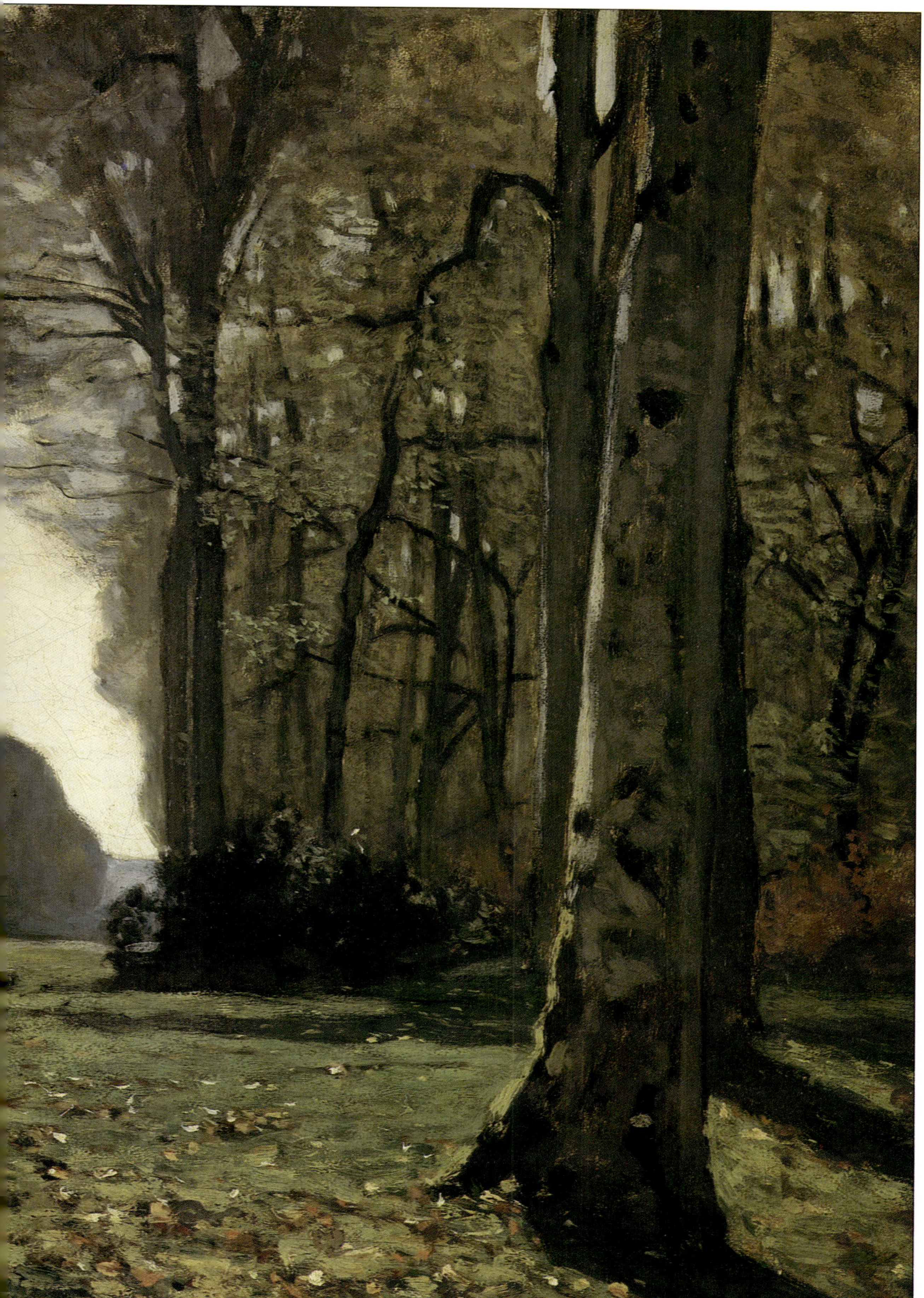

normally put down the cash needed to buy their sons out of the service and provide a substitute. The army held few attractions for them, as it was run by and for an aristocratic officer caste, offering no reasonable prospects of promotion; and the term of service was a daunting five years. Understandably, no young man who hoped to make a career for himself would want to spend such a large part of his prime as a common soldier; yet this was to be Monet's fate.

It is hard to understand why Adolphe Monet allowed his son to be taken. One theory is that Claude's overlong stay in Paris and bohemian lifestyle made Adolphe feel that he needed to be rescued from bad habits and bad company. It is also possible that, once chosen, Claude was swept away by the romance of military life and actually decided to go. He certainly displayed his characteristic forcefulness in pushing to gain admission to a cavalry regiment, the Chasseurs d'Afrique, whose splendid scarlet uniform he donned to great effect. Service with the Chasseurs also meant a posting to Algeria, a land recently conquered by the French and, viewed through the paintings of a great Romantic artist such as Eugène Delacroix, the quintessence of oriental exoticism.

Monet's period of service in Algeria was largely uneventful, even offering him opportunities to paint. Although he liked to claim that the colours of the Algerian landscape influenced his later development, the entire episode seems an odd irrelevancy in a life whose dedication to art gives it an almost novelistic unity. After a year or so, Monet fell ill with typhoid, was sent home to convalesce and never went back into the army – bought out with 3,000 francs largely provided by his ever-helpful aunt.

Monet spent his six-week-long convalescence painting and sketching around Le Havre. For much of the time he was accompanied by Boudin or by a new friend, Johan Barthold Jongkind (1819–91). Although Dutch, Jongkind had worked mainly in northern France since 1846, producing many views of the Normandy coast and the Seine estuary, areas later to be closely identified with Monet. He also experimented by painting the same subject in different lights, an approach that Monet would take to its logical conclusion in his celebrated series paintings (see Chapter 9). At this time, Jongkind, already 42 years old, served as the younger man's master, teaching in the way that Monet found easiest to assimilate, by example rather than precept; Jongkind's watercolours were particularly impressive.

On the other hand, he could be a distinct social liability, letting slip while dining with the highly proper Monet family that his lady companion was not his lawful wife; the incident certainly deepened Adolphe Monet's reservations about his son's way of life. Monet himself remained sufficiently middle class to be alarmed by Jongkind's alcoholic excesses, of which rumours had reached him even before their meeting. At one point he wrote to tell Boudin that the Dutchman was in such a bad way that he had 'become dead to art'. Jongkind seems to have been as tough as he was erratic and came back to life and art with no apparent ill effects. Monet introduced his new friend to Boudin, and in 1864, the three artists made a joint painting expedition to Honfleur on the other side of the Seine estuary.

A Student in Paris

In the meantime, Monet's family had become increasingly uneasy about the company he was keeping and the apparent aimlessness of his lifestyle; even Aunt Lecadre felt that the kind of work he was doing in the open air – mere sketching, after all – was leading nowhere. Threatened with the loss of his allowance and lured by visions of Paris and independence, Monet agreed to return to the capital. This time, however, he was to report to his cousin, a medal-winning painter named Auguste Toulmouche, who would ensure that he took all the proper steps to establish himself as a successful professional artist. In November 1862, almost 22 years old, Monet set off for the capital again. Toulmouche was to figure less prominently in Monet's life than the family expected, but he did give the young painter a suitably respectable start. At his cousin's direction, Monet became a pupil in the studio of the Swiss painter Charles Gleyre. Around this time, as a small gesture of independence, he dropped the name 'Oscar' and henceforth signed all his works 'Claude Monet'.

Gleyre had made his reputation as a painter of historical-sentimental subjects in the nineteenth-century manner, their story content emphasized by titles such as *Lost Illusions* (which actually was Gleyre's most celebrated work). Nothing could have been more unlike Monet's art, which was always inspired by what he was able to see with his own eyes.

Successful painters like Gleyre were exponents of what is now known as academic art – that is, art of the kind that was taught and promoted by the official academies. In France, where patronage and publicity were very largely controlled by the state-established

Academy of Fine Arts, it was difficult for a painter without private means to survive at all outside the system – as Monet and other Impressionists would discover.

Generally speaking, academic paintings were smooth-surfaced and meticulously detailed. Superficially, they look almost as truthful as photographs in their rendering of people and places, although to modern eyes their sentiments are quite obviously overblown or false. Actually, they were not intended to be realistic in any broad sense, as it was held that the aim of art was to dignify and ennoble existence, presenting ideal types and exemplary situations. Charles Gleyre told Monet's fellow pupil, Pierre-Auguste Renoir, that it would be wrong to paint the big toe of Germanicus, a Roman hero, in the same way as you would paint the big toe of a coalman; although the example was ludicrous, it accurately represented the academic viewpoint.

Not surprisingly, the academic authorities – and a biddable general public – regarded large-scale historical and mythological paintings as the highest forms of pictorial art. Certain types of moralistic and anecdotal subjects were also acceptable, and so were landscapes, provided they were painted in the approved, highly finished style; however, since they were not morally elevating, they occupied a relatively low place in the artistic hierarchy.

The Academy was even able to control what the public saw, since the exhibits at the one major art show – the Salon – were chosen by an officially appointed jury. The Salon had no rivals, for there were, as yet, no dealers or independent galleries or exhibitions of any great consequence. Even the painter whose work was selected for exhibition could fail – often by simply passing unnoticed if his pictures were hung too high on the crowded walls ('up in the sky', as the habitués said). There seemed to be no appeal against failure at the Salon, which was held only once every two years (once a year after 1863), except to try again. Every painter, however rebellious by temperament, hoped for success at the Salon, and Monet was to be no exception.

Working at Gleyre's was intended to be a first step in an official career-progress that would lead to prizes, medals, lucrative state commissions and an official decoration. But even during his first week in the studio Monet found it hard to conform. While he was diligently painting the nude male model provided for the students, the master stopped, sat down, and scrutinized his pupil's work. 'Not bad at all! but it's too much like the model. The man you can see is short and broad, so you paint him as short and broad; he has big feet, so you show them as they are. That sort of

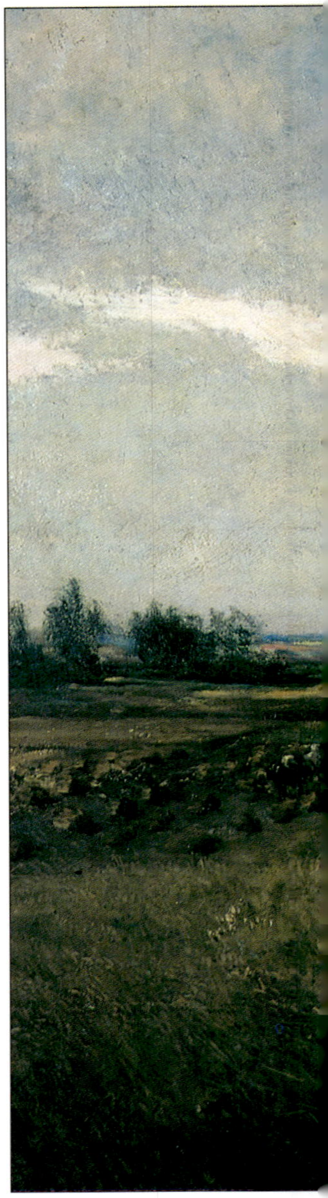

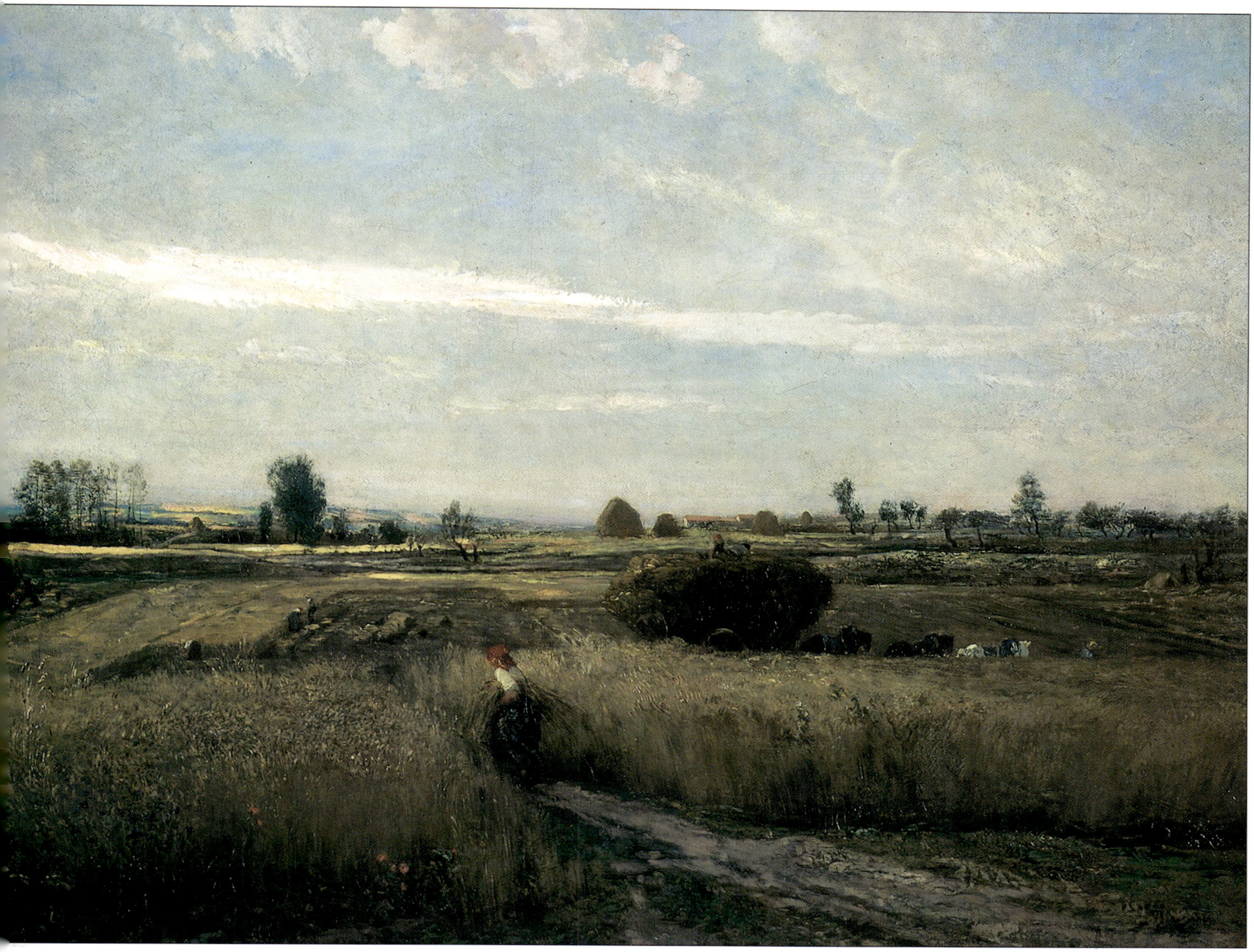

thing's terribly ugly!' When working, Gleyre urged, Monet should always bear in mind the classic figures of Greek and Roman sculpture. Nature was all very well in its place, but 'Style, you see, is everything!'.

Monet is unlikely to have received such advice very graciously, although his dependence on family funds made it unwise to fall out with Gleyre. Besides, the master, already ailing, put in fewer and fewer appearances, leaving his charges to get on by themselves. Moreover, by an extraordinary stroke of luck, Monet found among his fellow students no less than three kindred spirits with talents and energies comparable to his own.

For a long time his closest friend was Frédéric Bazille (1841–70), an unusually tall southerner from a wealthy family,

ABOVE:
Harvest Time
Charles-François Daubigny
(1851)
MUSÉE D'ORSAY, PARIS

who divided his time between art and the medical studies that his family still hoped would bear fruit. Alfred Sisley (1839–99), the son of wealthy English parents, was a quiet character and, according to his friend Pierre-Auguste Renoir, 'a delightful human being'; his attractiveness to women is captured in Renoir's double-portrait of *Sisley and his Wife* (page 13), in which the husband's tender protectiveness is palpable.

The third of Monet's new friends was Renoir himself (1841–1919), the odd man out in that he sprang from the Parisian working class and had been employed as a porcelain decorator before enrolling at Gleyre's. His curiously nervy, unworldly personality was particularly apparent during his young manhood (page 14), concealing a formidable dedication.

Over the next few years these four friends were to work side by side, in various permutations, and eventually to develop the distinctive Impressionist technique of landscape painting. Only Bazille, a casualty of the Franco-Prussian War, was unable to fulfil his promise. Even at Gleyre's, Monet emerged as the leader of the group, almost certainly becoming the first to challenge the wisdom of what they were being taught. Photographs of him as a young man show that he affected a romantic personal style, and Renoir in his old age enjoyed telling his son Jean about his friend's 'lordly' ways and dandyism: 'he didn't have a sou, but he wore shirts with lace cuffs'. At this stage in his life Monet was evidently trying to shake off his provincialism and pass himself off as a Parisian sophisticate; when one of the girls in the studio made advances to him, Monet is said to have rejected her with polite disdain, asserting rather implausibly that he never slept with any women but duchesses or maidservants!

Monet's pretensions to sophistication were soon abandoned, but he remained forceful and sometimes arrogant – characteristics which proved invaluable in carrying him through years of rejection and poverty. Renoir's later verdict was that they also helped his friends, nerving them to go on with the struggle. Without this evidence, we might take a more sceptical view of Monet's personality, since many of the stories he told about himself were questionable or even downright false. Once, having described his instant aversion to Gleyre's ideas, he even claimed to have walked out of the studio only two weeks after entering it. However, the truth was more banal: he remained for over a year, leaving early in 1864 after Gleyre's eye ailment had prompted the master's decision to close the studio and retire.

Still, there seems no reason to doubt that Monet and his friends thought of Gleyre's misfortune as a liberation. Over the next few years, while still based in Paris, they made a series of painting expeditions into the French countryside. In 1863 and 1864 Monet returned to his home territory, where he painted *Farmyard in Normandy* (pages 16-17); it is the earliest of his post-Algerian paintings known to have survived. In the summer of 1864 Bazille accompanied him on a trip to the coast, where they worked in the area around Honfleur. Among the paintings produced by Monet were *Village Street in Normandy* and *The Road to Saint Siméon Farm.* Like many of his works from this period, both rely on the simple perspective device of a road receding more or less diagonally into the distance; such a conventional arrangement, easily recognized as 'artistic', may indicate that he was consciously trying to create works that would be acceptable to the Salon and the wider public. In the course of this trip, Monet shrewdly took Bazille to meet his family, who were deeply impressed by this tall, well-bred young man and so became a little more inclined to view 'Oscar's' activities with tolerance.

After a few days Bazille left Normandy for the south. Monet stayed on at Saint Siméon's, a homely eating-place popular with artists where he enjoyed the convivial bohemian atmosphere and once more spent time with his friends Boudin and Jongkind. At some point he realized that he had run out of money and began to make frantic efforts to raise enough to pay his bill and get back to Paris. His friends failed to find buyers for any of his work, but a Monsieur Gaudibert providentially turned up and commissioned two paintings. Gaudibert was the artist's first patron; the finest memorial to their relationship is an elegant full-length portrait of Madame Gaudibert (page 55), painted four years later.

Monet and his friends also broke new ground in their wanderings. In 1863, while they were still at Gleyre's, Monet and Bazille made their first trip to the village of Chailly in the forest of Fontainebleau. The forest was famous for its varied and picturesque scenery and had already served to inspire the older generation of landscape painters. Camille Corot was still to be seen working there, and the village of Barbizon, only a few miles away, had become a virtual artists' colony, not only by Charles-François Daubigny (1817–79), Théodore Rousseau (1812–67), and Jean-François Millet (1814–75), and but by other painters

RIGHT:
Cart, Road under the Snow at Honfleur
(1865)
MUSÉE D'ORSAY, PARIS

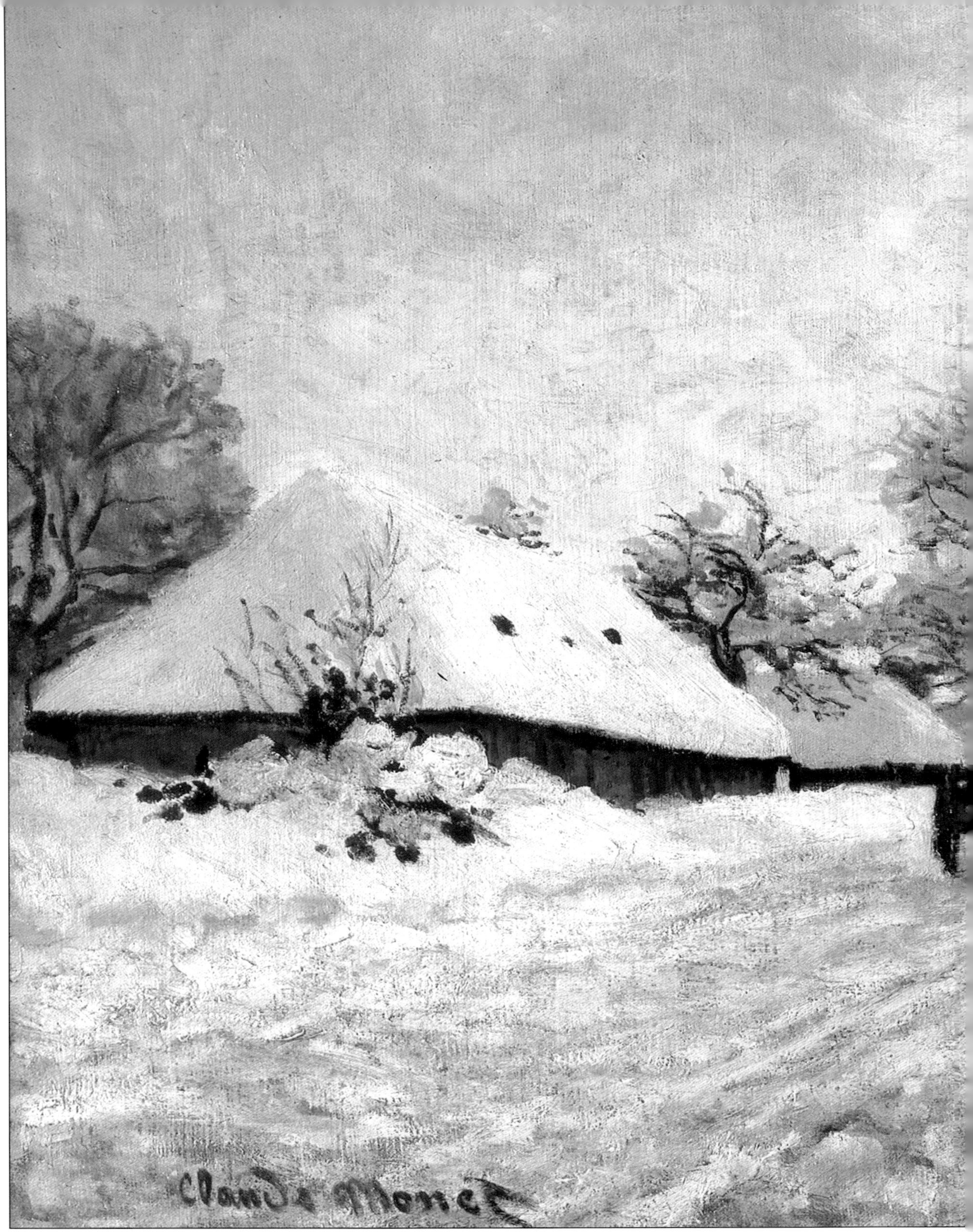

who became known collectively as the Barbizon School.

Monet, too, succumbed to the leafy loveliness of the forest, so effectively captured in *The Road to Chailly* (pages 18-19). Although strongly influenced by the Barbizon painters, his work is less romanticized and already shows a greater awareness of the play of

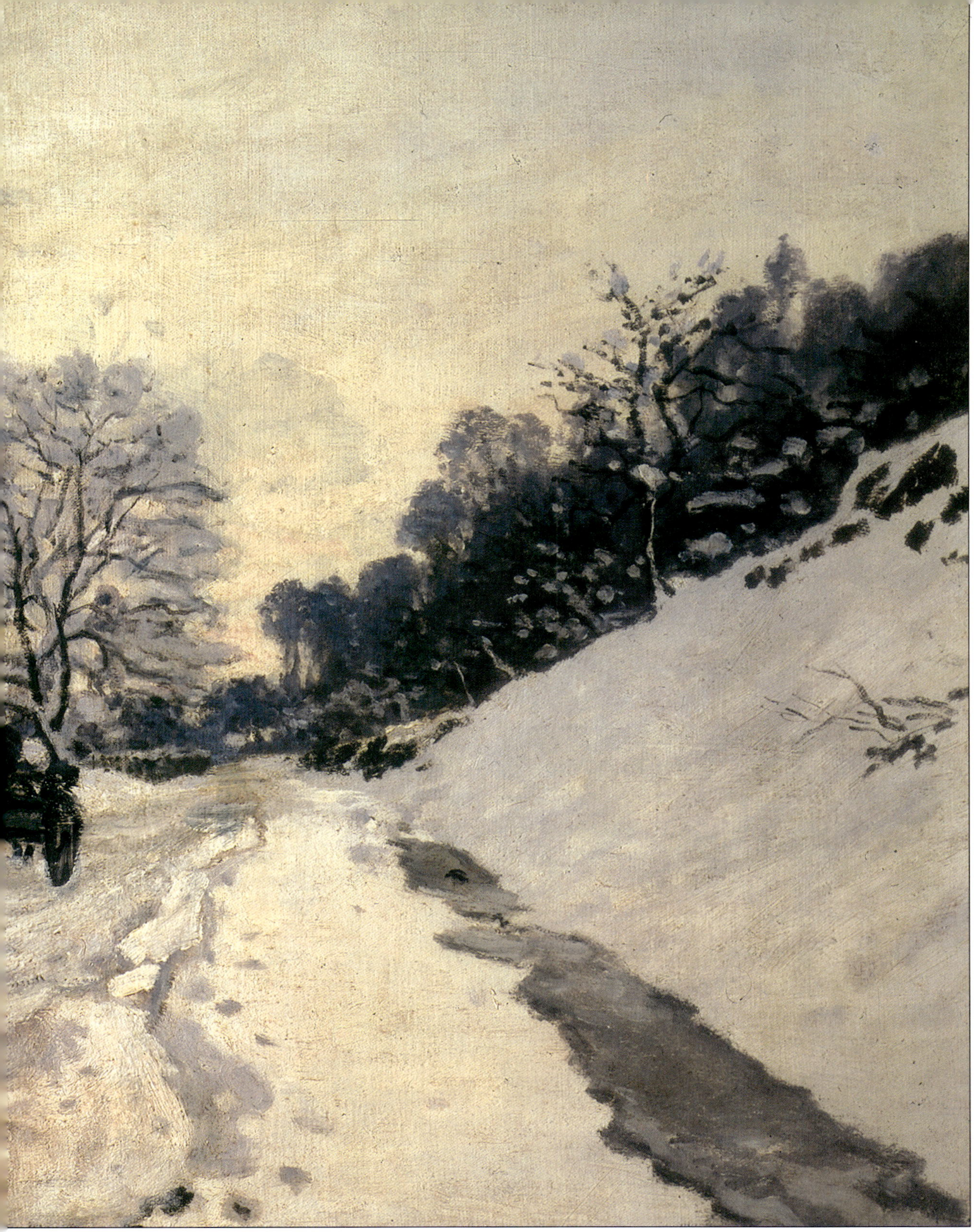

light on objects, than, for example, that of Daubigny in a typical landscape such as *Harvest Time* (pages 22-3). Monet returned to Chailly in 1864 and again, meditating great things, in 1865, by which time it seemed that he might, after all, become a credit to his family and cut a figure in the official art world.

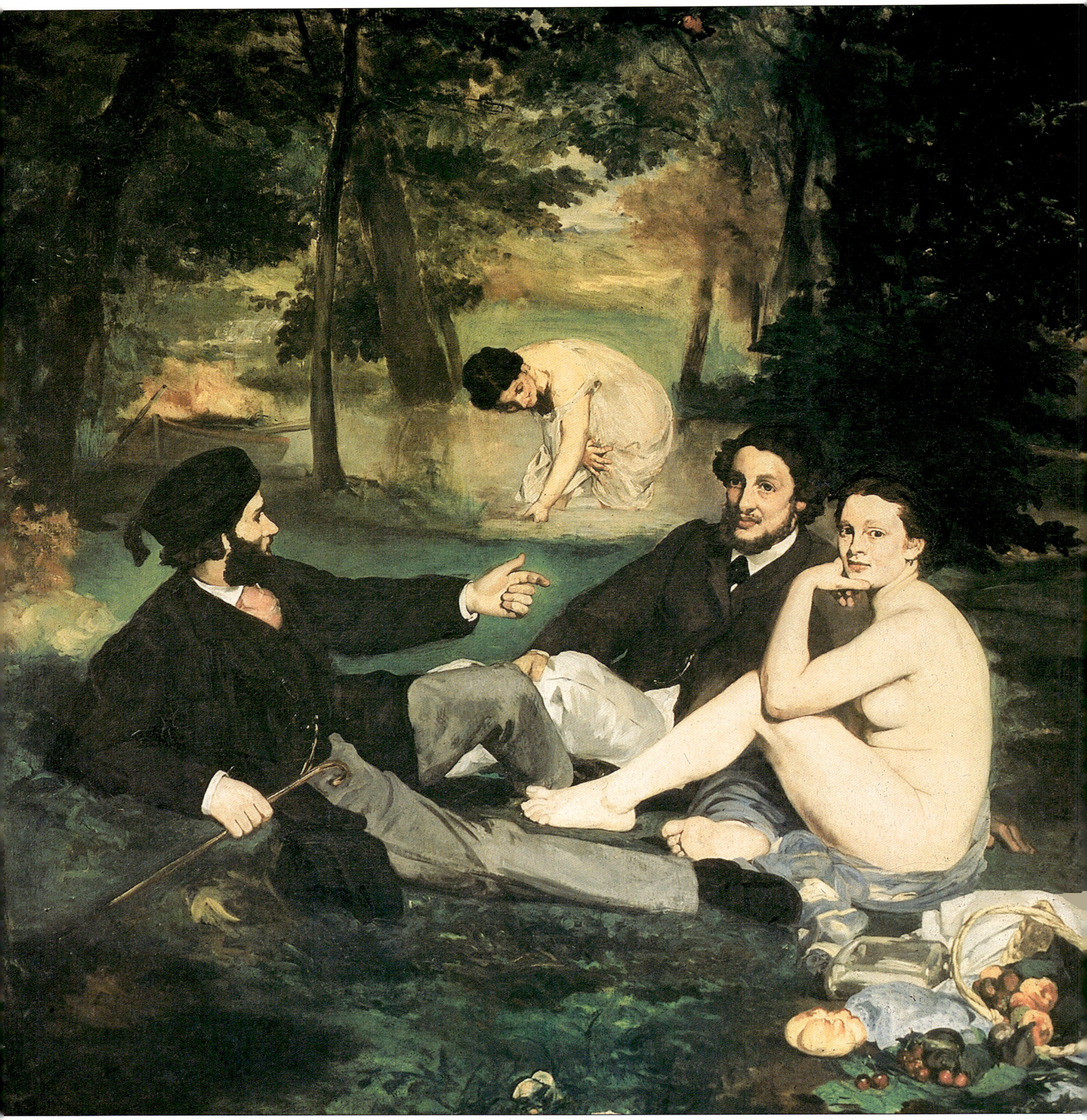

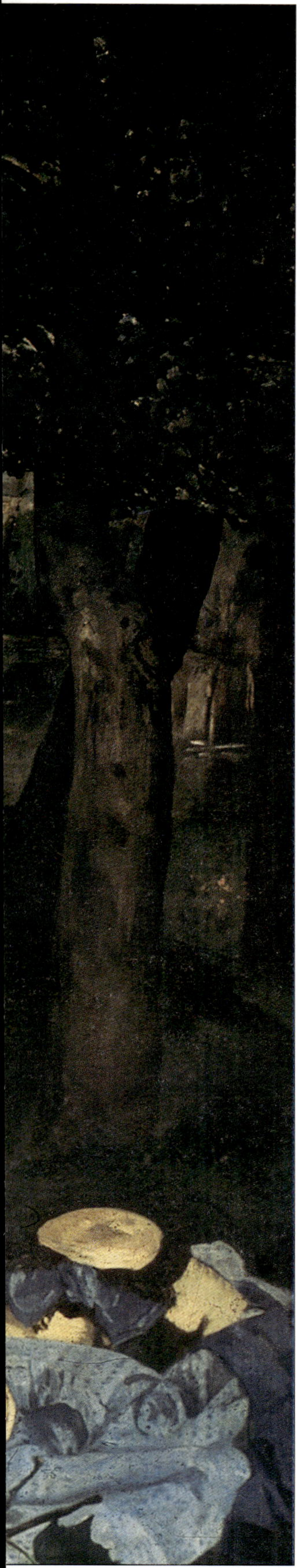

CHAPTER TWO

LEFT:
Le Déjeuner sur l'Herbe (1863)
Edouard Manet
MUSÉE D'ORSAY, PARIS

Ambition and the Salon

IN JANUARY 1865 Monet moved into a studio on the Rue Furstenberg, which he shared with his friend Bazille. There he put the finishing touches to two canvases which he had painted the previous summer in Normandy: *The Mouth of the Seine at Honfleur* and *The Pointe de la Hève at Low Tide.* He intended to submit them to the Salon jury, and they were carefully calculated to please – not too bright or 'sketchy' for contemporary taste, but conveying a fine, wind-blown romantic sense of northern atmosphere, with big cloud-filled skies and surging waves. Even when working in relatively conventional style, Monet already had the ability to capture the mesmerizing pulse of moving waters.

He was successful at his first attempt. Both paintings were accepted for exhibition at the Palais d'Industrie and subsequently singled out by the critics as the work of an exceptionally promising artist. Monet was even invited to make a drawing of *The Mouth of the Seine* so that it could be turned into an engraving and reach a wider public by being sold in multiple copies.

One of the more entertaining results of this triumph was that another painter, Edouard Manet (1832–83), found himself congratulated by an acquaintance on the reception of 'his' landscapes. As thousands of people have since confused the similar-sounding names of Monet and Manet, the mistake may have been genuine. However, it seems rather more likely that it was prompted by malicious amusement; already well known, Manet was widely regarded as the leader of the rebellious modern-life school, and his current Salon exhibit, the nude *Olympia*, was being assaulted on all sides as a moral and artistic outrage. At this time in Manet's life, congratulations were definitely not in order and he touchily assumed that some opportunist was trying to make capital out of his own celebrity – or notoriety.

RIGHT:
Man with a Parasol (1865)
KUNSTHAUS, ZURICH

Déjeuner vs. Déjeuner

Manet soon realized that his suspicions were unfounded and in later years proved a generous friend to Monet. Ironically, at this time Monet did see himself as a rival to Manet and had started work on a project through which he hoped to replace the older artist as the leader of the modern school. Manet had caused a sensation in 1863, when he had exhibited *Le Déjeuner sur L'Herbe* ('Luncheon on the Grass', pages 28/9). Although the subject and treatment were based on reputable art-historical precedents, Manet had given the subject a contemporary turn that deeply offended nineteenth-century prudery: two young men, unmistakably modern, were shown lounging at their ease in a glade after a picnic, accompanied by girls whose clothing lay all too obviously discarded on the grass. The completely naked young woman sitting at her ease in the foreground was even shameless enough to look out at the spectator, not invitingly but with a friendly amusement that wickedly belied her fallen state.

Championed by a minority but reviled by conventional opinion, Manet's *Déjeuner* was an artistic landmark, and Monet cannot possibly have contemplated painting a picnic picture of his own without knowing full well that the two works would be compared. That he not only intended comparisons to be made, but also aimed to outdo Manet, can be inferred from the extraordinary scale on which he chose to work: the finished canvas was to be about six by five metres, over four times as big as Manet's painting.

It was an audacious bid for early fame, not necessarily doomed to fail. Monet's *Déjeuner* was a modern-life subject and so might be deemed suspect in the eyes of conservative opinion, but at least its modernity was discreet and decent. For, unlike Manet's

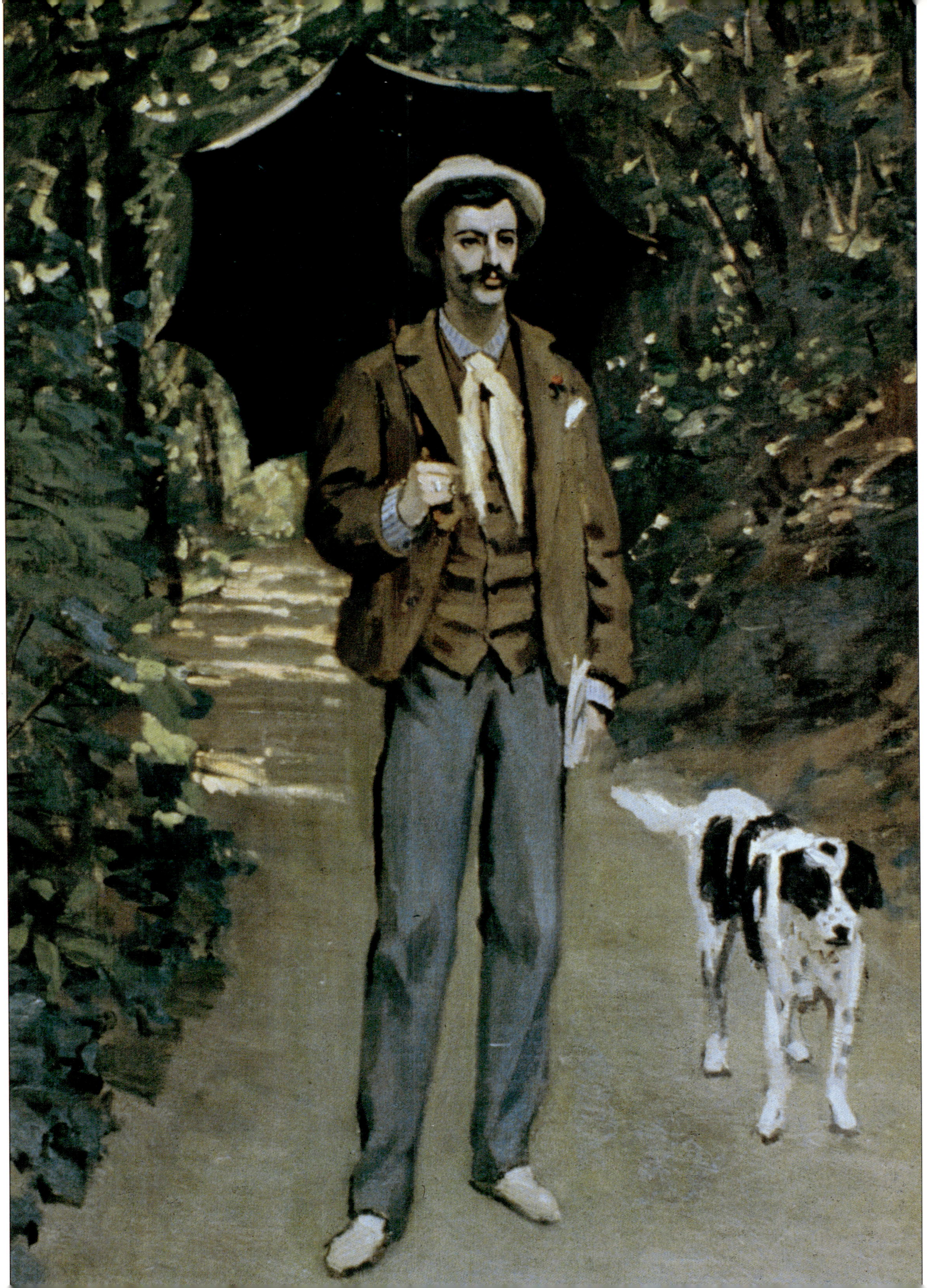

picnickers, Monet's would be fully clothed and apparently interested in nothing more than food and conviviality. This was not necessarily a concession to prudery, since Monet never showed much interest in the nude as an artistic subject; and it did seem to guarantee that the new *Déjeuner* would not be condemned for moral reasons. On the other hand, Monet's conception was unorthodox in other important respects for which he might not be forgiven: in picturing an informal middle-class outing on a scale associated with heroic and historic canvases, and in painting with vivid, natural colours that made Manet's dark tones seem quite conventional.

Monet threw himself into the project as soon as possible. He left Paris well before the Salon ended (pursued by letters congratulating him on his success) and settled once again at Chailly, which was to provide the woodland setting for the *Déjeuner*. A portrait of the artist Jules Ferdinand Jacquemart, *Man with a Parasol* (page 31), was probably executed at this time, as Monet shaped up to the new challenge of figure painting. A pleasant but tentative work, it shows the evident influence of Manet in its firm outlining and Monet has clearly not yet worked out how to integrate the figure convincingly with the dappled, leafy background.

Although he was able to make preliminary studies in the forest of Fontainebleau, Monet had to wait for weeks until Bazille turned up to model for him. By the time he did so, Monet had injured his leg, and the first service Bazille performed was to use his medical training to make his friend comfortable. He fixed up an ingenious device which directed a steady, soothing drip of water from a large jar onto the inflamed limb; then he – Bazille, not Monet – was able to get on with some painting, notably a doleful portrait of the injured artist, with jar and leg prominently displayed, gazing out from a mass of bedding.

When Monet had recovered, he began to make studies and sketches again, culminating in a large oil study (page 33) almost a third the size of the final canvas. Monet dated it 1866, probably after touching it up and signing it, but the costumes as well as artistic logic indicate that it was done earlier, before the full-scale painting. Most of the male figures were based on Bazille, while the women were versions of Camille Doncieux, an 18-year-old who became Monet's mistress. Monet insisted that the reason why he used only these two models was that they were all he could afford – that is, they were free. Perhaps there is also something to be said for the view that, as an artist, he was not greatly interested in the individual characteristics of human beings, so that a variety of models was not

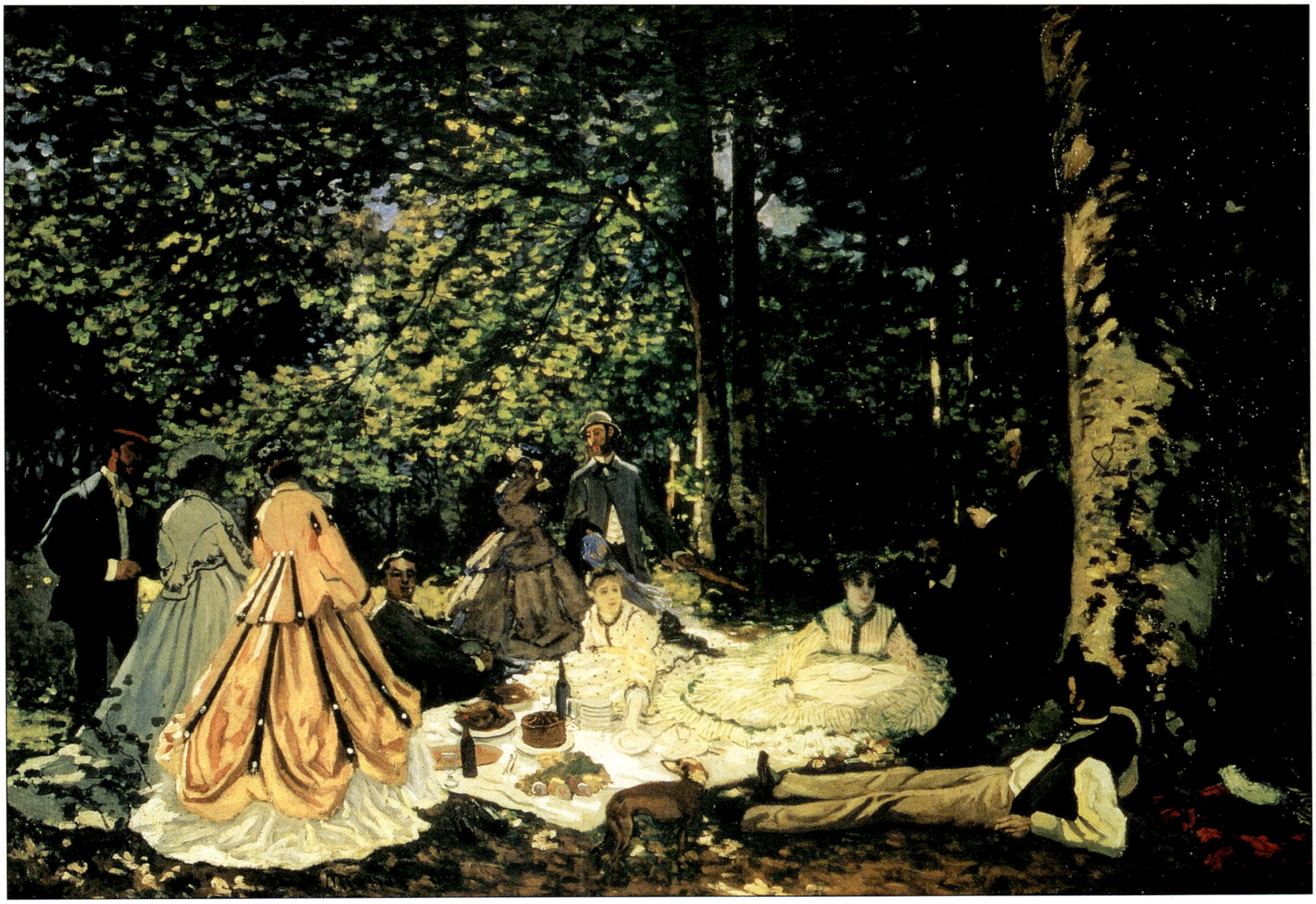

a high priority. Arguably Monet's large-scale figure painting of 1865–66, coinciding with his urgent efforts to win over the Salon and the public, were the product of ambition rather than a purely artistic impulse. Certainly there is very little that resembles them in his later work.

In the autumn of 1865 Monet returned to the Rue Furstenberg with his sketches and studies and began work on the final canvas. Finishing a picture in the studio was normal artistic practice, and although Monet later claimed to regret this decision, he evidently felt at the time that painting such a huge canvas out of doors would involve insuperable difficulties. Even so, the work went slowly, partly because Monet had to leave the Rue Furstenberg early in 1866 and move to less spacious quarters. When it became apparent that the *Déjeuner* would not be ready for the 1866 Salon, Monet abandoned it and worked on a painting of Camille that could be completed in time. Although the *Déjeuner* had reached an advanced stage, Monet did not return to it, although he kept it by him for years. In 1878, down on his luck, he left it as a pledge with

ABOVE:
Oil study for Monet's **Déjeuner sur l'Herbe** (1865)
PUSHKIN MUSEUM, MOSCOW

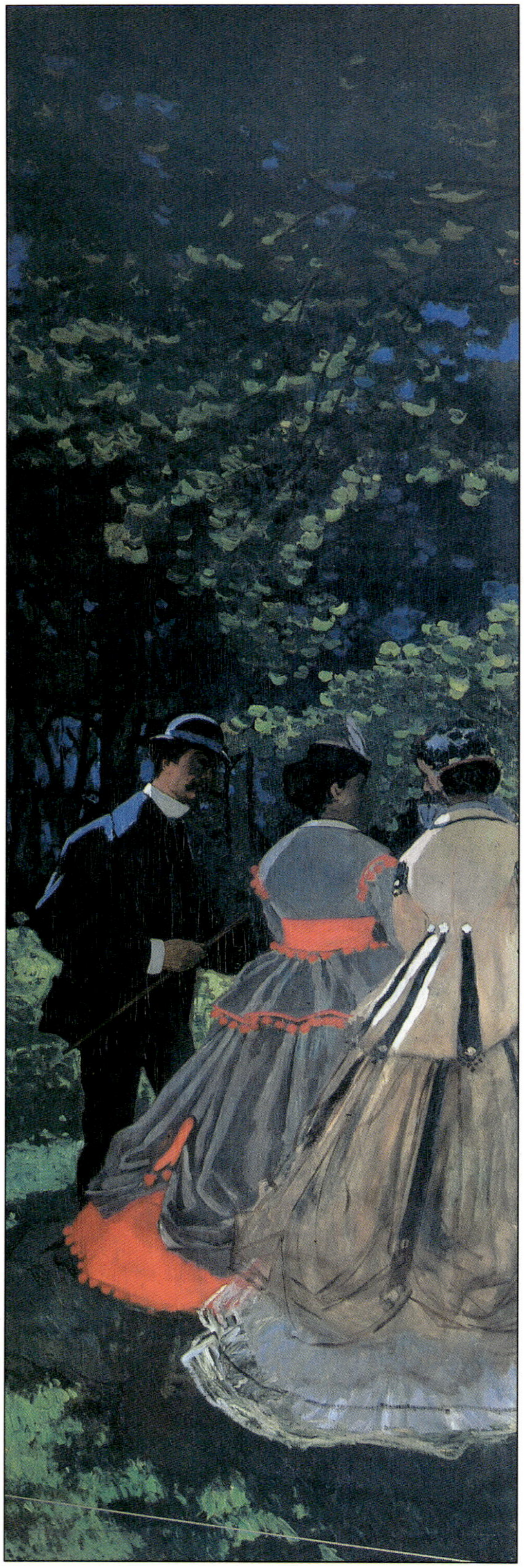

ABOVE:
Fragment of Monet's **Déjeuner sur l'Herbe** from the left-hand side (1865)
MUSÉE D'ORSAY, PARIS

his landlord at Argenteuil. When he reclaimed it, six years later, parts had rotted away. He was only able to salvage two substantial fragments, which still survive, featuring seven of the twelve figures shown in the large oil study.

The smaller fragment (page 34) is a narrow vertical which shows Bazille (cleaner-shaved than the equivalent figure in the oil study) and two ladies who are seen from behind. Remarkably, it was discovered – in Monet's studio! – only in the 1950s. It originally belonged just to the left of the large central section of the composition (page 35) which comprises the other fragment. Bazille, still with his own whiskers, reappears in this at the back, just as he does in the oil study. However, the seated man in the large fragment, burly and bearded, is nothing like the young man in the study. This is almost certainly a portrait of the painter Gustave Courbet, the radical and realist who had led the opposition to academic art in the 1850s, before the emergence of Manet. Although the *Déjeuner* was most obviously designed to challenge Manet's painting, it also drew on aspects of Courbet's works and, more generally, may be thought to have taken its cue from his celebrated *Burial at Ornans* (1850), the first painting to present an everyday event – a peasant funeral – on a canvas of heroic size. Courbet certainly saw Monet's work in progress and may well have sat for his portrait, but contradictory reports make it hard to be sure what he thought of the *Déjeuner*. The friendship between the two artists, although poorly documented, was certainly important to Monet during the 1860s.

In its mutilated state the *Déjeuner* remains a fascinating might-have-been, impossible to judge with any confidence. By comparison with the oil study, the fragments are less leafily poetic, with greater vitality and, above all, colours that are far brighter and more intense; at this point Monet has patently gone beyond the Barbizon school. If, finally, there appears to be something a little stolid and characterless about the picnic-party in the *Déjeuner*, that may be because we now see them in too narrow a focus. If we could examine the picture in its entirety, it is possible that we should be overwhelmed by its scale and dazzling colours and that nothing else would matter.

On the other hand, by abandoning the *Déjeuner*, Monet appears to have made the implicit judgement that it was not fully satisfactory or, at any rate, not suited to his purposes. His decision not to finish the painting – let alone show or sell it – was truly extraordinary and remains inexplicable. Apart from some forest

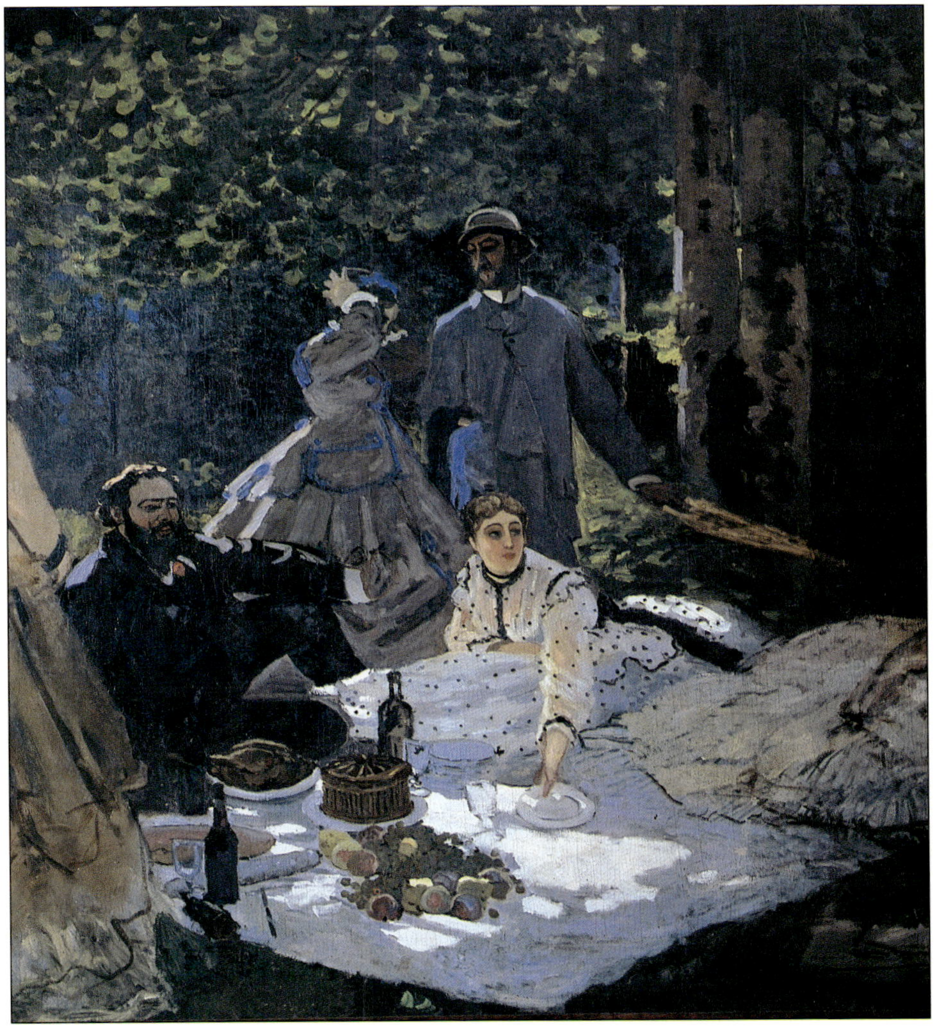

LEFT: Fragment of Monet's **Déjeuner sur l'Herbe** from the central section (1865) MUSÉE D'ORSAY, PARIS

landscapes, the *Déjeuner* had been his exclusive concern for a year – even for a young man a heavy investment of time, energy and money. Moreover, In addition, in spite of this particular renunciation, for some time to come Monet would continue to see himself as a 'painter of modern life' like Edouard Manet.

The Girl in Green

Setting aside the *Déjeuner*, Monet hurried to stake his claim at the Salon by painting *Woman in a Green Dress* (page 37). Camille again served as his model and her name is often used as the title of the picture. Legend has it that, to meet the deadline for submissions, Monet took only four days over the entire work. As the picture is a big one (Camille is shown life-sized), this is almost certainly a romantic fiction. Nor does it square with Monet's ambitious, but sober and steady attempts to conquer the Salon and become famous.

As usual, artists were allowed to enter only two works for the Salon. Monet submitted *Woman in a Green Dress* and, in striking contrast, the large *The Road to Chailly* (pages 18-19). Both were accepted, viewed and widely applauded. In fact *Woman in a Green Dress* was one of the great successes of the show. A Paris dealer bought a copy from Monet. The rising young journalist Emile Zola, not yet known as a powerful and controversial novelist, declared 'I do not know Monsieur Monet, but he already feels like an old friend'. Other reviewers and even the cartoonists were encouraging; one magazine published verses hailing Camille's image as that of a 'queenly Parisienne'.

This suggests that its evocation of fashionable life was the key to the picture's success. Its tones were acceptably dark and the solidity with which Camille's figure is rendered conveyed an impression of seriousness; but the smart and stylish clothes, three-quarter back view and elegant pose, involving a gloved hand making some minor adjustment, were all redolent of the fashion plate. Consciously or otherwise, Monet had created a painting in which the controversial 'modern-life' style was seen at its most acceptable. With its neutral background and well-defined colour areas, the portrait of Camille had strong affinities with some of Manet's portraits (though not with the outrageous Manet of the *Déjeuner* and *Olympia)*. The resemblance did not go unnoticed and one cartoonist produced his own version of *Woman in a Green Dress* to which, still vastly amused by the similarity between the two painters' names, he gave the title 'Monet or Manet? - Monet!' The caption read: 'But it is to Manet that we owe this Monet. Bravo, Monet! Thank you, Manet!'

Monet can hardly have been pleased at being labelled a follower of Manet, but his success must have been a powerful consolation. Thanks to the favourable publicity his works had received, he found buyers for a number of his canvases and his family's attitude towards him softened; for the time being he could again count on receiving a small allowance. He was by now living just outside Paris, at Ville d'Avray, having originally left the capital to escape his creditors. The upturn in his fortunes enabled him to plan an ambitious new assault on the Salon. Although most of Monet's canvases were later to be modest in size, at this stage in his career he seems to have believed that success at the Salon could be achieved only by working on a near-epic scale and to have acted accordingly. There was a good deal to be said for his view, since the walls of the Salon were crammed with pictures, and sheer size

RIGHT:
Woman in a Green Dress (1866)
KUNSTHALLE, BREMEN

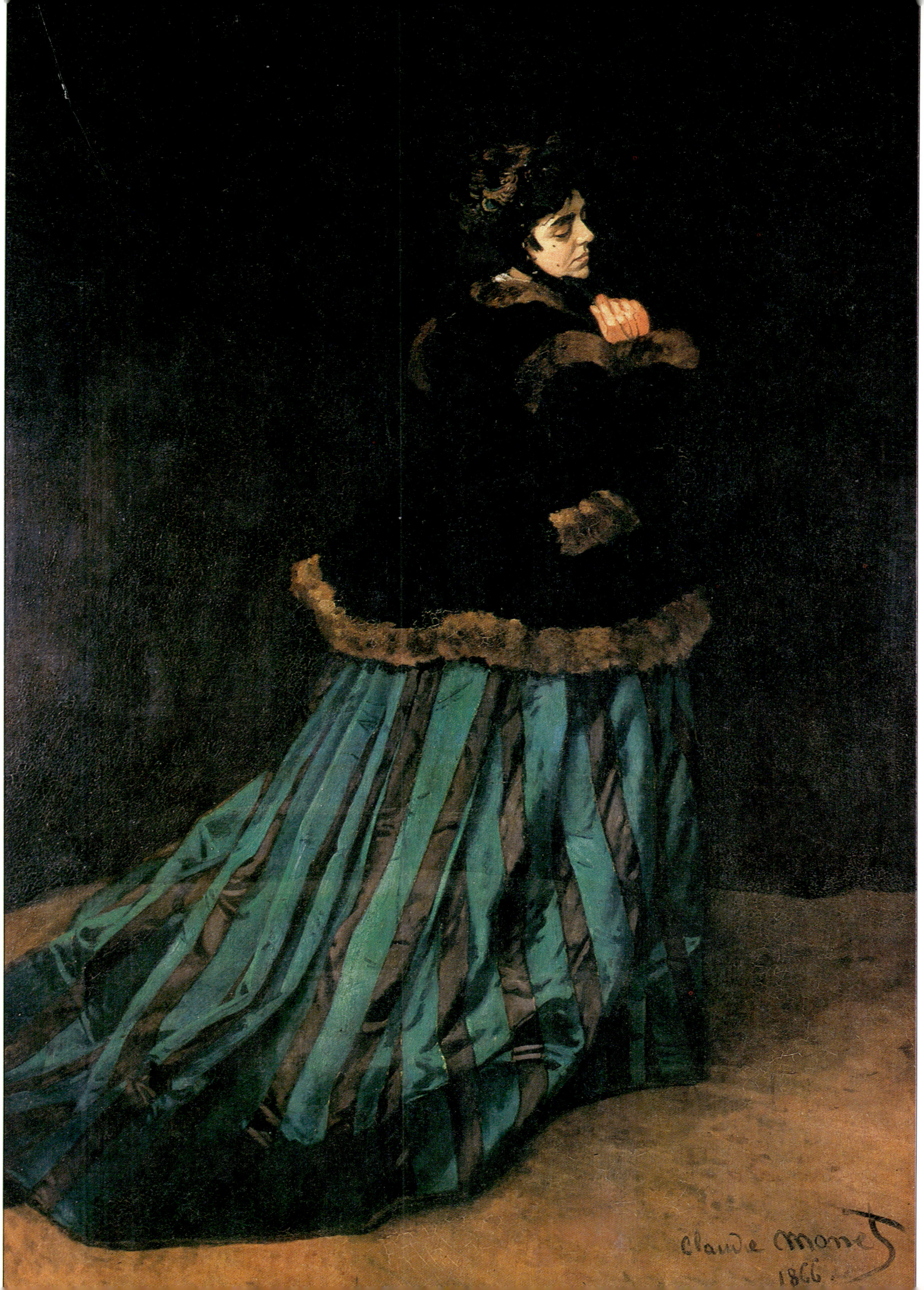
Claude Monet
1866.

RIGHT:
Flower Garden
(c.1866)
MUSÉE D'ORSAY,
PARIS

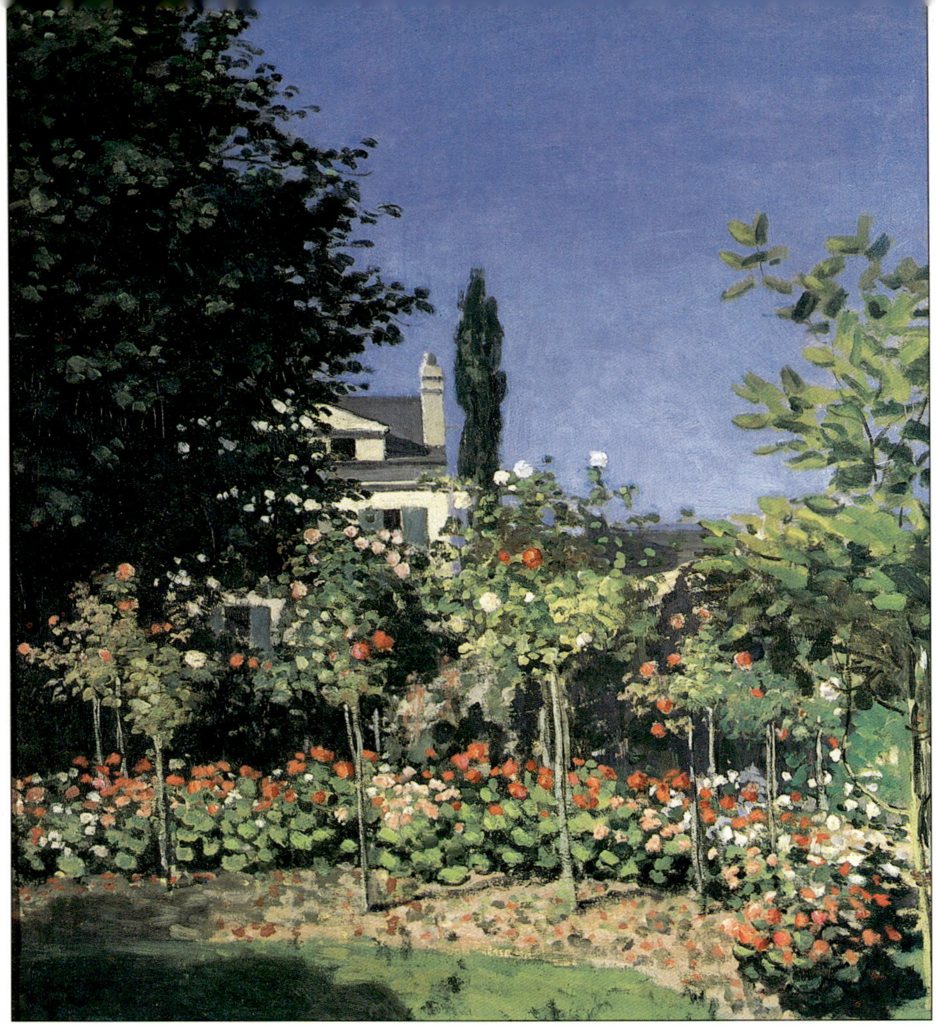

must at least have ensured that an exhibit could not be entirely overlooked. Moreover, the contemporary taste for huge, grandiose history paintings probably did encourage people to feel that size and quality were much the same. Notoriously, a public that was unsure of its own taste tended to admire works that at any rate exuded one of the Victorian virtues, in that their creators had obviously worked long and hard on them.

Women in the Garden

Encouraged by the Salon's unexpected tolerance of uncontroversial modern-life subjects, Monet proceeded to paint a large *Women in the Garden* (page 39), featuring four young women in contemporary dress. Evidently funds were still not so very plentiful, since Camille Doncieux seems to have been the model for all four. Although he hoped that *Women in the Garden* would make its mark at the Salon, Monet was determined that his work on the picture should play a part in his artistic progress. In creating *Déjeuner sur L'Herbe* he had followed normal practice by assembling his sketches and studies in the studio and executing the finished work there, but the new

RIGHT:
Women in the Garden (1867)
MUSÉE D'ORSAY,
PARIS

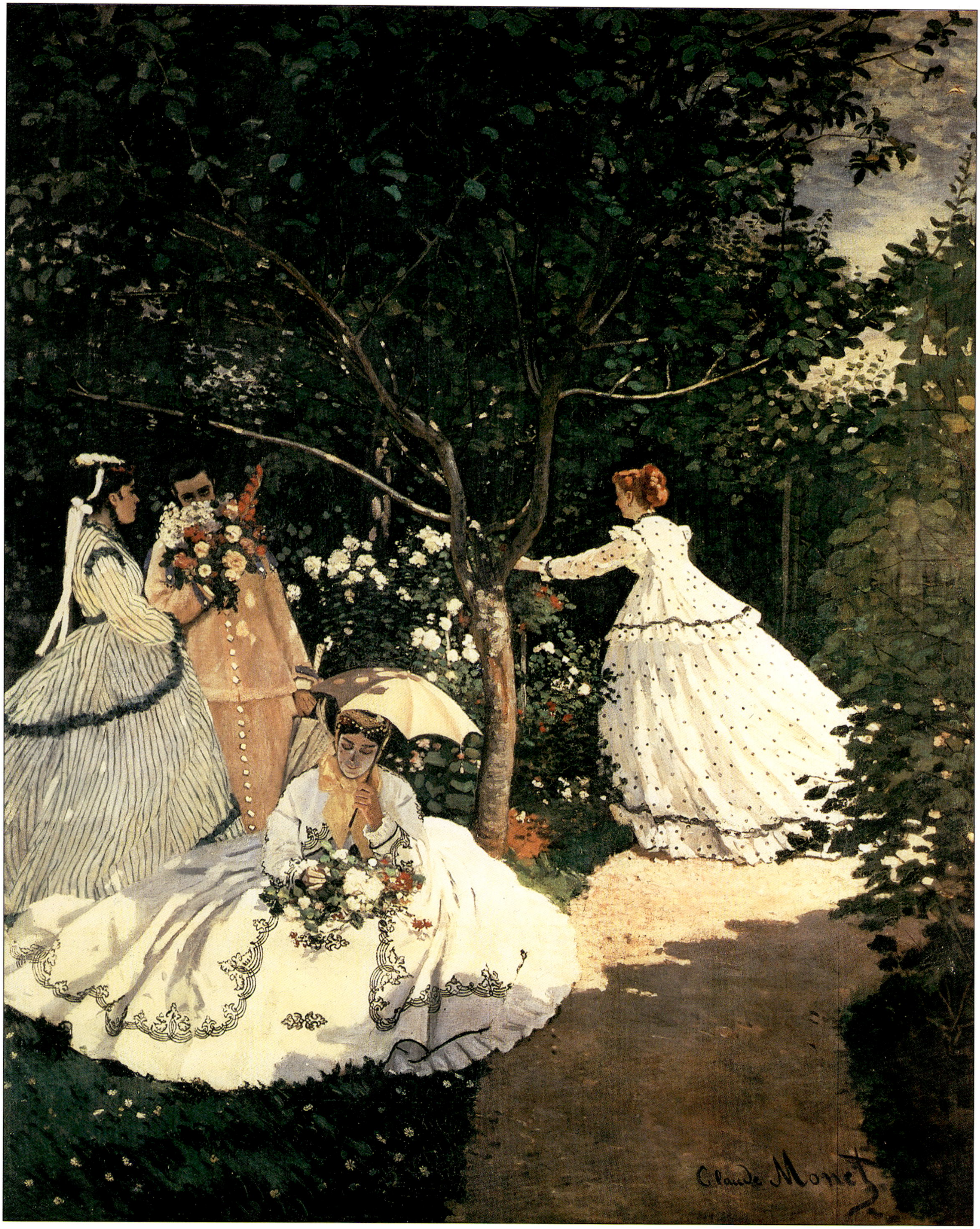
Claude Monet

painting was to be done entirely in the open air, despite its unwieldy size (approximately 2 x 2.5 metres). According to his own account, Monet dug a trench in his garden at Ville d'Avray and then rigged up a contraption that allowed him to raise the canvas or lower it into the trench; this enabled him to bring any part of the surface within reach of his brushes.

The arrangement sounds impossibly clumsy, and despite Monet's remarkable doggedness in matters of artistic practice, it is difficult to believe that he made no compromises at Ville d'Avray during the spring and summer of 1866. Furthermore, the evidence of a fellow artist makes it certain that, once he had left the village and settled in at Honfleur, he worked in the studio and finished the picture there. Of course such details are not really important, except that in later life Monet was always reluctant to admit that his mature output owed anything to work done in the studio – a curious indication of the way in which, for him, *plein air* painting acquired the status of a cult, closely associated with his public image as an artist.

Like the *Déjeuner, Women in the Garden* was a project that left little time for any other work, as well as involving quantities of materials that had to be paid for. Monet was soon deep in debt again and his exit from Ville d'Avray was another flight from pressing creditors. In Normandy matters went from bad to worse and by the end of the year he was so short of ready cash that he asked Bazille to send on his old canvases, intending to scrape them off and use them again. At about the same time, he learned that Camille was pregnant. Quite apart from the unfortunate timing of the event, such evidence as there is suggests that Monet, at once intensely ambitious and accustomed to a life of bohemian freedom, faced the prospects of fatherhood and family responsibilities with considerable trepidation.

Moreover, unknown to Monet, his luck had turned, and there were bitter years of poverty and failure ahead. In the spring of 1867 he submitted *Women in the Garden* and a very large landscape, *The Port of Honfleur,* to the Salon. For the previous three years, the mood of the selection jury had been influenced by the presence of liberal-minded members such as Daubigny. In 1867 a reaction set in that would last for years and Monet was one of the early victims: both his submissions were rejected and were, therefore, not seen by the general public. After such an investment of time and effort, this was a crushing blow. Almost the only consolation was that Monet again found an eloquent defender in Emile Zola, who was

RIGHT:
Le Jardin de l'Infante (1867)
ALLEN MEMORIAL ART MUSEUM, OBERLIN COLLEGE, OBERLIN, OHIO

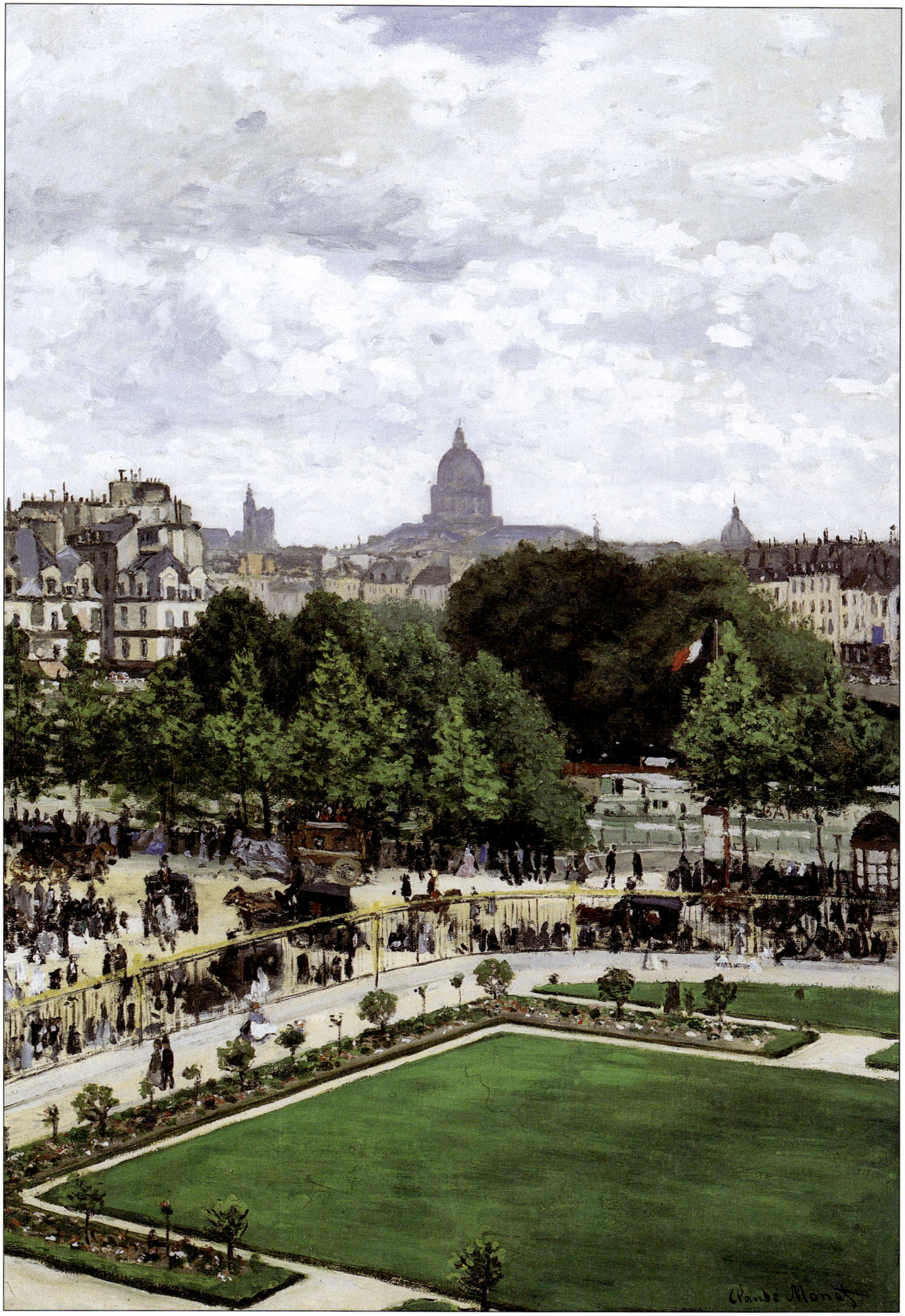

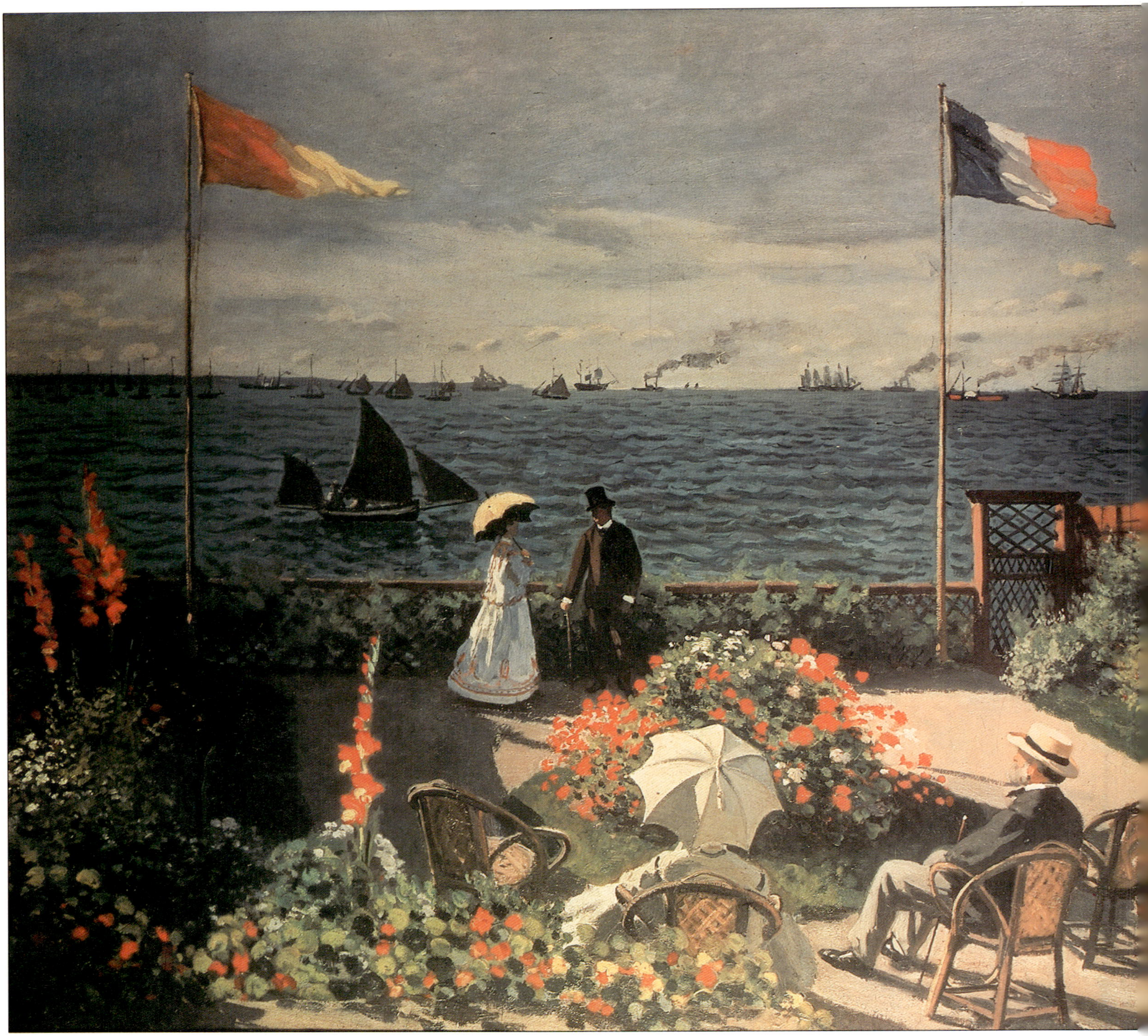

ABOVE:
Terrace at Sainte-Adresse (1867)
METROPOLITAN MUSEUM OF ART, NEW YORK

steadily making a name for himself as the champion of the moderns against academic artists. In some respects Zola misinterpreted Monet, seeing him as a true Parisian who always tried to introduce a human presence and urban values into his rural scenes. More important, however, was the fact that Zola, employed to write reviews of the Salon, chose to comment at length on works that did not even feature in the show. If nothing else, Monet's name was kept before the public.

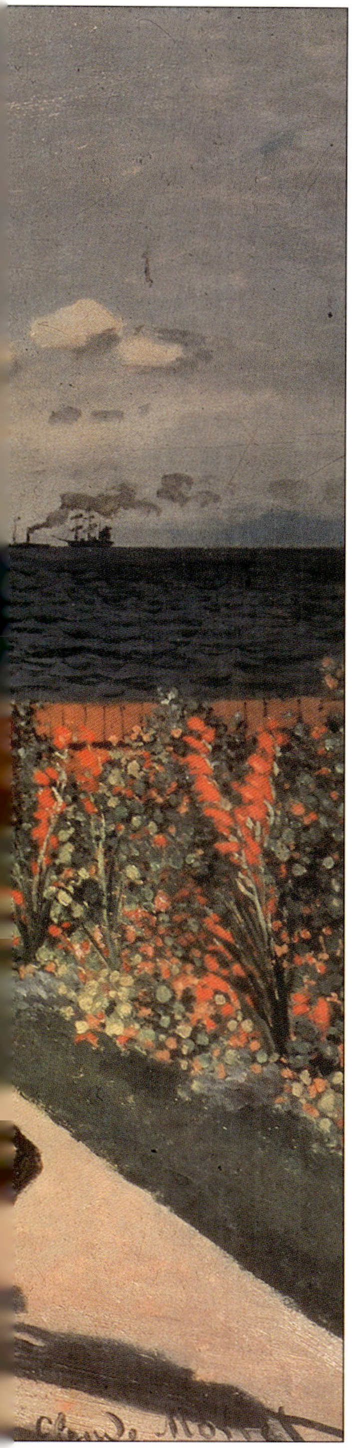

Women in the Garden has both admirers and detractors, but its rejection – the decision that it was not worthy to hang beside hundreds of mediocre works – still seems astonishing. A similar comment would almost certainly be appropriate in the case of Monet's other submission, *The Port of Honfleur*, if we could see it. (The work is now known only in reproduction, having vanished – presumed destroyed – during World War II.)

The jury may well have been disconcerted by the very qualities in Monet's painting that give *Women in the Garden* such an appeal for us. The light colours and fresh, open-air feeling are in marked contrast to the acclaimed *Woman in a Green Dress*; to the academic sensibility they may have made the new canvas seem lacking in the seriousness which its great size implicitly claimed for it. Nor did it live up to expectations by telling a story or presenting an emotionally-charged situation. These are not demands that most modern spectators would make, but all the same it must be admitted that there is a certain confusion of purpose in the scene, which combines an idyllic, leisured atmosphere with an uneasy sense that there may be more going on than we can make out. There is something wilfully enigmatic about the figure standing in the shade, holding a bouquet of flowers like a mask, and our curiosity is also aroused – but not satisfied – by the red-headed woman wholooks as though she is rushing across the gravel. The almost life-size figures are neither as natural nor as convincing as Monet later made them in intimate paintings such as *The Luncheon* of 1868 (page 60). Nevertheless, when all is said and done, *Women in the Garden* is a remarkable work that lingers in the memory, with an audaciously placed tree as its axis, and the women, like large pale butterflies, circling it in never-failing sunlight and shadow.

Cityscapes

Having finished his work at Honfleur, Monet returned to Paris at the beginning of 1867. Still desperately short of money, he moved in for a time with the long-suffering Bazille, who now had a studio in the Rue Visconti. He already shared it – almost certainly paying most of the bills – with Auguste Renoir, who was also struggling to make ends meet. One result of this get-together was that the friendship between Monet and Renoir, hitherto superficial, became closer. During the spring the two artists worked side by side, once more painting on the spot, but not from 'Nature', since their subjects were not landscapes but city scenes. Unlike Monet's earlier pictures of village streets in Normandy, these were not 'close-ups' but more or less panoramic views in the manner of the traditional landscape.

Monet's Parisian cityscapes, *Saint-Germain l'Auxerrois*, *The Jardin de l'Infante* (page 41) and *The Quai du Louvre*, show his taste for plunging views. They were all painted, by special permission, from the balconies of the Louvre – a richly ironic fact if there is any truth to the story that, during their student days, Renoir had dragged the vehemently anti-traditionalist Monet round the Louvre, France's greatest museum, in an attempt to make him appreciate the glories of the past. Some writers have even seen a symbolic significance in the fact that, while working on his cityscapes, Monet necessarily kept his back turned on the treasures of the Louvre.

At this stage Monet was still very much the 'painter of modern life'. The people of Paris, although dwarfed by the buildings around them, play an important part in the atmosphere of these pictures and, especially in *The Quai du Louvre*, Monet has picked out in the crowd some distinctively contemporary details of costumes and carriages. It is certainly instructive to compare the semi-documentary treatment of this view with a full-fledged Impressionist Monet, *The Boulevard des Capucines* (pages 104-5), painted only six years later.

The rejection of Monet's Salon submissions was a blow that must have made the future seem bleak, but it was a misfortune that Monet shared with Renoir, Bazille and others, thanks to the hardened attitudes of the Salon jury. For the first time, the friends were sufficiently disillusioned with the art establishment to contemplate holding their own separate and independent show (something their elders, Courbet and Manet, were doing at that very time, erecting individual pavilions outside the 1867 International Exhibition), but funds were too short and the idea was dropped for the time being.

Summer at Sainte-Adresse

In the summer Monet went back to Normandy, staying with his aunt at Sainte-Adresse, just along the coast from Le Havre. He was again on poor terms with his family, although by now, despite his recent Salon failure, even his father had begun to believe in his talent and his future. The painter's way of life was another matter. His chronic inability to earn a decent living gave rise to suspicions of

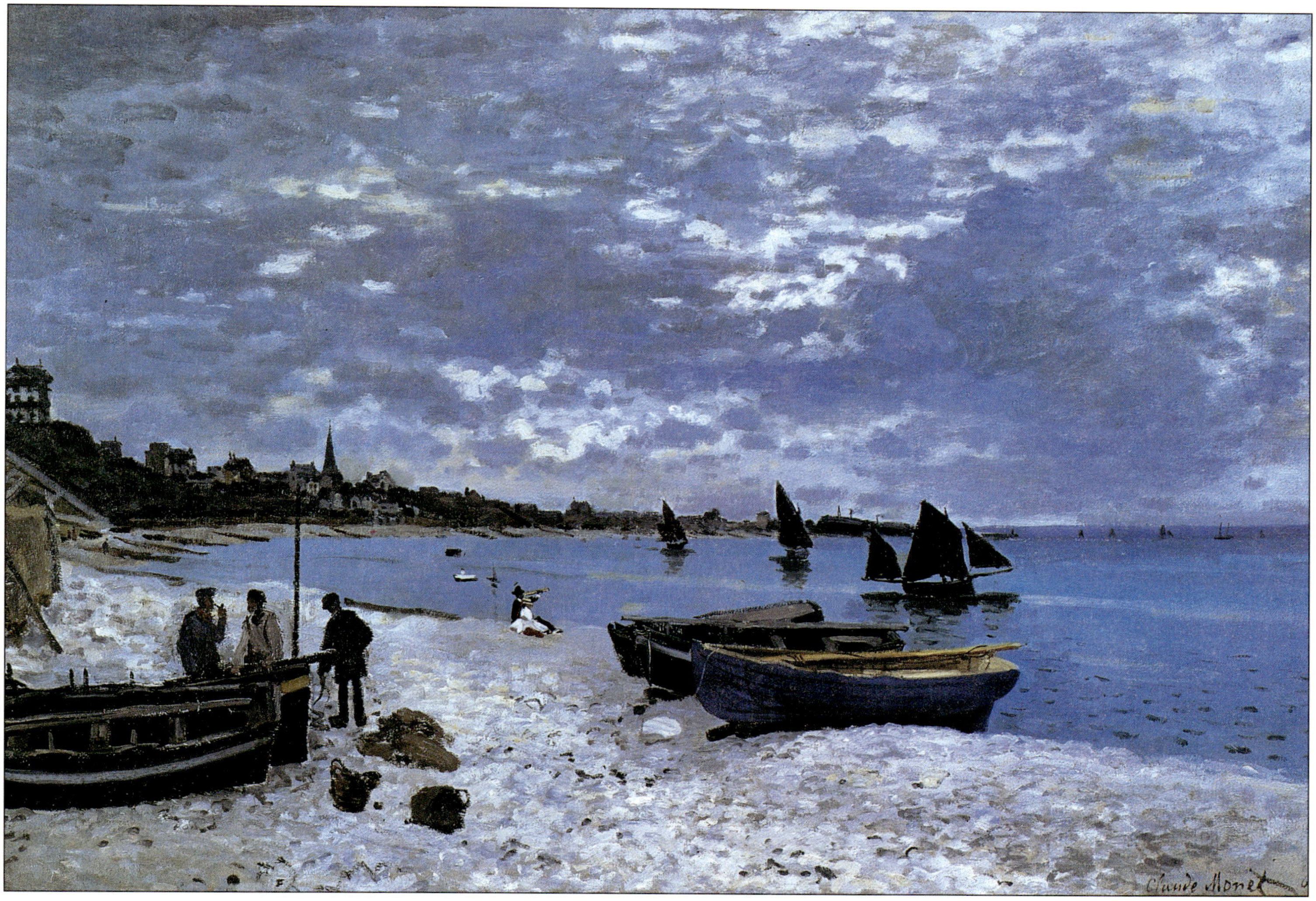

ABOVE:
The Beach at Sainte-Adresse
(1867)
ART INSTITUTE OF CHICAGO

improvidence and dissipation, and the family's worst suspicions were confirmed when Monet broke the news that his companion, Camille, was about to have a baby. By making him welcome at Sainte-Adresse while keeping him financially on a short leash, Monet's relations probably hoped to keep him away from Camille and bring an unsuitable, immoral relationship to an end.

Monet's feelings about the situation are hard to interpret. Poverty may not have been the only reason why he spent months at Sainte-Adresse, leaving Camille to wonder whether he intended to abandon her for good. He seems to have been daunted by the prospect of fatherhood, perhaps understandably in a young man whose way of life was necessarily unsettled, and who was simultaneously poor, ambitious and self-absorbed. His letters show that he was worried about Camille's welfare and discomfited by the realization that he had left her, at the most vulnerable time in her life, alone and destitute. However, the coolly objective tone of his remarks –

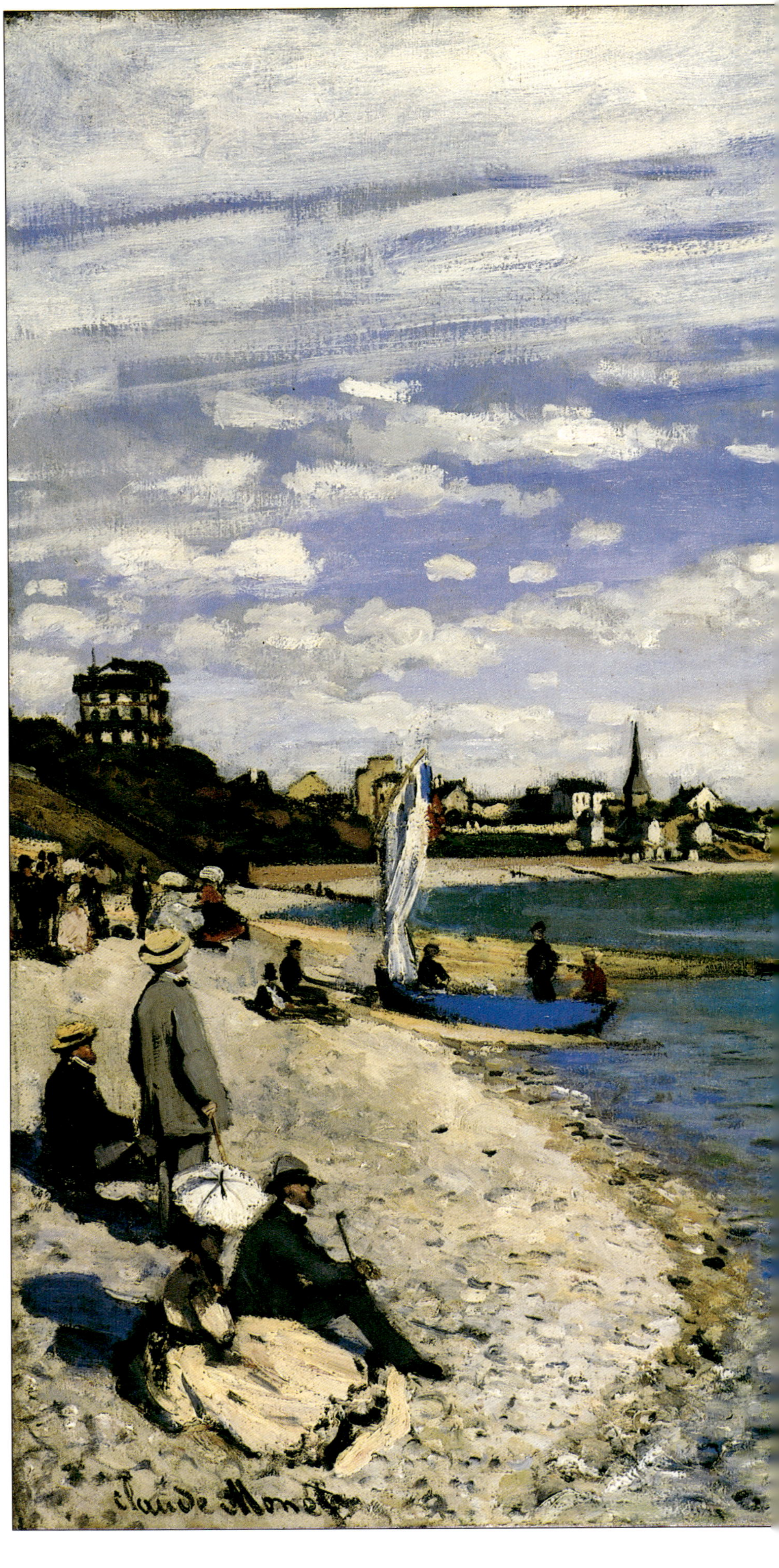

RIGHT:
Regatta at Sainte-Adresse
(1867)
METROPOLITAN MUSEUM OF ART, NEW YORK

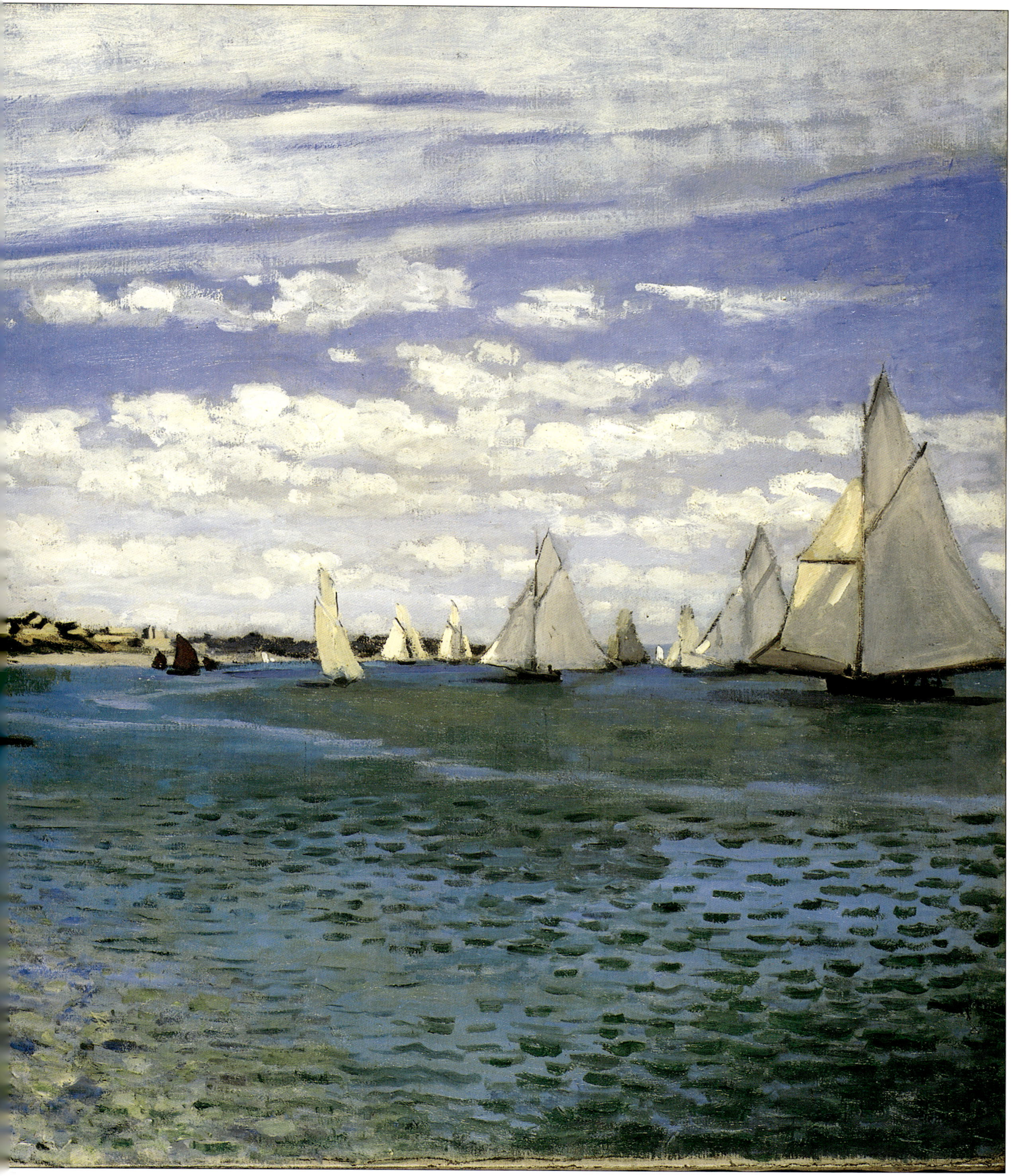

more like those of a concerned family friend than a lover – suggests that duty rather than love prompted his concern.

In any event, Monet did pay a flying visit to Paris, timed so that he could be present at the delivery. He wrote to tell Bazille that when his son Jean was born, on 8 August, 1867, he was surprised to feel a surge of love for the child. Nevertheless, within days he had dutifully gone back to Sainte-Adresse.

Among the canvases Monet completed during the summer was *Terrace at Sainte-Adresse* (pages 42-3), which is believed to show Adolphe Monet and Aunt Lecadre in the garden of the aunt's house. The picture has been analysed and used as evidence of Monet's state of mind during the summer of 1867, but such close approximations of life and art are always of debatable value – just how much so in Monet's case is suggested by the fact that his painting became ever-brighter and freer from the later 1860s, without any equivalent improvement in his personal situation.

Terrace at Sainte-Adresse is certainly one of Monet's less characteristic works. He once referred to it in a letter to Bazille as 'my Chinese painting where there are flags', and it has been suggested that it may owe something to Japanese prints – on the very questionable assumption that Monet, with European arrogance, made no great distinction between the arts of China and Japan. However, the most striking features of the picture are not crisply linear, like Japanese designs, but painterly. This is most notable in the exceptionally strong colours, which convey the almost uncanny appearance of objects lit up by a low, late afternoon sun; in places, Monet's use of pure primary colours for the flower blossoms anticipates his fully developed Impressionism. The division of the surface into three horizontal strips, and the smoky, vessel-strewn skyline, have the rather naive charm of a postcard or souvenir. Monet's father is easily the most important person in the picture, seated very prominently and very solidly in the foreground. Monet himself noted that the way he used flags and poles as a compositional device was considered very daring at the time; they are important as verticals, breaking up the schematic horizontals, and also as areas of strong colour, introduced into the upper part of the canvas to balance the floral effusion below.

Monet's other surviving paintings from the summer of 1867 were less idiosyncratic but of excellent quality. *The Beach at Sainte-Adresse* (page 45) presents an out-of-season view of the place, featuring local fishermen and their boats. In effect, it evoked an earlier time before the railways brought tourists to the Normandy coast; Monet has painted the scene in a consciously old-fashioned style with a very subdued palette. By contrast, everything is lighter and brighter in *Regatta at Sainte-Adresse* (pages 46-7), in which the beach is occupied by city folk in their smart clothes, watching the elegant manoeuvres of expensive private craft. The two paintings are almost identical in size and it is easy to believe that Monet intended them to be seen together and compared. Although he became fond of declaiming 'I should like to paint as a bird sings,' any notion that Monet was a 'natural', unselfconscious artist is refuted by the variety of devices he used to create appropriately contrasting atmospheres: the lower horizon and wider shoreline in *The Beach at Sainte-Adresse* is set off against the moving diagonal lines where the clouds break in the regatta painting, along with the curving sweep of the sea and the more involving closeness of the spectator to both people and boats.

Monet was highly productive during the months he spent at Sainte-Adresse, and no one would have supposed from the atmosphere of his work that he was anything but contented. His letters to Bazille, both before and after Camille's confinement, tell a different story. They are full of despairing descriptions of his helpless state and Camille's desperate need.

Bazille was his best friend and Jean's godfather, so it was natural that Monet should pour out his heart to him, but it is also obvious that, aware of the southerner's wealthy background, Monet looked to him for regular help and never really believed that Bazille, although on an allowance, could not lay his hands on spare cash or supplies. Bazille did often come to the rescue, but at times he evidently grew tired of being pestered and, rather than excuse himself further, sent no answer to Monet's appeals. This made Monet more urgent and he fired off one missive after another, his impatience intensifying until he came perilously close to insulting his friend. Aggressively self-centred and shamelessly cadging, the letters make uncomfortable reading; they show Monet at his worst or, from a different view, show just how desperate his situation was.

Although we have no hard evidence concerning his finances in 1867, enough is known of Monet's income in the 1870s to suggest that he may not have been as hard up as he protested to friends such as Bazille or, at any rate, that his poverty was largely of his own making. The root of his difficulties appears to have lain in his 'lordly' attitude to life. If not positively a spendthrift, he seems to have been a man who believed himself entitled to live in a certain style that it would be unthinkable to modify: if the money to pay

RIGHT:
Jeanne-Marguerite in the Garden
(1868)
HERMITAGE MUSEUM, ST. PETERSBURG

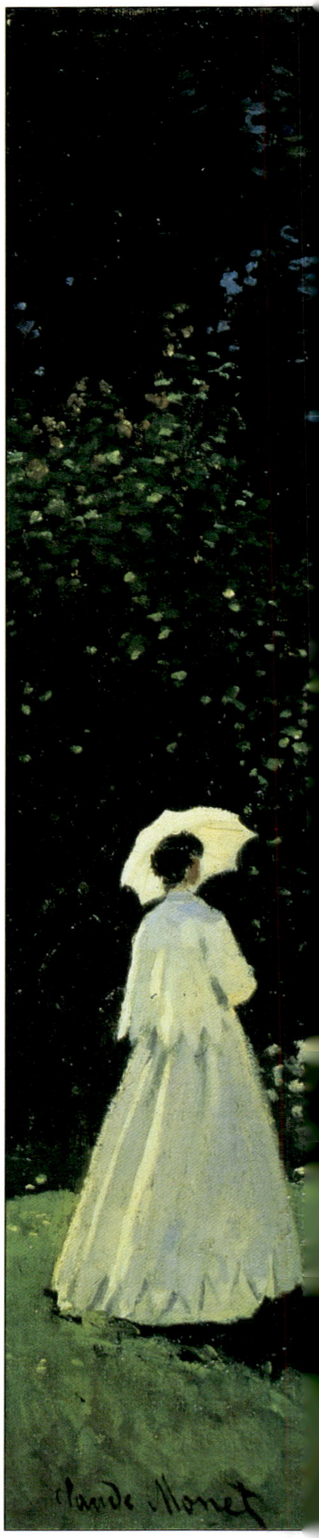

for it was not available, he suffered, borrowed or begged, but never seriously considered a change in that style. In other words, Monet's attitude was egotistical and irresponsible – justifiable, if at all, only by the possession of genius and the achievement of ultimate success.

Whatever Monet may have sometimes thought, Bazille was his active ally, using his influence with Adolphe Monet on Claude's behalf and finding a buyer prepared to pay 200 francs for a still life. In addition, having greatly admired *Women in the Garden*, Bazille finally offered to purchase it himself for 2,500 francs, far more than Monet can have hoped to get elsewhere. However, the boost to Monet's morale was probably greater than the financial benefit, since Bazille could only afford to buy it on the instalment plan, paying a useful but hardly thrilling 50 francs a month.

Meanwhile, Monet continued to spend most of his time in Normandy, finding occasional pretexts to enable him to spend a few days in Paris with Camille and Jean. He finally returned to the capital in March 1868, effectively throwing in his lot with his new family. His hopes were still fixed on the Salon, to which he submitted two harbour views, a splendidly wind- and wave-battered *Jetty at Le Havre* and *Boats leaving the Quay at Le Havre*; both were, as usual with his Salon submissions, very large. Only *Boats leaving the Quay* was accepted, and then only as a reluctant concession to one jury member, the Barbizon landscapist Daubigny, who championed it with an angry passion that silenced all opposition. This was a small success for Monet, and although the picture created no great stir, his name was still well enough known to make his contribution worth caricaturing. Ironically, the cartoons in the *Journal Amusant* and the *Tintamarre* have outlived their target, for the painting itself disappeared long ago. The *Journal Amusant* mockingly asserted that, since Monet was four and a half years old when he began it, he must be regarded as quite a promising artist. Monet was no longer a favourite of the art establishment, but even so the magazine's joke was probably flung out with no very serious intent; nevertheless, it did anticipate the years of relentless abuse to come, in which Monet and other artistic pioneers would be cavalierly dismissed on all sides as childish daubers.

Master in the Making

The cartoonist's attitude becomes easier to understand in view of Emile Zola's description of *Boats leaving the Quay*, which concluded,

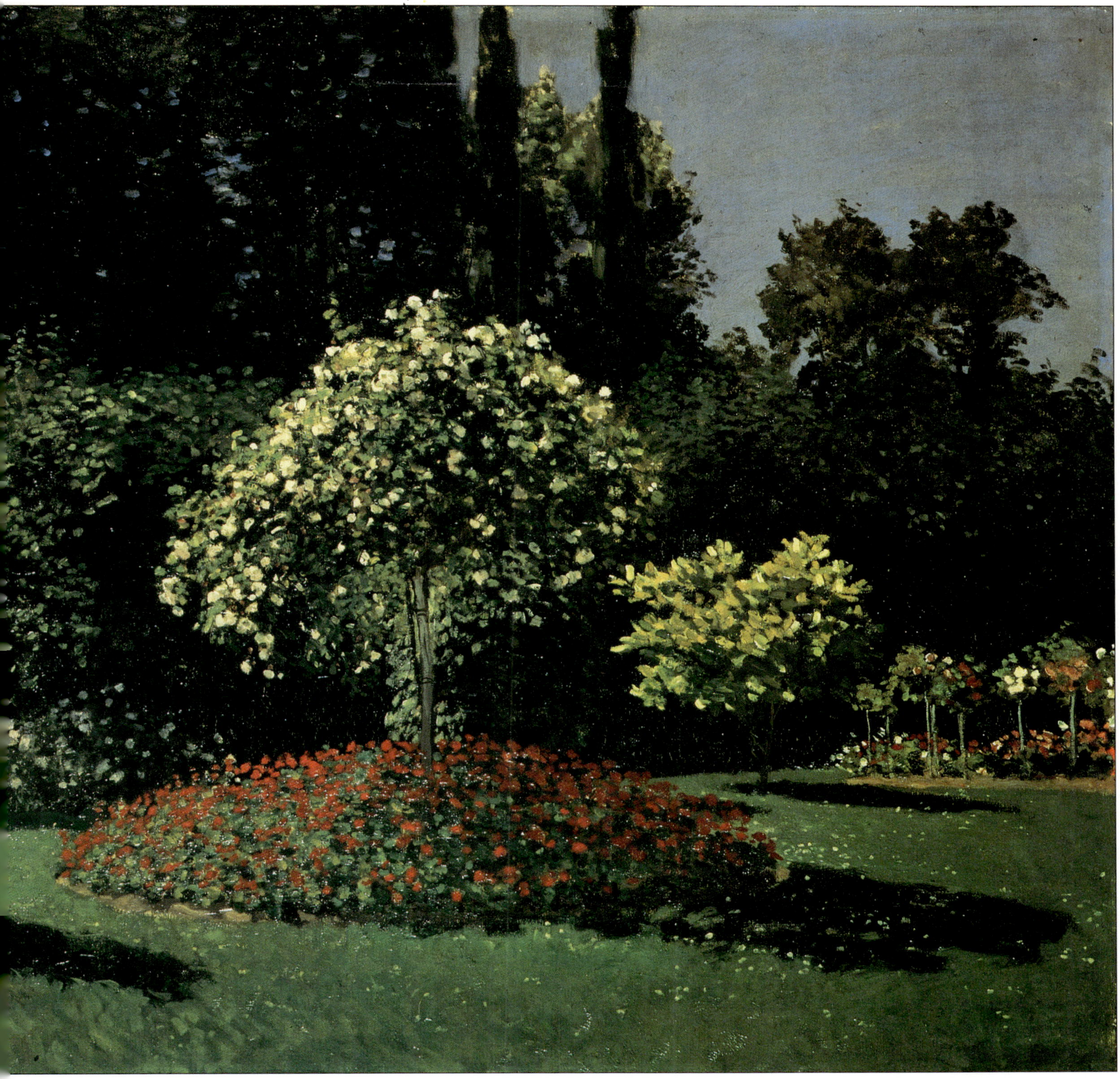

'What struck me about this painting was its immediacy and the roughness of the artist's touch'. Zola admired this 'roughness', but such brushwork was the reverse of the academic ideal, in which the strokes were carefully blended into invisibility, so that the painting presented a perfectly smooth surface within its frame, like a scene viewed through a window. To eyes accustomed to the

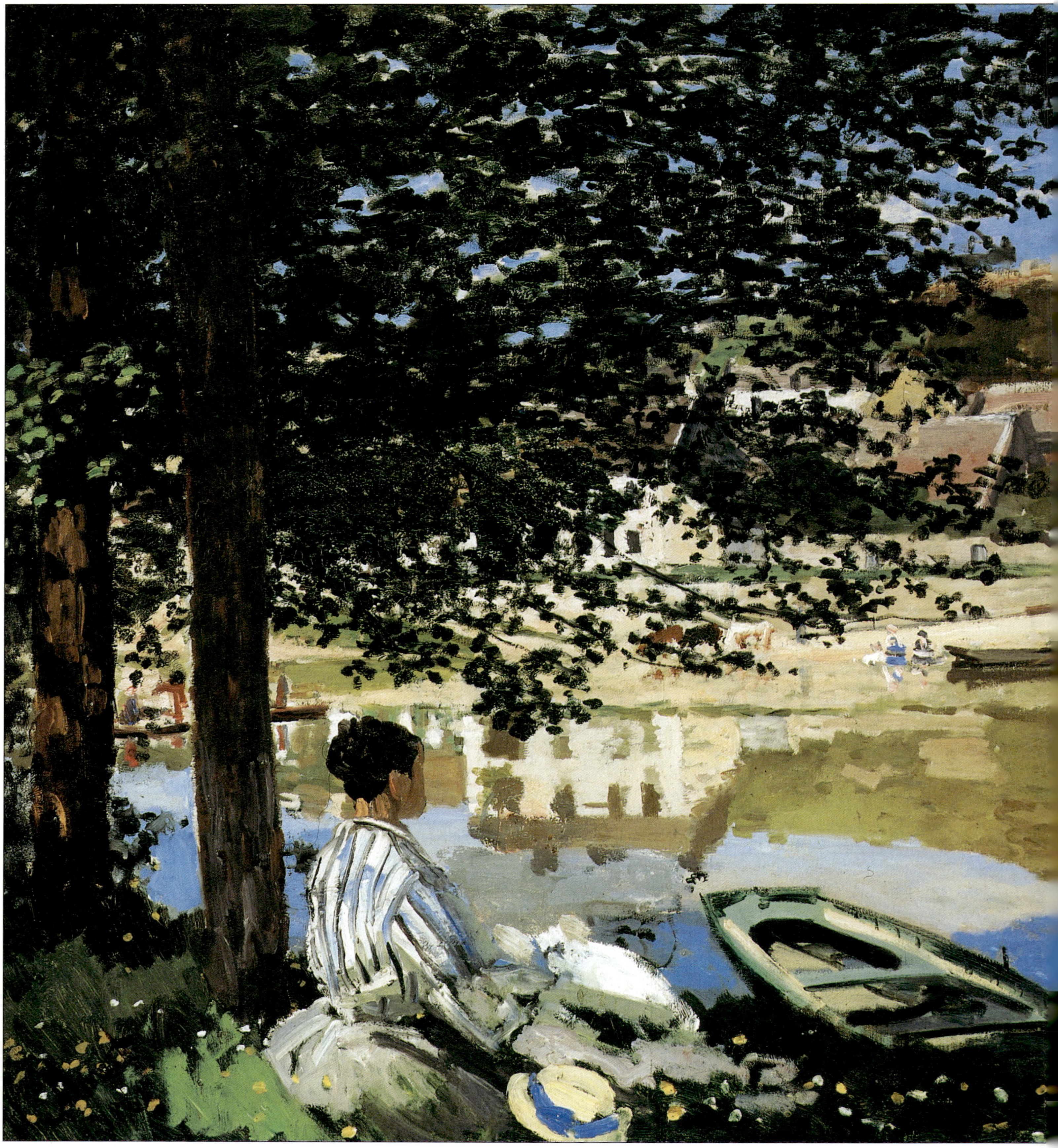

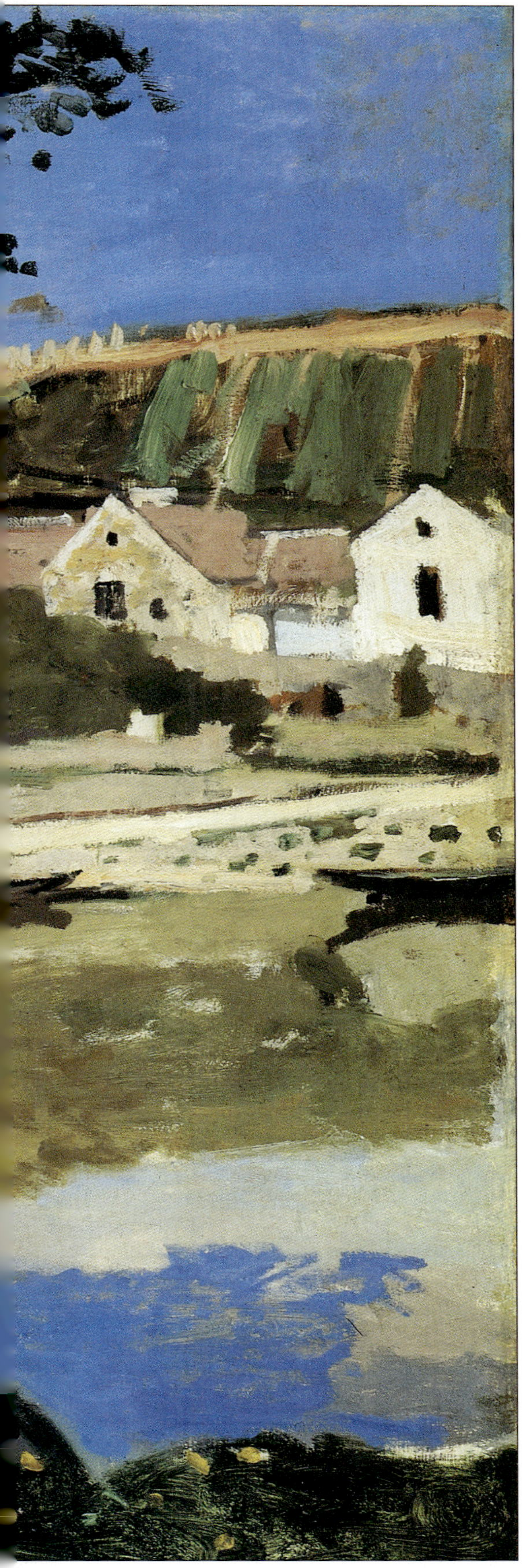

academic convention, vigorous, visible brushwork seemed merely a sign of negligence or incompetence.

The increasing freedom of Monet's style became even more striking in the work he accomplished at Bennecourt, a little place some 40 kilometres up the Seine, probably recommended by Zola; 15 years later Monet would settle for good at nearby Giverny, the most celebrated of his homes. Monet, Camille and Jean arrived at Bennecourt in May 1868, even before the Salon closed, and put up at an inn. During their stay, Monet painted *The Seine at Bennecourt*, often called simply *The River* (pages 52-3). This might well be called the first Impressionist painting because of its brusque, rapidly executed brushwork and also for its subject: although there is more to Impressionism than an evocation of light and wate,r and of leafy riverside pleasures, that is certainly the single most potent image associated with it. The slashes and dabs of colour convey a sense of the intense assault of the summer sun under which forms dissolve; and some of the painting, such as that of the woman's head and blouse, is remarkably cursory. In effect, for the first time, Monet reveals his delight in the broken and distorted reflections on the water, which offered a challenge that he would strive to meet for most of his life.

At the end of June, Monet went on his own to Le Havre, where an art show was being held in association with the local event of the year, an International Maritime Exhibition. His old teacher, Jean-François Ochard, was on the jury and his friend Boudin was one of the exhibitors. Monet must have felt that, as a local boy, he was likely to do well, and in the event he was awarded a silver medal – 'worth 15 francs', he noted with disgust, having failed in the much more important task of selling some of the canvases he had shown.

He was more successful in his other aim, which was to secure help from his former patron, Louis-Joachim Gaudibert. Gaudibert responded generously, commissioning portraits of himself and his wife Marguerite. The painting of Gaudibert, if it was done, has not survived; but the *Portrait of Madame Gaudibert* (page 55) has a unique place in Monet's life's work. It is his only commissioned portrait – that is, the only canvas by him that was intended to capture individual characteristics and satisfy a client. The result was a painting of sumptuous elegance. Madame Gaudibert is dressed in fashionably voluminous splendour, the narrow format and the verticals of the curtains adding to the impression of a tall, queenly presence. Her costume, the carpet and the other fabrics which

PREVIOUS PAGES 52-3:
The River
(1868)
ART INSTITUTE OF CHICAGO

occupy most of the picture space are enlivened by Monet's 'rough' treatment. The pose, half turned away from the spectator, is unusually self-effacing in a commissioned portrait, but it would be unwise to read too much into it, since the realization of Monet's conception must, from the very beginning, have been dependent on the sitter's consent.

All the same, the style of this portrait, along with the way in which Monet almost always painted Camille and his children, tends to confirm that he saw people as figures in a landscape rather than individuals who demanded special attention. If this is so, there are no good grounds for believing that the hostility of the art establishment prevented him from becoming a great portraitist. Although modified by the circumstances of his time, Monet's visual responses – the selectivity imposed by his temperament – were what determined the nature of his art.

In August, Monet arranged for Camille and Jean to join him at the Norman port of Fécamp, and soon afterwards they all moved further down the coast to the village of Etretat. Evidently Le Havre, only a short distance away, was still territory that the woman and child were forbidden to enter and Monet, in spite of his refusal to abandon them, seems to have accepted this verdict. Although the exact motives of all concerned are now hard to fathom, the intimidating influence of Victorian morality – and the authority of overbearing bourgeois parenthood – are all too clear.

In his letters to Bazille, Monet claimed that his father and aunt had refused to do anything more for him and again he sent off one desperate plea for help after another. He was 'naked', destitute, even momentarily suicidal: 'I was so depressed yesterday that I was stupid enough to throw myself in the water. Luckily there were no ill effects.' Since Monet so often wrote in an impassioned style – all heights and depths – it is possible that he exaggerated his plight (Bazille, at the other end, may have thought so too). At any rate, the situation improved. The Gaudibert portrait was done and *Woman in a Green Dress* at last found a buyer. Appropriately, he was the man-about-town and man of letters Arsène Houssaye, editor of the very periodical, *L'Artiste*, that had praised the painting so lavishly. Houssaye paid the very respectable sum of 800 francs for it.

Perhaps the most surprising revelation of the episode is that it had remained unsold for such a long time; even acclaim at the Salon did not guarantee a sale for a canvas or its painter. If that was so, what chance had an artist who failed or, like Monet, lost favour with the authorities? Such incidents bring home the precariousness

RIGHT:
Portrait of Madame Gaudibert
(1868)
MUSÉE D'ORSAY, PARIS

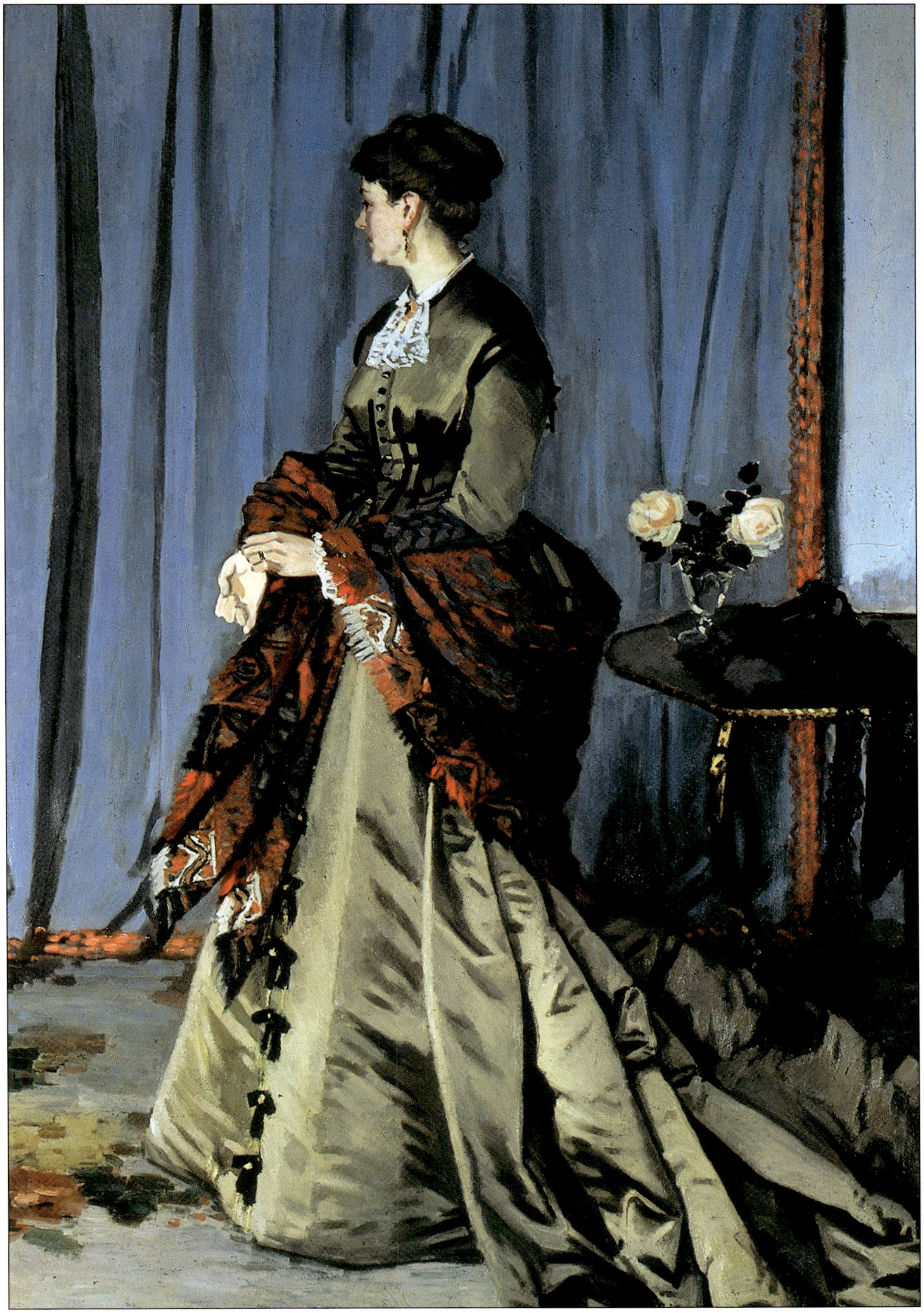

of nineteenth-century artists' careers, explaining both the widespread and apparently craven desire to conform, and the extremities to which outsiders such as Monet and Van Gogh were driven.

From December 1868 Monet began to write to his friends in an entirely different vein. He was enjoying the fierce, moody weather at Etretat, whose spectacular cliff formations and strong seas would draw him back again and again in years to come. He was also relishing a cosy domesticity – for the first time, it seems – in the little, winter-besieged house he had rented. Money cannot have been plentiful; several of the canvases Monet had shown at Le Havre were seized by his creditors and sold for knockdown prices. Luckily, Gaudibert came to the rescue again, bought them back for 80 francs apiece and probably gave Monet further assistance.

During these happy winter months Monet painted a number of seascapes and a snow scene, *The Magpie* (pages 58-9). This, like the slightly earlier *Cart, Road under the Snow at Honfleur* (pages 26-7), is an early example of a genre that the Impressionists, with their sensitive, feathery brushwork, were to make peculiarly their own. Monet met the challenge with great confidence, creating a symphonic arrangement of shades of white, with the small black presence of the bird providing an off-centre focus in stark contrast to the prevailing tones.

Much of Monet's happiness in his 'little cottage where there is a good fire and a nice little family' probably stemmed from the fact that he was working indoors as well as out. He had set himself to paint one more big canvas for the Salon – his only indoor scene of the kind and, as it turned out, his last major figure painting for years. This was another *Déjeuner*, customarily translated as *The Luncheon* (page 60) to distinguish it from the picnic scene (*Déjeuner sur L'Herbe*, pages 33-5) which he had painted three years before.

Like Monet's other Salon efforts, *The Luncheon* represented an attempt to conciliate the authorities without any essential sacrifice of principle. The subject was contemporary and everyday but eminently respectable: the kind of midday meal that millions of middle-class French families sat down to every day. The presence of the child and the abandoned toys on the floor in the foreground provided a touch of sentiment that was designed to appeal, while stopping well short of sentimentality. Moreover, if Monet's brushwork was too free in places to pass the test of academic purity, his use of earth colours created a brown-toned interior, reminiscent of the Dutch and other Old Masters, that might be expected to sway opinions and earn the approval of a Salon jury.

These points explain why *The Luncheon* is so unlike almost every other canvas by Monet; they are not criticisms and, in fact, add to the interest of a painting that is certainly admirable in its own right. On first viewing, the mother and child seated at the table in the light hold the attention. They are depicted with great tenderness, while the spread in front of them – in effect a superb still life – is painted with a gusto that makes the everyday foods seem extraordinarily succulent. The third place at the table, still undisturbed, awaits the master of the house, along with his copy of the newspaper *Le Figaro*, which he has not yet had time to open and read. If we could believe that this is any middle-class household, we might suppose that the man has not yet left his study or has not yet returned from work; but, given the setting and the sitters, it is more likely that he is too busy painting the scene to come to the table. Monet probably found it amusing to mix reality and illusion by implying that, while he was creating the picture, his presence was expected inside it! Flourishes of this sort were quite common in the past, and an artist with a more marked taste for elegant artifice would not have hesitated to hang a mirror on the back wall of the scene, showing a reflection of himself in the act of painting it.

Some other unusual features in *The Luncheon* emerge once the spectator's attention leaves the mother and child. The visitor has not been seated, has not even taken off her gloves and leans right back against the window, as if to put a distance between herself and the proceedings in the crowded little room. Since the meal has not even started, she cannot be a friend or relation who is waiting to go out with the family, yet it is difficult otherwise to account for her presence in the room and her attitude of self-chosen discomfort. The servant, too, plays an ambiguous role in the scene, standing close to the partly opened door, in a pose that usually signifies eavesdropping or a sly, malevolent presence. Such apparent mysteries may be accidental effects, or may indicate the presence of tensions within the 'nice little family'.

These seem rather feeble and implausible explanations, and there is a powerful objection to them: similar incongruities can be found in Monet's earlier paintings (especially *Women in the Garden*) and in directly contemporary paintings by Monet's peers, a fact that seems not to have been remarked on before. In an interior of 1868–69 by Degas, the atmosphere is so fatefully heavy with violence and alienation that it has often been labelled *Rape*; yet there is no authority for the title and, overtly, all that the scene shows is a

RIGHT:
The Magpie
(1868-9)
MUSÉE D'ORSAY,
PARIS

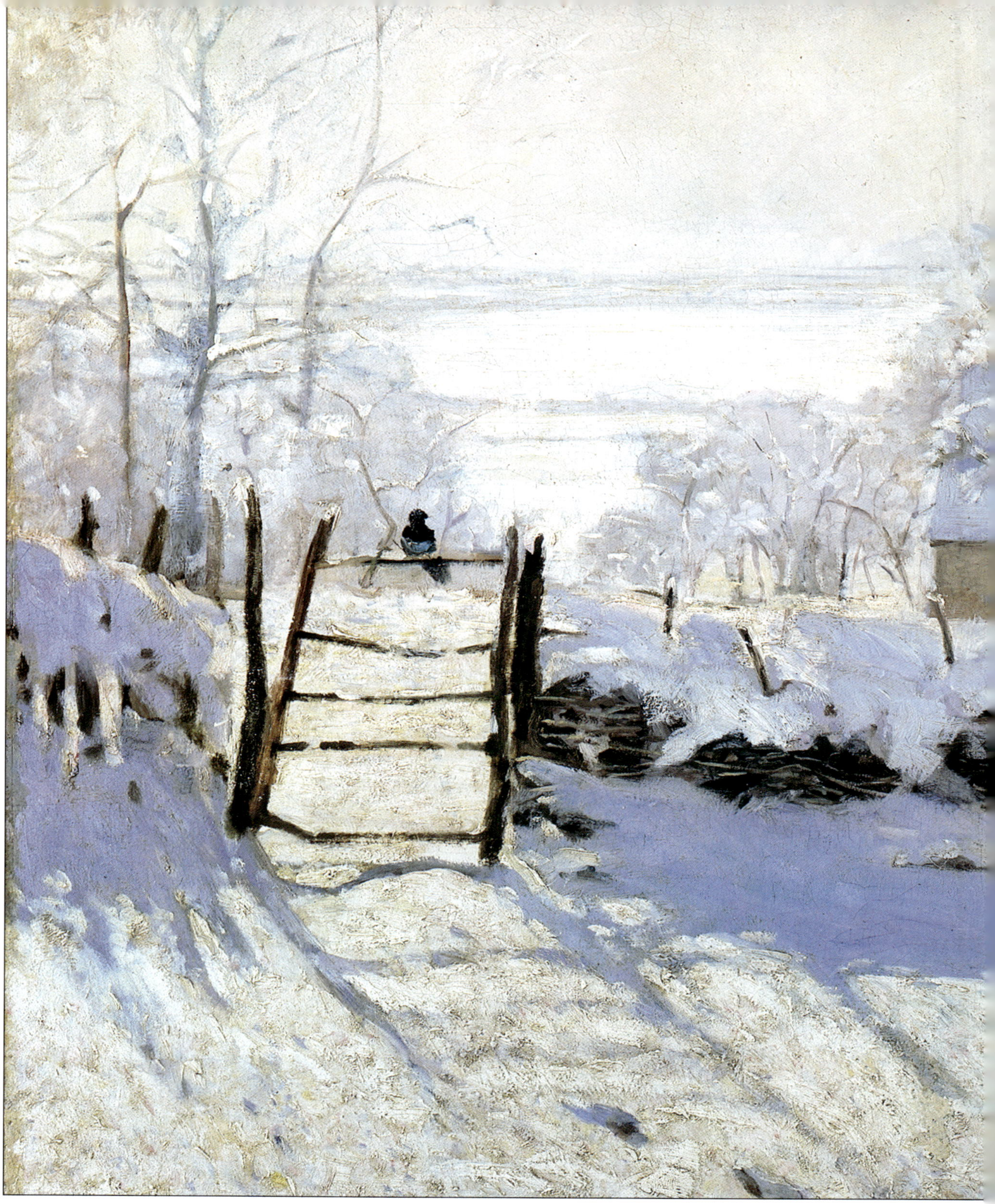

saturnine man leaning against a door and, across the room, a woman slumped in a chair with her back to him. Even more striking are the affinities between Monet's work and one bearing the same title, *Luncheon,* that was painted in the same year by Manet. Indeed, it has often been asserted that Monet knew of the older master's project and, as in 1865, deliberately set out to surpass

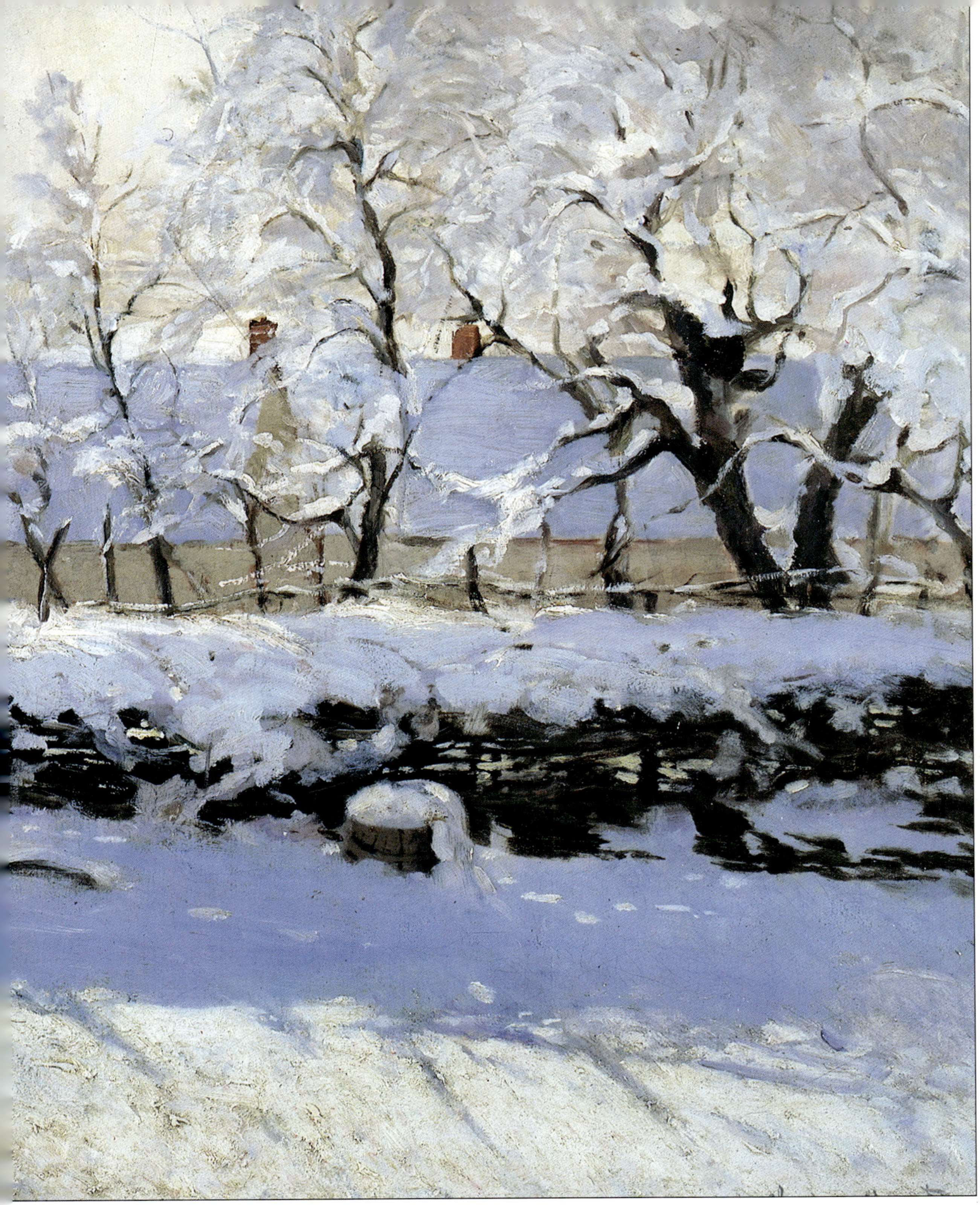

him, but no hard evidence has so far emerged to support this contention. As it happened, both canvases featured the artist's illegitimate son (although Manet's child, Léon Koëlla, was 16 years old), as well as a lingering maid and an outsider whose presence is not entirely in keeping with the setting; but whether these amount to anything more than some unsurprising correspondences

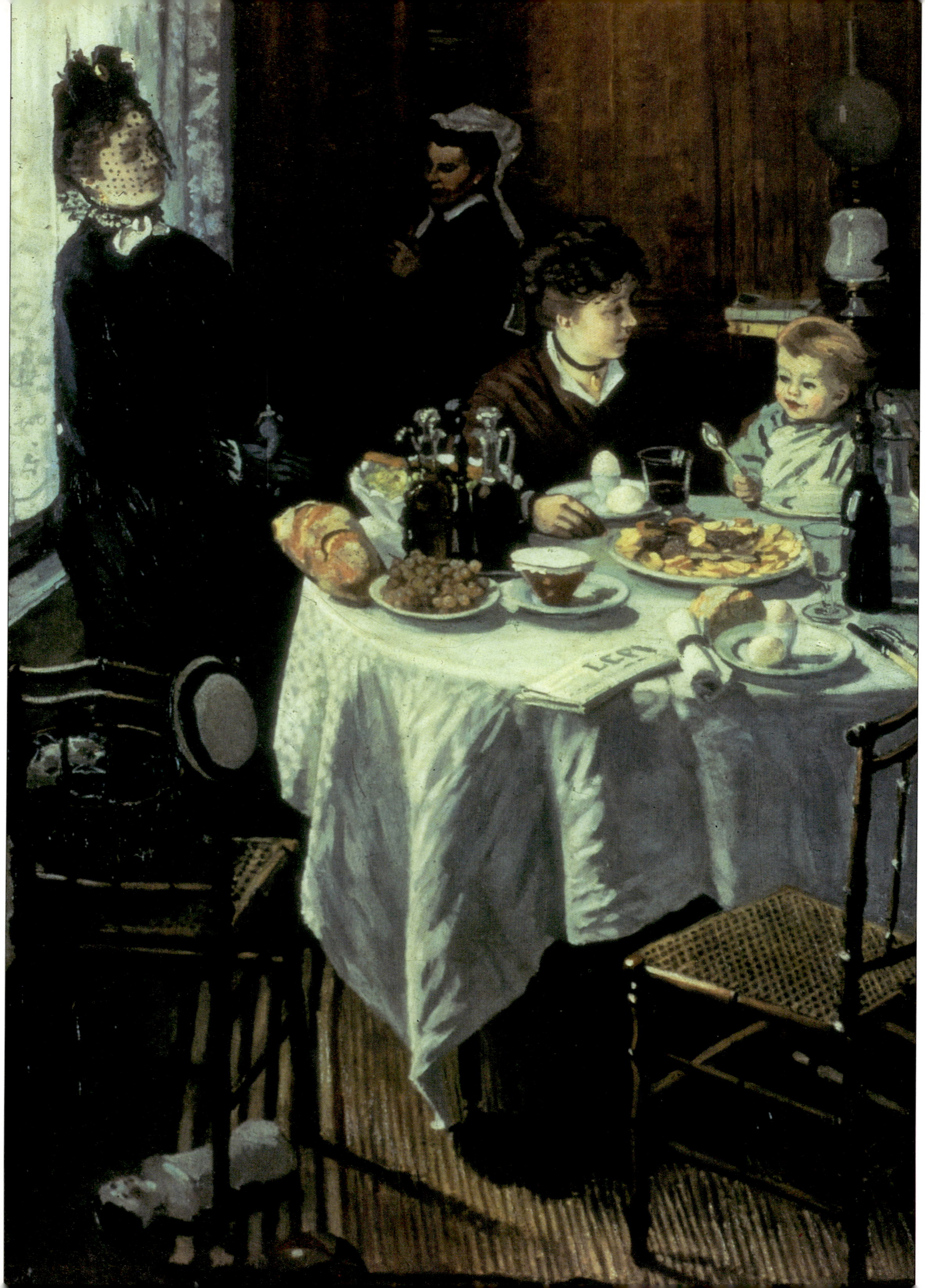

LEFT:
The Luncheon
(1868)
STÄDELSCHES
KUNSTINSTITUT,
FRANKFURT

between the work of contemporaries is another matter.

What remains beyond doubt is the mildly enigmatic atmosphere of Manet's *Luncheon*, in which a stylish young man is posed in front of a lunch table, flanked by people and things (including pieces of armour) that are subtly out of key with his clear, bright person. As in Degas' *Rape* and Monet's *Luncheon*, the spectator is led to interpret the scene as a snapshot from some untold story.

In Monet's case, one possible explanation is that he was trying to combine his modern-life subject with elements from the kind of anecdotal picture that was admired by the general public, while drawing back from blatant story-telling. If *The Luncheon* were re-titled in nineteenth-century fashion – for example, *The Unwelcome Visitor* - most of the enigma (even the absence of the head of the family) would immediately disappear, although Monet's more fanatical admirers might be angered to see one of his paintings put on a par with *The Awakening Conscience*!

However, it must be admitted that such an explanation does not account for the existence of similar enigmas in the work of Manet and Degas. An alternative that would at least cover Monet and Manet is that the paintings in question represented, in part, tributes to the great exponents of genre (everyday-life interiors), notably a host of seventeenth-century Dutch artists and the eighteenth-century French master Jean-Baptiste-Siméon Chardin. We know that Manet and Monet shared an admiration for them, although Manet always made more overt references to the Old Masters in his work. On this occasion, perhaps both took their cue from the classics of the genre whose grave beauty was often accompanied by hints that the apparently peaceful scenes concealed complex situations and relationships. The mystery may have been an illusion based on an ignorance of the allusions and symbols in the pictures, but by the nineteenth century it had become part of their appeal and, therefore, part of the 'Dutch' quality of a painting such as Monet's *Luncheon*.

The Luncheon is the last painting by Monet in which this kind of formal inquiry can be conducted with very much profit. From this point onwards the influence of tradition and the academies became virtually non-existent in his work, and his art became essentially a dialogue conducted between the painter and the visible world. As the winter of 1868–69 came to an end, he encountered a new crisis and unwittingly prepared for a momentous artistic breakthrough.

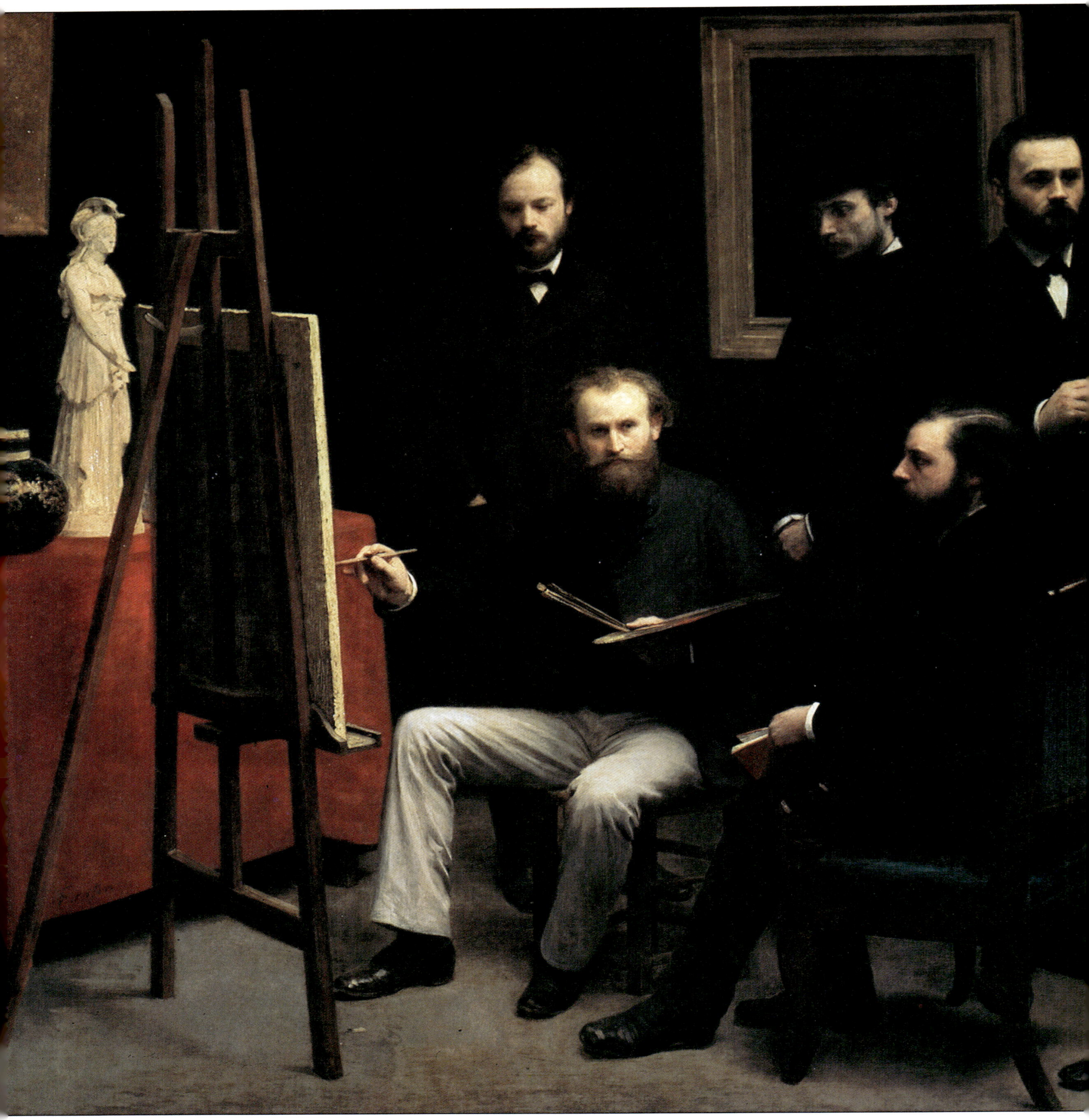

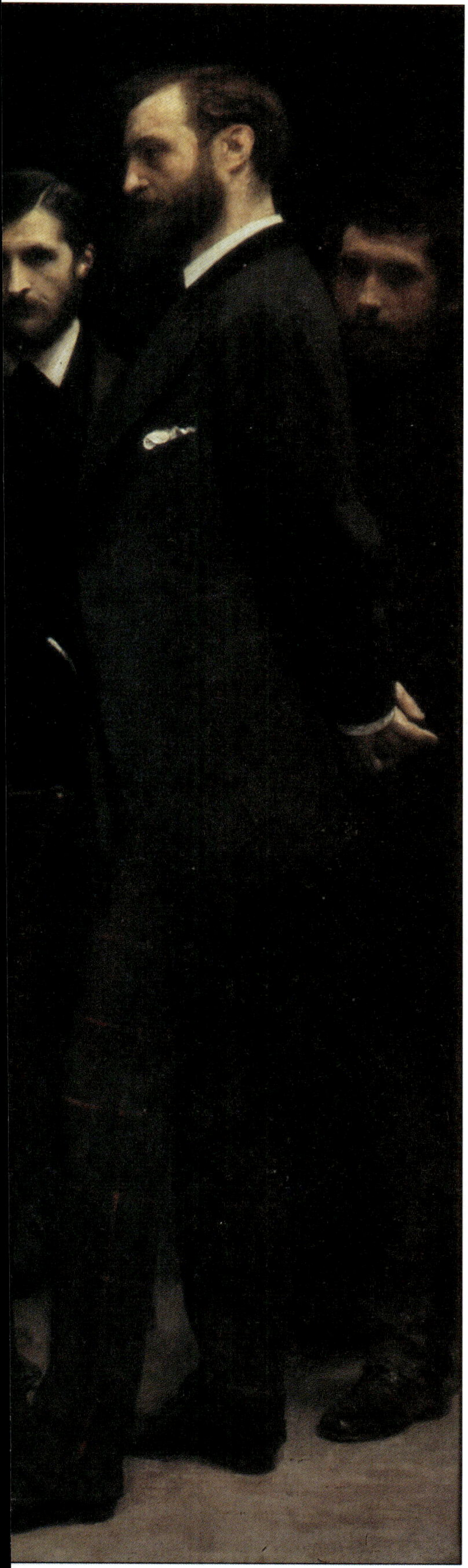

CHAPTER THREE

Years of Discovery

SPRING BEGAN BADLY. For reasons that remain unclear, Monet had second thoughts about submitting *The Luncheon* to the Salon jury, and eventually substituted two substantial views, the magpie snowscape and *Fishing Boats at Sea*, in which the boats sail through the early morning mist towards a brightening horizon. Incomprehensibly, these fine – and not markedly subversive – works were rejected by the jury. What made its decision even more difficult to understand was that, in most instances, its choices on this occasion were relatively liberal. Canvases by Renoir, Pissarro and Bazille were accepted, and even Manet – still regarded as the arch rebel of his generation – was allowed to show *The Balcony*, a painting somewhat less conventional than Monet's submissions. The jury was obviously singling out Monet for punishment, although it is not clear why they should have done so. A plausible reason would seem to be that he was regarded as the worst of the troublemakers, that is, the most original and subversive member of the younger generation. If so, the decision can be interpreted as a back-handed compliment. Naturally Monet failed to see it in that light, and

PREVIOUS PAGES 62-3:
A Studio in the Batignollies Quarter (1870)
Henri Fantin-Latour
Musée d'Orsay, Paris

RIGHT:
La Grenouillère (1869)
Metropolitan Museum of Art, New York

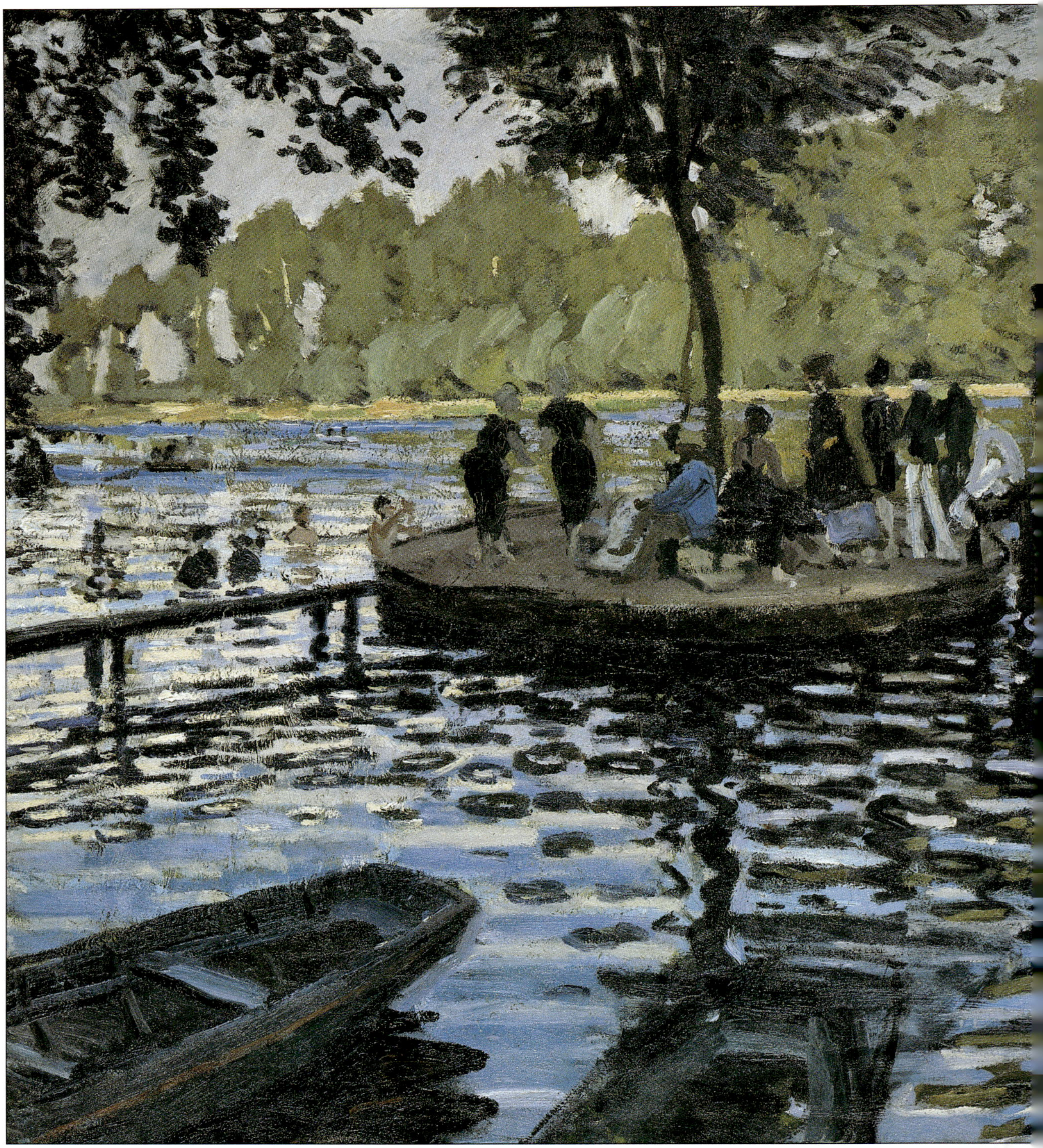

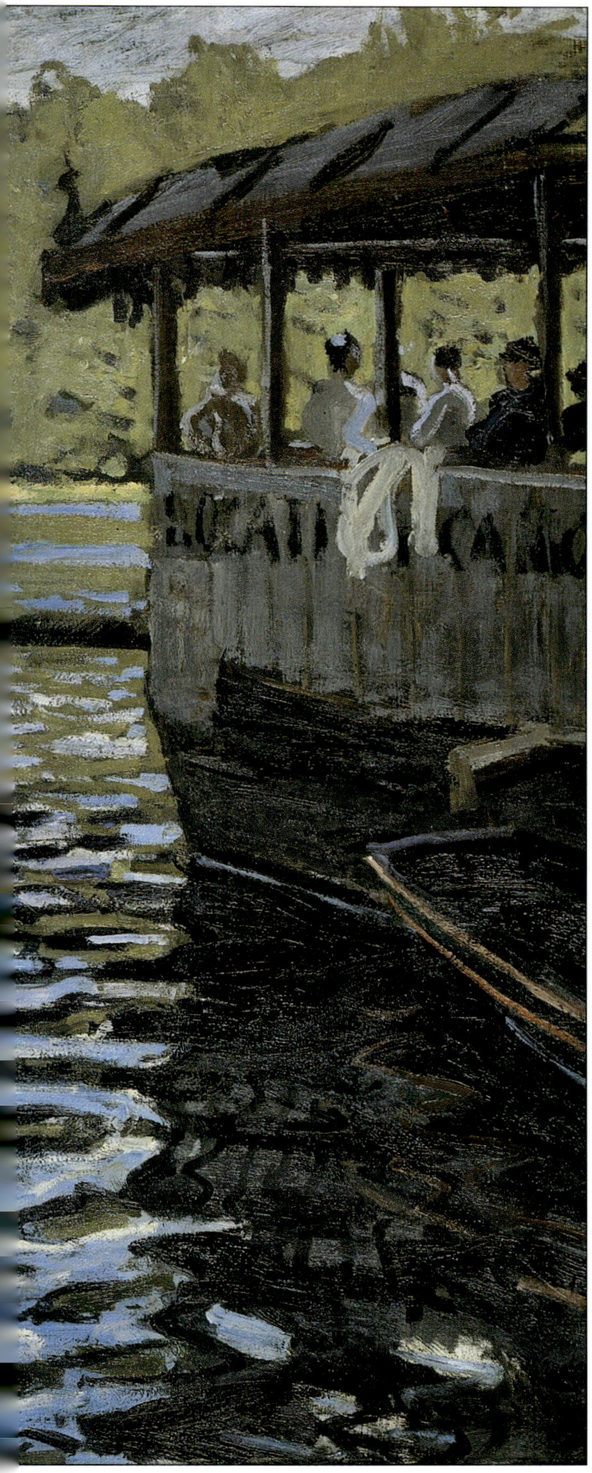

felt – as he had probably been intended to feel – humiliated by the contrast between his friends' success and his own rejection.

Although mortified, Monet was powerless, since there was no rival institution that might show his work and allow him to appeal directly to the public. The best he could manage in the way of a protest was to display *The Terrace at Sainte-Adresse* in the window of a well-known dealer in art equipment, Louis Latouche, who had a shop on the corner of the Rue Lafitte. Latouche, himself a painter of some skill, was sympathetic to the new trends that were emerging in the arts and bought a number of paintings from Monet over the years. By the standards of the time, *The Terrace at Sainte-Adresse* was luridly coloured and certainly much more unconventional than Monet's rejected Salon pictures. It attracted crowds who blocked the pavement outside Latouche's. In a letter to a friend Eugène Boudin claimed that the painting had gained its creator a 'fanatical following' among the young – unluckily for Monet, a group that had little money and no present influence.

Days at Bougival

Helplessness remained the theme of the months that followed, although Gaudibert once more came to the painter's assistance. By June Monet, Camille and Jean were established at Saint-Michel, a village just outside Bougival, in the area that he already knew well around the Seine north-west of Paris. However, he remained downcast and shortly after his arrival wrote to Houssaye (angling for a commission, it is true) that 'this fatal rejection has almost taken the bread out of my mouth, and although my prices are reasonable, the dealers and collectors turn their backs on me'.

Three months later he was still writing as though in despair to Bazille, rising to a moment of wrath when his friend suggested some ways in which he might economize. Monet's sharp response was that only someone in Bazille's position – who would never have to do it – could talk of walking instead of taking the train or of chopping the wood for oneself. Although Monet's exasperation is perhaps understandable, reading such a letter confirms the suspicion that his poverty was borne with – and accentuated by – a certain middle-class style, no doubt related to the 'lordly' manner of his student days that Renoir recalled so vividly.

However, Renoir was also on the scene in the summer of 1869 and could bear witness to the reality of Monet's poverty. Renoir and his companion Lise Tréhot had themselves fallen on hard times and had taken refuge with Renoir's parents at Ville d'Avray, not far from Bougival. The two artists once more made painting trips together and Renoir, blessed with a happy-go-lucky temperament, enjoyed himself most of the time in spite of the dearth of food. Sometimes Monet and his family were on such short commons that Renoir purloined provisions from his parents' house and took them over to Saint-Michel. Yet, if Renoir is to be believed, the Monet who was his companion during that summer was nothing like the Monet who wrote begging letters: it was he who kept up their spirits and, however desperate things seemed, never gave way to despair.

Between June and October 1869, Monet and Renoir set up their easels and worked side by side whenever they had enough materials to paint with. The area around Bougival was only a few kilometres from the capital and, especially since the development of the railways, had become immensely popular with Parisians who felt like a day out in the country. For much of the time Monet and Renoir positively sought out the trippers, thereby creating a type of landscape very different from the peaceful, nature-dominated views of the Forest of Fontainebleau painted by Daubigny and the Barbizon group. In this sense the geography of landscape painting is decisive and it is no accident that Impressionist painting is associated above all with the area along the Seine below Paris, and with riverside holiday pleasures.

Impressionism as a term had not yet been invented, but in the summer of 1869 Monet and Renoir pioneered the key techniques of the Impressionist landscape. Their most remarkable canvases were painted at a highly fashionable place on an arm of the Seine known as La Grenouillère ('The Frog Pond'), which combined bathing and boating areas with excellent facilities for dining and dallying. During the period when Monet and Renoir were working at La Grenouillère, it acquired the official stamp of approval when it was honoured by the French Emperor, Napoleon III (Louis-Napoleon), and his wife, the Empress Eugénie. No doubt with a view to exploiting the fact, Monet planned to make the place the subject of a painting for the Salon. Like Manet, he still regarded the Salon as 'the real battleground' for any artist who hoped to make a name for himself.

Nevertheless, the two friends were soon working with an extraordinary freedom that they must have suspected would make their canvases unacceptable at the Salon. It is possible that, at first, they even thought of themselves as 'sketching' rather than

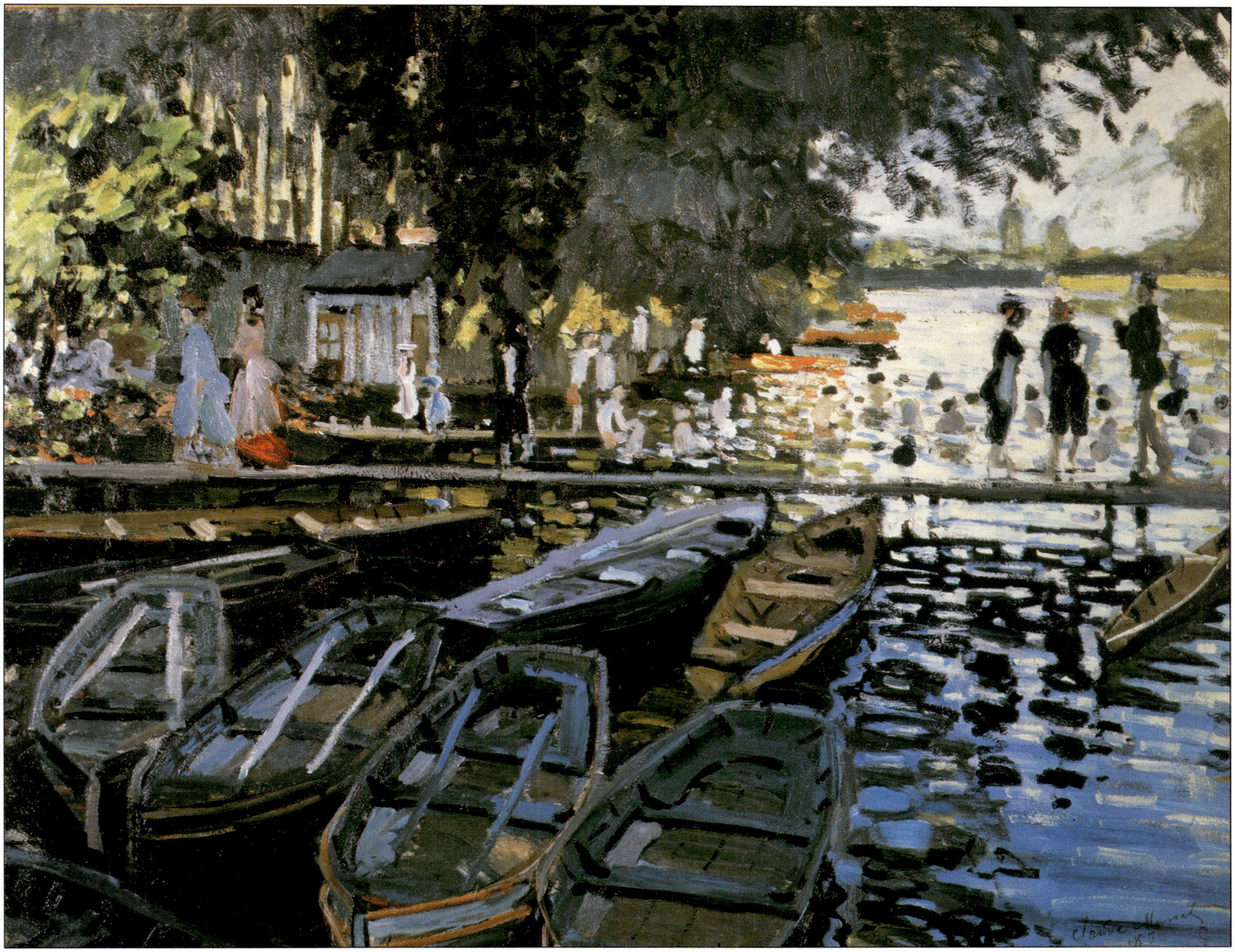

executing proper paintings – until they realized that the 'sketches' were so vivid and atmospheric that they were more exciting than conventionally admired landscapes. In Monet's case, the work he accomplished in the summer of 1869 was not an entirely new departure, but a powerful surge forward from a well-prepared base. In outdoor canvases such as *The River* (pages 52-3), he had deployed areas of broad, unmodified colour, making no attempt to convey smooth, gradual changes of tone, leaving the brushwork visible, eliminating many details and only here and there defining an object with 'drawn' outlines. The avant-garde character of *The River* becomes even more apparent when it is compared with the relatively conventional technique he used for his Salon-oriented interior *The Luncheon* (page 60).

Now, in the summer of 1869, he began to paint in an even more distinctive way, although he was too intuitive an artist ever to

ABOVE:
La Grenouillère
(1869)
NATIONAL GALLERY, LONDON

translate what he did into an inflexible system. His most radical innovation was to paint with small brushstrokes of pure colour. Instead of mixing two or more pure colours on his palette, he grouped together the different little touches of individual colours in such a way that the spectator's eye perceived them as blended into a single colour. The effect of this 'optical mixing' was livelier and more vibrant than conventional shading could give, but a canvas painted in this way needed to be seen from a little distance; close up, it dissolved into an undifferentiated jumble of colours. Unfortunately, the public and the critics were used to a very different type of painting, so highly finished that the brushwork was invisible and the details of the scene remained crisp and clear even when the eye was brought right up to the canvas. In fact, one way in which people praised a work was to remark that 'you'd hardly know it had been painted'. So the kind of canvas that Monet and Renoir were creating looked to most of their contemporaries as if they had not bestirred themselves to finish it: it was a preparatory sketch or, if seriously intended as an exhibition painting, an incompetent daub. This misunderstanding dogged Monet and his comrades for decades until their persistence had re-educated the public.

The 'broken brushwork' practised by Monet and Renoir was ideal for working in the open air, enabling the artist to record his perceptions swiftly and truthfully before there was a change of light or atmosphere. In practice, some later work in the studio might be needed, but the process was fundamentally different from the academic routine of working up sketches and studies into a separate, highly finished painting. The directness of the Impressionist method also meant that the artist could register actual appearances with an unfamiliar exactness – the way in which the light modified or even changed the colours of objects, for example, and the range of hues present in shadows, which were popularly supposed to be black. Here, too, convention blinded spectators, so that in 1876 a critic, writing of a Renoir nude whose body was dappled with reflections from the surrounding foliage, jeered at the greenish tints as evident signs that the girl was a putrefying corpse.

In the 1860s, Monet had been a more daring innovator than Renoir, who was in many ways a traditionalist, not unhappy at times to tackle mythological subjects with which he could hope to win favour at the Salon. During the summer of 1869 the two artists worked together on a basis of equality, so much so that it is now

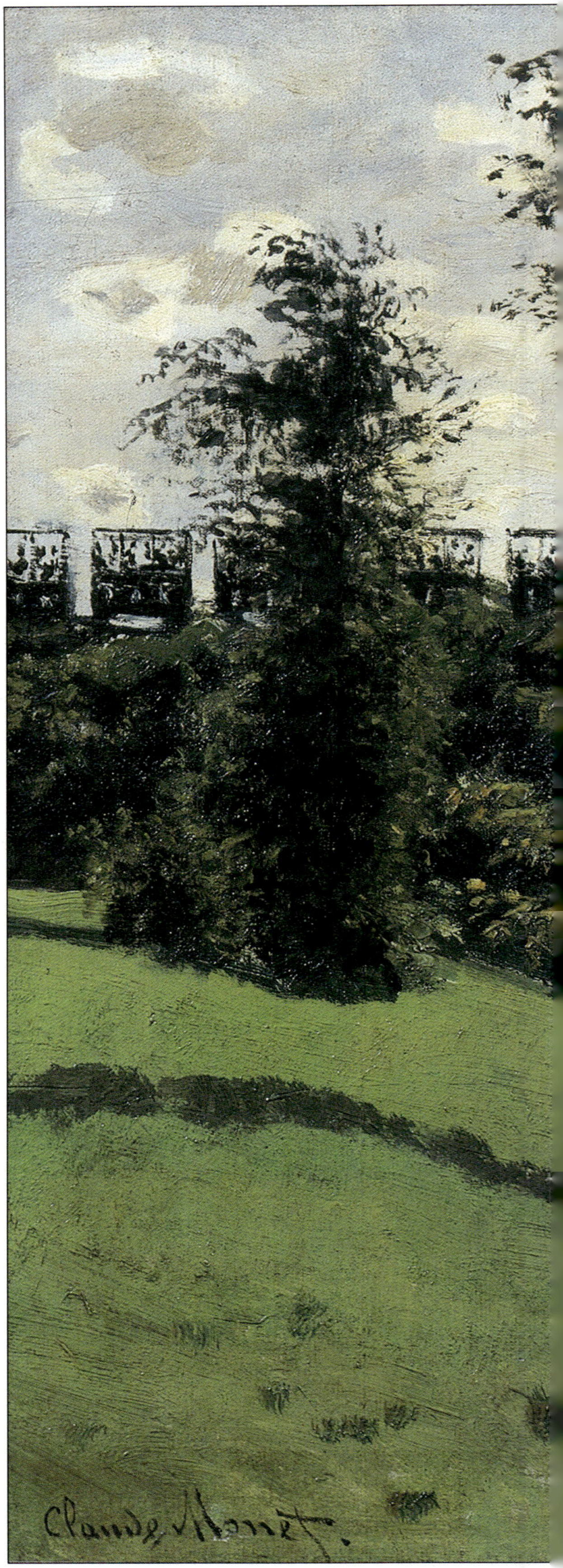

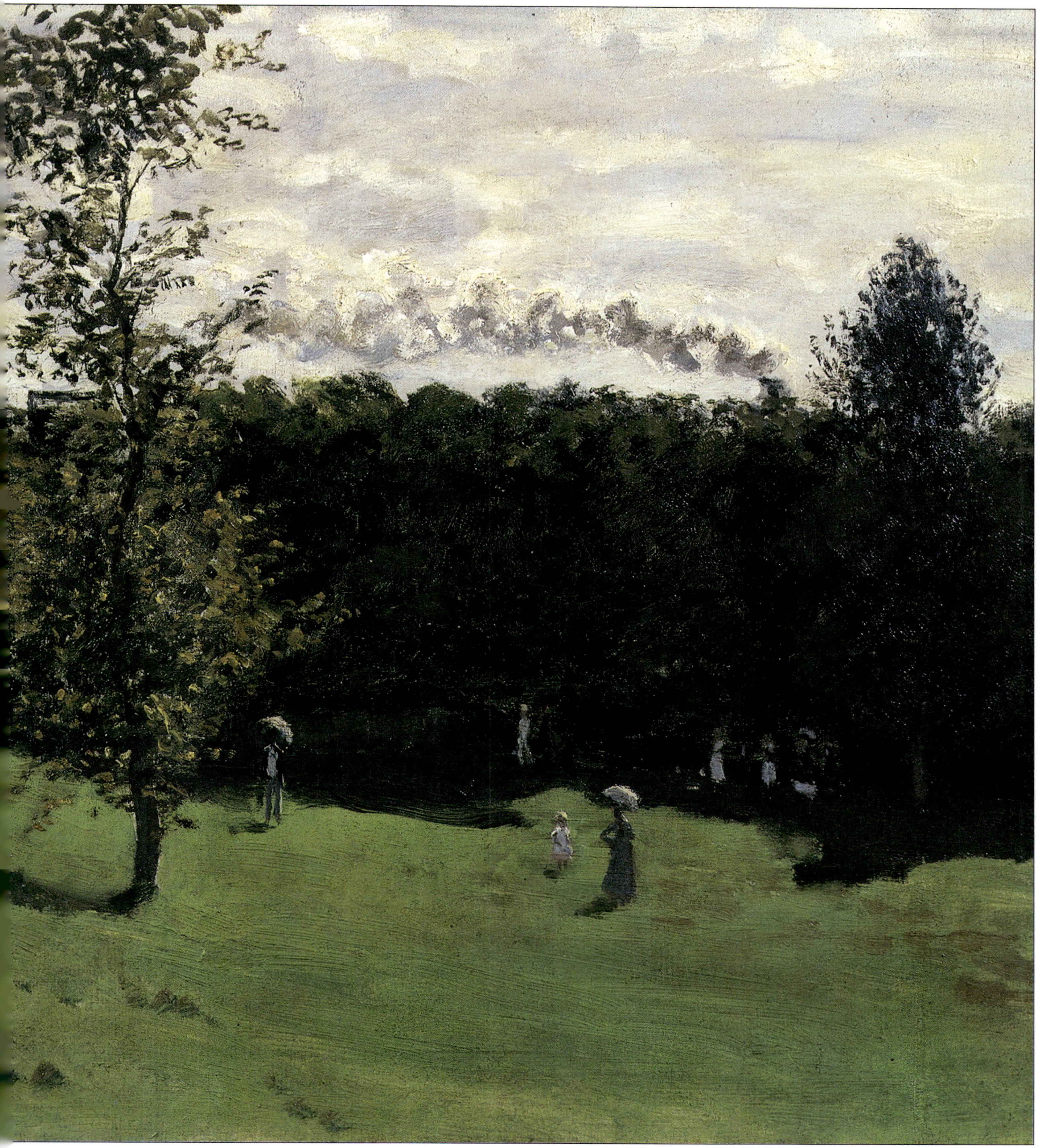

PREVIOUS PAGES 68-9:
The Train in the Countryside (1870)
MUSÉE D'ORSAY, PARIS

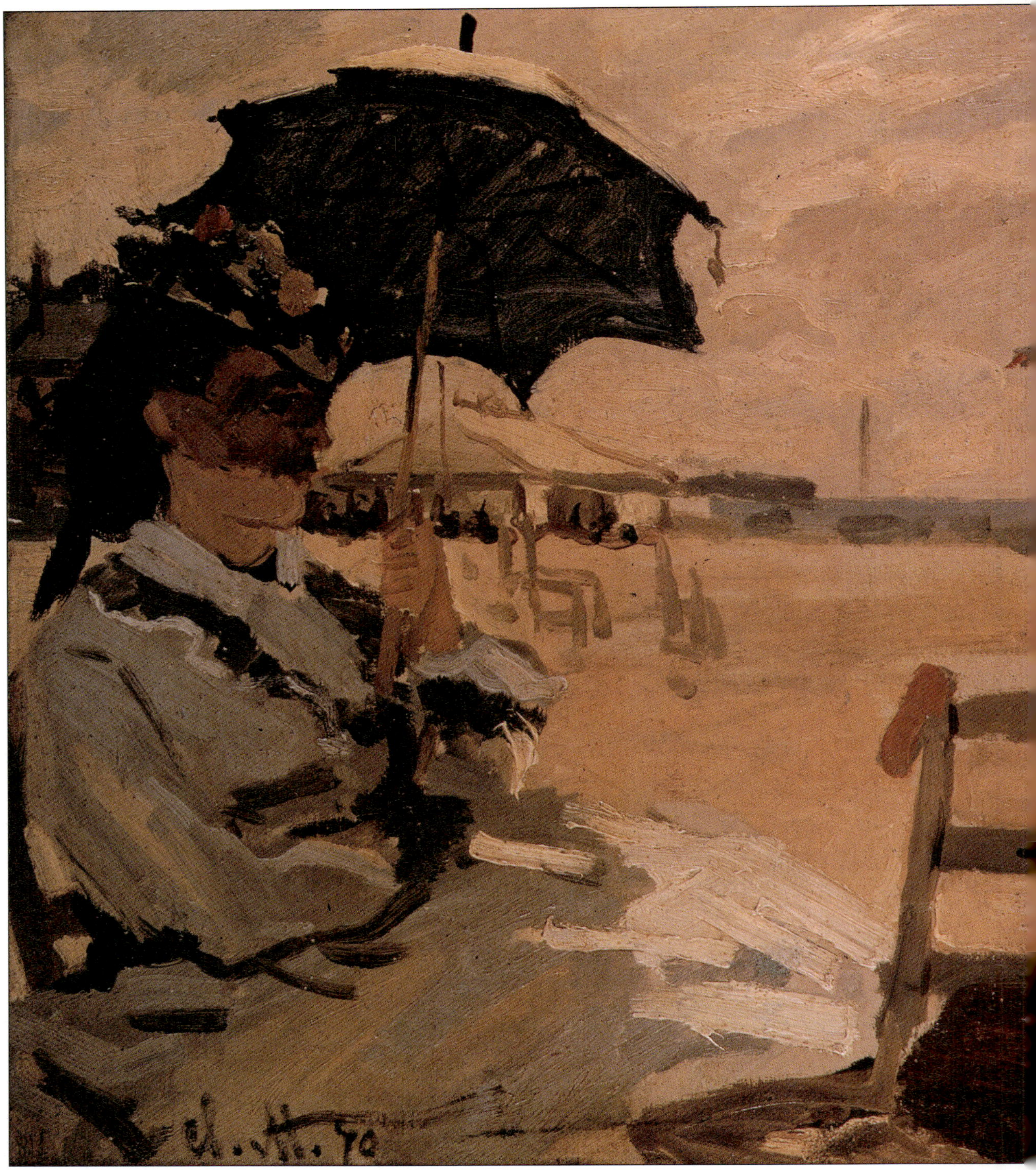

RIGHT:
The Beach at Trouville (1870)
NATIONAL GALLERY, LONDON

impossible to evaluate their contributions separately. Moreover, it is said that in later life, when confronted with a canvas from this period, they were not always certain which of them had painted it. Between them Monet and Renoir created what later became known as the Impressionist landscape. Other friends, notably Camille Pissarro and Alfred Sisley, were moving in the same direction and would bring their distinctive talents to the Impressionist movement. How much of the Impressionist technique each found

out for himself, and how much stemmed from Monet and Renoir, we are never likely to know.

All four artists were certainly in contact with one another and ready to exchange ideas. Apart from individual encounters, they met fairly frequently at the Café Guerbois in the Grand Rue des Batignolles, near Monet's studio. Manet was still regarded as the leader of the younger generation on the basis of his daring 'modern life' subjects, and a table at the Guerbois was permanently set aside for him. Artists and writers, including all the most important future male Impressionists – Degas, Monet, Renoir, Sisley, Pissarro, and Cézanne, but not, for reasons of propriety, the woman Impressionist Berthe Morisot – turned up at the café to gossip and debate. When reminiscing in later life, Monet sometimes paid warm tribute to the encouragement he derived from meetings at the Guerbois, but at other times he implied that his own appearances there were rare because he had little patience with theoretical discussions. In view of his frequent absences from Paris this cannot be too far from the truth, but he probably exaggerated a little to emphasize his role as the lonely, independent, intuitive man of genius.

In the winter of 1869–70 he was certainly in Paris often enough to be included in two group portraits: Bazille's *The Artist's Studio, Rue de la Condamine*, and Fantin-Latour's *A Studio in the Batignolles Quarter* (pages 62-3). In Fantin's painting, Monet is a rather shadowy figure on the far right, behind his enormously tall friend Bazille. Renoir and Zola are also in the group, but the focus of the picture is Manet, who is shown seated and painting a portrait of the writer Zacharie Astruc; in fact, the painting is often called *Homage to Manet.* At this time Monet obviously did not object to being portrayed as a member of a group. His presence in both paintings, unlike Pissarro and Sisley, who were in neither, suggests that contact with fellow artists and mutual support were still of considerable importance to him – as, indeed, all the evidence of the next few years confirms.

Rejection at the Salon

Monet found himself artificially isolated when submissions were made for the Salon in the spring of 1870. His friends were again quite successful – Manet, Degas, Bazille, Pissarro and Sisley were all represented – while both his paintings were rejected. In the case of *La Grenouillère* this was not surprising, as it was one of the

PREVIOUS PAGES
70-1: **Bathers at La Grenouillère**
1869
Claude Monet
© DACS 1996
NATIONAL GALLERY, LONDON

rapid fashion in order to capture the light and atmosphere of the moment, applying the paint in small patches of pure colour that created a vibrantly lively surface; as we have seen, this was a radical departure from the traditional method of mixing paints to achieve carefully graduated tones and a smooth final effect.

The liveliness of the technique was matched by the liveliness of the scenes it was used to record. Whereas the Barbizon painters had tended to concentrate on virtually unpeopled woodland views which appeared 'timeless', the Impressionists painted a countryside inhabited by unmistakably contemporary citizens who were more often than not visitors from a town, and at leisure rather than at work. Generally speaking, Impressionism was modern, urban and middle-class. In the La Grenouillère canvases of both Monet and Renoir (pages 76-91 and 203-11) the human presence is important, although the temperamental difference between them is already apparent. When painting for himself (and not for the Salon), Monet pulls back from human beings, rendering them as no more than 'figures in a landscape', whereas Renoir's inclination is to get close enough for the figures to dominate that same landscape, imbuing it with characteristic gaiety. The difference, small but definite until the early 1870s, later widened until there was not the slightest resemblance between their styles.

Monet may initially have regarded his La Grenouillère canvases as 'sketches'. However, when he submitted a presumably finished painting of the place to the Salon jury in the spring of 1870, it was done in very much the same style, although the scene was more panoramic and, with the addition of sailing boats, more picturesque. (Or so it appears in black-and-white reproduction: like a number of Monet's canvases, this *La Grenouillère* is presumed to have been destroyed during World War II, although it is just possible that it will reappear among the works carried off by the Soviet army, which have now begun to be shown in Russia.) With *La Grenouillère*, Monet sent in the *Luncheon* of 1868, which had a much better chance of being shown and liked; but the majority of the jury were still resolutely hostile and, despite vehement protests by Corot and Daubigny, both pictures were rejected. Once more, for reasons that are still unexplained, Monet was singled out for humiliation while most of his friends were moderately successful. Understandably, after this rebuff Monet gave up any ambitions he may have entertained to become a star of the Salon and painted the subjects he liked in the style that suited him.

Although the La Grenouillère episode seems to have been

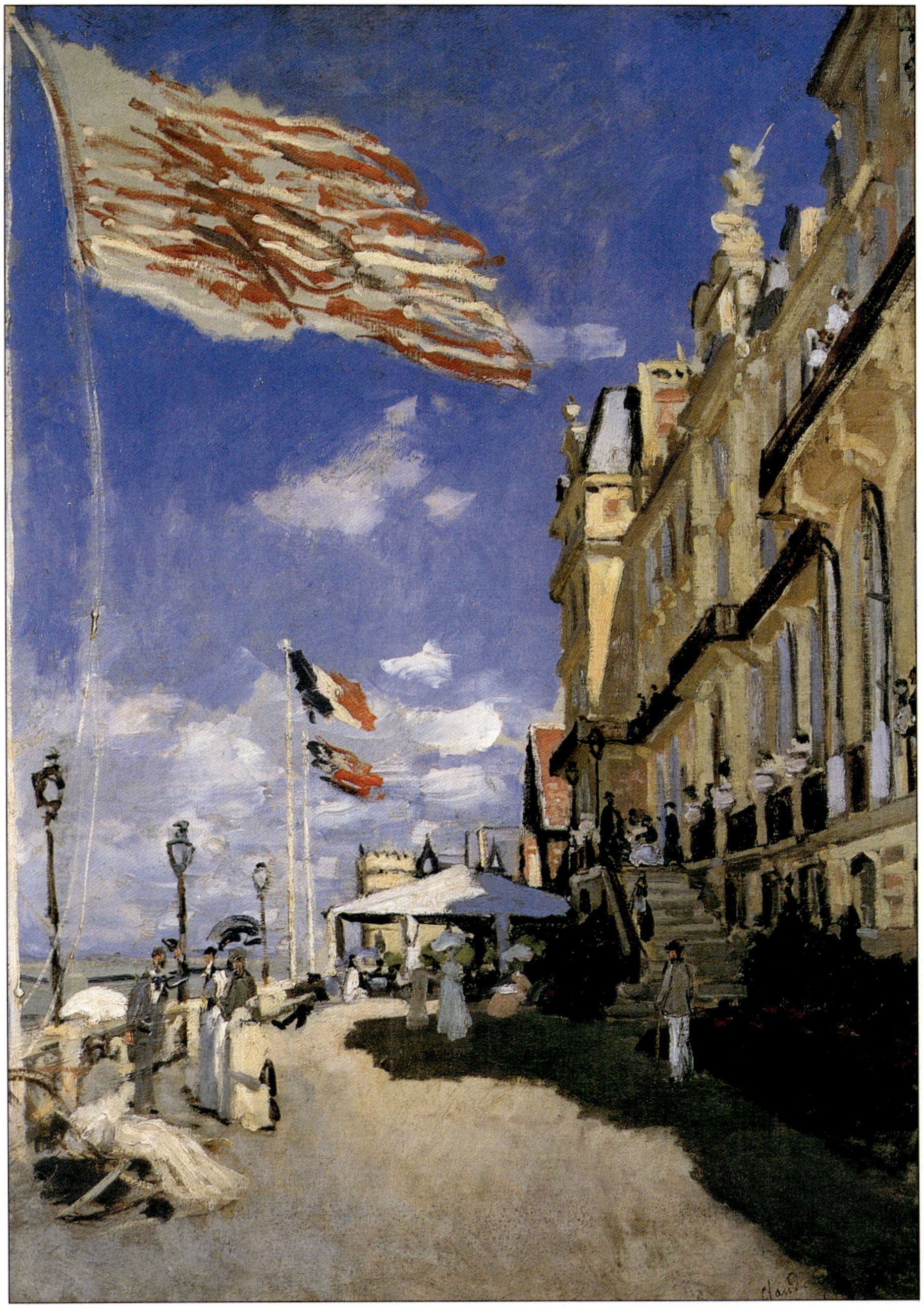

LEFT: **The Hôtel des Roches Noires** 1870
Claude Monet
© DACS 1996
MUSÉE D'ORSAY, PARIS

decisive in the development of the Impressionist landscape, it is not possible to trace the spread of ideas and techniques in any detail. All of the major male Impressionists were in contact with one another, not least in the informal atmosphere of the Café Guerbois. Monet himself was in Paris frequently enough to make up one of the admiring group in *A Studio in the Batignolles* (pages 34-5), where he is the small, neat-looking figure on the extreme right.

In June 1870 Monet and Camille were married quietly in

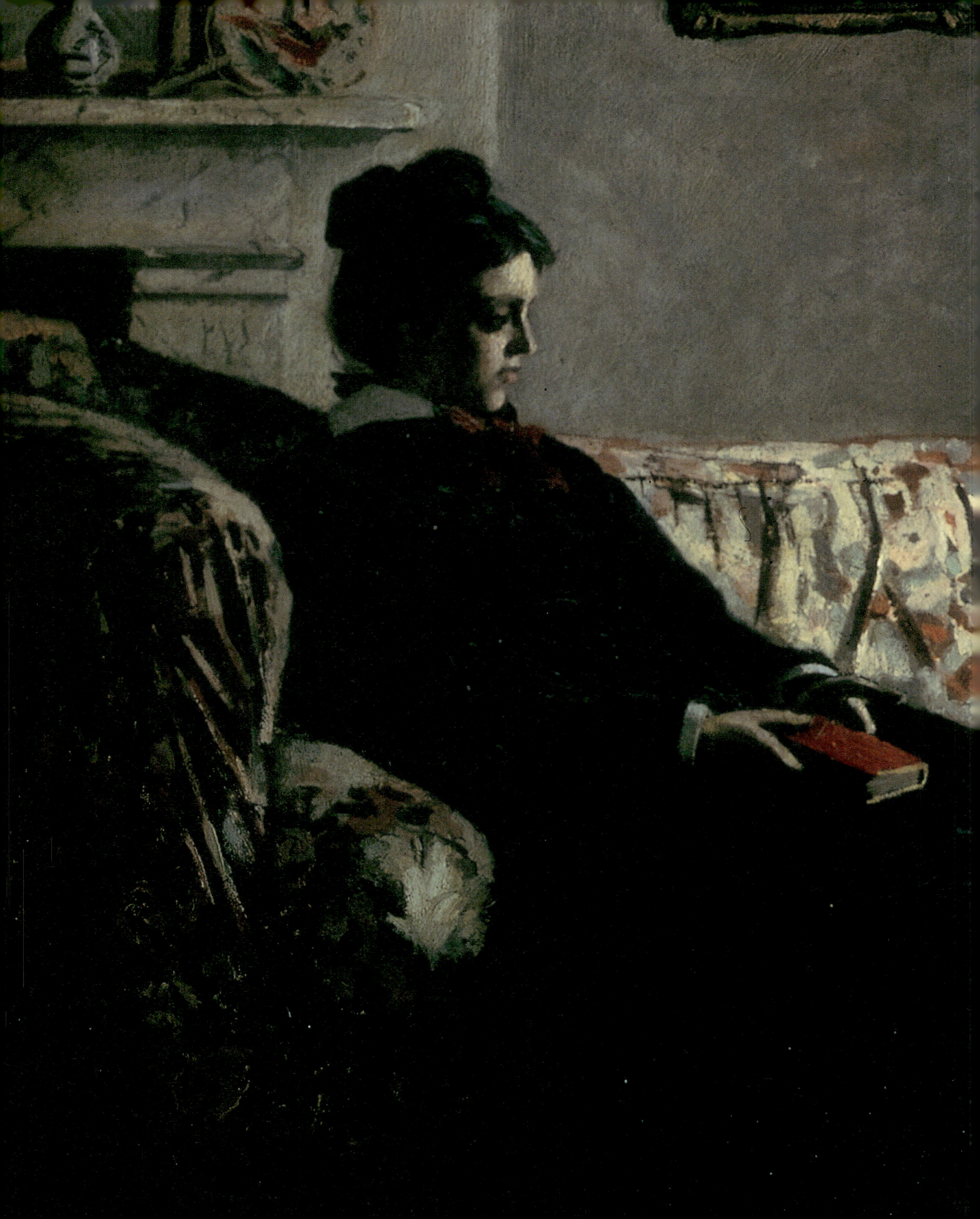

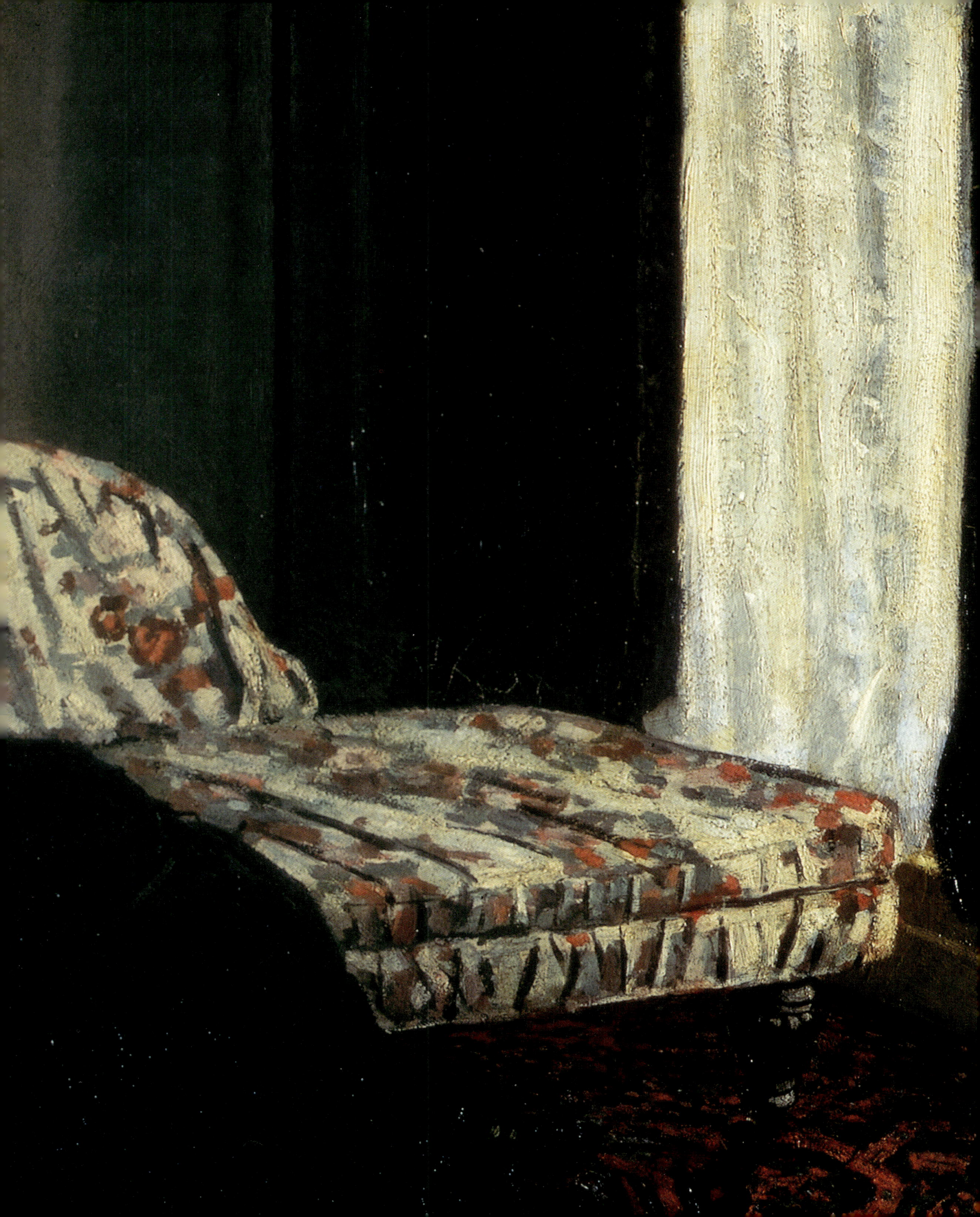

falling due only on their deaths), and shortly afterwards the newlyweds went off to spend the summer at Trouville.

Trouville was in familiar Norman territory, lying just down the coast from Honfleur. The atmosphere of the town was distinctly sophisticated and cosmopolitan, as befitted a smart, modern seaside resort with a sandy beach and a line of grand hotels along the esplanade. Monet must have set up his easel and started work almost at once, for he finished at least eight canvases during his few weeks at Trouville. Most of them are seafront subjects which admirably capture the breezy, sunny, sandy atmosphere; they also preserve miniscule parts of it in the form of wind-blown grains of sand which have lodged in the paint. As usual, Camille seems to have been Monet's chief model, although none of his Trouville paintings can be called portraits of her. In *The Beach at Trouville* (pages 70-1), she probably represents a type very much in evidence at the resort, the fashionable young woman, determined to see and be seen, her elegance set off by the subdued clothing and demeanour of an older companion or relative.

The Beach at Trouville is a small picture, painted with an extreme freedom which suggests that it was initially intended as a study for a more finished work. However, even a canvas such as *The Hôtel des Roches Noires* (page 73), whose size makes it certain that it was intended to be a complete, saleable work, is almost as suggestively cursory and free. This is most obvious in the large United States flag at the top of the picture and the 'squiggle' rising from the top of the hotel – actually a well-known landmark, a large gilded figure of Neptune. In both instances, it is almost as if the breeze had agitated and blown away some of the paint.

All the same, the picture is not simply an 'impression of the moment' in the sense of being unplanned or accidental, although that was how many of Monet's contemporaries regarded Impressionist paintings. The magisterial American novelist Henry James, for example, wrote with characteristic amplitude that he viewed the Impressionists of 1876 as 'partisans of unadorned reality and absolute foes to arrangement, embellishment, selection, to the artist's allowing himself, as he has hitherto, since art began, found his best account in doing, to be preoccupied with the idea of the beautiful'.

Up to a point James was right, in that Monet did not attempt to create an ideal beauty, although he sought it in the world around him. Nevertheless, *The Hôtel des Roches Noires*, with its balanced masses and inward-running diagonals, provides a particularly clear

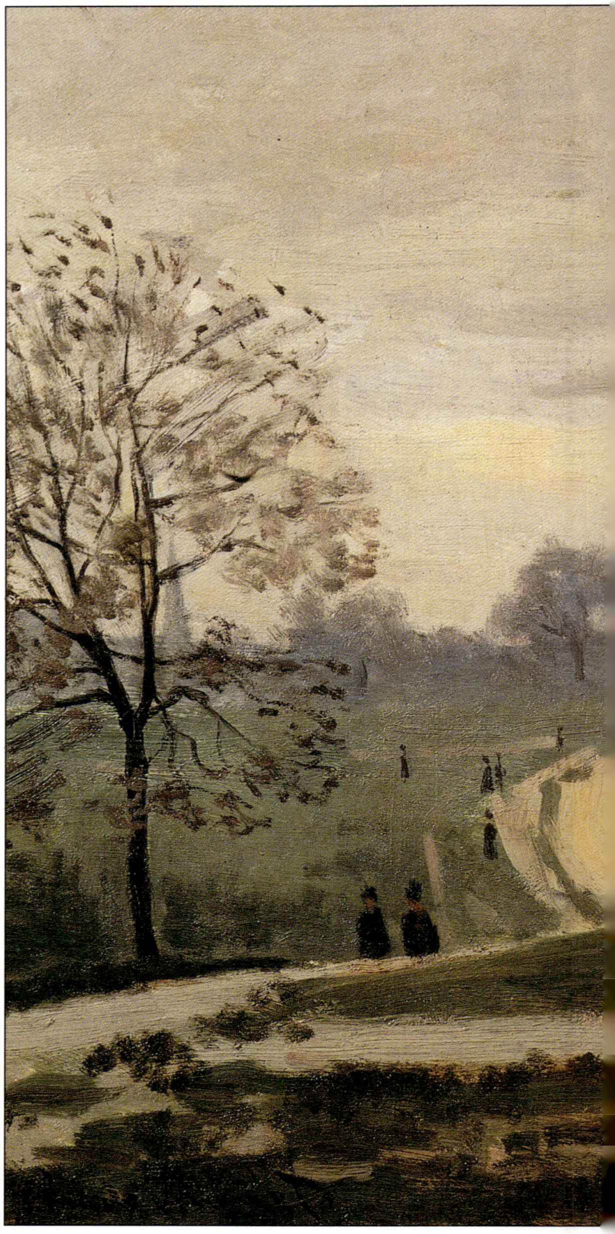

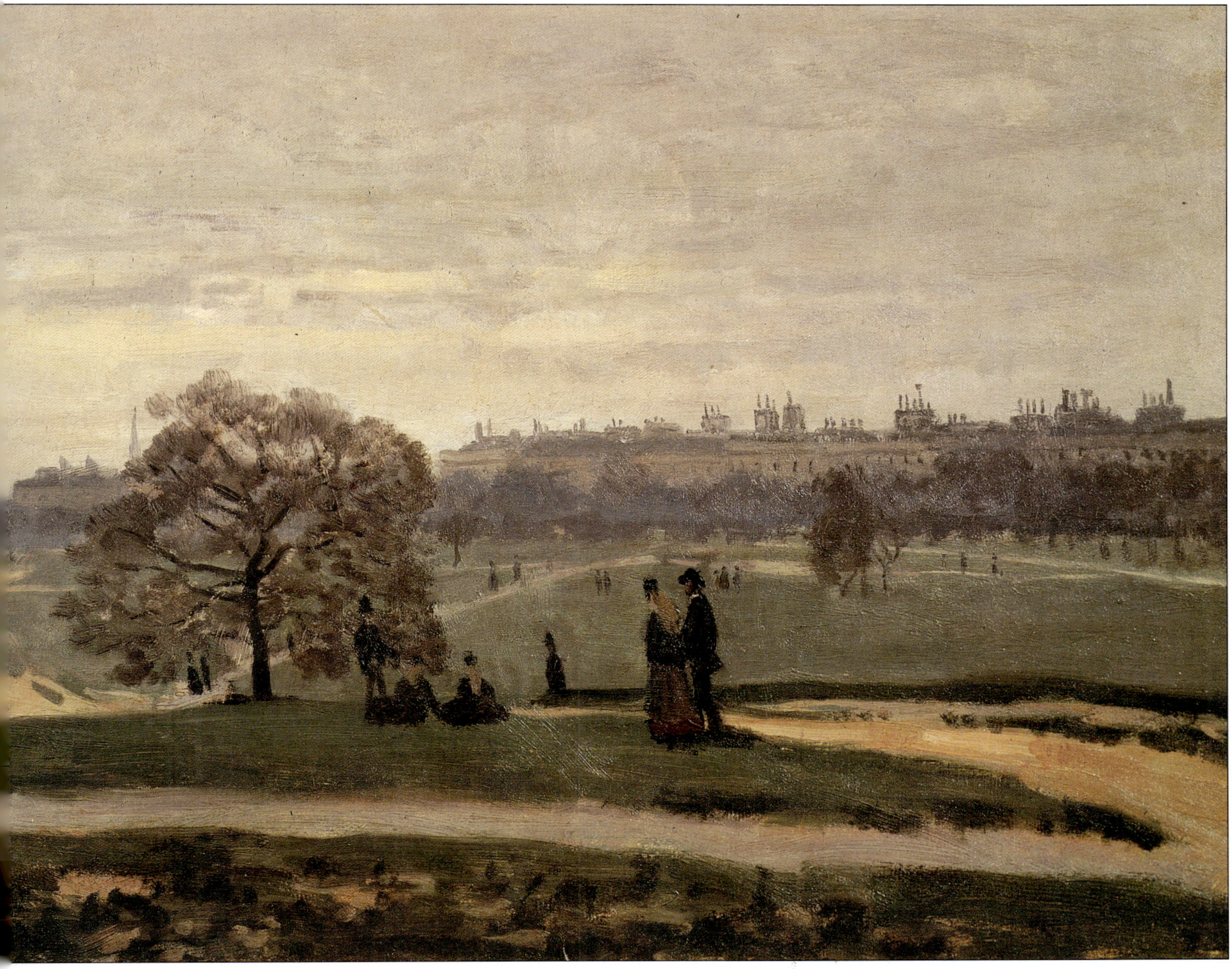

example of a composition that has been worked out to the last detail, whether done laboriously beforehand or by means of intuition or experience as the artist put paint onto canvas. At the same time, the arrangement of the scene reflects its theme of fashionable life; unlike some other Trouville paintings by Monet, *The Hôtel des Roches Noires* excludes the sea and concentrates on the hotel itself and the well-off tourists on the terrace; even the inclusion of the flags of three nations serves to emphasize the cosmopolitan character of the setting. In other words, despite its unorthodox brush technique, the picture is a traditional, well-ordered composition with a subject about which the artist has 'something to say'.

ABOVE:
Hyde Park
(1871)
RHODE ISLAND SCHOOL OF DESIGN

This is less immediately apparent in some other works by Monet, such as the La Grenouillère paintings. Yet, despite his references to them as 'sketches', they too are composed, and at this point it is worth taking another look at them. Monet, like so many nineteenth-century artists, learned much from the Japanese colour prints that were starting to reach the West in quantities. The Japanese had devised a method of composition in which the line of the frame often cut off a figure or object so that only part of it appeared in the picture. The effect was like that of a photographic snap, taken too hurriedly to get the entire subject inside the frame – except, of course, that the Japanese masters used it consciously as part of an overall design. When that was done, the 'cut-off' fostered the illusion that the scene represented an instant of life casually caught on the wing. The link between such a technique and Impressionism is obvious, the point being that, in the works of the western artists too, the apparent casualness was calculated. In the paintings of La Grenouillère, walkways, boats, the boathouse and tops of trees are all sliced in this fashion, by contrast with the conventional full-framing of slightly earlier paintings such as *The River* and *The Luncheon.* It seems likely that it was in 1869 that the Japanese technique entered Monet's repertoire, although he may well have known about it some years earlier. From this time he used both traditional and cut-off compositions, switching from one to the other even in the course of a series such as the *Poplars* paintings (pages 193-5).

London Exile

At Trouville the Monets stayed at the Tivoli, a hotel which, although not as grand as the Roches Noires, was more expensive than they could afford. Monet's funds were soon exhausted and he was forced to make a trip to Le Havre, where he hoped to borrow enough from his father to pay the bill. Meanwhile Boudin and his wife took care of Camille.

Monet may have been reluctant to return to Paris for fear of being taken back into the army, as he was a reservist. For while he, Camille and Jean enjoyed the amenities of Trouville, France had gone to war against the rising power of Prussia, whose policy was being directed with spectacular success by Otto von Bismarck. All the same, Europe expected that France – the greatest military power for the past two centuries – would emerge victorious; but Europe was wrong. The Prussians thrust rapidly into France, winning success after success, and by early September the French emperor, Napoleon III, had been captured. Thoroughly discredited, Napoleon's regime, the Second Empire, fell apart. For the third time in its volatile history, France was declared a republic. Meanwhile the Prussians continued to advance and had encircled Paris by 19 September.

Monet's response to these shattering events was to apply for a passport and then cross the Channel to England. Clearly he had no intention of becoming involved in the conflict. There is no reason to suppose that this was an act of cowardice; many other French artists made the same decision. In fact, during a disturbed period when no one was likely to be buying pictures, going to London may have seemed an act of commercial common sense to those who were unwilling or unable to take part in defending the nation. Politically Monet was a man of the Left, entirely out of sympathy with the Second Empire and not sorry to see it go. In any case, his later attitudes to political events suggest that, whatever the nature of his opinions, he would always regard painting as the only activity that had any claims on him.

In London, Monet was soon joined by Camille and Jean. They spent almost nine months in the city, but very little is known of their activities. Camille Pissarro had also chosen exile and together he and Monet visited the South Kensington Museum, where they admired the paintings of Constable and Turner, British masters of the earlier nineteenth century whose landscapes were the equal of anything that had so far been done in France. Turner, in particular, had painted with extraordinary freedom, bathing and dissolving his subjects in light of a blazing intensity that has still never been matched. At the very least, his example must have given heart and hope to the two future Impressionists.

From a material point of view, Monet made one very significant contact in London. Another French artist in exile, Daubigny, introduced him to the dealer Paul Durand-Ruel, with whom he was to have a long, often acrimonious, but rewarding relationship. Dealers were still of relatively minor importance in France and there was as yet no real international art market, but Durand-Ruel was one of the enterprising few who would soon change this situation. One of his first important steps was to open a gallery in London's New Bond Street shortly after his meeting with Monet, who contributed to the inaugural exhibition. This initial contact appears not to have resulted in any commissions or sales, yet in his old age Monet expressed the profound gratitude he felt towards

RIGHT:
The Thames below Westminster
(1871)
NATIONAL GALLERY, LONDON

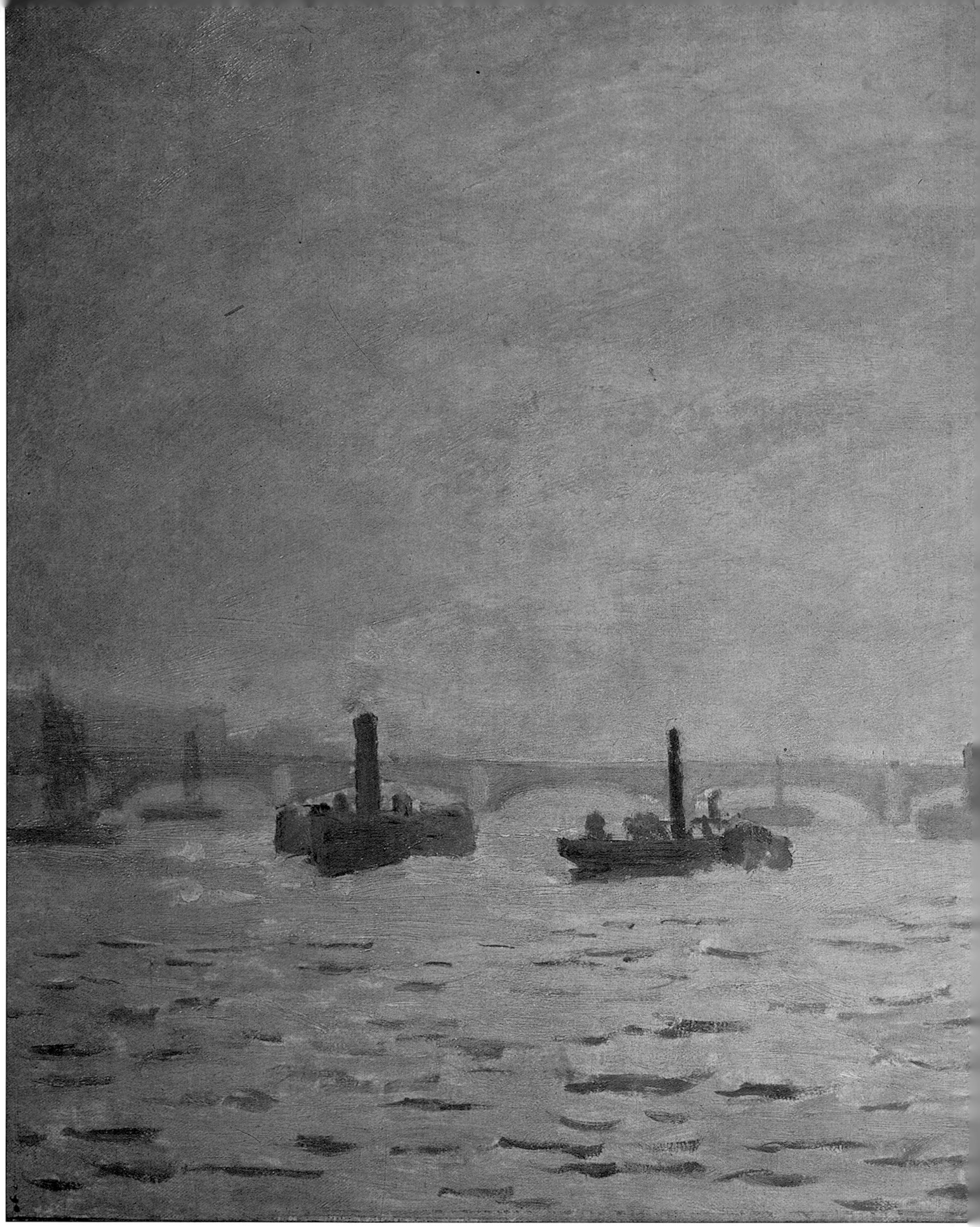

Daubigny because he had introduced him to Durand-Ruel and later stood up for his work at the Salon. He expressed similar warmth towards Durand himself, who 'saved me and several of my friends from dying of hunger'; in context the reference seems to be to the period 1870–71.

Monet also exhibited at a show in the South Kensington

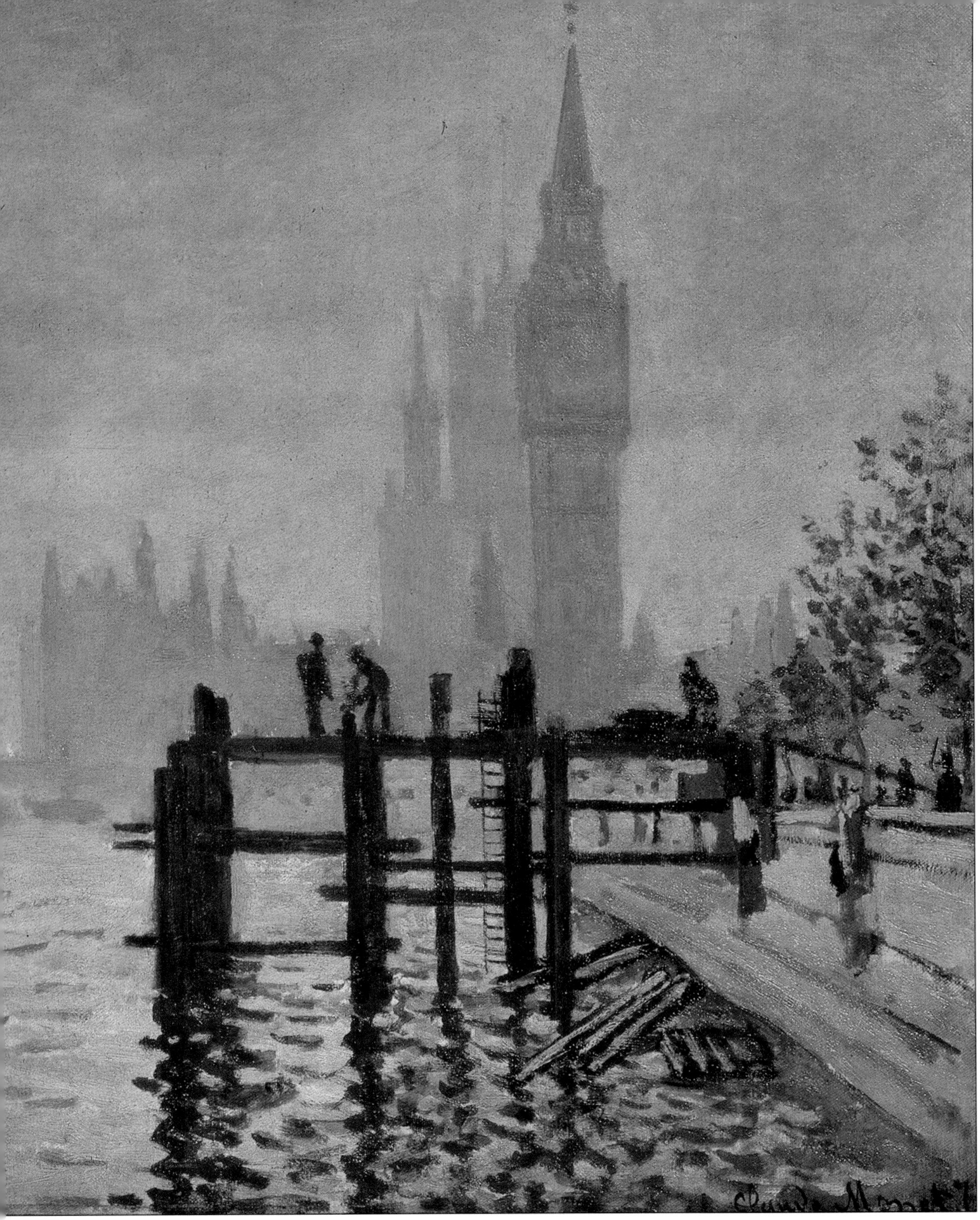

Museum, but he failed to sell anything in spite of the shrewd conservatism of his entries, *Madame Monet on a Sofa* (pages 74-5) and *Woman in a Green Dress.* Unless Durand-Ruel did, in fact, help him, it is difficult to imagine how Monet, who had run out of money after a few weeks at Trouville, could have supported his family during their long stay in London, or even how he occupied his

RIGHT:
Zaandam
(1871)
MUSÉE D'ORSAY,
PARIS

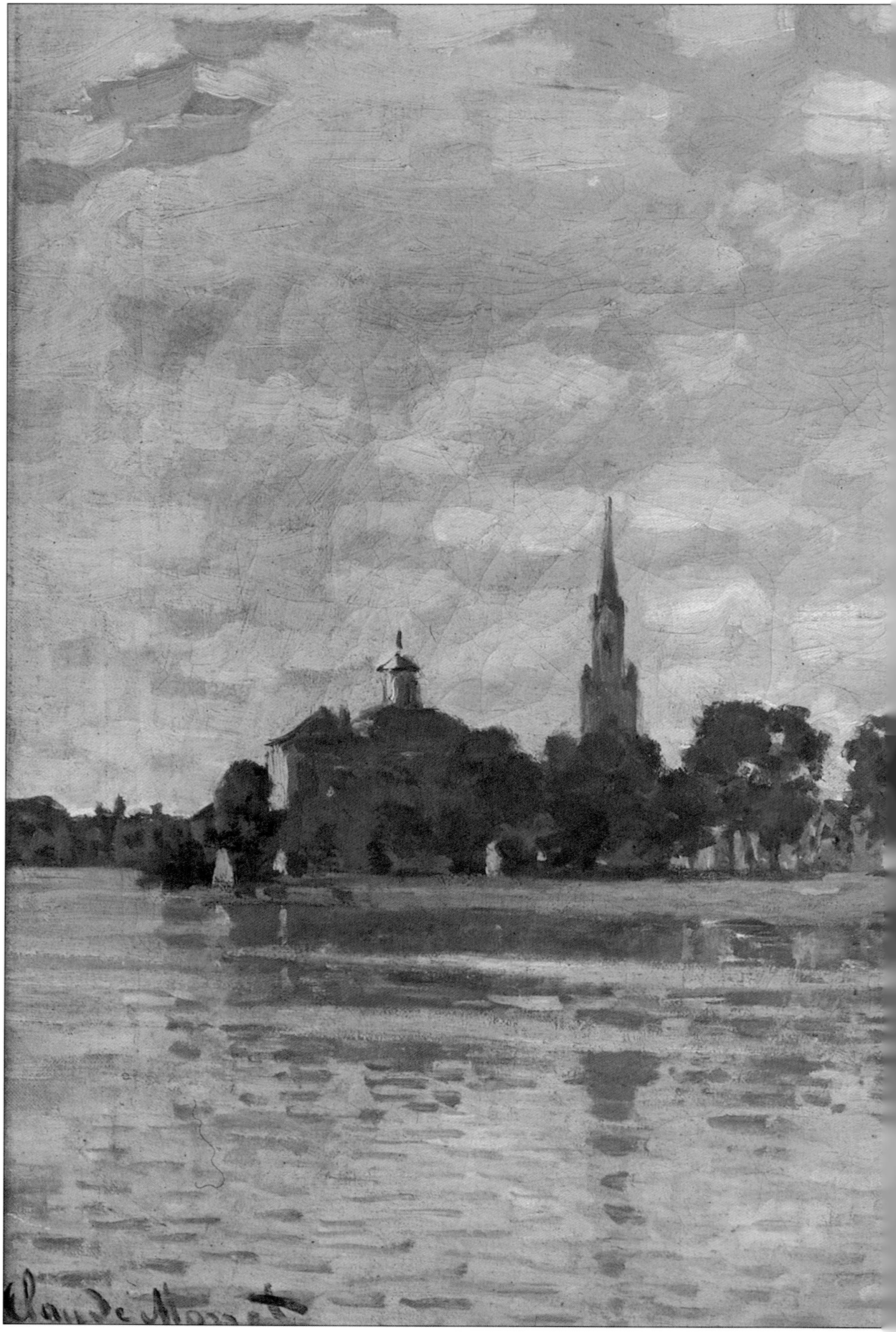

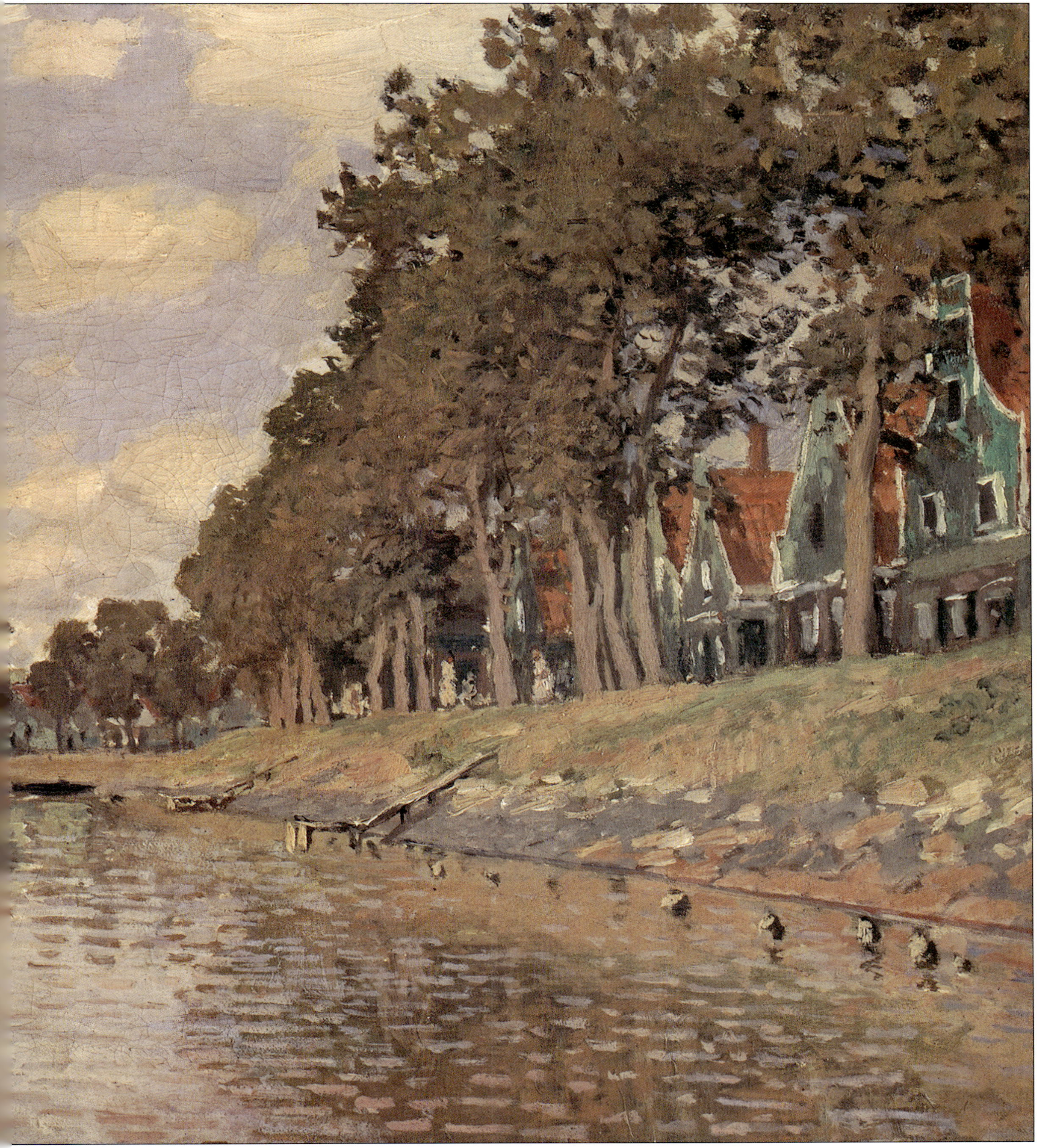

time, since only half a dozen canvases by him are known from these months. They include charming views of Hyde Park (pages 76-7) and Green Park, and three paintings of scenes on the River Thames including *The Thames Below Westminster* (pages 80-1). London was notorious for its yellowish fogs, and Monet captured one very effectively in this atmospheric picture. The Houses of Parliament and Westminster Bridge appear in the background as murky, unreal silhouettes, yet they dominate the scene. Two tugs occupy the middle distance, but only the landing stage and the embankment, closest to the viewer in the bottom right-hand corner, have the definition and sense of movement that make them seem part of the living world; even their reflections in the Thames create a darker, more urgent stretch of water.

Monet's unproductiveness during his stay in London may well have been related to the terrible times through which his native land was passing. The capital held out against the besieging Prussians for four months while its increasingly desperate inhabitants consumed horses, domestic animals, rats and even the elephant in the Paris Zoo. On 28 January, 1871, the city was forced to capitulate and armistice terms were agreed that would be followed in May by a peace treaty depriving France of Alsace and Lorraine and condemning her to pay a heavy indemnity.

This was not the end of the agony. The Parisians, embittered and radicalized by their sufferings, refused to accept defeat and declared the capital an independent Commune, hostile to the new French government at Versailles (ironically, the seat of the Bourbon kings who had been overthrown by the French Revolution). A savage conflict followed, with atrocities committed on both sides, culminating in the storming of Paris by the Versailles forces in 'Bloody Week' (21–28 May). Some 20,000 Communards were slaughtered and many more were subsequently executed or deported. Fires, begun accidentally or in an attempt to slow down the advance of the troops, destroyed a number of historic landmarks and gutted the famous Rue de Rivoli.

From a distance, Monet seems to have sided with the Commune, perhaps influenced by the fact that his old friend Gustave Courbet had become the radical regime's minister for the arts. News from across the Channel was intermittent and unreliable and on 27 May, 1871, Monet, believing that Courbet had been shot by the victors, wrote to Pissarro denouncing the 'vile', 'atrocious' and 'sickening' behaviour of Versailles. As Pissarro was even more left-wing in outlook (he became a self-proclaimed anarchist),

Monet was quite safe in expressing himself so vehemently, but there is no reason to believe that he was being insincere. By this time he was ready to leave England but, unwilling to confront the immediate aftermath of civil war, crossed to Holland and settled in the pretty little town of Zaandam, about 13 kilometres from Amsterdam.

Monet's spirits seem to have improved rapidly in Holland. The people were friendly, the picturesqueness of the Dutch countryside pleased him, and he was evidently not deterred by the fact that the windmills and canals had become visual clichés in the hands of lesser artists. During his four months or so in Holland he completed at least 25 canvases, among them lively harbour paintings as well as quieter scenes such as *Zaandam* (pages 82-3), in which green-gabled houses in the old Dutch style line the banks, adding touches of colour to the distant view of the church and houses. As usual, Monet's painting of water is superb; here, although it fills the entire foreground, its mild ripples and broken reflections are in harmony with the general tranquillity.

Monet returned to France towards the end of 1871, moving into a hotel in Paris. Although he had avoided the months of privation and bloodshed, his own life had been changed by recent events. His great friend Bazille had been killed in action. Courbet was in prison, where Monet visited him; faced with ruinous fines for his part in the Commune, he would soon flee abroad and, after a rapid physical decline, die in exile in 1877. The scars of war and civil war were still visible in the streets of Paris, among them the ruins of the Tuileries (henceforth only gardens, not a palace) and the Hôtel de Ville. Moreover there was no longer an older generation of Monets for the painter to rebel against and depend upon: Aunt Lecadre had died shortly after Monet's marriage, and his father had followed her during the war.

Perhaps as a response to all these events, Monet did very little work during his few weeks in Paris. By December he had arranged his escape. He and his family moved to a rented house at Argenteuil, where his life as an artist would enter a new, productive and publicly controversial phase.

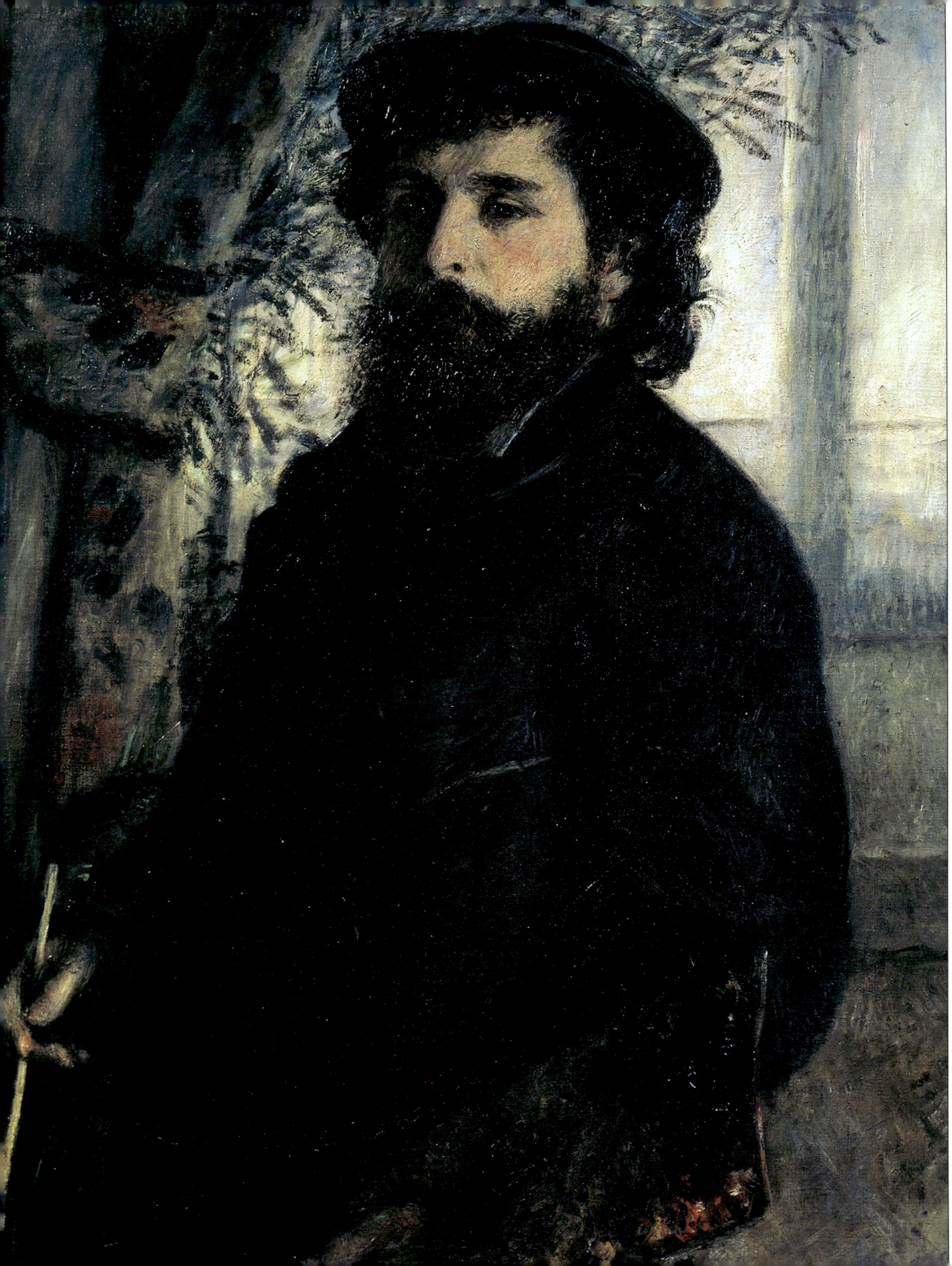

CHAPTER FOUR

By the River at Argenteuil

ARGENTEUIL WAS A SMALL TOWN on the River Seine, some eight kilometres from Paris. It had been steadily growing since the 1850s, thanks to the coming of the railway, which brought it within 15 minutes of the capital. This was certainly one of its attractions for Monet, who remained in touch with Parisian life and kept up a studio near the Gare Saint-Lazare. At the far end of this same line lay his home town of Le Havre, which he still visited from time to time. Argenteuil itself had a little of almost everything needed to interest an artist of Monet's wide-ranging sensibility, from picturesque streets and river views to a railway bridge and factories with smoke-belching chimneys.

LEFT:
Portrait of Claude Monet (1875)
Pierre-Auguste Renoir
MUSÉE D'ORSAY, PARIS

Although he may not have known it at the time, Monet had settled down at last; Argenteuil was to be his home for the next six years. Surprisingly, he was undaunted by the fact that his house, the Maison Aubry, was large and expensive (the rent was 1,000 francs a year), standing close to both the railway station and the river. It had been found for him by Edouard Manet, who knew the area well because he maintained a holiday home just across the river at

Gennevilliers. Inevitably, he saw a good deal more of Manet during the years that followed, and especially in the summer of 1874, when it was the older master who was most obviously influenced by their contacts, making his first extended experiments with open-air painting and producing some highly distinctive works. Nevertheless Manet remained at heart a Parisian and a painter of people and interiors.

However, several of Monet's fellow artists did opt, like him, to settle in the countryside, where the living was cheaper and there were abundant landscape subjects. Renoir and Sisley remained particularly close to Monet, coming to stay with him during his early years at Argenteuil and strengthening the artistic and personal ties that bound them together. He also saw his old friend Boudin and his wife. Boudin noticed that Monet had lost none of his ambition: 'We often see Monet and went to his housewarming recently. He is thoroughly settled, and seems to have a powerful urge to make a name for himself. He has brought back some really beautiful studies from Holland and I think he is bound to become one of the leaders of our school.'

Trains and Bridges

If the evidence of Monet's works can be relied on, Argenteuil delighted him. He had never before been so prolific, painting well over 50 canvases in 1872 alone. Most of them were done at Argenteuil, but there were also subjects taken from Le Havre and Rouen, where his older brother Léon lived. During this early phase, Monet's 'landscapes' included such distinctly unromantic subjects as factory sites and the two bridges over the river at Argenteuil, which had been badly damaged during the war and were under repair. He continued to paint the bridges after the work was finished, and also the trains that rushed over the railway bridge to and from Paris (pages 88-9).

Despite the calls that had begun to be heard in some sections of the art world for more timely, realistic works, few painters could bring themselves to tackle such 'ugly' subjects, but Monet went boldly ahead. As an artist he appreciated the compositional possibilities of bridges and similar structures, and the spectacular visual effects obtained by the passage of a steam engine. This last effect had already been captured by the English artist Turner in his celebrated *Rain, Steam and Speed* of 1844 and, in more subdued fashion, by Monet himself in *The Train in the*

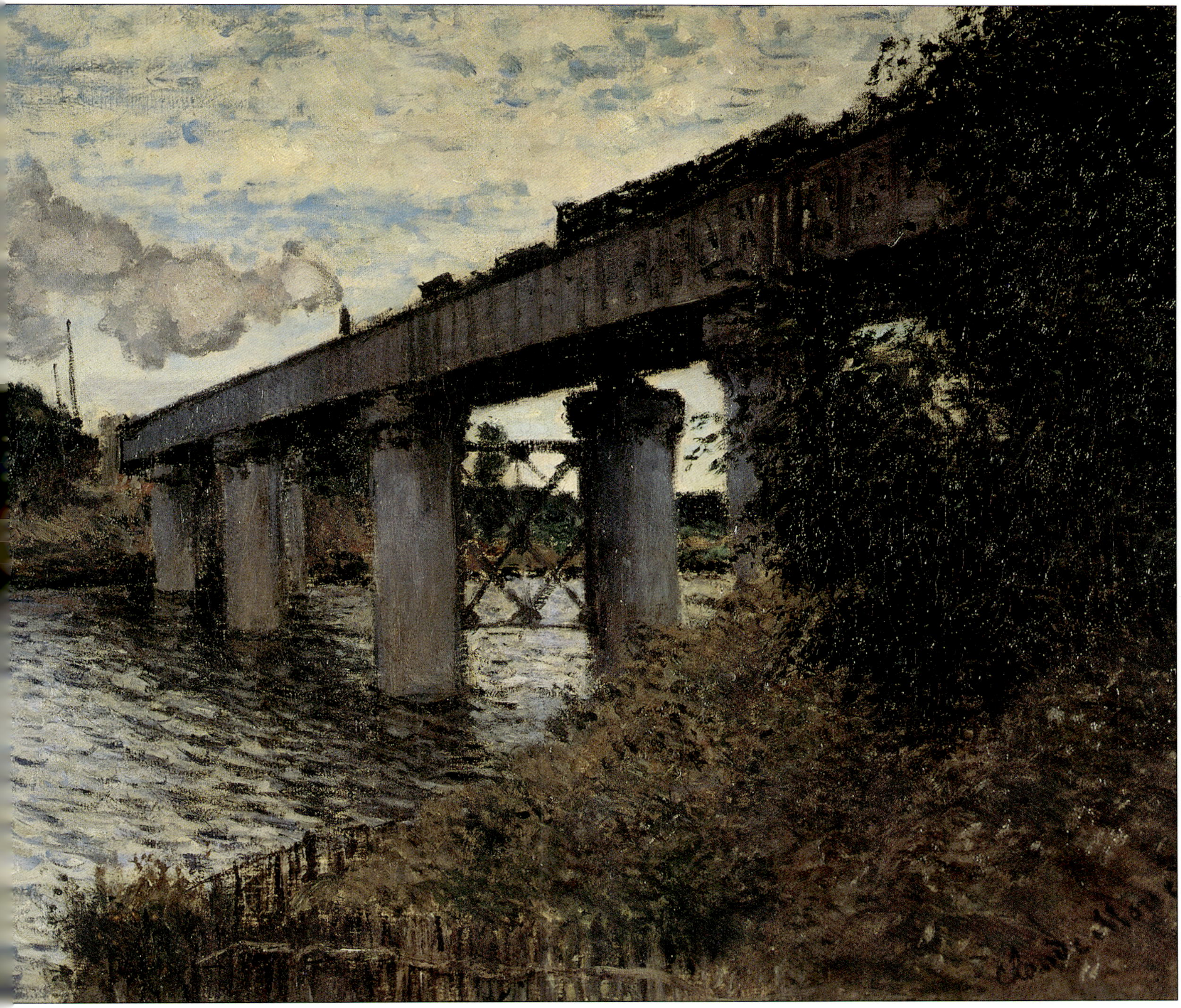

Countryside (pages 68-9), painted during his years at Bougival.

The pictorial possibilities of train and bridge are superbly combined in *Railway Bridge at Argenteuil* (pages 88-9), in which the iron monster, half-hidden by the sides of the bridge, is shown as though plunging down its vertiginous diagonal. Similarly, on a visit to Normandy, Monet turned his attention to the new industrial world, painting factories near Rouen and, in the famous *Impression: Sunrise* (page 109), captured the heady atmospheric mixture of mist, smoke and sunshine in the port of Le Havre. Moreover, as an ambitious man Monet was aware that modern-life

ABOVE:
The Railway Bridge at Argenteuil
(c.1873)
MUSÉE D'ORSAY, PARIS

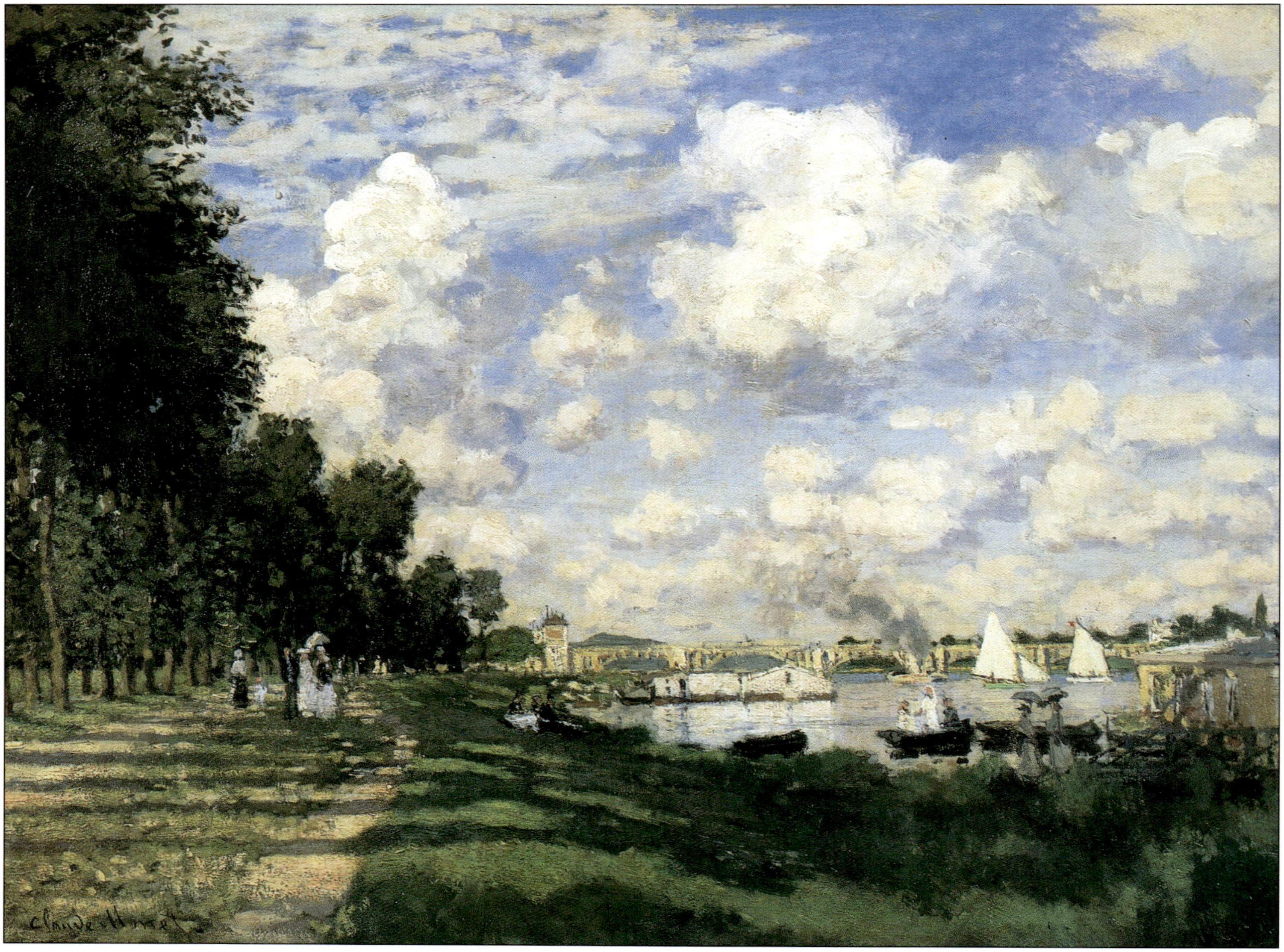

ABOVE:
The Basin at Argenteuil
(1872)
MUSÉE D'ORSAY, PARIS

subjects, although still the taste of a minority, did have a considerable sales potential.

The proof was that, during his years at Argenteuil, Monet was not only prolific, but also sold a respectable percentage of his output (38 canvases in 1872 alone) and for most of the time earned a very substantial income. As usual, he seems to have spent it recklessly, putting aside nothing for a rainy day and meanwhile bemoaning his poverty and ill-success to his correspondents. The legend of Monet's sufferings persisted down the generations, until the publication of his own account books proved that, at Argenteuil, he was making something between an admittedly meagre nine- and a princely twenty-four- thousand francs every year. The dealer Durand-Ruel regularly bought Monet's canvases and the artist also sold to a number of perceptive private collectors, ranging from the local doctor, Georges de Bellio, to the opera singer Jean-Baptiste Faure and the wealthy Gustave Caillebotte (1848–94), a painter of

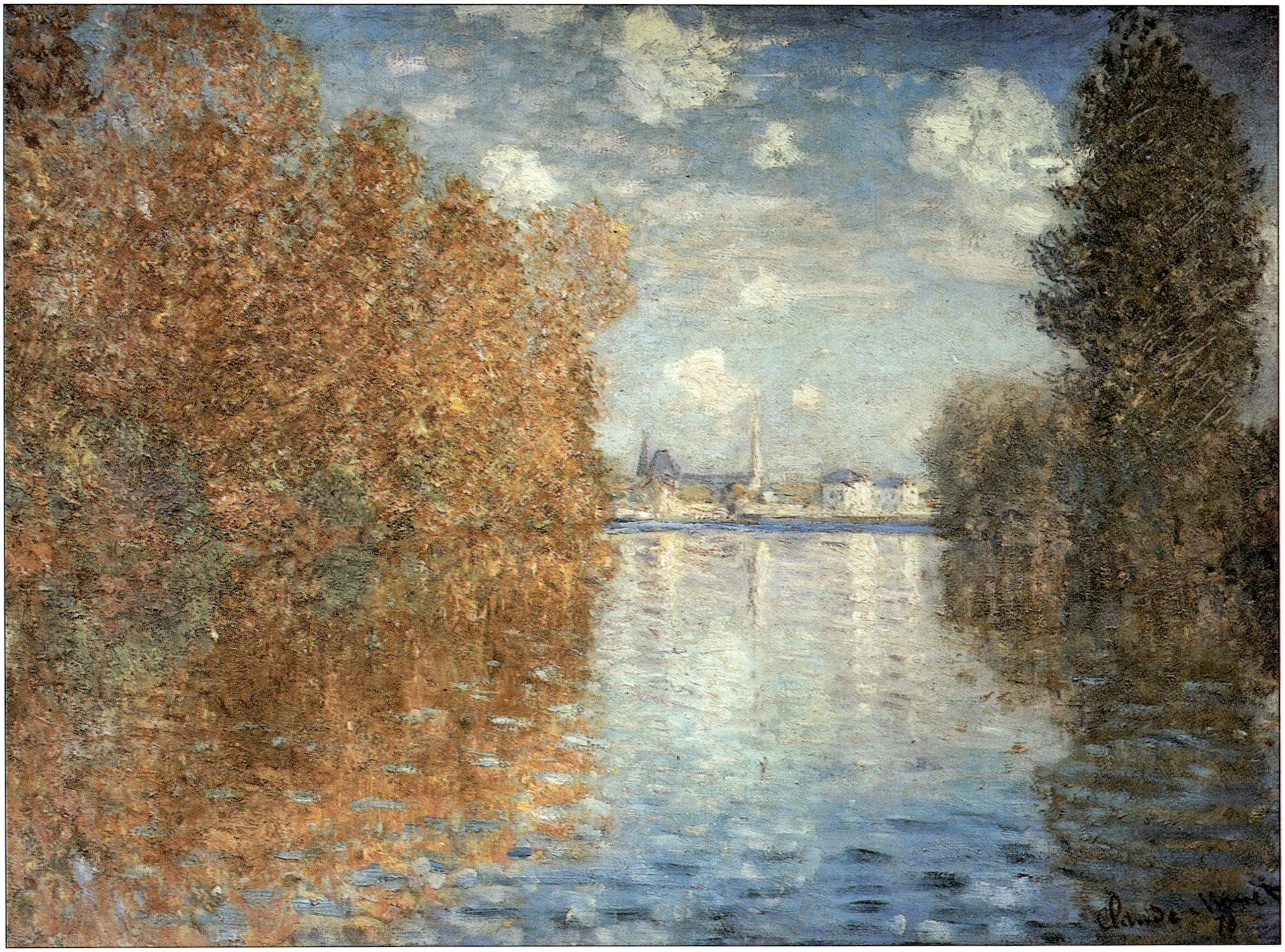

great ability who also frequented the Argenteuil area and became a close friend of Monet's.

Visual and commercial motives aside, Monet was not driven by an urge to be a 'painter of modern life' in quite the same programmatic sense as his friend Manet or another slightly older artist with whom he would later be associated, Edgar Degas (1834–1917), whose paintings and pastels took in subjects such as backstage ballet scenes, café-concerts and musicians in performance. So, as Argenteuil took hold of him, Monet increasingly devoted himself to representing its beauties, old as well as new: the quainter parts of the town, the surrounding countryside and, above all, the river at every season and in all its moods. Even in *The Basin at Argenteuil* (page 90), painted during his first year of residence, the view is unashamedly idyllic, and the same can be said of several otherwise very different riverside canvases such as *Autumn Effect, Argenteuil* (page 91).

ABOVE:
Autumn Effect, Argenteuil
(1872)
COURTAULD INSTITUTE GALLERIES, LONDON

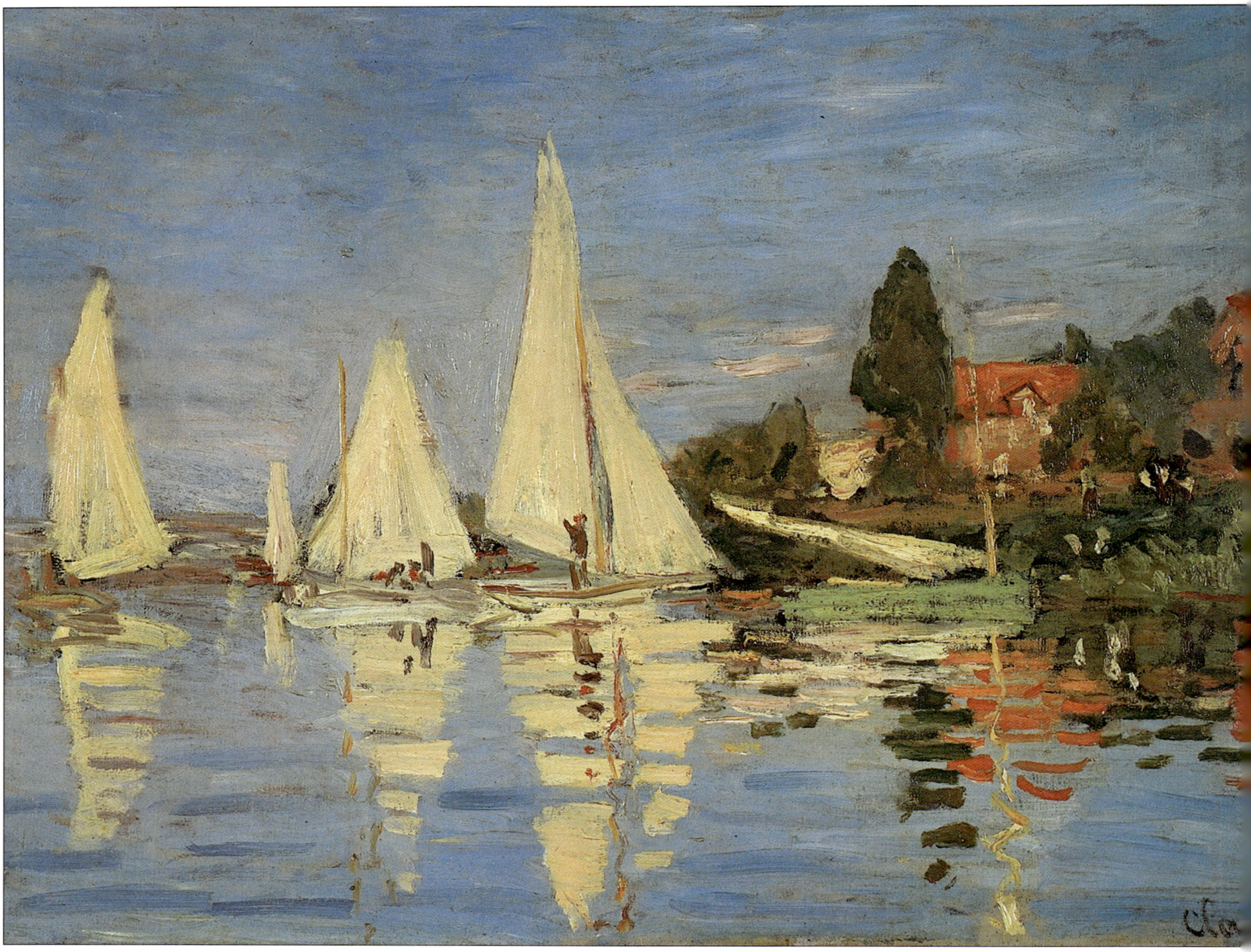

ABOVE:
Regatta at Argenteuil
(c.1872)
MUSÉE D'ORSAY, PARIS

Boats and Boating

When he took the river itself as his main subject, Monet almost always turned the canvas into a celebration of pleasure boats and sailing. These are among his most enchanting works and have helped to fix the image of Impressionism as an art of bright colours, sparkling reflections on water and peaceful, light-filled leisure. By accident or design, Monet had come to live in the most important boating centre in France. At Argenteuil the river widened into an ample basin that offered ideal conditions for sailing without hazards or irritating obstructions, and the municipality had encouraged the provision of suitable facilities. Argenteuil

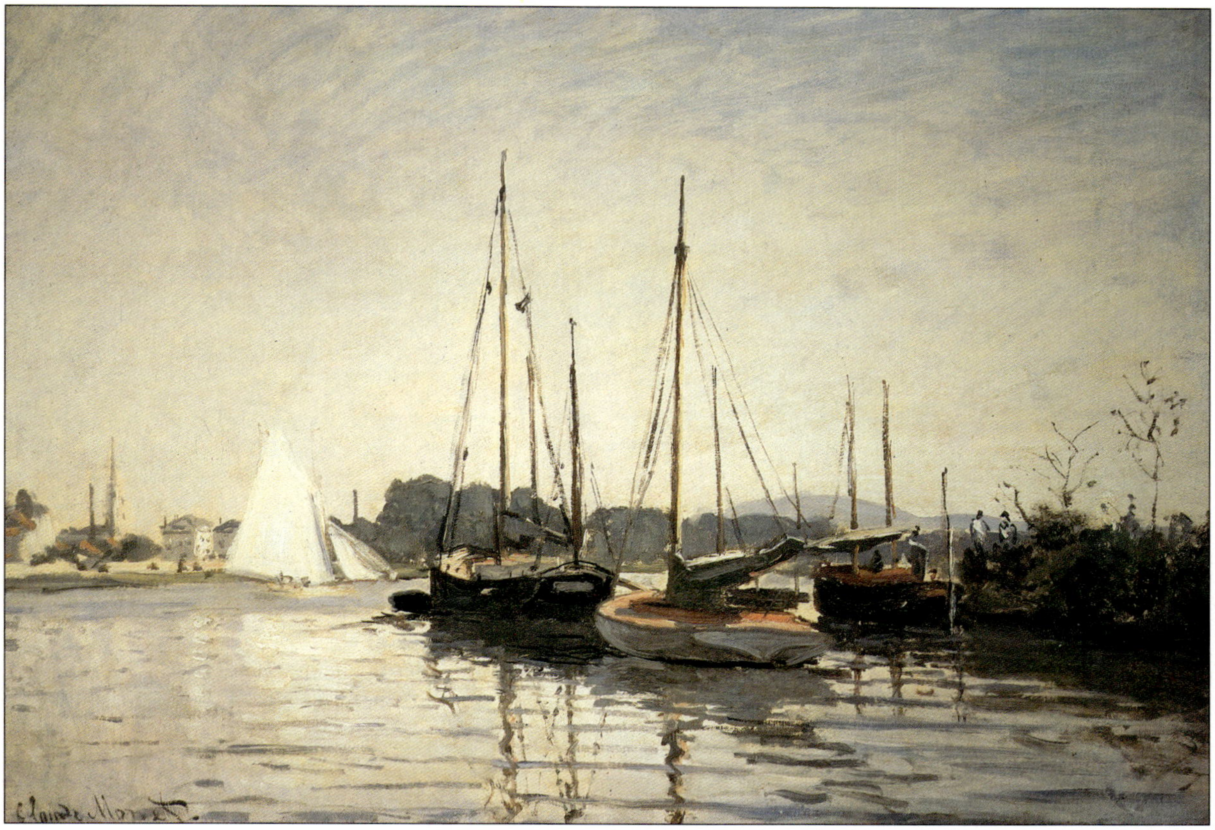

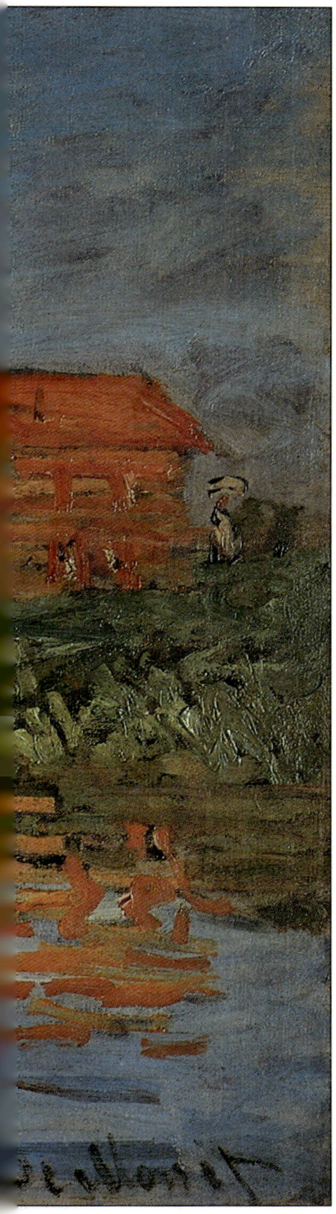

ABOVE:
Boats at Argenteuil
(1872)
MUSÉE D'ORSAY, PARIS

became a place where regattas and even international competitions were held. It was also welcoming to the day tripper or weekender, who was able to hire a boat by the hour or use one of the moorings available for his – perhaps occasionally her – own craft.

In this kind of boating, respectable householders put on casual clothes and guided their own craft. It was a relatively recent and in some ways surprising development – in fact, one of the earliest informal leisure activities that was socially acceptable in a world that was still governed by strict codes of dress and behaviour. Like several other features of Monet's time, boating could have become widely popular only after the railways brought places such as Argenteuil within easy reach of city-dwellers. So although Monet's paintings of boats and regattas have, to our eyes, a timeless look, in their own day they were picturing an essentially modern activity, one practised by the boaters with a zestful consciousness of being very much in fashion. Although it is hardly possible to doubt that Monet painted these scenes with delight, he was too interested in self-promotion not to be aware of their potential appeal as contemporary vignettes.

Unfortunately, the *way* in which they were painted was so unfamiliar to most art-lovers that years had to pass before they came to be appreciated. At Argenteuil, Monet took to its limit the Impressionist technique of rapid working with dabs of pure

RIGHT:
Red Boats
(1875)
MUSÉE D'ORSAY,
PARIS

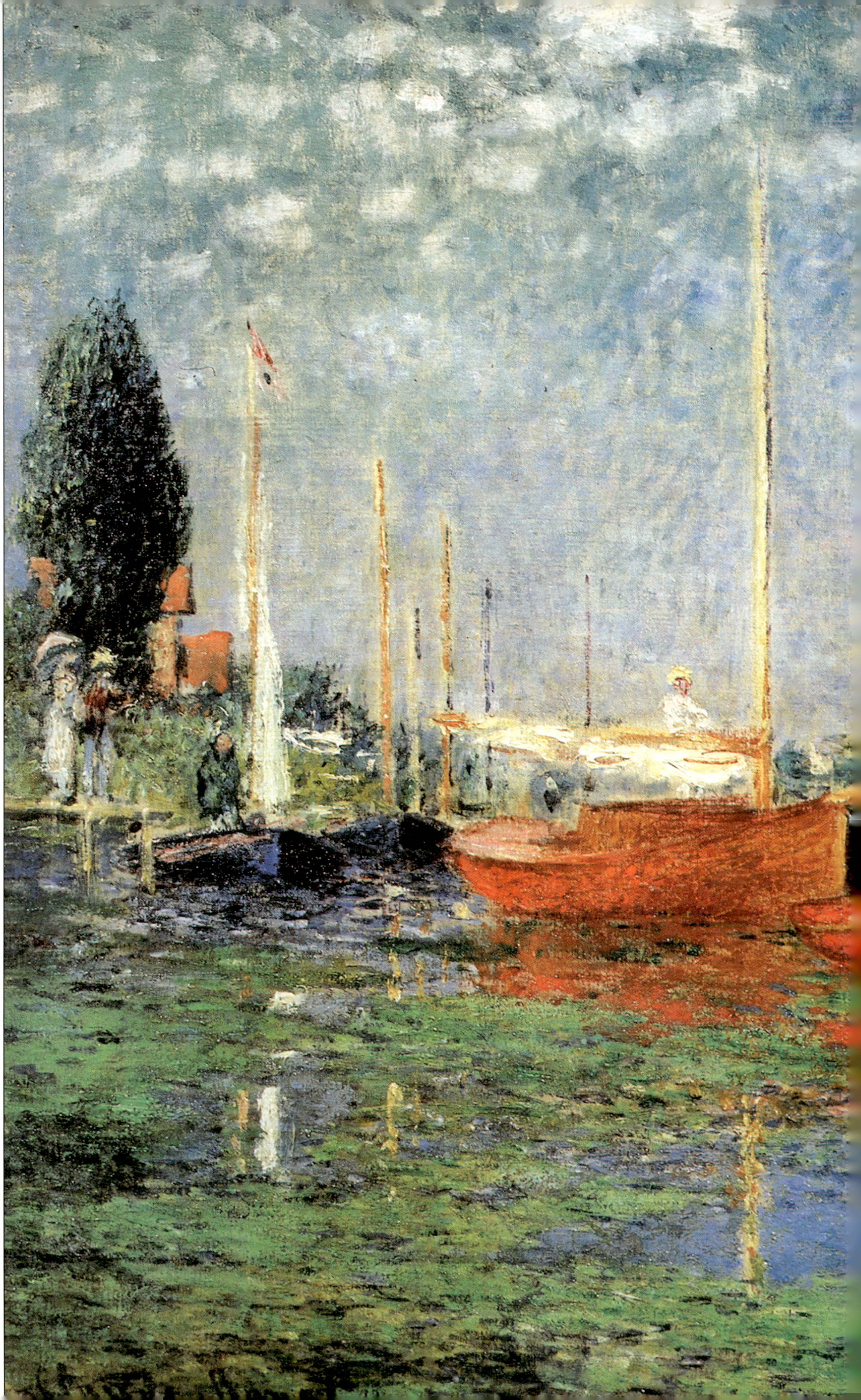

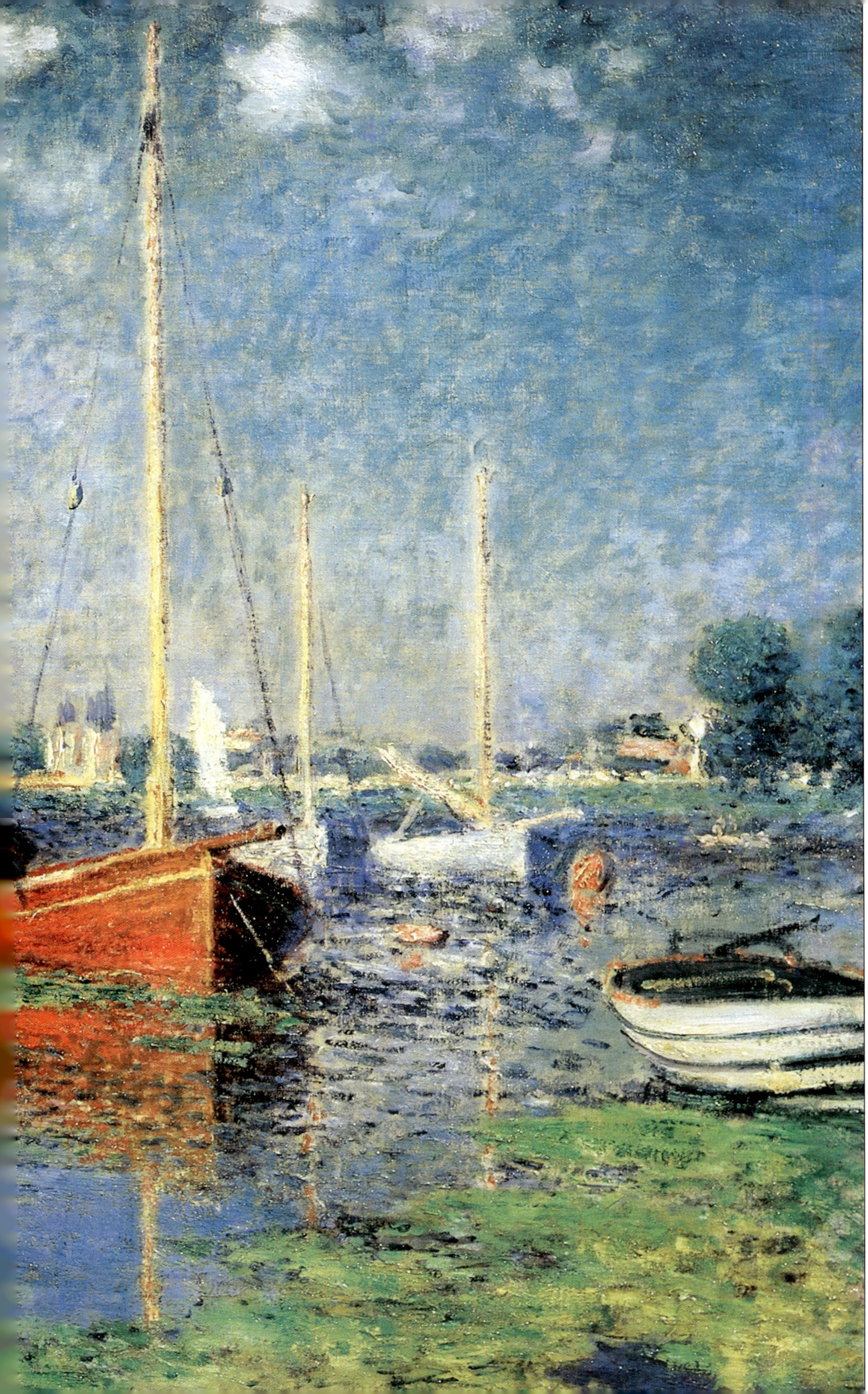

RIGHT:
Monet Painting in his Studio Boat (1874)
Edouard Manet
BAYERISCHE STAATSGEMALDE-SAMMLUNGEN, MUNICH

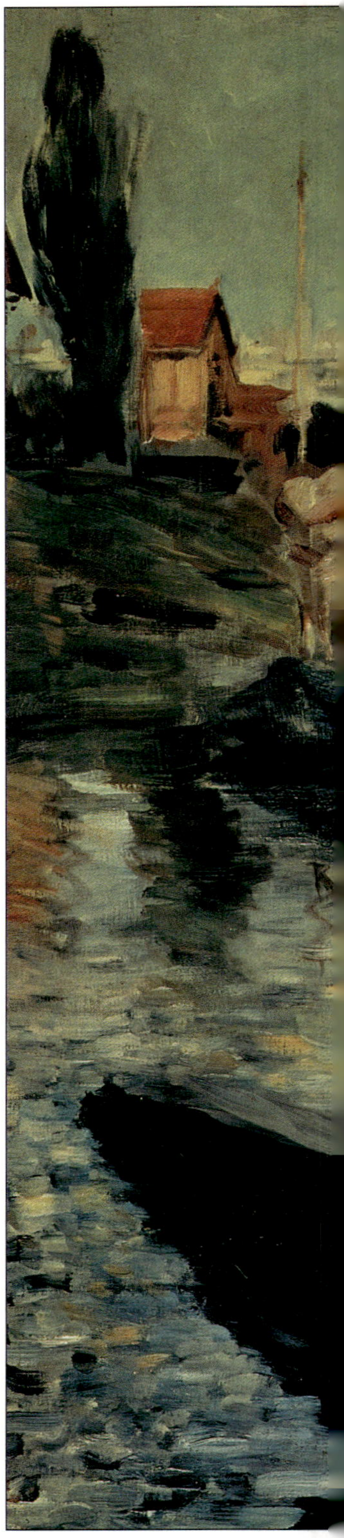

colour, eliminating detail in an effort to capture the breeze, glitter and movement of the occasion. A triumphantly successful work such as *Regatta at Argenteuil* (pages 92-3) seemed deeply shocking to many of Monet's contemporaries. We can summarize the kinds of objections they would have made: there are no drawn outlines defining objects, the boats merge into their own reflections, which are themselves only vertical patches or slashes, the human figures are mere blurs, there is no subtle transition from one tone to another (for example on the roofs of the houses) and, painted in too high a key (from the conventional point of view), the entire picture lacks dignity. By these standards, even a quieter scene such as *Boats at Argenteuil* (page 93) had to be dismissed as a failure; at best, it might pass as a sketch or study, useful to the artist but of no interest to the public. Moreover, a person who bought a painting that had been executed rapidly, with no substantial investment of time and labour, was not getting value for money! Given the standards on which such an evaluation could be made, it is perhaps more surprising that Monet and his colleagues did find a handful of perceptive patrons, and a committed dealer in Durand-Ruel, than that they were heartily abused by the majority.

Of course, use of the open-air technique did not mean that there was no element of advance planning. Common sense tells us that even the most rapid brushwork could not fix the image of a boat on the canvas before it had changed position. There was no reason why fidelity to light and atmosphere, achieved by working on the spot, should have involved a literal reproduction of the scene, even if that had been possible. As we know, Monet composed his works with great skill and in doing so he was, if necessary, prepared to take liberties with the scene in front of him. In *Red Boats* (pages 94-5), for example, the factory buildings that actually stood on the skyline are simply omitted, because the composition demanded it, because they spoiled the mood of the picture or, most likely, for both reasons.

Renoir shared Monet's enthusiasm for boating as a subject, and during his visits the two men again set up their easels side by side, painting the same scene. However, Monet soon found his earthbound viewpoints too constricting and took to the water. He bought a boat and, with some help from his friend Caillebotte – another sailing enthusiast – added a cabin just large enough to hold an easel and a roll-up sun canopy which would enable him to work on deck. The idea of a floating studio was not quite new, however; the Barbizon painter Daubigny had designed his own '*botin*' some years

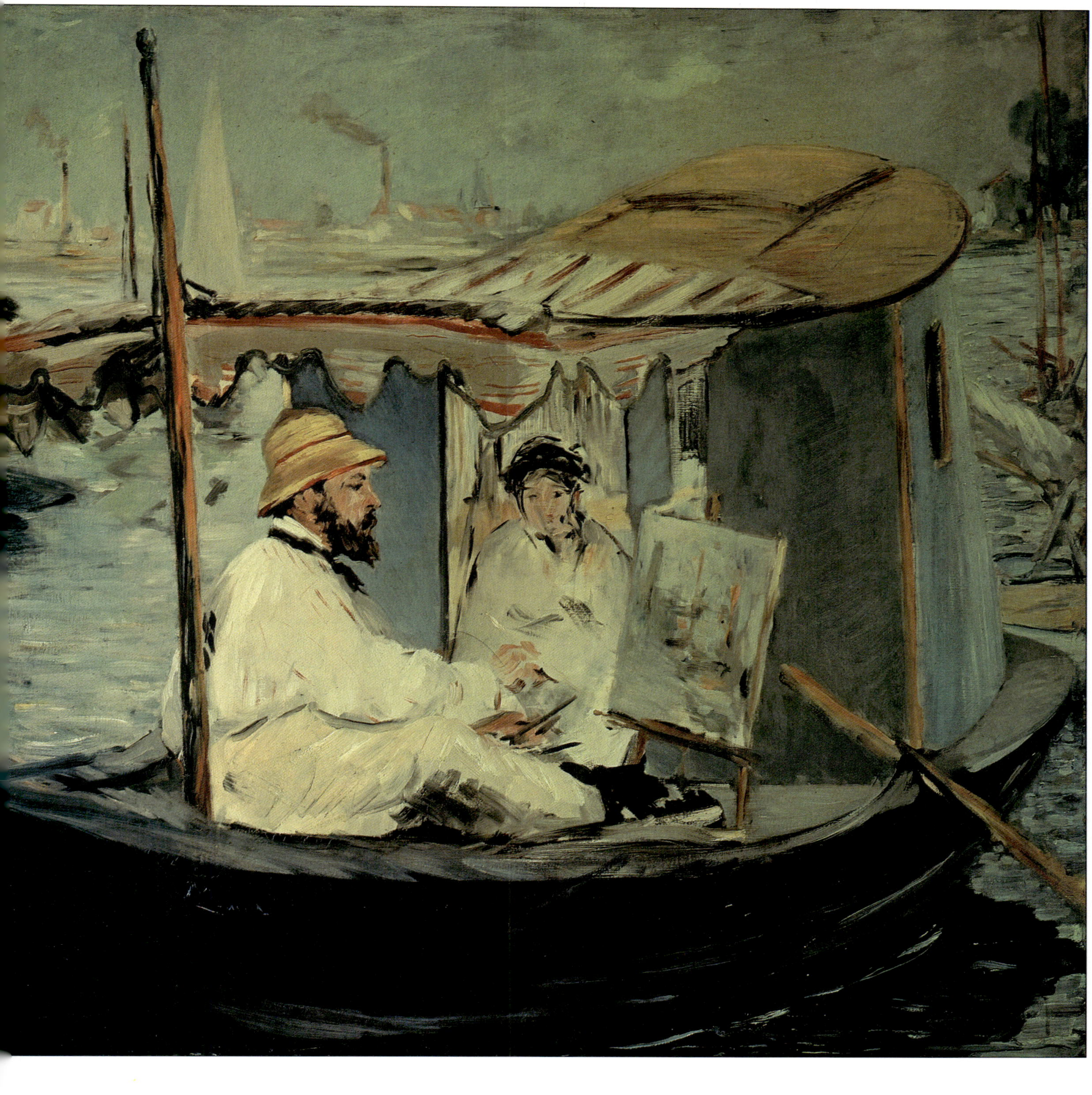

earlier and had made long trips in it. Monet was less intrepid or better able to make use of the materials to hand, since he never ventured far from Argenteuil in his little craft. Manet, who spent much of the summer of 1874 with Monet, has left a lively canvas (pages 96-7), showing his friend at work under the canopy while Camille sits in the door of the cabin.

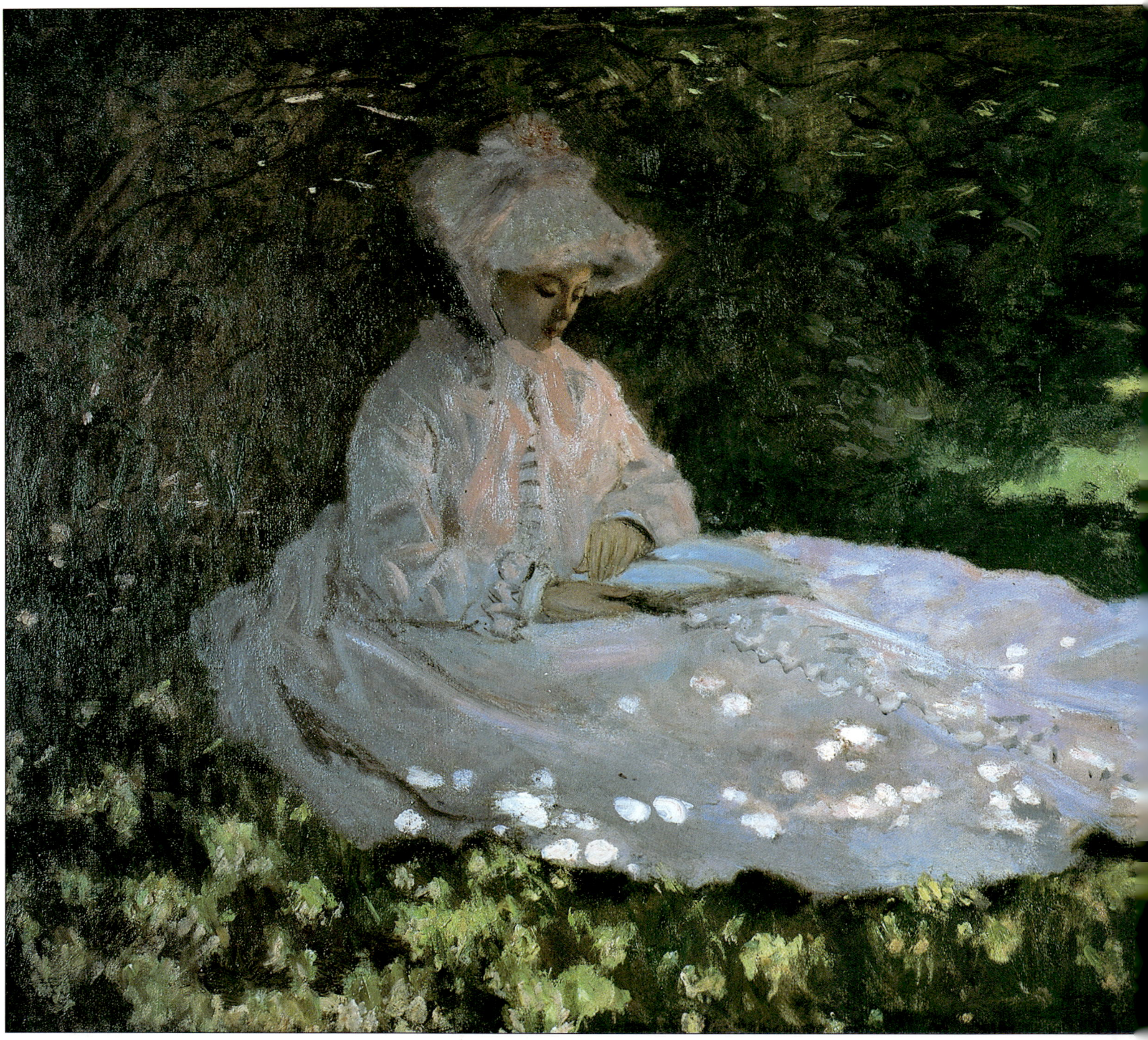

ABOVE:
Woman Reading
(1872)
WALTERS
ART GALLERY,
BALTIMORE

Garden Figures

During that same summer, Manet also painted a family scene set in Monet's garden. Monet is shown bent over, engaged in some horticultural task. After years of living in apartments, lodgings and hotels, he was delighted to have a garden of his own in which he could indulge his passion for flowers. Gardening became his principal hobby, closely linked with his work since his garden provided a convenient subject or setting for a painting when he

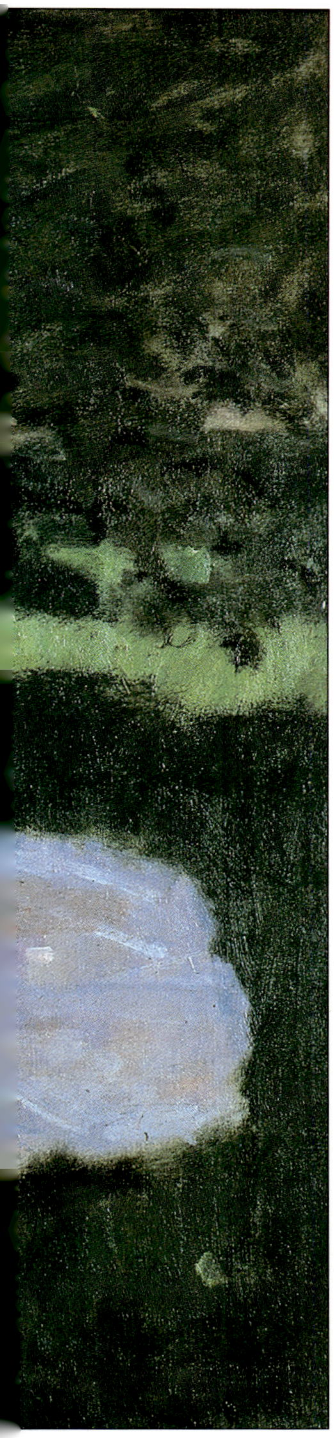

did not choose to venture beyond the house. Eventually, at Giverny, he would create a garden so large and lavish that it became all the world he needed for his art. Even during his first summer at Argenteuil, Monet was inspired by his flowers to attempt a new departure, painting two identical studies of lilacs in different light conditions; this anticipation of the celebrated series paintings of his later career was evidently an idea whose time had not yet come.

Monet's treatment of garden subjects already went back several years, notably to the brilliantly colourful *Flower Garden* of about 1866 (page 38) and *Jeanne-Marguerite in the Garden* of 1868 (page 50-1), which was painted at Sainte-Adresse; Jeanne-Marguerite, a female relative, is another of Monet's figures in the landscape rather than a distinct individual. Finally, the very large *Women in the Garden* (page 39) was Monet's least characteristic treatment of the setting; never again would he produce a work on this scale, dominated by the human presence. Even in *Woman Reading* (pages 98-9), where the figure occupies a large proportion of the picture surface, she is very much part of the glade, a delightful blossom of sun-dappled lavender and lilac.

BELOW:
Le Déjeuner
(1873)
MUSÉE D'ORSAY, PARIS

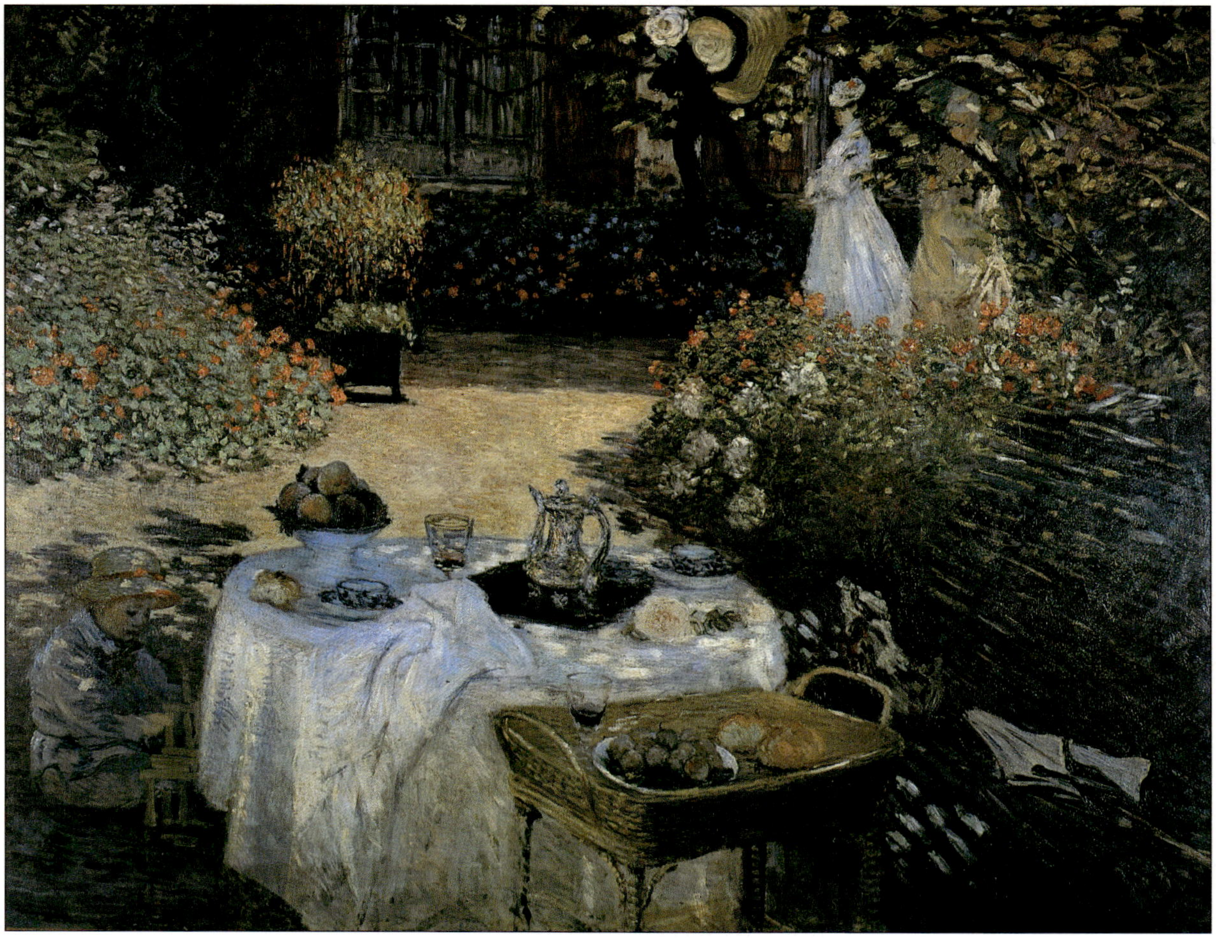

RIGHT:
Interior of an Apartment
(1875)
MUSÉE D'ORSAY, PARIS

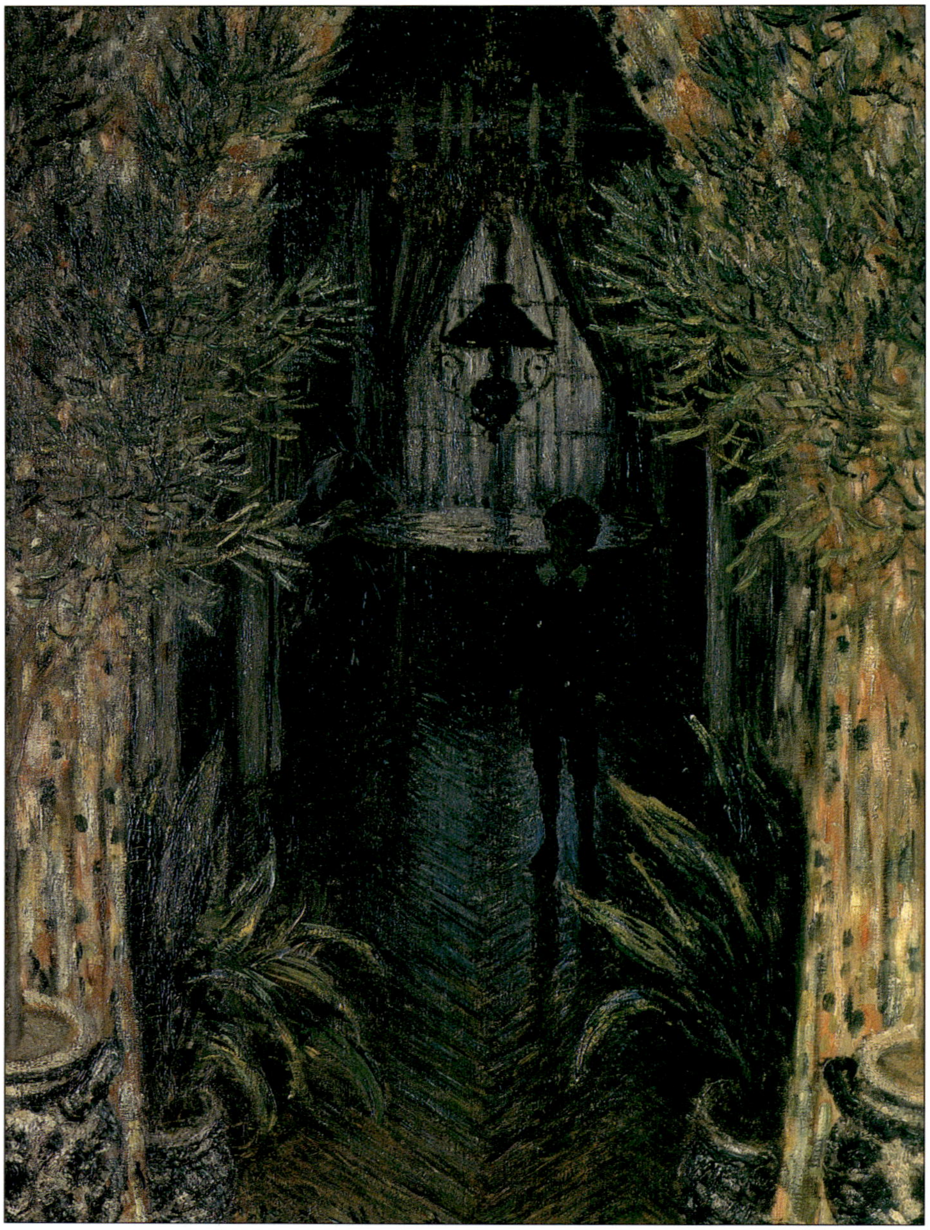

In many paintings of the Argenteuil garden the figures are very small, but some do strike a more domestic note. The lovely *Le Déjeuner* (page 99) conveys the special, relaxed character of alfresco dining, but it is noticeable that Monet has chosen to set the scene immediately after the meal. Where Renoir would have painted a table crowded with happy people, Monet disperses them; table and trolley, the diners, even the straw hat dangling saucily from a bough, become parts of the garden, unified by sunshine and shadow. *Le Déjeuner*, of course, has the same title as *The Luncheon* (page 60), although it is convenient to distinguish between them by translating only one into English; but the contrast between them

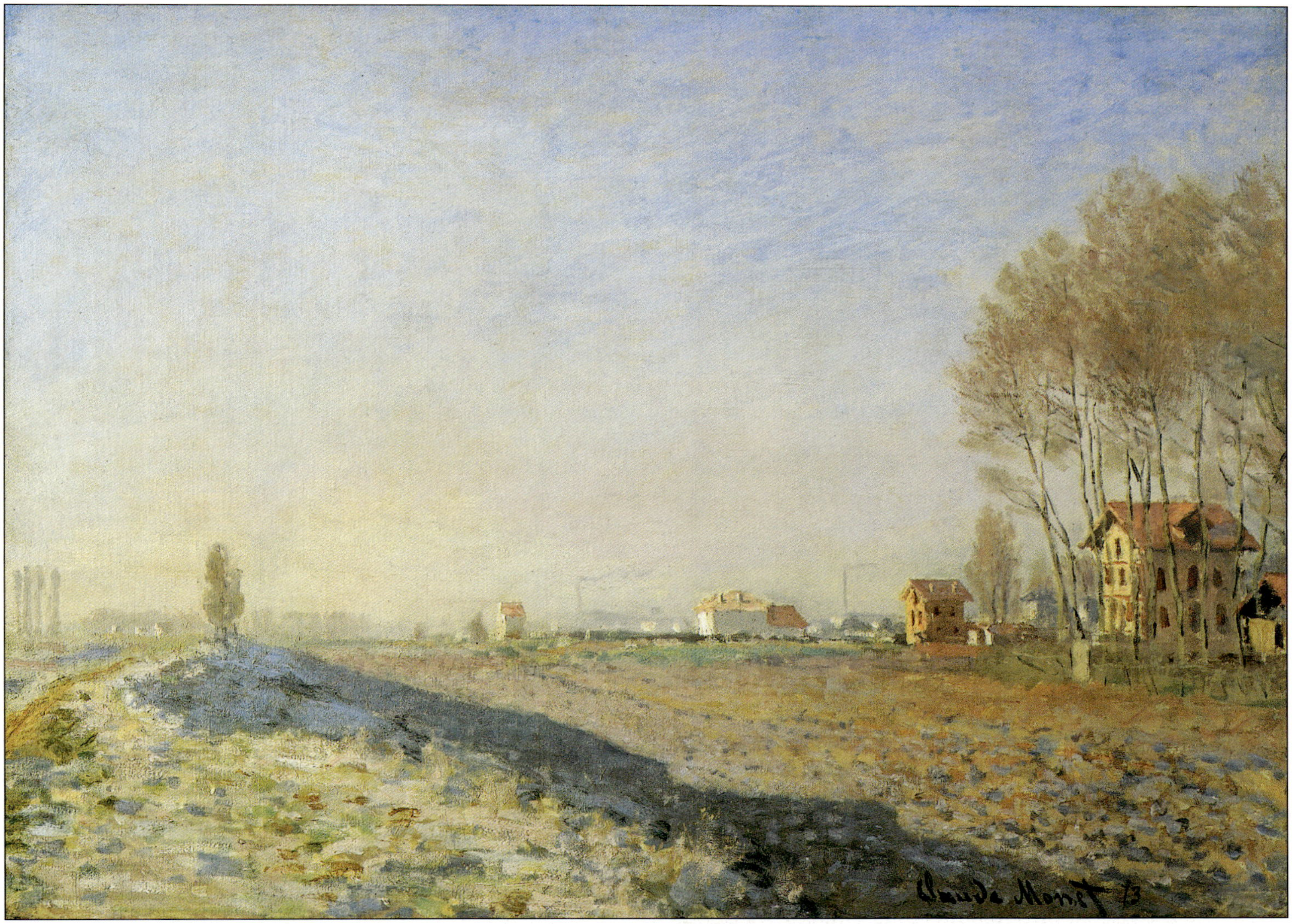

ABOVE:
The Plain of Colombes, White Frost
(1873)
PRIVATE COLLECTION

in almost every other respect – intention, setting, mood, technique and colour – is extraordinary and fascinating.

The impersonal quality of Monet's treatment of individuals persists even in paintings such as *Jean Monet on his Mechanical Horse* (1873), which shows the little boy mounted on a stuffed or wooden horse that is fixed onto a kind of iron tricycle. In *Interior of an Apartment* (page 100), with its theatre-like side curtains and adult's-eye downward view of the room, Jean might be any small boy, isolated in a rather sinister, oppressive setting. Camille, too, is generally a figure in a landscape (in many instances it is impossible to be certain whether she was the model). However, in a handful of canvases Monet does give her an individual presence, although of a surprising kind: she is pale, hollow-eyed, with what appears to be an air of anxiety, even in a cheerful, fanciful picture such as *The Japanese Girl* (page 115). As she died young, these may be no more than signs of ill-health, although it is possible to interpret them as indicators of Monet's hidden discontent or of tensions between the couple.

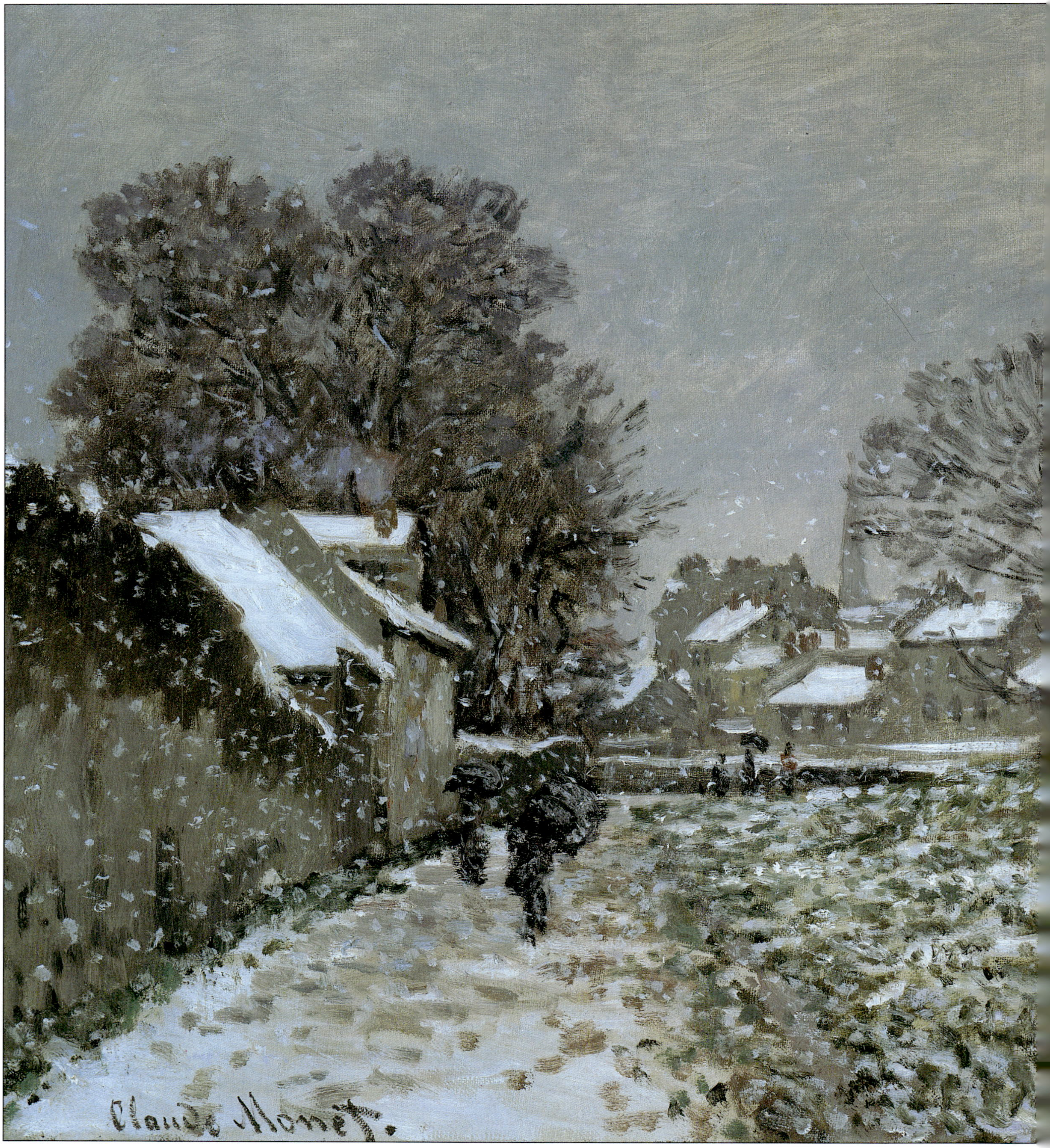
Claude Monet.

This is particularly tempting in the case of *The Red Cape*, where Camille looks into the room through the French windows like a forlorn ghost who has been forbidden to enter. Nevertheless, readings of this kind are notoriously unreliable unless supported by other evidence, and that is lacking. All it is possible to say is that, as a painter, Monet, the former caricaturist, was curiously uninterested in human individuality, whether expressed in terms of the model's personality or in a set of distinctive physical traits. Such was the nature of his art; it may or may not tell us something significant about the man.

Camille and Jean also appear in a number of the landscapes Monet painted in the countryside around Argenteuil. They are one (or both) of the couples shown coming down a flowery slope in *The Poppy Field at Argenteuil* (pages 106-7), perhaps the most frequently reproduced of all Monet's paintings. The dazzling vermilion of the poppies provided the opportunity for an explosion of colour that Monet exploited again and again during his years at Argenteuil and afterwards. However, he was hardy and resolute enough to work in all weathers, and if the low sunlit landscape in *Plain of Colombes, White Frost* (page 101) looks too pretty to be unbearable, *Snow at Argenteuil* (pages 102-3) is almost blizzard-like (although, naturally, we need not believe that it was painted while the snow was actually falling). The forms of human figures are barely suggested and yet convey an authentic sense of being drawn in on themselves to resist the assault of the elements.

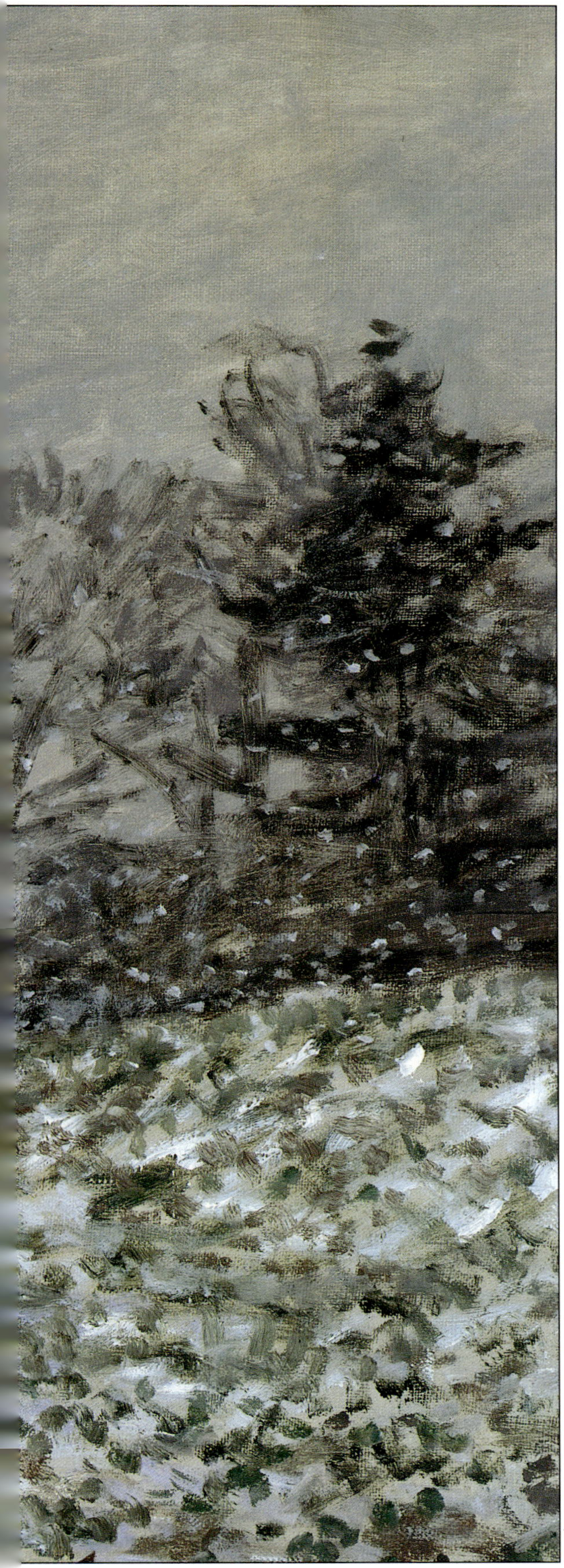

LEFT:
Snow at Argenteuil
(c.1875)
MUSEUM OF FINE ARTS, BOSTON

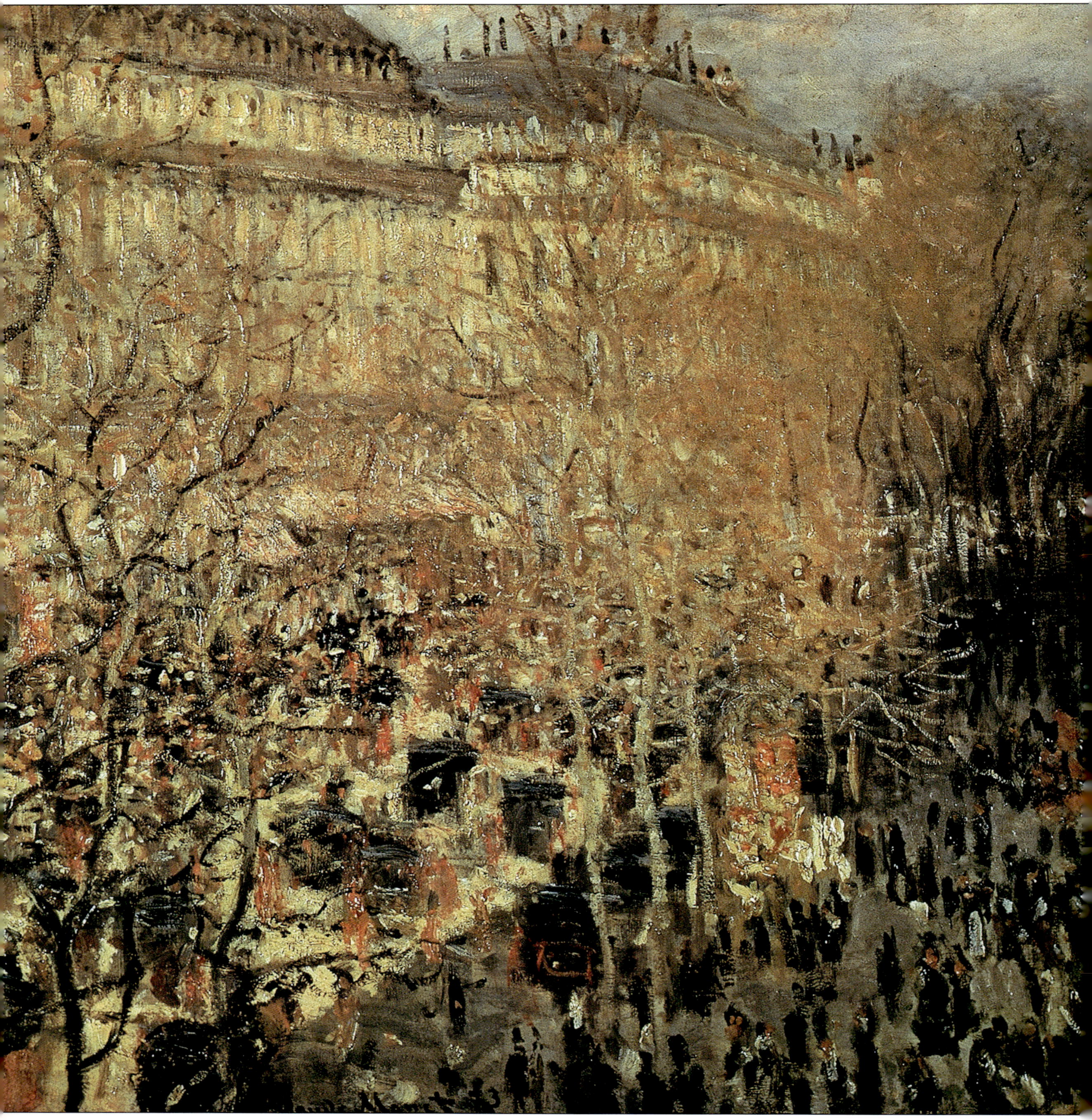

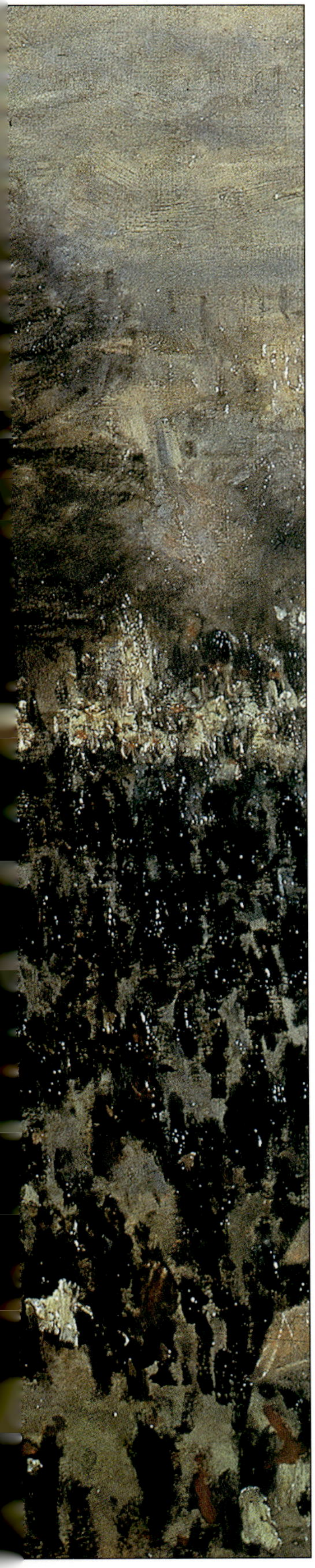

LEFT:
The Boulevard des Capucines
(1873)
Pushkin Museum, Moscow

CHAPTER FIVE

The Birth of Impressionism

DURING HIS FIRST THREE YEARS at Argenteuil, Monet was furiously productive and quite successful in finding buyers for his work. After the humiliating rejections of 1869 and 1870, he had decided to submit nothing more to the Salon. Of his fellow artists working in a similar vein, Pissarro and Sisley had also given up, but Renoir continued to try his luck, even though the results were not particularly encouraging.

Despite their apparent aloofness and physical absence from the capital, Monet and his friends still hoped to win wider public recognition, and closely followed events in the art world. One encouraging development was that in the early 1870s the Salon's prestige seemed to be waning. The 1872 show was criticized for its mediocrity and in 1873 the severity of the jury caused such an outcry that a separate exhibition of rejected works – a Salon des Refusées – was authorized. This had happened only once before, in 1863, when the rejects had included two major works, Manet's *Déjeuner sur l'Herbe* and *The White Girl,* by the American James McNeill Whistler. In 1873, with the exception of a canvas by Renoir,

RIGHT:
Poppy Field at Argenteuil
(1873)
MUSÉE D'ORSAY, PARIS

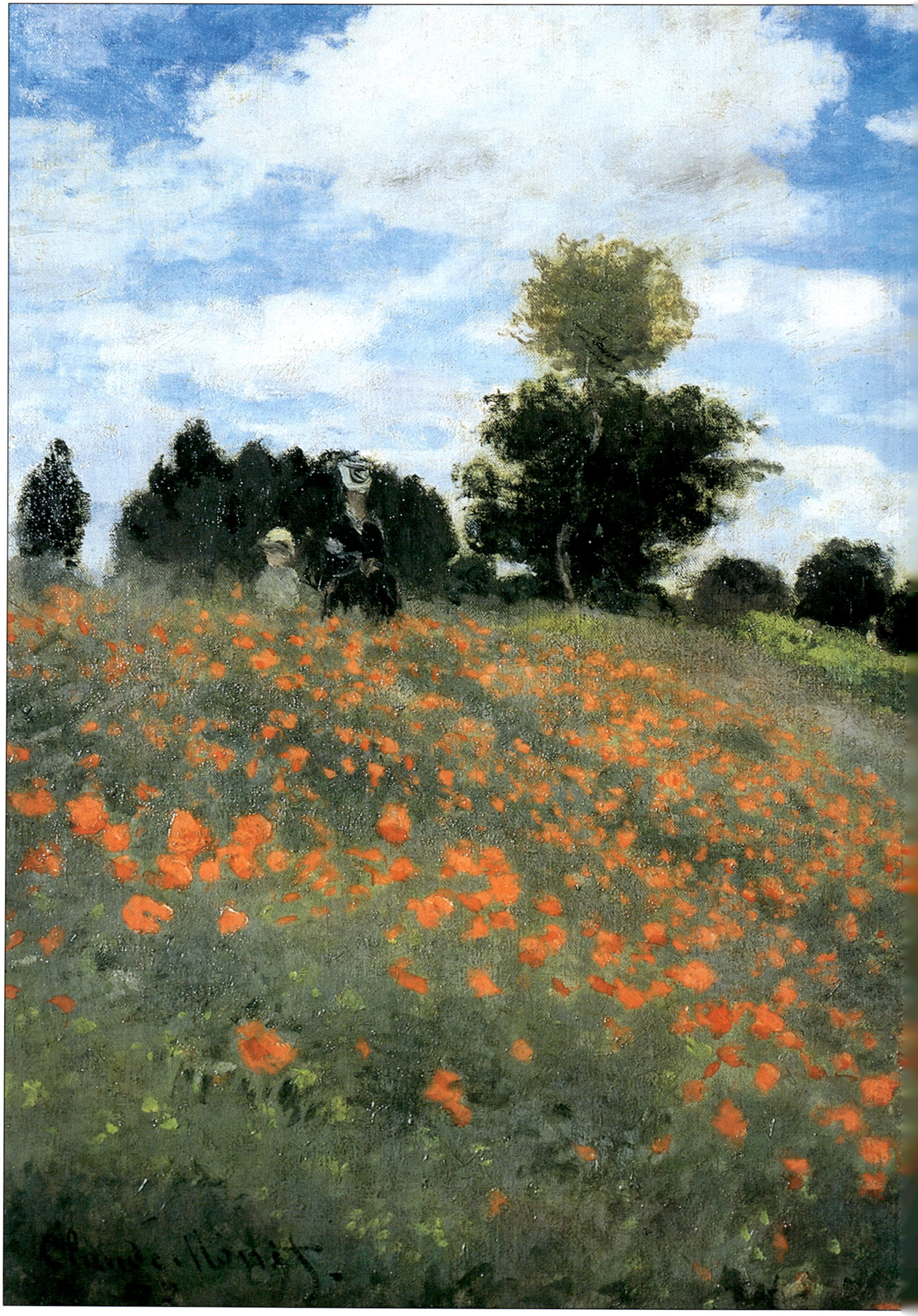

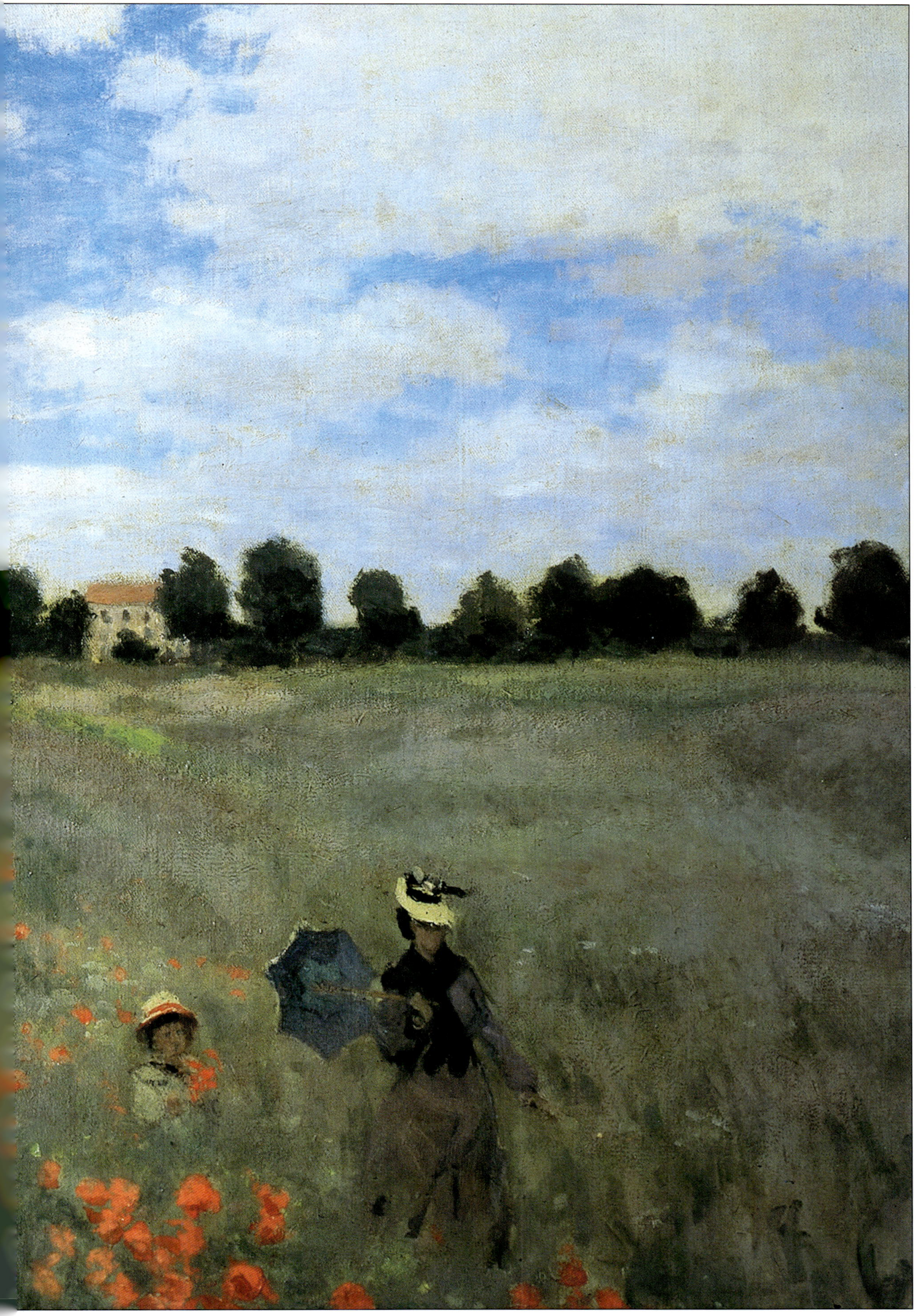

works of comparable quality were shown at the Refusées, so that Monet and his friends remained the leaders of the younger generation of anti-academic painters. It seemed at least possible that they were on the point of winning general acceptance, for Durand-Ruel was not only buying from them, but was preparing a three-volume catalogue of his collection in which Monet and the rest appeared side by side with Corot and other hallowed names. With prices for their own works rising and the 'enemy' in disarray, perhaps the time was ripe for an assault on Paris.

Putting on a Show

The campaign began in May 1873 with a pre-arranged newspaper article by Paul Alexis, a writer friend of Emile Zola, who denounced the jury system and called on independent-minded artists to organize their own shows. Monet was able to send a letter in prompt reply, stating that he and a group of like-minded painters were planning just such an exhibition and looked to the newspaper, *L'Avenir National*, for support. The principal figures in the group, apart from Monet himself, were Degas, Pissarro, Renoir, Sisley and Berthe Morisot (1841–95), who was closely associated with Manet, but was increasingly using the open-air technique of painting on the spot. Manet himself remained hopeful of conquering the Salon, which he still considered 'the real battlefield', and consequently refused to join a venture that seemed likely to alienate the art establishment for good. His attitude is understandable, since the proposed exhibition would be the first ever held independently by a group of artists and was clearly intended as a direct challenge to the monopoly of the Salon.

Over the next few months a good deal of manoeuvring and negotiating took place in order to keep the project alive, with Monet, Pissarro and Degas taking many of the initiatives. A number of other artists were persuaded to join the original nucleus, including Gustave Caillebotte, Monet's old friend Boudin and the touchy, eccentric Paul Cézanne (1839–1906), a future great master, still far from his maturity, who had become a landscapist under Pissarro's influence. In December 1873 the group set up a limited company to organize and finance an exhibition. Spacious premises were rented from the famous photographer Nadar in the Boulevard des Capucines, in the heart of fashionable Paris, and the show opened on 15 April, 1874. The date was obviously selected with an eye to maximum publicity and provocation, since it fell

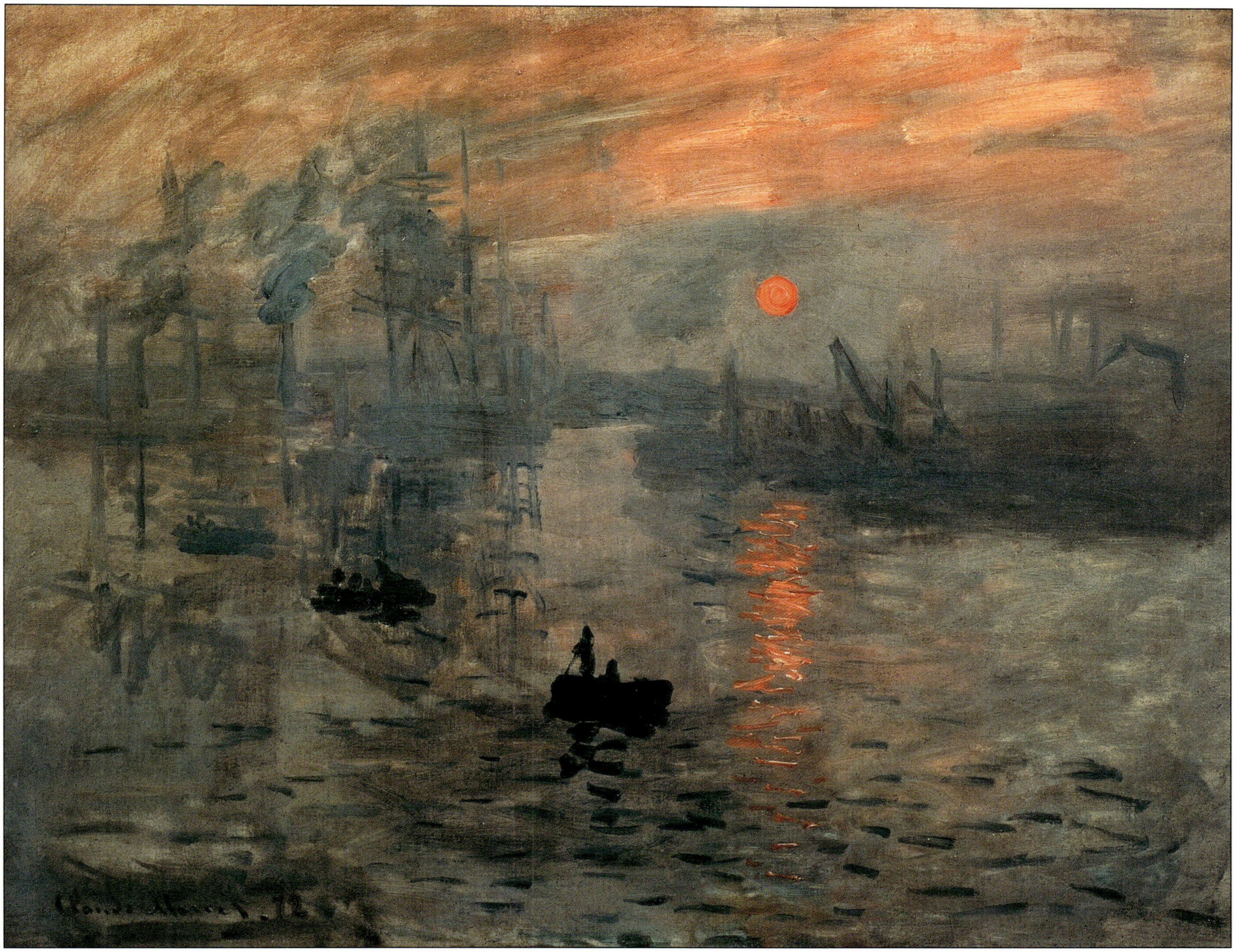

ABOVE:
Impression: Sunrise (1874)
MUSÉE MARMOTTAN, PARIS

just before the opening of the official Salon in May.

Monet chose to exhibit five paintings and seven pastels. The pastels may well have been included because they were relatively low in price and consequently more likely to sell to ordinary members of the public. Among the paintings was the large Salon candidate of 1868, *The Luncheon*, which established that Monet could, if he chose, deploy all the conventional skills. Perhaps he hoped that this would persuade the spectators to look without prejudice at works in which he had deliberately abandoned such conventions, such as *Boulevard des Capucines* (pages 104-5), *The Poppy Field at Argenteuil* (pages 106-7) and *Impression: Sunrise* (page 109). *Boulevard des Capucines* represents Monet at his most publicity-conscious, deliberately attempting to steal a march on his colleagues. A few months earlier, he had come to Paris, obtained access to the future exhibition room and painted two views of the

RIGHT: **Men Unloading Coal** (1875)
MUSÉE D'ORSAY, PARIS

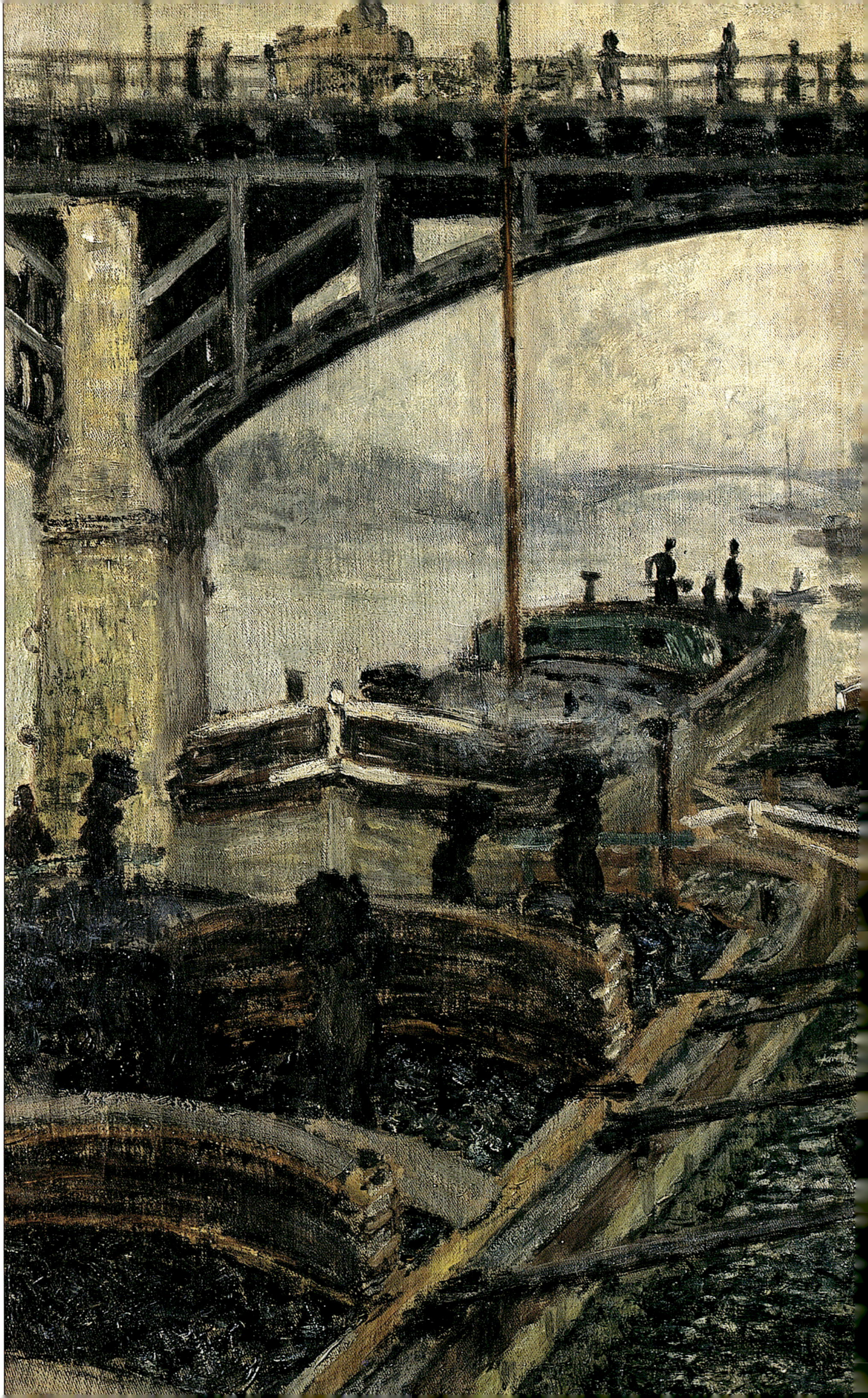

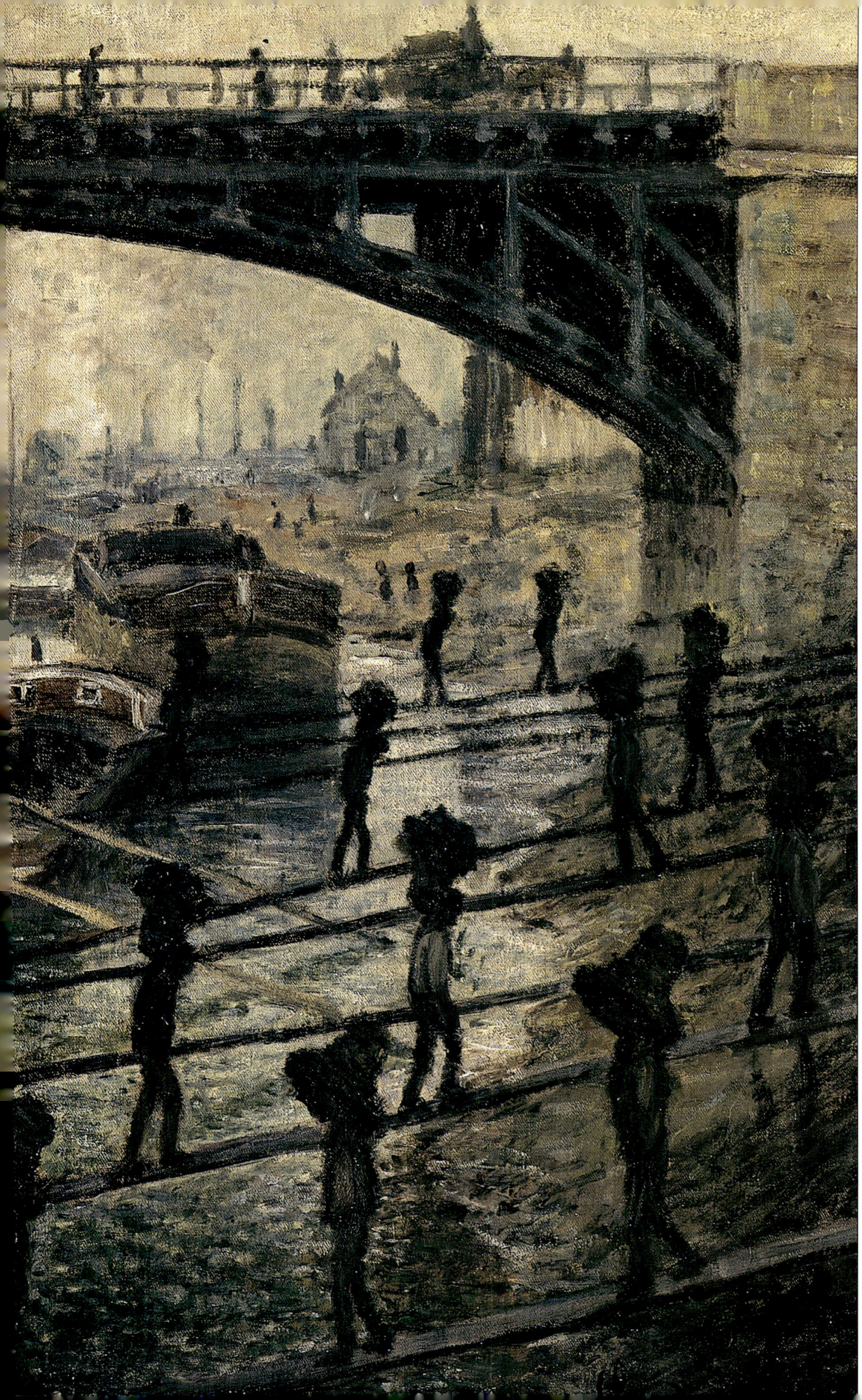

boulevard from the window. One of them (pages 104-5) was put on show at Nadar's, so that visitors to the exhibition were able to take in both the view and the painting of it at almost a single glance. Unfortunately, this splendid coup made less impact than the cursory treatment of the crowd shown on the canvas: their figures were dismissed as black blobs, although one critic did comment on how perfectly the picture conveyed 'the ant-like scurrying of the crowd'.

The show itself went off smoothly enough, attracting a very respectable total of 3,500 visitors. Financially it was a disappointment, with few sales, partly at least because the economic climate was changing for the worse. Monet sold nothing, although he soon afterwards got a good price – 800 francs – for *Impression: Sunrise,* purchased by a wealthy new patron, Ernest Hoschedé. The painting had attracted a good deal of attention, largely because of a vicious satirical magazine review entitled 'Exhibition of the Impressionists' by the journalist Louis Leroy. He had made great play with the word 'impression', which he used as a synonym for something hurried, smudged and incompetent. The review is cast in the form of a dialogue in which Leroy represents himself as defending the 'impressions' conveyed by the paintings of Renoir, Pissarro and Sisley, while an imaginary academic artist, Joseph Vincent, fulminates against them so violently that he shows signs of becoming mentally unhinged.

'A catastrophe seemed to me to be imminent', writes the narrator, 'and it was left to Monsieur Monet to provide the final impulse'.

Vincent stops in front of exhibit no. 98. 'What is it supposed to be? Have a look at the catalogue.'

'Impression: Sunrise.'

'Impression: I was certain of it. I was just thinking that as I was impressed, there had to be some impression in it. Andwhat freedom! What ease of handling! A preliminary drawing for a wallpaper pattern is more finished than this seascape!'

Eventually Vincent experiences a kind of nervous breakdown, imagines that he too is an impressionist, criticizes the face of a municipal guard, who is standing nearby, on the 'impressionist' grounds that it is too detailed, and begins to dance frenetically in front of Monet's paintings. Singing 'Ho-ho! I am impression on the warpath!' he is led away.

Leroy wrote for *Charivari,* a satirical magazine that would not normally have been read for its revealed truths about the arts; but the journalist's relentless use of 'impression' and 'impressionism' caught the public fancy. Its aptness was confirmed by a review published a few days later in which Jules Castagnary, not an unsympathetic critic, deployed the term 'Impressionists', apparently unaware of Leroy's use of the word. 'If we must characterize them with one explanatory word, we should have to coin a new term: *impressionists*. They are impressionists in that they render not the landscape but the sensation evoked by the landscape.' Evidently the label expressed a genuine response to the new art; and it stuck hard. The 1874 exhibition became known as the first Impressionist Exhibition, and Degas, Monet, Pissarro, Renoir, Sisley, Morisot and Cézanne, along with the absent Manet, became the 'Impressionists', despite the considerable differences between the outlook and techniques of the primarily modern-life painters (Manet and Degas), Monet and the landscapists, and artists like Renoir whose works can be seen as belonging to both categories or neither. As a result, defining Impressionism has been a problematic task ever since. As we have seen, even Monet, the quintessential Impressionist in the open-air-working sense, was also intermittently concerned with distinctly modern subjects.

Hard Times

Reviews of the Impressionist Exhibition ranged from magisterial condemnation, through Leroy's rather silly satire, to a number of positively encouraging articles. Statistically the tally was not unsatisfactory, yet somehow it was Leroy's point of view that became paramount. Over the next few years Impressionism became a favourite target for cartoonists: the pregnant young woman is advised to stay away from an Impressionist show for fear of the obstetric consequences ('Madame! It would be unwise to enter!'), an Impressionist painter declares that he learned his skills in the morgue, and in battle the terrible Turks use a new secret weapon – they hold up Impressionist paintings and their horror-struck foes take to their heels! In other circumstances the jokes might have provided the Impressionists with good publicity, but for most of the 1870s they reflected a real hardening of attitudes and public derision.

The financial consequences were all the more serious because the post-war boom had passed and even friendly patrons were becoming cautious about purchasing. Worst of all, the recession had hit Durand-Ruel, who had been forced to close his London galleries and put an abrupt end to his lavish buying of Impressionist paintings. Yet the artists themselves were slow in sensing the changed atmosphere. Warning signs appeared early in Monet's case, as his income for 1874 fell drastically to a no more than adequate 10,554 francs. Yet in October of that very year he moved into the house next door to his home at Argenteuil – a building that was even grander, cost much more to rent (1,400 francs) and, in his mind, could only be satisfactorily run with the assistance of a maid and a gardener. No wonder that Renoir was so impressed by Monet's 'lordly' ways! In 1873 he had made a princely income of 24,000 francs from his paintings, but he ran through the money – along with Camille's dowry and everything he had inherited from his father – at an alarming rate.

RIGHT:
The Japanese Girl (1876)
MUSEUM OF FINE ARTS, BOSTON

If Monet and his friends approached 1875 with any optimism, their hopes were soon shown to be ill-founded. At Renoir's urging, Monet and Sisley agreed to a bold new stroke: following the successful example of Daubigny, they would sell their works at auction. Berthe Morisot was also persuaded to take part. On 24 March, 1875, the sale was held at the Hôtel Drouot, the capital's leading auction house. Durand-Ruel conducted the proceedings and according to his own account, took the precaution of making the pictures more enticing by putting them in expensive frames. The mood of the public at large was indicated by the number of people who turned up simply to laugh and hoot: Impressionism had become riotously funny, and at one point the riot became so close to a reality that police had to be called in to restore order. Worse, the bidding was unenthusiastic and almost everything on offer was knocked down at a heartbreakingly low price; Monet was not the greatest sufferer, even though the 20 canvases he sent in were sold for an average of about 200 francs apiece.

In the event, 1875 was the worst year of the decade for Monet. His earnings fell again, to 9,765 francs, and halfway through the year he was writing to Manet, claiming that his credit at the butcher's and baker's was exhausted, and begging for immediate relief in the form of a 20 franc note. Yet the atmosphere of his paintings of boats and snowscapes was, if anything, more tranquil than ever, as in the well-known *Red Boats* canvases. Among all these idyllic works, there is a single odd-painting-out, *Men Unloading Coal* (pages 110-11). It has attracted a certain amount of attention just because it was unlike Monet to tackle such a grimly realistic, 'industrial' subject. One plausible view is that it reflects Monet's increasing unease at the growing industrialization of Argenteuil; but if so, he concealed the fact by turning the picture into a highly organized work of art, pulled tightly together by multiple

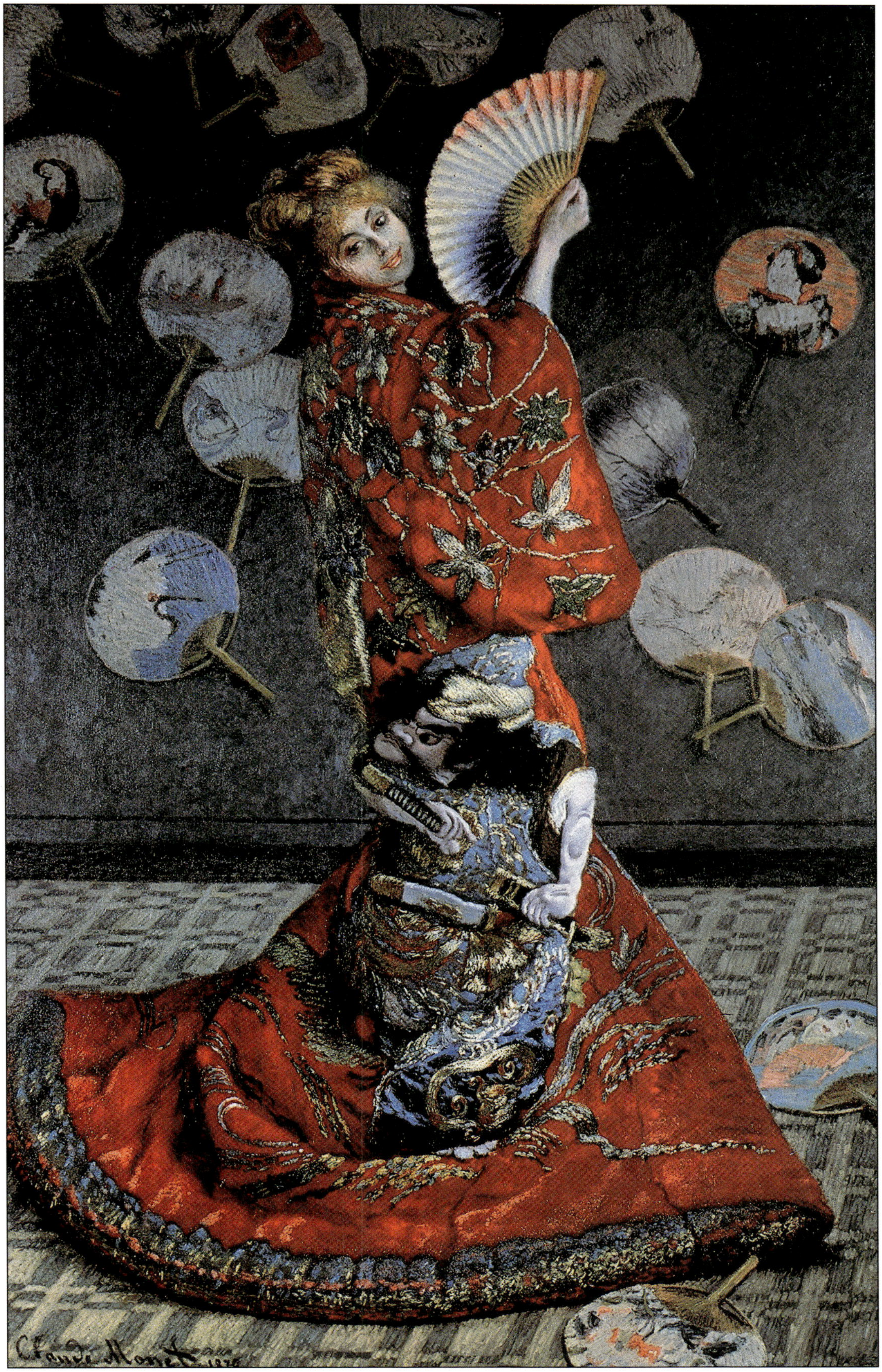
Claude Monet

RIGHT:
A Corner of the Garden at Montgeron
(1876)
HERMITAGE MUSEUM,
ST. PETERSBURG

horizontal, vertical and diagonal lines: the bridges, masts and oars of the boats, the planks along which the toilers move backwards and forwards, and even the near-identical shapes of the men themselves. Far from being a raw, earnest study of nineteenth-century industrialism, *Men Unloading Coal* is, for Monet, an unusually formal, patterned composition.

Although their limited society had been wound up, the Impressionists decided to hold another show, which opened in April 1876 on the Rue Le Peletier. There were more visitors than in 1874 and the press reaction was fairly respectful. Monet showed 18 works, and managed to sell the charming *The Japanese Girl* (page 115). Japanese art had enjoyed a long vogue in avant-garde circles and had certainly influenced Monet's painting. However, *The Japanese Girl*, although over life-size, is a consciously fanciful exercise in *japonaiserie* (that is, European pseudo-Japanese art). By picturing Camille in a reddish-blonde wig, Monet appears to insist upon the fact that she is not Japanese and that the painting is a friendly salute to the Orient rather than an imitation. The scattering of fans is a tribute to their popularity as decorative objects, but there is something almost cheeky in the way that Monet has shown Camille's kimono from the very angle at which we can see the embroidered warrior figure in the act of drawing his sword.

Monet stayed on in Paris that spring, but rather than cityscapes he painted urban greenery – the Tuileries Gardens, where no sign now remained of the palace burned down during the Commune, and the Parc Monceau. During the visit (partly, perhaps, set aside for drumming up business), Monet renewed his contacts with the department-store magnate Ernest Hoschedé. The outcome was the stroke of luck Monet must have been hoping for: he was invited to stay at Hoschedé's magnificent country house, the Château de Rottembourg, at Montgeron, not far from Paris. In return, Monet executed a commission on the grand scale, to paint four very large canvases (all about 172 cm high by 140–193 cm. wide) as decorations for the salon of the château. He had done nothing of this kind since the 1860s, and he remained essentially faithful to his current style and preoccupations in *A Corner of the Garden at Montgeron* (pages 116-17) and *The Pool at Montgeron* (page 119); the brilliant flowers and, above all, the melting reflections in the pool foreshadow the wonderful effects achieved by Monet in his old age in his own garden at Giverny. *Turkeys* (page 120) is a more unusual, endearing work, avoiding portentousness by putting the birds in the foreground, leaving the château to be glimpsed in the distance.

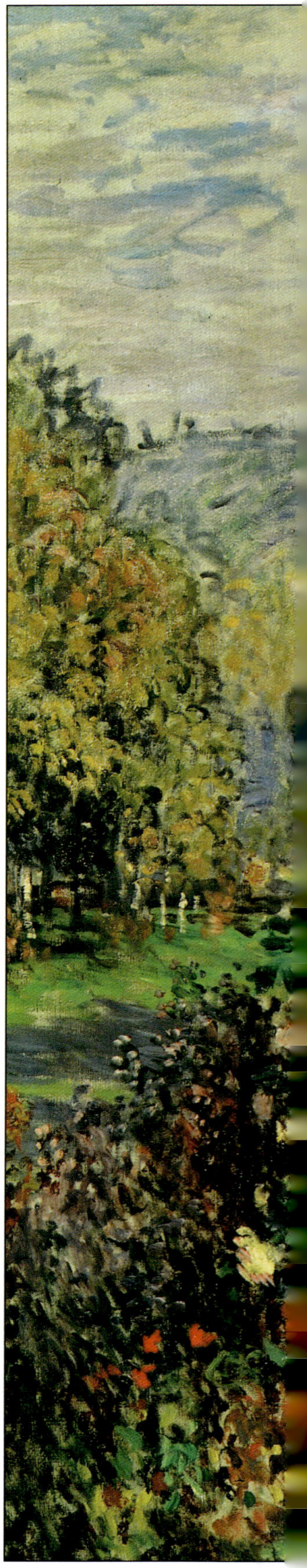

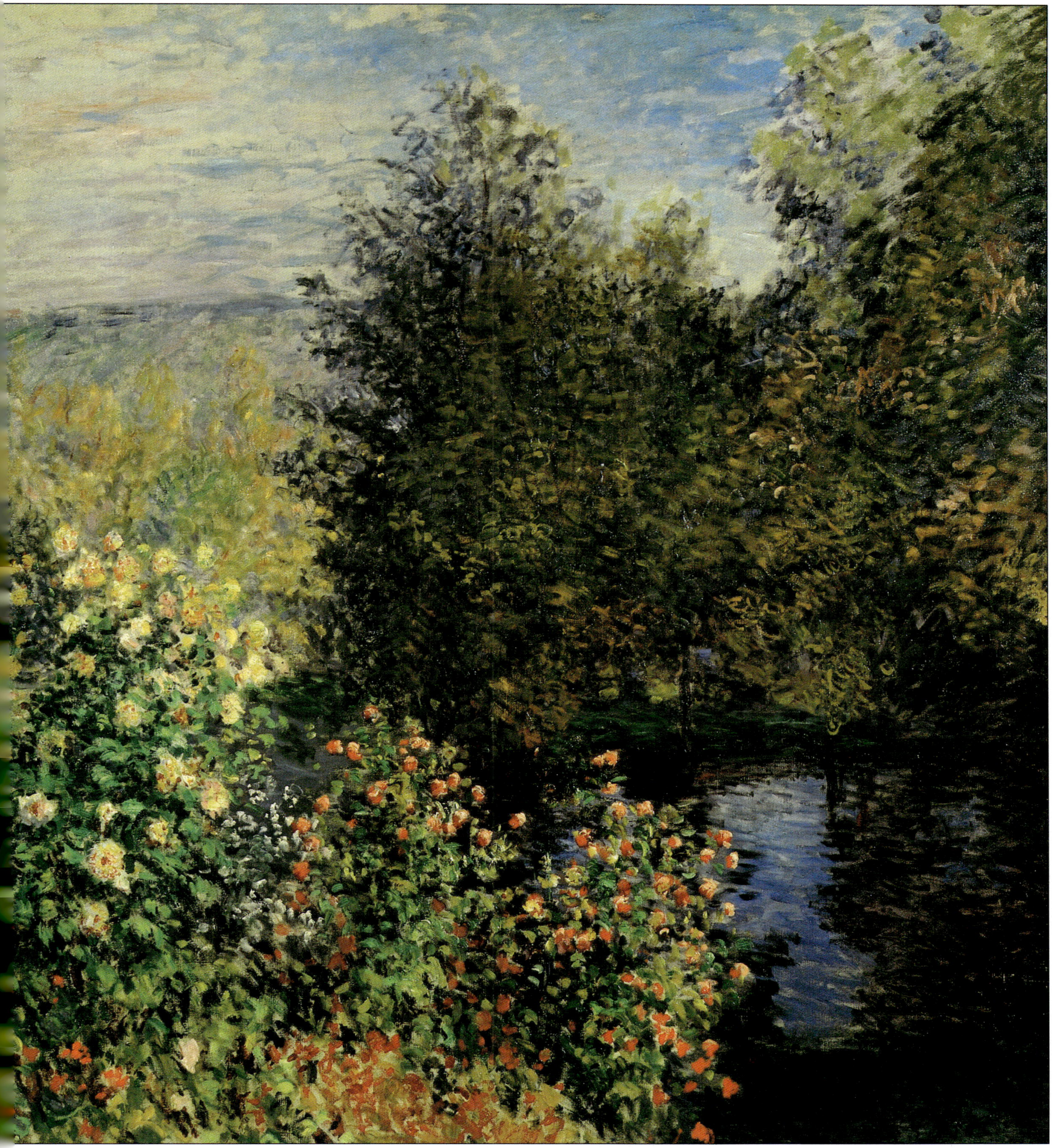

Only the fourth canvas, *The Hunt,* makes a concession to traditional country pursuits, although even in this scene the ardent hunters are almost overwhelmed by the surrounding woods, being pictured as a small party lined up so that they recede into the distance down a leafy tunnel.

At Montgeron, Monet was lavishly entertained but left to work without interruption in a studio specially set up for him in the grounds. He remained there for most of the summer and autumn of 1876, painting a number of smaller landscapes as well as the four large panels for the château. By this time the Hoschedés had become his close friends, and Monet and Camille saw a good deal of them in Paris during the following winter. Monet's relations with Hoschedé's wife Alice in 1876 have been a subject of considerable speculation – naturally enough, in view of their later connection, although there is no real evidence for the existence of a liaison at this stage. In August 1877 Alice Hoschedé had a child, Jean-Pierre, who might have been fathered by Monet, although the supposition seems based mainly on Jean-Pierre's later fantasies. Those who doubt Monet's involvement point out that Alice was deeply devout, an argument that, given the known history of human piety and human frailty, seems equally unpersuasive. Like many aspects of Monet's personal life, his extra-marital activities, if any, have remained outside the public domain.

Keeping such grand company may not have helped Monet's financial position. His earnings had crept back up to 12,313 francs, making 1876 his best year since 1873. Such a sum should have been adequate, but was not; he was in debt and, whether quite truthfully, claimed in letters to his better-off friends that he lived in dread of being evicted from his house at Argenteuil. Over the next few years he would receive generous help from Manet, Caillebotte, Dr de Bellio and other friends, but in spite of gradually increasing earnings, he seemed unable or unwilling to manage while his income remained anything less than a tycoon's.

At the Gare Saint-Lazare

In January 1877 Monet made another extended trip to Paris. There were signs that Argenteuil had lost some of its appeal for him and he evidently felt the need to tackle a new kind of subject in a new kind of way. Consequently he rented an apartment in the capital and obtained permission to set up his easel inside one of the great Parisian stations, the Gare Saint-Lazare; he already knew

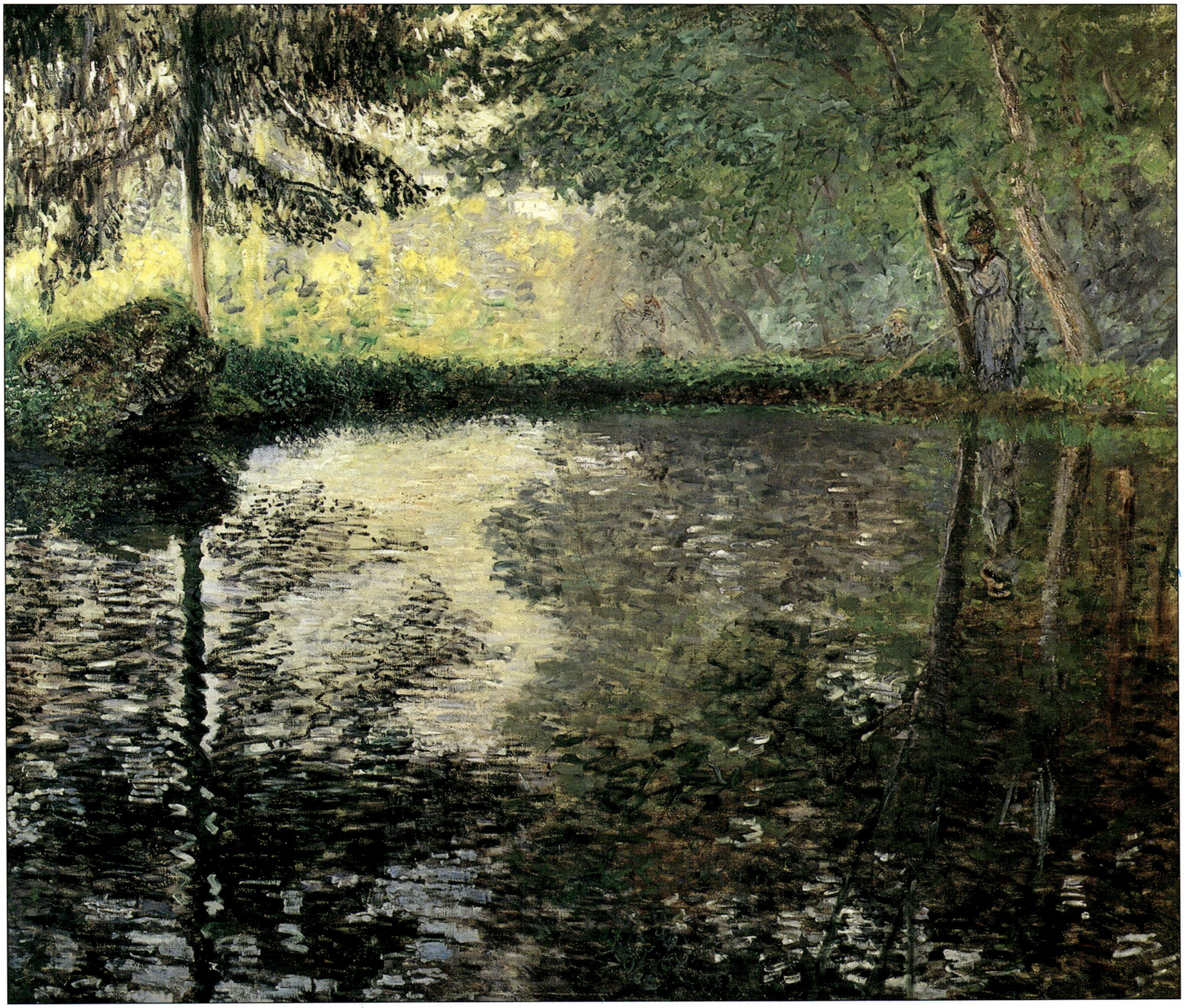

ABOVE:
The Pool at Montgeron
(1876)
HERMITAGE MUSEUM, ST. PETERSBURG

it very well, since it was the terminus of the line that passed through Le Havre and Argenteuil. The project marked the culmination of his interest in trains as a pictorial subject and constituted one of his most daring innovations. Although Monet's own subjects had included trains speeding through the countryside, and Manet and Caillebotte had painted scenes linked with stations and their iron-monster inhabitants, no one before Monet had tackled directly this sooty, murky environment, apparently lacking every element of traditional dignity or romantic appeal.

Monet worked obsessively at Saint-Lazare, finishing 12 canvases by April 1877. Here, five years after the garden lilacs he had painted at Argenteuil, the idea of a series of linked views had re-emerged.

RIGHT:
Turkeys (1876)
MUSÉE D'ORSAY,
PARIS

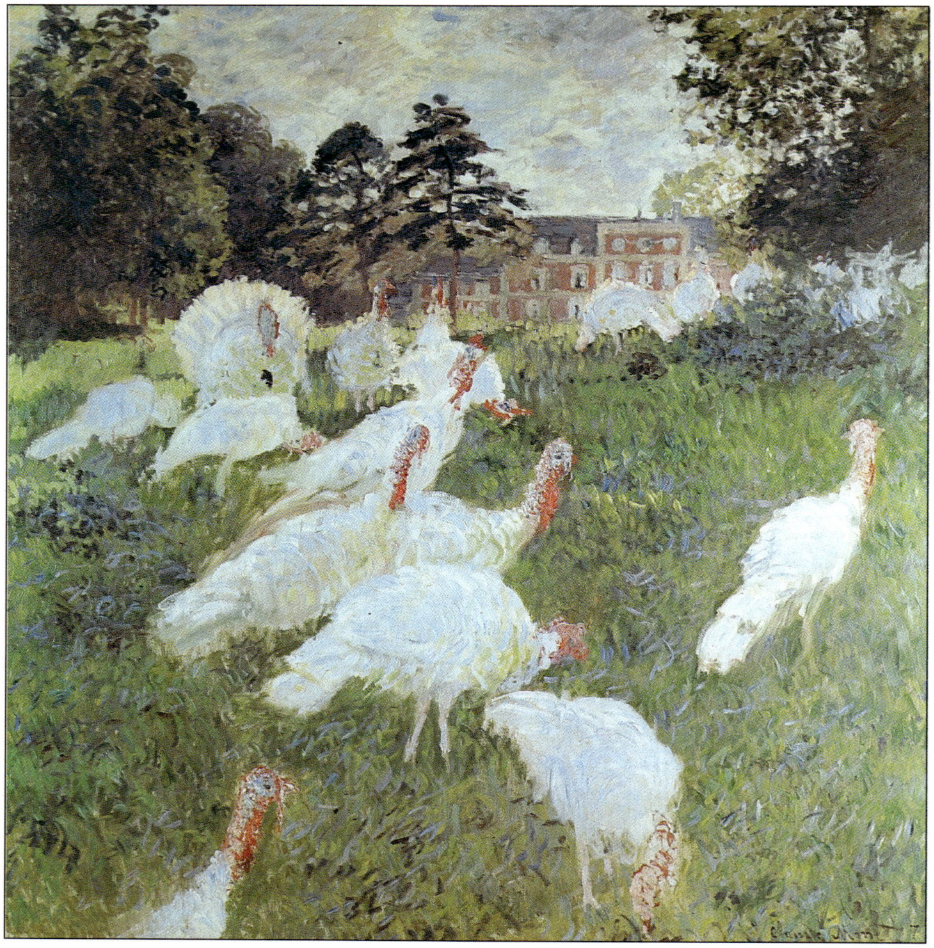

It almost certainly embodied an urge to wring every drop of pictorial interest from a subject, perhaps in order to exhaust it and be done with it for ever. By contrast with the Rouen Cathedral paintings (pages 197-98 & 201) and similar series from later in his life, the Gare Saint-Lazare canvases are unalike in size and subject: the intention is not to exhaust a single view, but to capture every aspect of the station. The 12 canvases include both exteriors and interiors, station sheds and sidings, with great clouds of steam and smoke as the common element, whatever the angle of vision. Even the basic treatment, although everywhere free, varies from picture to picture; in *The Signal*, Monet has laid on the paint with such urgent rapidity that the scene takes on an air of mystery, with all of its contents so smokily indistinct that they seem on the point of dissolving and disappearing. Throughout the series, Monet deploys steam and smoke with such mastery that they become a form of audio-visual shorthand, conjuring up a world of human bustle, abrupt mechanical movements and discontinuous noises, piercing whistles, shrieking brakes, clanking iron and pounding locomotives.

Inevitably, the best-known canvases from the series are those in major museums, such as the Musée d'Orsay in Paris (pages 122-3), which also happen to be views of trains in or approaching the great station sheds that covered the interior. One exception is the Musée Marmottan's splendidly atmospheric *Gare Saint-Lazare: Pont de l'Europe* (pages 124-5), which shows the road-bridge crossing the lines just outside the station. The sheds of great termini were iron-and-glass marvels of nineteenth-century technology, often described as the equivalent in the industrial age of the great medieval cathedrals; their presence in these paintings suggests a 'social realist' intention on Monet's part that seems less convincing in the context of the entire series. Although he certainly appreciated the pictorial possibilities of such non-traditional subjects and was admirably prompt in exploiting them, there is little evidence that Monet had any particular interest in the social or economic problems associated with industrial growth, or even that he saw himself in any programmatic way as a 'painter of modern life'. Moreover, even in the most prominently peopled Gare Saint-Lazare scenes, the human element is given no special importance and is represented in a distinctly neutral fashion, from which it would be impossible to say whether we are looking at the oppressed masses in grimy squalor or happy travellers enjoying the blessings of progress. As a matter of fact, Monet was reaching the end of even this limited commitment to the distinctively modern. Having finished the Gare Saint-Lazare paintings, he began to turn back to traditional subjects and, with only a handful of exceptions, even including family portraits and figures in landscapes, modernity virtually disappeared from his work. His art remained avant garde, but in technique and compositional effects rather than subject matter.

This important development must have seemed unlikely in April 1877, when eight of the Saint-Lazare views were hung at the third Impressionist exhibition. Funded by Caillebotte, the event was again staged in the Rue Le Peletier, but in new premises. By this time the Impressionists had half-embraced the group name that the malicious Leroy had given them; the show was called the Exhibition of Impressionists, and while it was running a young supporter, Georges Rivière, published a weekly with the title *L'Impressioniste.* Many of the earlier, more conventional exhibitors had dropped away, so that the group gained in coherence but possibly seemed even more outrageous than before. It was still bitterly attacked in some journals, but had begun to find defenders among writers and intellectuals, as well as a few perceptive clients.

Monet exhibited 30 canvases, including *Turkeys* and other works done at Montgeron, the views of the Tuileries and the Parc Monceau from the previous spring and the eight Gare Saint-Lazare paintings. The immediate results were disappointing, but in the course of the year he managed to drive his income up to 15,197 francs; in fact, he seems to have spent more and more time trying to sell existing works rather than painting. Nevertheless, money was still short, Camille was ill and Monet was deeply depressed by his failure to win the kind of fame and fortune he craved. His prospects looked all the bleaker when his most munificent patron, Ernest Hoschedé, went bankrupt. The event may not have been entirely unexpected, as in 1874–5 Hoschedé's wild speculations had forced him to sell the family textiles firm and his own art collection, but he had kept afloat by dubious expedients and had even founded a new company. This time, however, he was wiped out and the Hoschedés lost everything including Alice's inheritance, the lovely château at Montgeron. The initial effect of the Hoschedé crash on Monet was to deprive him of a client, but soon there were further repercussions that changed the entire course of his life.

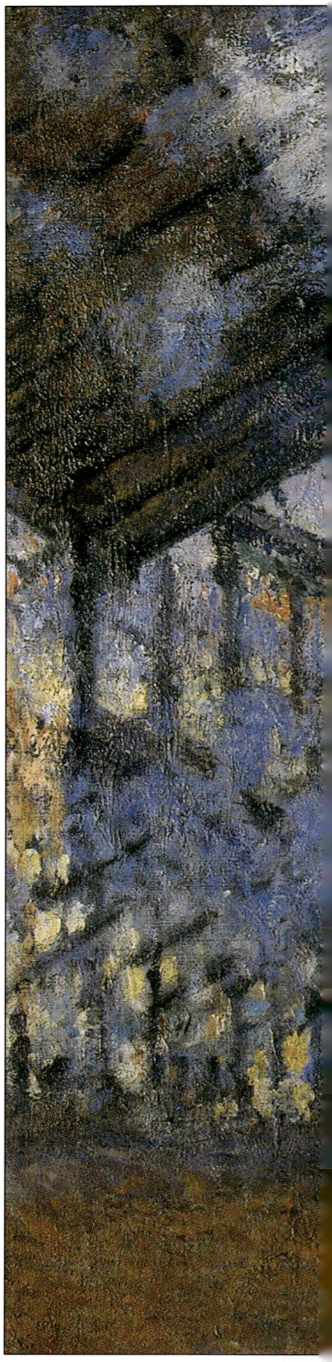

Back to Paris

In the meantime, he made the drastic decision to quit Argenteuil, although his reasons for doing so are not entirely clear. Perhaps it was because the once idyllic riverside was becoming industrialized and polluted; perhaps Monet had finally exhausted the subjects it offered him; or perhaps he left for the more banal reason that his perpetual financial difficulties were, by now, well known in the town, compounding a low credit-rating with considerable social embarrassment. If Monet's letters, mostly written to raise money, can be believed, he had come close to being evicted and/or sold up on many occasions over several years. If nothing else, leaving the scene of these torments and making a fresh start must have seemed worth doing.

Even going away proved to be difficult for a man with outstanding debts in Argenteuil, and Monet was still trying to disentangle himself in January 1878. Once more Manet and de Bellio came to the rescue, but even so Monet had to leave behind his youthful *Déjeuner sur l'Herbe* (pages 34-5) as a surety. As we have seen, he failed to redeem it for six years, during which time it rotted in a cellar until only fragments could be salvaged.

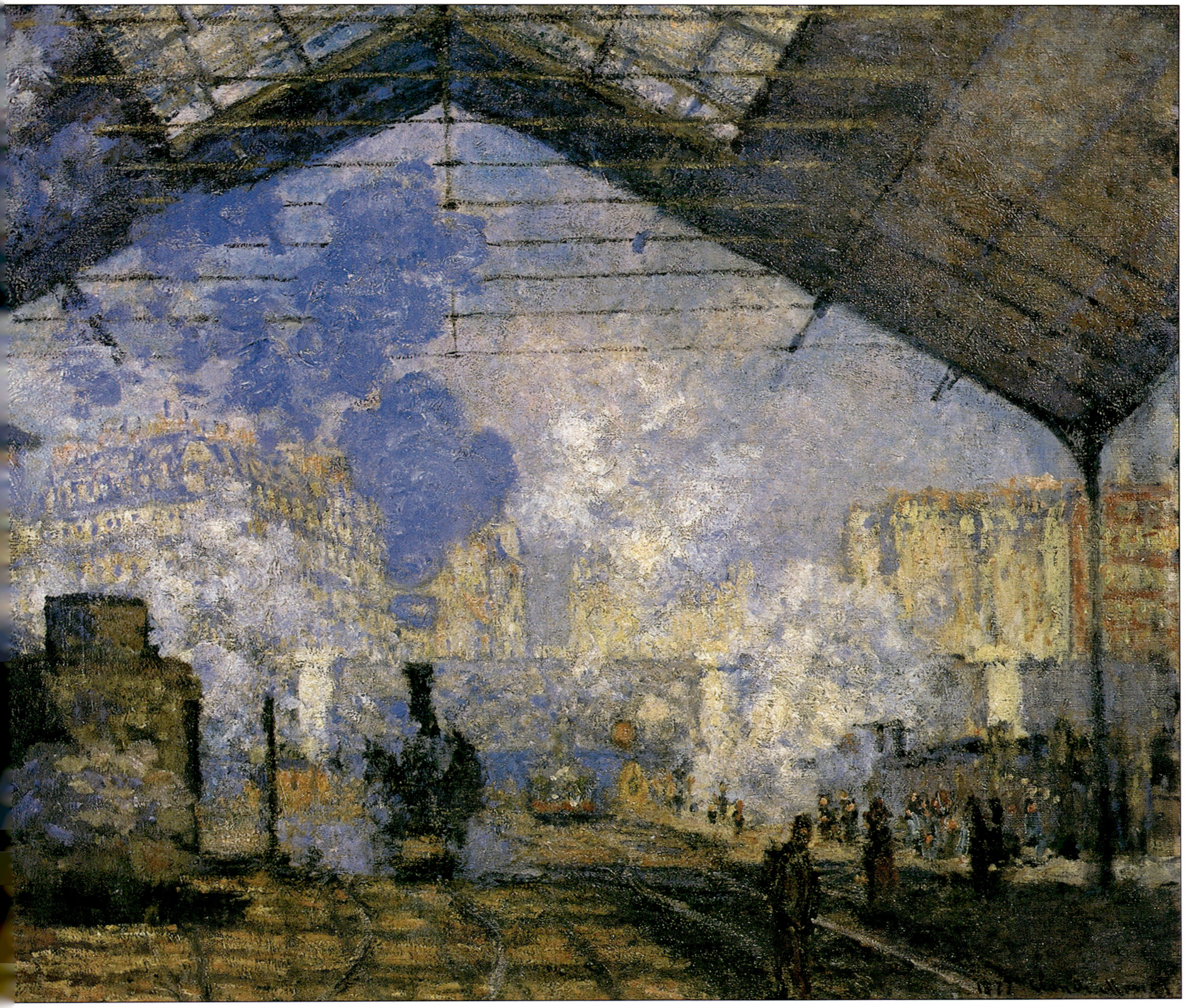

Initially Monet and his family moved to Paris, spending several months at 26 Rue d'Edimbourg, where Camille gave birth to another child, Michel, on 17 March, 1878. Monet wrote desperate-sounding letters to friends and clients, claiming that he could not afford the medical care needed by mother and child. Meanwhile the family remained in their expensive six-roomed apartment and he still kept on the studio in the Rue Moncey that he had rented in order to paint the Gare Saint-Lazare series . . .

Plans for a fourth Impressionist show in the spring came to nothing, but in May the publication of Théodore Duret's book

ABOVE:
The Gare Saint-Lazare
(1877)
MUSÉE D'ORSAY, PARIS

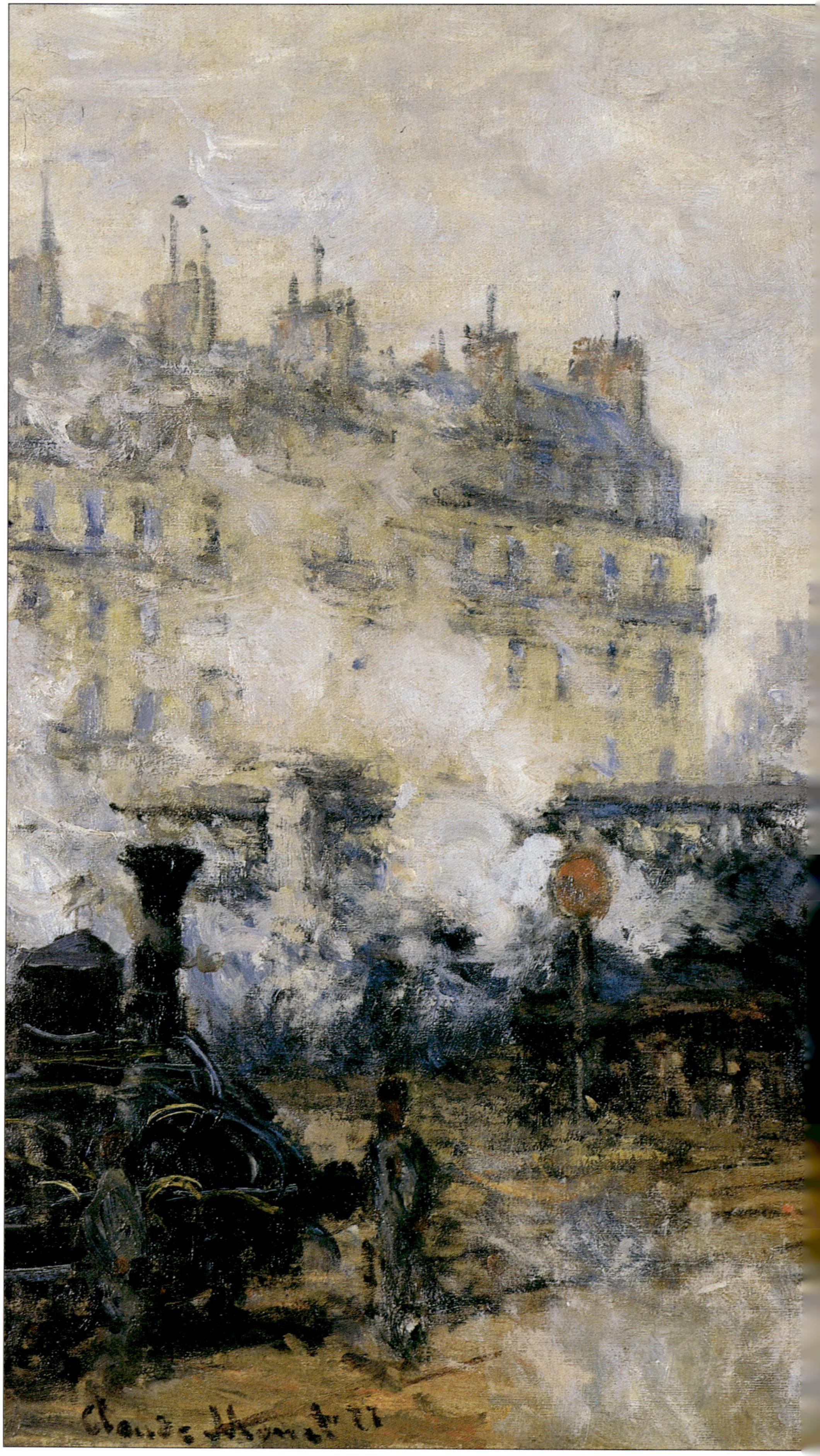

RIGHT: **The Gare Saint-Lazare: Pont de l'Europe** (1877)
MUSÉE MARMOTTAN, PARIS

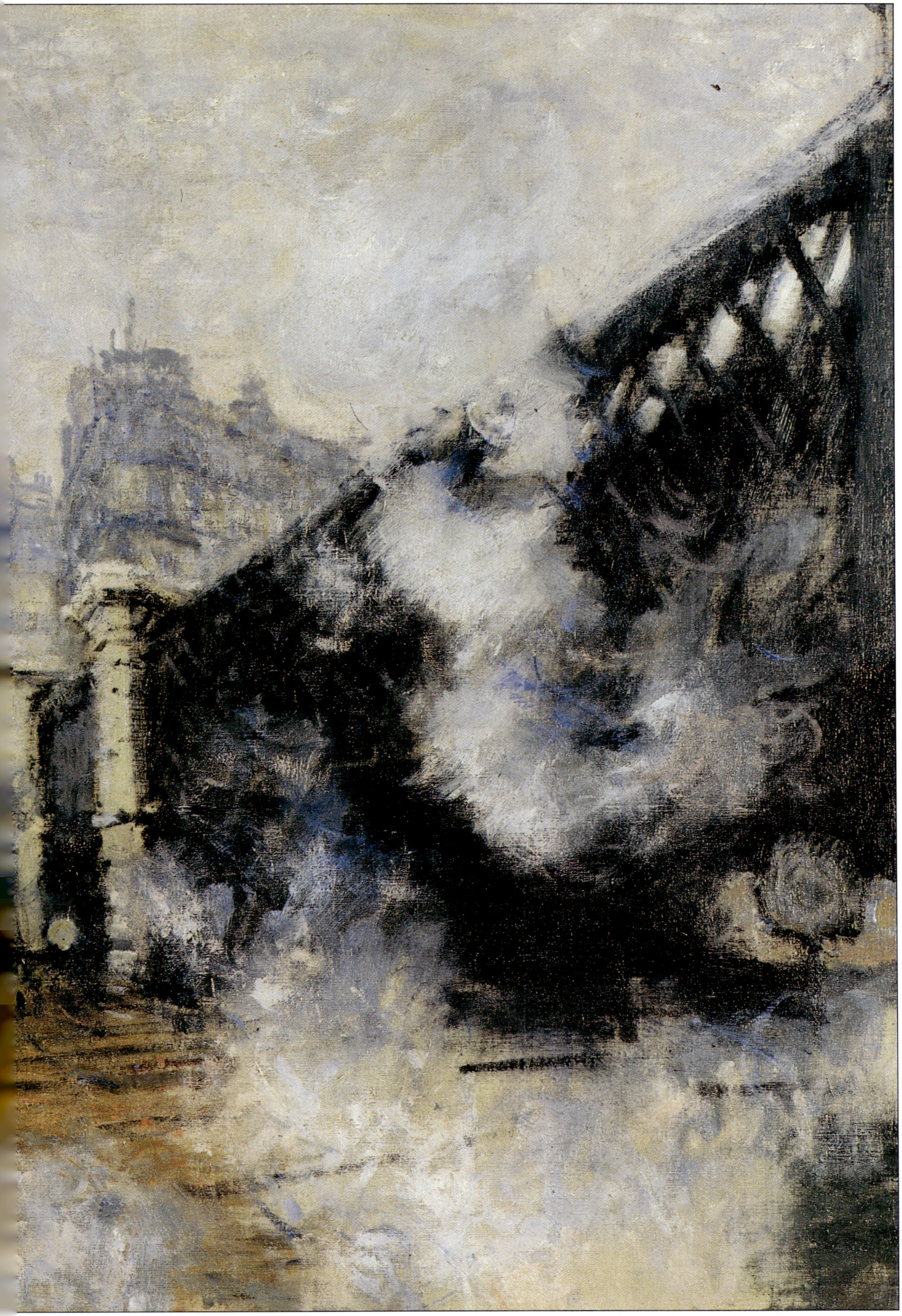

Les Peintures Impressionistes struck a blow on behalf of the group. Duret, a wealthy writer-collector, had met Manet in Madrid 13 years before and had been a staunch defender of the painter and his 'gang' ever since. Duret's book was the first to survey the Impressionists as a group that would inevitably become part of the history of its time, including brief biographies of the individual members as well as general discussion. Duret identified Monet as the most thoroughgoing Impressionist of all, concerned not only with the unmoving, permanent features of nature, but also with 'the elusive aspects it assumes with changes of atmosphere', so that he was always alert to seize upon 'thousands of nuances' of light, colour and reflections. As well as remarking that 'Monet is the painter of water par excellence', Duret perceptively drew attention to the specific features of the artist's landscapes, including what he chose to omit or ignore: he was not a painter of rustic life, hardly ever including peasants, cows or sheep in his canvases, but was attracted by 'ornamental nature' in the form of parks, gardens and buildings. Two years later Duret wrote the preface to the catalogue of Monet's first one-man show at the offices of *La Vie Moderne*, in which he placed the painter firmly in the great French tradition of landscape art.

Meanwhile, during his stay in Paris, Monet painted mainly gardens and views of the Seine. However, earlier in the summer, knowing that he would not be in the capital for much longer, he made a superbly flamboyant gesture, recording the festive scene on 30 June, the first national day celebrated in France since the Franco-Prussian war. Combined with the holding of an International Exhibition that year in Paris, this constituted a reassertion of French national pride and, significantly, Monet also painted the scene in the streets on 30 June. According to Monet's own account, written in his old anecdote-age, he made his way through the throng on the Rue Montorgeuil, carrying his equipment, until he spotted a likely balcony, then simply asked and was granted permission to paint from it. For once, the story is entirely credible, coming from a man for whom the departures from Saint-Lazare were delayed! On the other hand, Monet painted two closely similar pictures, *The Rue Montorgeuil* (page 127) and *The Rue St-Denis*, which are both dated 30 June, 1878; as the two streets run parallel, it is doubtful whether there was any single viewpoint from which both could have been painted on the same day!

Whatever their origin, these are gloriously cheerful works, alive with wildly flapping flags and jostling crowds in the street below.

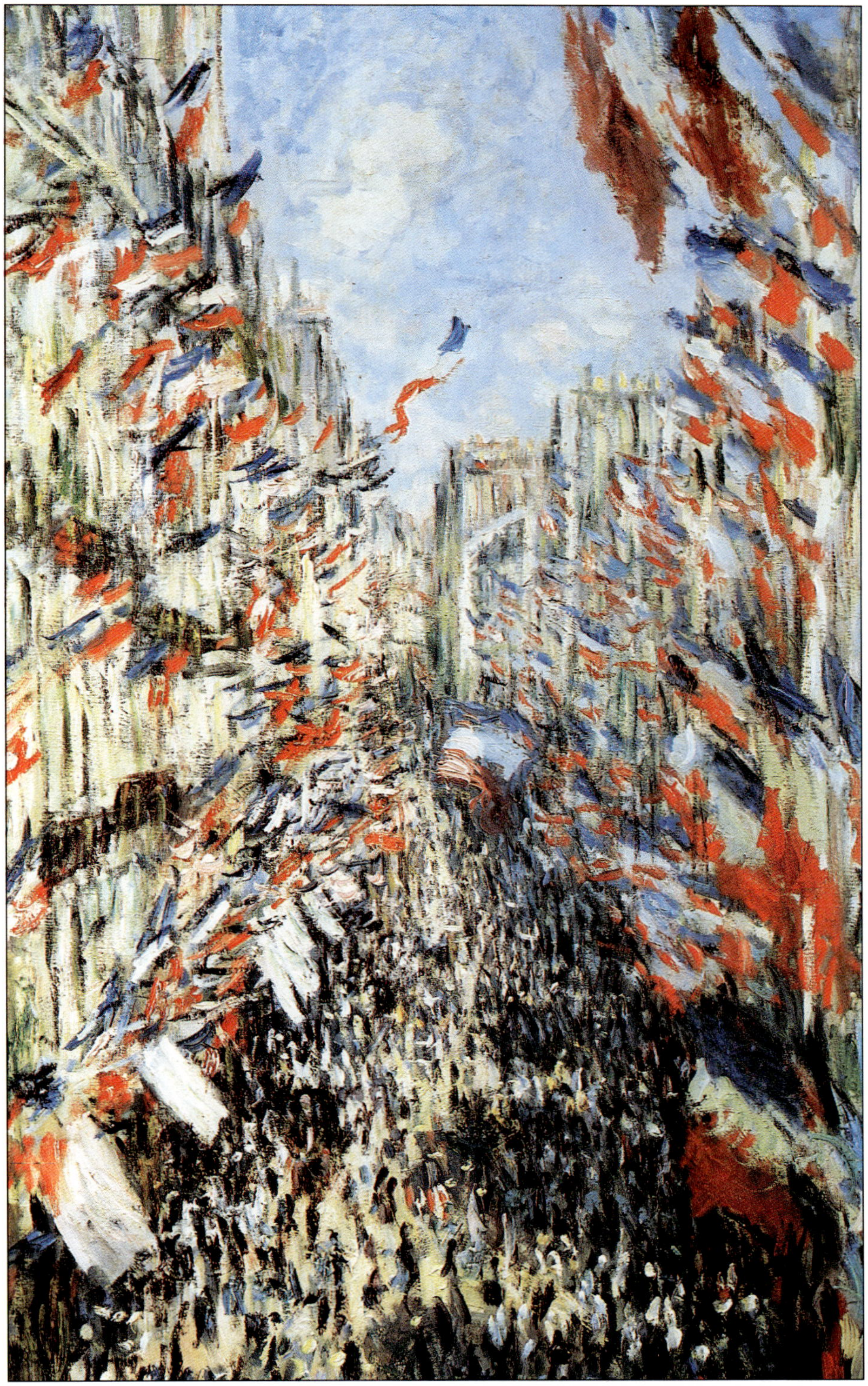

LEFT:
The Rue Montorgeuil, 30 June (1878)
MUSÉE D'ORSAY, PARIS

The Rue Montorgeuil is particularly impressive because the plunging view has enabled Monet to introduce strong diagonals and make the painting as striking in composition as it is powerful in expression. These canvases have often been seen as Monet's rousing farewell to the Parisian scene, which he would never again attempt to paint. Set in the city and fixed in date, they were also the last of his works that can meaningfully be called modern in subject matter.

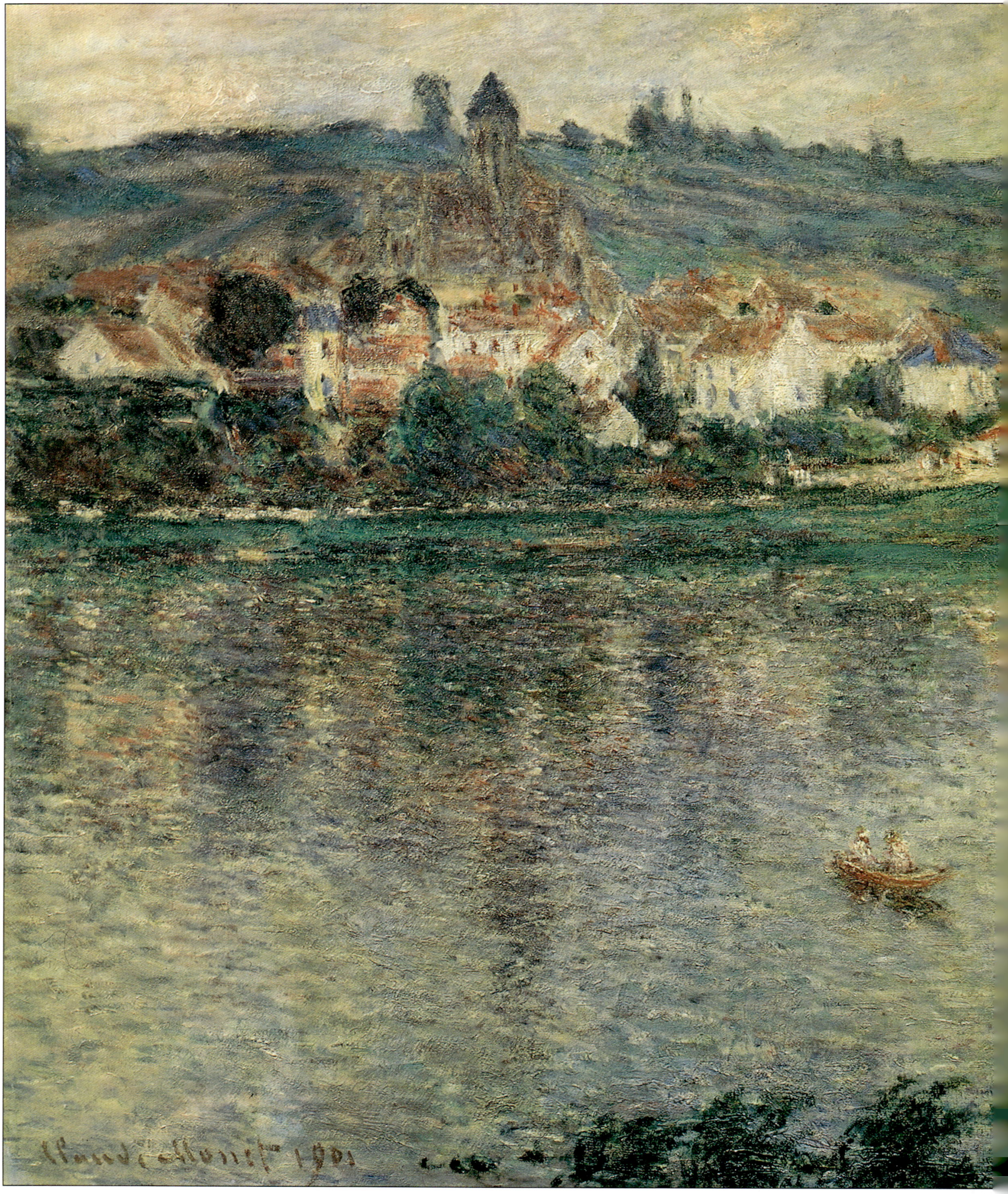
Claude Monet 1901

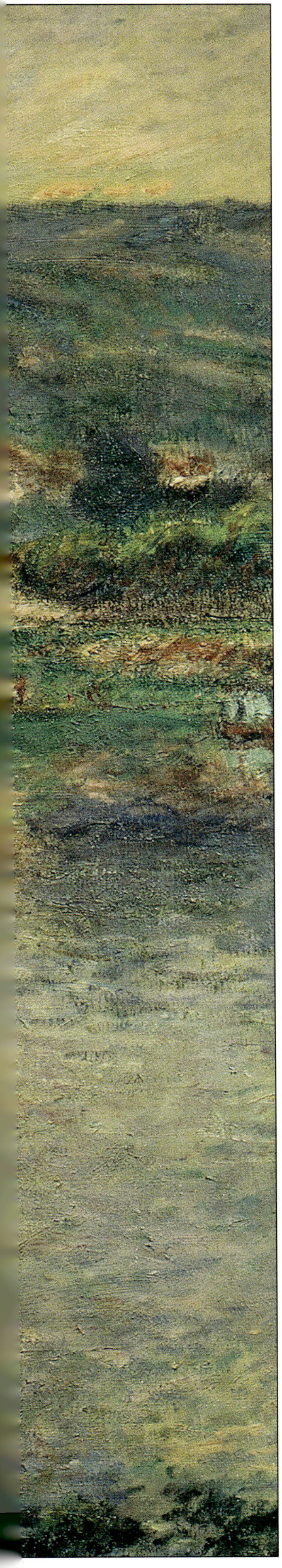

LEFT:
The Town of Vétheuil (1881)
PUSHKIN MUSEUM, MOSCOW

CHAPTER SIX

Break up at Vétheuil

BY THE 1ST SEPTEMBER, 1878, Monet was able to write to one of his patrons, Eugène Murer, with the news that 'I have pitched my tent at Vétheuil, a ravishing place on the banks of the Seine'. He had spent a long time looking in the Seine valley for a place to live, so the fact that he fixed on Vétheuil tells us a good deal about the sort of life Monet wanted to lead and the sort of work he planned to do.

Argenteuil had been a lively little town, closely linked to the capital and thronged in summer with trippers and boating enthusiasts; it represented the urban dream of country life rather than its reality. By contrast, Vétheuil was little more than a village of some 600 residents, too far from Paris to suit commuters or attract Parisian holidaymakers. The people were mostly farmers, set in an apparently unchanging way of life. By choosing to settle among them, Monet was rejecting not only the city but also such distinctively contemporary phenomena as tourism, regattas, trains and railway stations engulfed in steam. He may have felt that tackling such subjects had proved a dead end, at least as far as conquering the art world was concerned. Perhaps, too, like so many men and

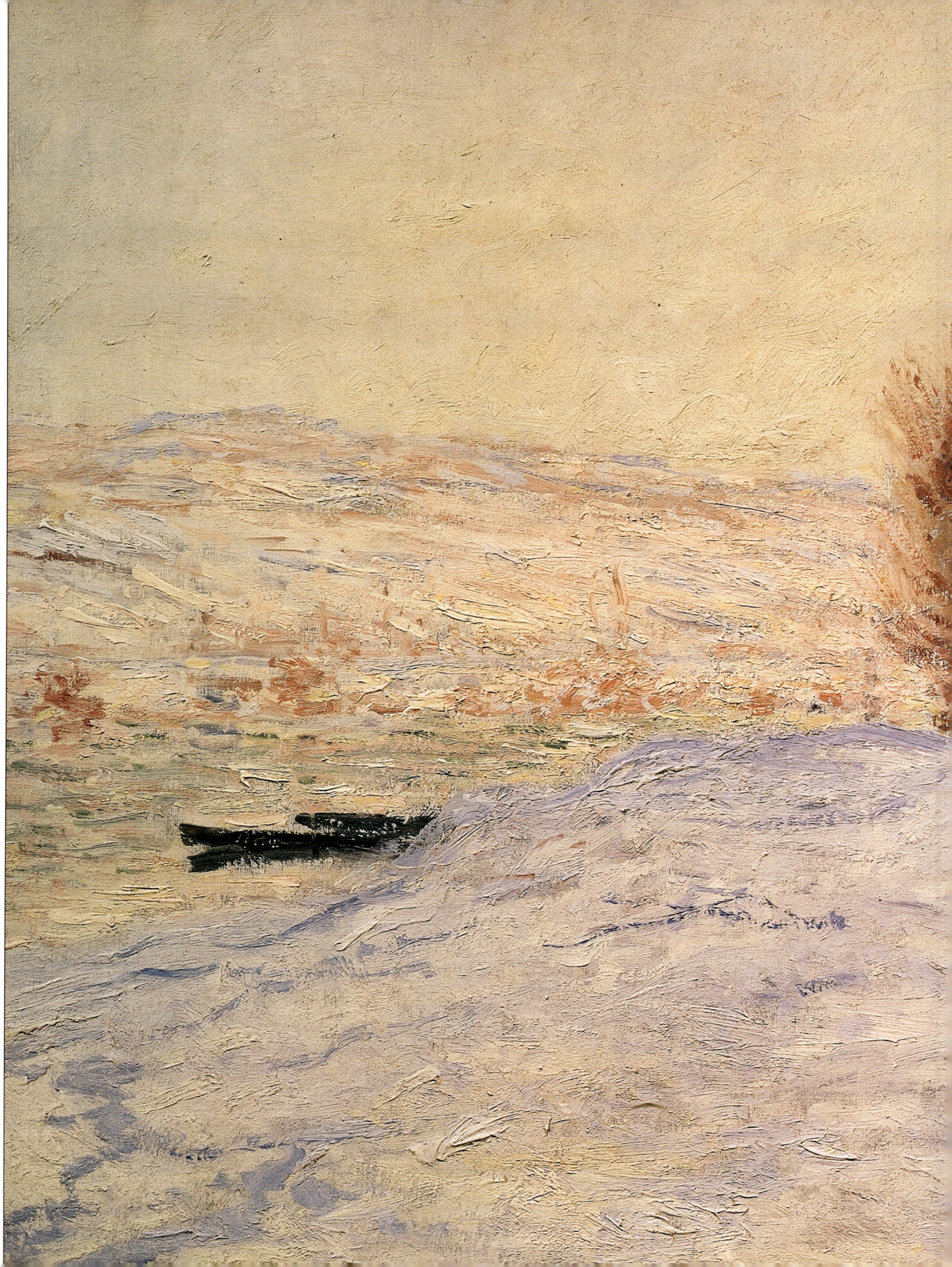

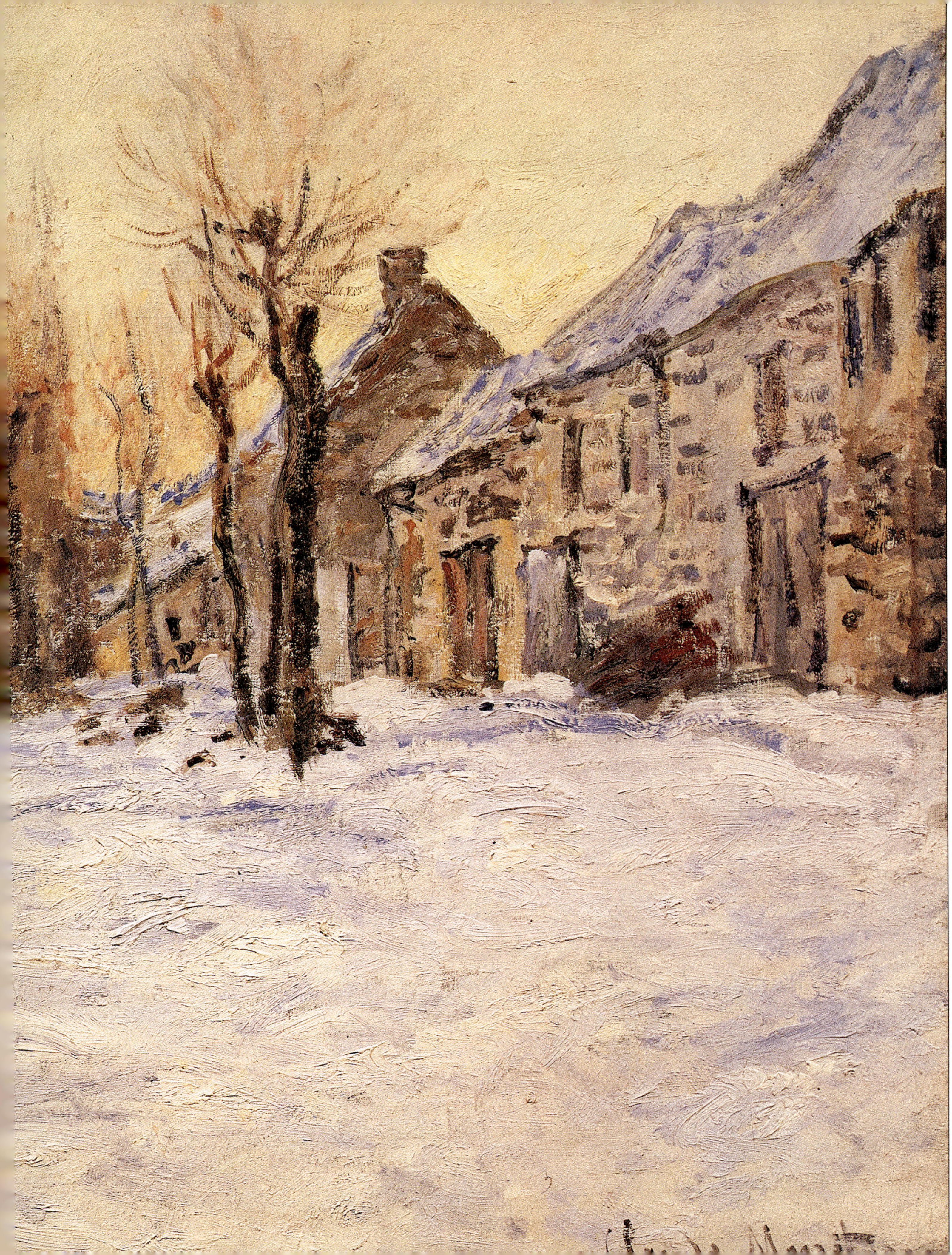

PREVIOUS PAGES 130-1: **Winter at Lavacourt** (1881) NATIONAL GALLERY, LONDON

women when they reach the threshold of middle age, he was becoming steadily less convinced of the benefits of change and fonder of traditional sights and values. In any case, his isolation was by no means complete, since he could always reach the wider world by taking a short trip to nearby Mantes, which was on the railway line to Paris – where, in spite of everything, he still kept on a studio near the Gare Saint-Lazare.

Vétheuil had the further advantage of being cheap: Monet's house, along with a big garden running down to the river, cost a modest 600 francs a year. This was all the more important because Monet's finances were in worse shape than ever, although this time through no fault of his own. Hoschedé's bankruptcy had been a blow, but the consequent auction of his art collection at the Hôtel Drouot proved a worse one. Paintings by Manet, Pissarro and Sisley went under the hammer for disastrously low prices, and a dozen canvases by Monet yielded an average of about 150 francs. The news was deeply discouraging: if this was an expression of public taste, then all the Impressionists' struggles had been in vain. The practical consequences were even more serious, since artists whose works could be picked up for such low prices at auction could hardly expect their clients to pay more for their current efforts.

Enter the Hoschedés

Hoschedé's bankruptcy had a further consequence, so improbable that it reads like fiction: Ernest, Alice and their six children went to live with the Monets at Vétheuil. This reversal of fortune, in which the tycoon of two years before was driven to share a house with his impecunious former protégé, says a great deal for the friendship that had developed between the two families, whether or not it yet included a special frisson between Monsieur Monet and Madame Hoschedé. It is hard to imagine life in this household consisting of four adults, eight children and several servants; poverty-stricken or not, the Monets and Hoschedés were middle-class Victorians who could always somehow afford 'help'. Hoschedé seems to have spent much of his time in Paris; Monet painted outdoors; Camille was ill and getting steadily worse. Exactly what subterranean currents of feeling washed through this menage, we have no way of knowing. Appearances were certainly kept up between Monet and Hoschedé, for as late as May 1879, the painter was writing apologetically to his friend, lamenting the fact that he and Camille were such poor company for Ernest and 'Madame Hoschedé' and

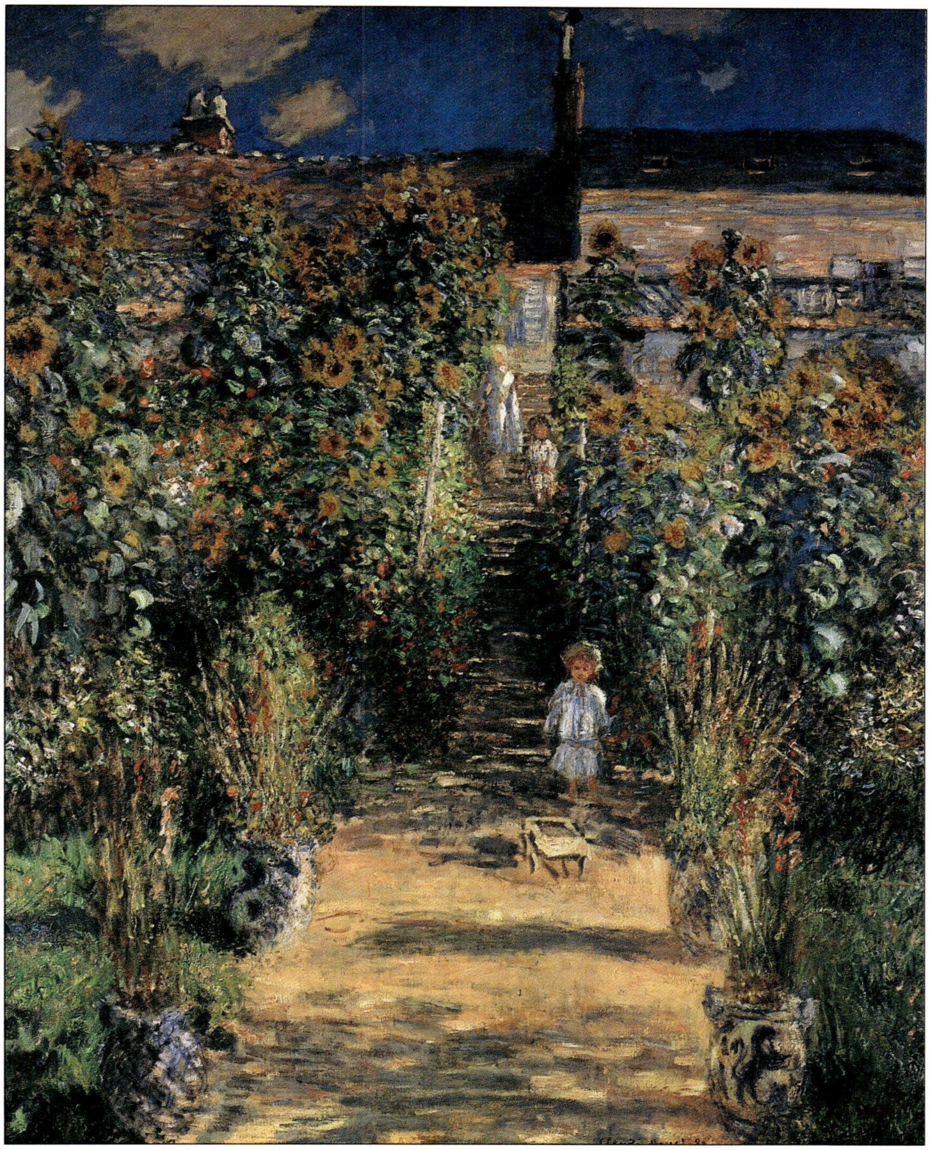

LEFT:
The Artist's Garden at Vétheuil (1880)
NATIONAL GALLERY OF ART, WASHINGTON, D.C.

even hinting that the Hoschedés might be better off without them. This last suggestion might be interpreted as deceitful or threatening, but might even have been, at the moment of writing, sincere.

As if mindful of nothing else, Monet painted with demonic energy, producing an astounding 300 canvases – about two every week – during his years at Vétheuil. One reason was, no doubt, his accumulated experience and ever-increasing virtuosity; but it is hard to avoid the impression that he also felt liberated by leaving Argenteuil and Paris behind. Apparently never at a loss, he managed to discover an endless variety of pleasure-giving possibilities in the picturesque townscape and the banks of the Seine. *The Town of Vétheuil* (pages 128-9) is only one of many such views, dominated by the church set on rising ground; although Monet was an unbeliever,

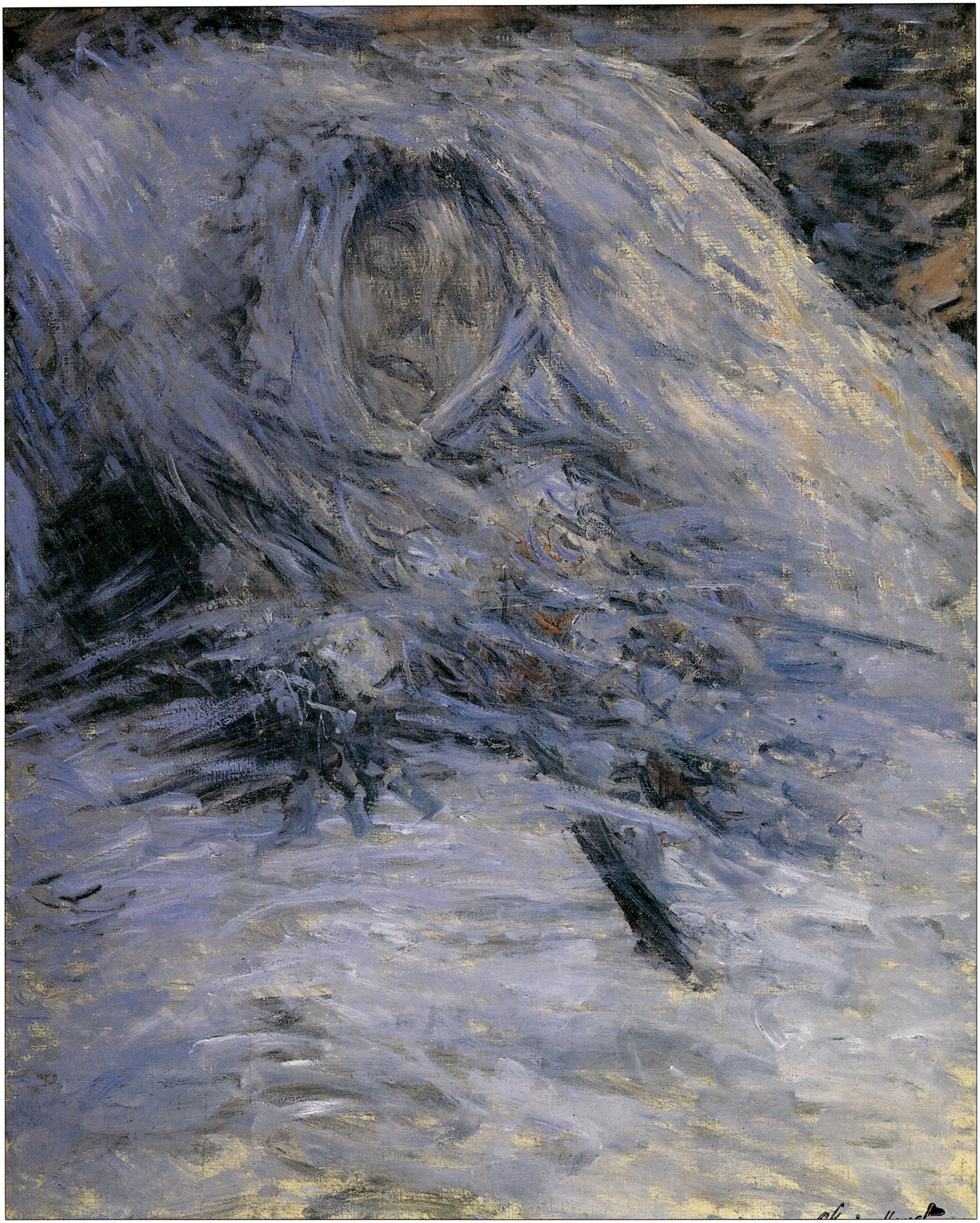

LEFT:
Camille on her Death-Bed
(1879)
Musée d'Orsay, Paris

it is possible to interpret this symbol of the traditional order as an unconscious expression of his changed outlook. Even more characteristic of his work at this time were panoramic views of the Seine or its banks. He continued to use his studio-boat, often anchoring it on one of the little islands in the river, and one of his favourite views was the hamlet of Lavacourt, on the other bank (pages 144-5). At home, now and later, the garden remained a delight, captured in all its summery excess by a web of brilliant, flickering brushstrokes (page 133).

By contrast, the winter of 1878–9 was a hard one, which Monet recorded in a number of snowscapes that feel a little cheerless. When spring came, he showed a certain disillusion with the prospect of another Impressionist exhibition, claiming that he would contribute only to avoid a charge of betraying his comrades – as Renoir was to do that very year by showing his works at the Salon again. When it came to the point, Monet sent in 29 canvases to the exhibition, mainly representing his recent work at Vétheuil. However, he stayed away from Paris, leaving Gustave Caillebotte to hang the paintings and look after his interests. In the event, Monet at least earned a 439-francs share of the gate money taken at the exhibition, which had been singularly well attended.

For most of 1878–9 tranquil beauty remained the keynote of Monet's art. However, as so often before, the tranquillity was hardly reflected in what we know of his life. He was, as usual, worse off than his accounts suggest he should have been, and sending off begging letters in which he spoke of giving up the struggle for good. One of his afflictions was authentic and undeserved: Camille, never well after the birth of Michel, sank rapidly and died on 5 September, 1879, at the age of 32. Monet's capacity for self-pity and self-dramatization makes it hard to be certain of his real feelings, but the death of his companion of 14 years does appear to have shaken him. *Camille on her Death-Bed* (page 134) is a harrowing work unlike anything else he painted. Even at the end, Camille is less of a person than a representative figure, her diminished and dimmed features intensely pathetic, as if shrouded within a cocoon of slashing brushstrokes that dim her bouquet of red flowers and seem about to float away with her.

Monet's friend, the statesman Georges Clemenceau, recorded a conversation in which the painter recalled that 'At the deathbed of a woman who had been and still is very dear to me, I caught myself instinctively tracing the gradations of colour that death was successively imposing on her motionless features.' The desire to

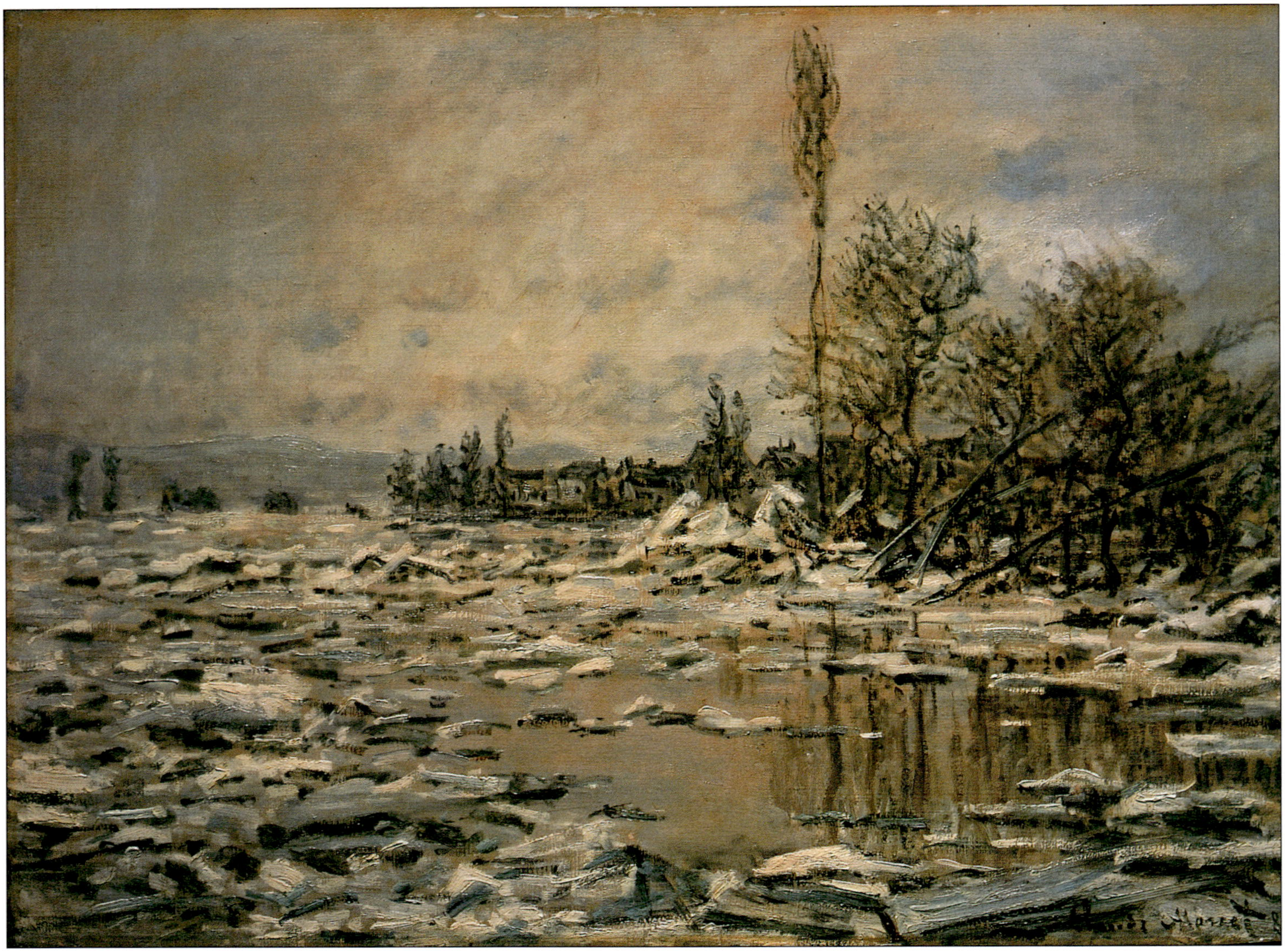

ABOVE:
Ice Breaking Up at Vétheuil
(1880)
PRIVATE COLLECTION

preserve her, said Monet, came after, not before, this exercise in artistic observation. Clemenceau was writing in 1928, a year after Monet's death, and may well have spiced up the story a little. However, there seems no reason to doubt that it is basically true, and on reflection it was not so very shocking that a life-long professional habit should continue to function in all circumstances, even in parallel with the experience of grief and loss.

Faced with the prospect of bringing up two motherless children, Monet fretted even more than usual. He could not be certain that Alice would stay with him, whatever the exact nature of their previous relationship. However, the situation was rapidly clarified. By the end of the year Hoschedé left – not very willingly, despite the bohemian existence he had begun to lead in Paris – while Alice remained at Vétheuil. Initially her presence was excused by the fact that somebody had to take care of the two sets of children, but it fairly soon became clear that the arrangement would be permanent.

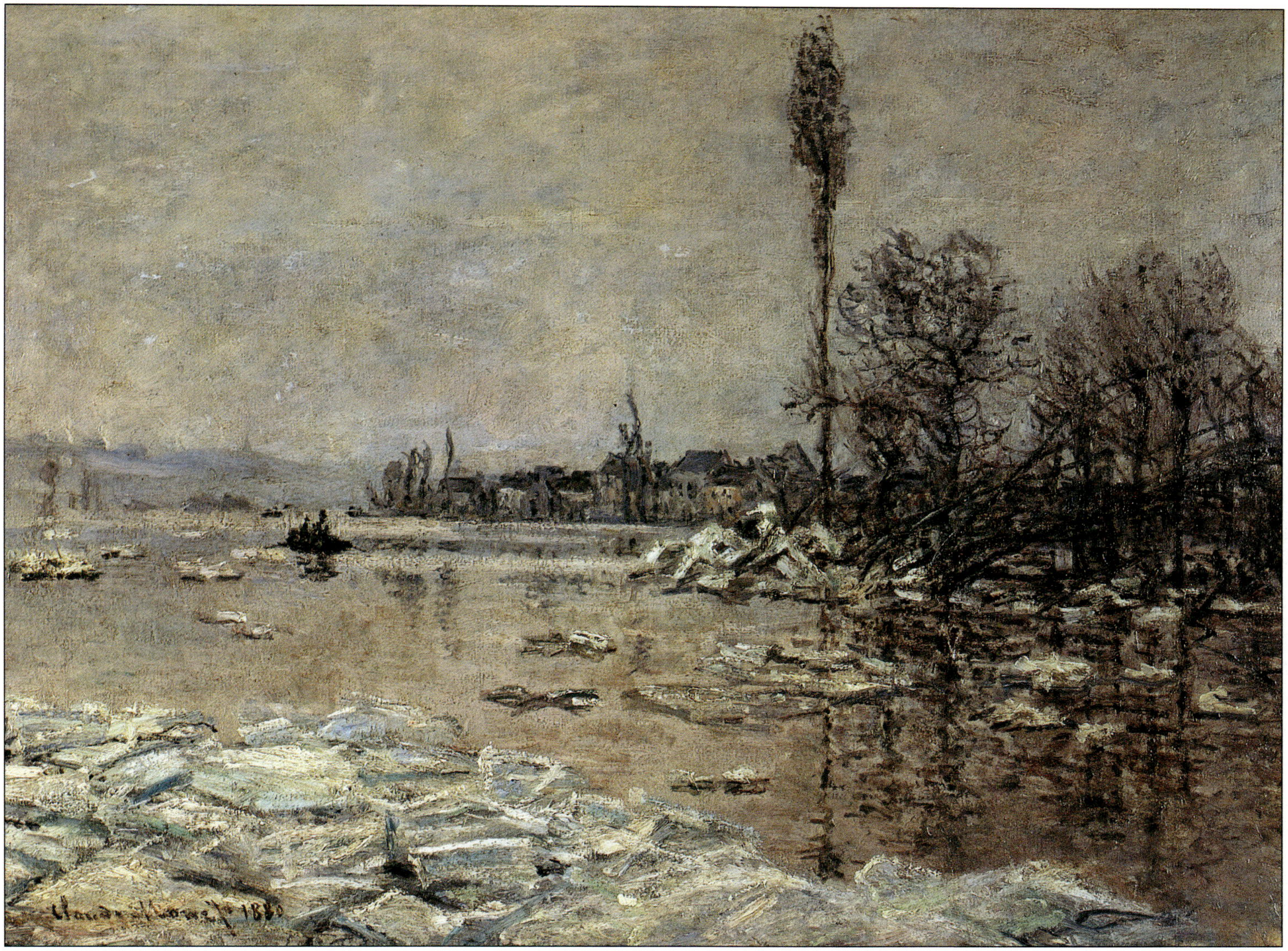

At Vétheuil the winter of 1879–80 was even fiercer than its predecessor. The Seine froze, and when the thaw came the ice broke up with a terrible rending noise that echoed through the streets of Vétheuil. Monet was alive to the rare, spectacular quality of the event and pictured its successive stages in a series of paintings which included *Ice Breaking up at Vétheuil* and many studies of the thawing river (pages 136-9). The movement of the water, rendered with Monet's usual mastery, is here broken by the ice floes, which he has painted with thick, agitated brushstrokes that capture their destructive presence. Since the break-up occurred in a matter of hours on 4–5 January, these superb canvases cannot all have been executed there and then, although Monet increasingly made *plein-air* painting central to the legend he wove about himself. Later in life, answering a question from one curious but credulous journalist, he made an expansive gesture indicating the great outdoors and declared with magnificent mendacity, 'My studio? *This* is my

ABOVE:
The Thaw, Vétheuil (1880)
MUSÉE DE BEAUX-ARTS, LILLE

studio!' In more prosaic vein he wrote to the dealer Durand-Ruel, 'whether my cathedrals, my Londons and my other pictures are done from life or not is my business, and in any case is not of the slightest consequence... I know lots of painters who work from life and produce nothing but horrors.' This, although rather ungracious, was a deadly accurate way of saying that what counts in a work of art is the final effect, not the means by which it is achieved.

Monet's winter scenes are highly expressive, whether they are regarded as objective records of a cruel season or as emotional statements charged with his grief for Camille. It is certainly the case that a new sense of drama and emotion would carry over into Monet's paintings of the 1880s in dozens of wonderful canvases painted on the Normandy coast. There is even an unexpected richness in a group of still-life paintings that Monet painted during his years at Vétheuil.

The still-life is a pictured arrangement of inanimate objects, ranging from skulls and dead game to fruit on a plate. Some great painters have had a special taste for the genre in which reality can be manipulated to achieve any desired effect. For most of Monet's life this held little attraction for him, as he preferred to confront nature directly, relying on his acute sensibility to respond with ardour to the motif – a response that would include framing and editing what he saw. However, between 1878 and 1882 he completed an unusual number of still-life paintings, perhaps because the severe winters kept him indoors more often than usual, but perhaps too because there was a ready market for the genre. Monet's still-life pictures, from *Chrysanthemums* (page 140), appropriately 'cut' by the frame (Japanese style for a Japanese flower), to the succulent *Pears and Grapes* (page 143), are painted with an unexpected warmth of feeling which may represent an implicit yearning for the sun.

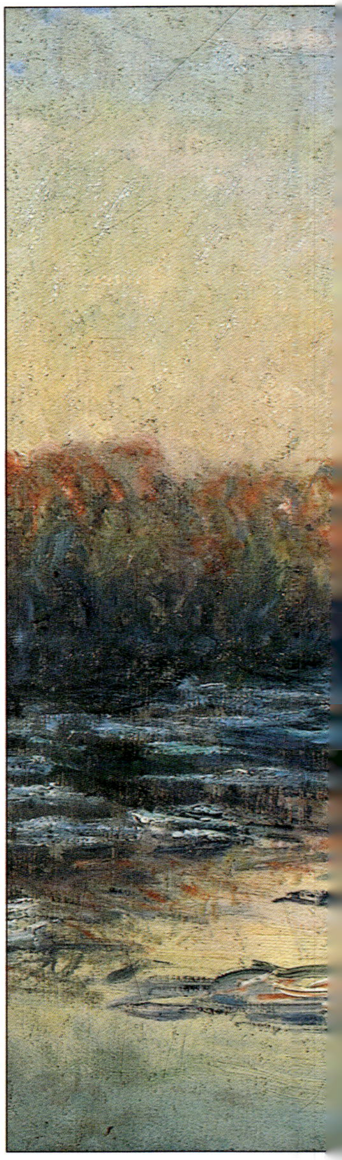

Return to the Salon

In the spring of 1880, Monet made two radical decisions. His disillusion with the Impressionist exhibitions reached a point at which he decided not to contribute to the next show, which was planned to run all through April in premises on the Rue des Pyramides. Dissension had been on the increase for some time, and Renoir and Sisley, the painters with whose work Monet was most in tune, had already withdrawn from the group shows. This left the 'realist' Degas and his friends – including a number of quite conventional talents – in the ascendant. However, there were

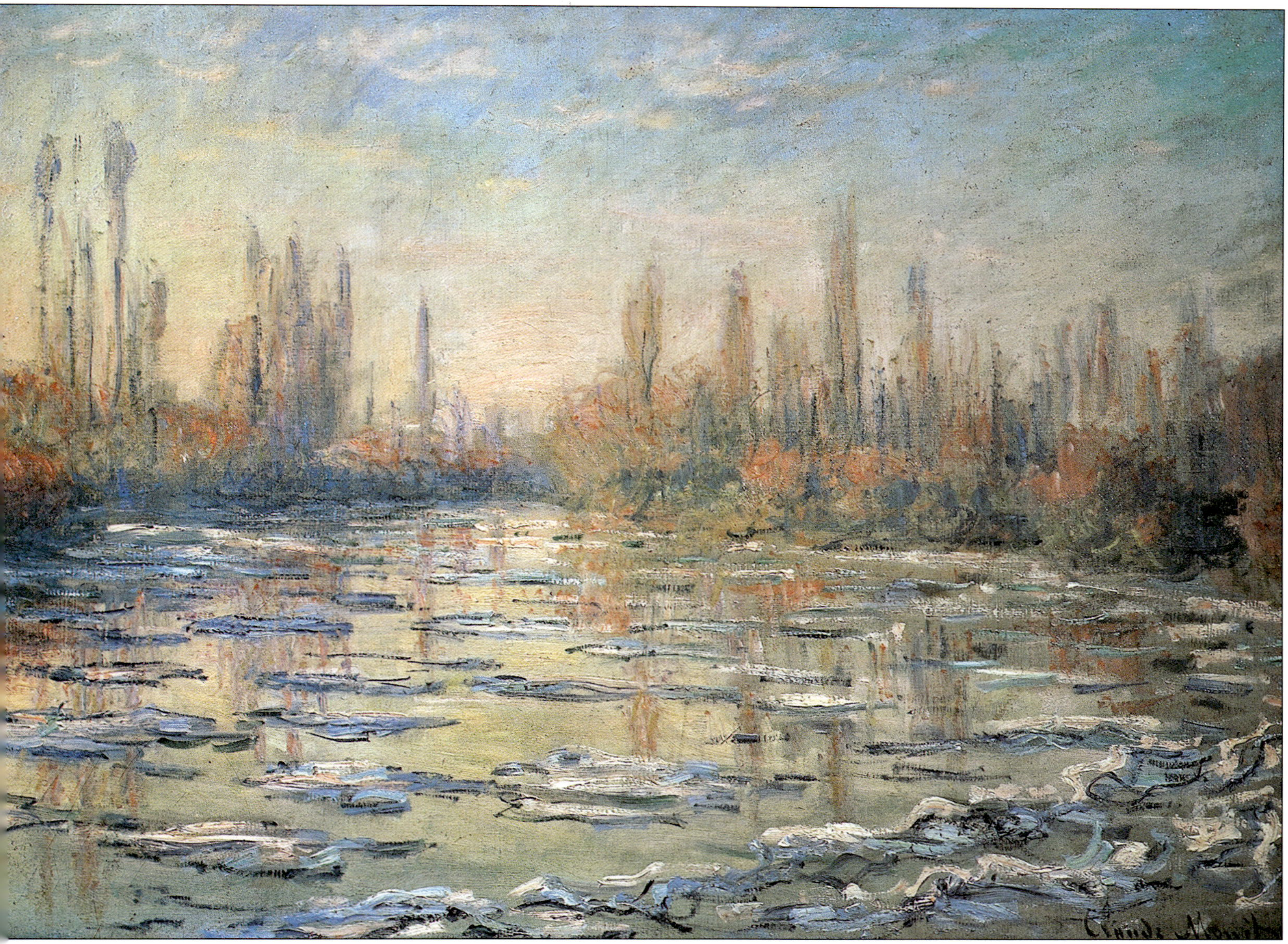

more material reasons for Monet's withdrawal. His friend Renoir was beginning to look like a success, having deserted the group shows, exhibited at the Salon, and had a one-man exhibition at the premises of a new periodical, *La Vie Moderne.* Hoping for a comparable change in his own fortunes, Monet decided not only to remain aloof from his former colleagues, but to send in works to the Salon again. In principle, defections of this kind were final, as would-be contributors to the Impressionist exhibitions were expressly forbidden to submit to the Salon.

ABOVE:
The Thaw, Vétheuil (1880)
MUSÉE D'ORSAY, PARIS

Monet's departure was a landmark in the progressive break-up of the Impressionist movement, and an enterprising journalist got wind of it at a very early date. On 24 January, 1880, *Le Gaulois* printed a mock funeral notice which showed that its author knew that Monet had broken with his colleagues and was even aware of his intention to exhibit at the Salon, which opened that year on 30

RIGHT:
Chrysanthemums
(1878)
MUSÉE D'ORSAY,
PARIS

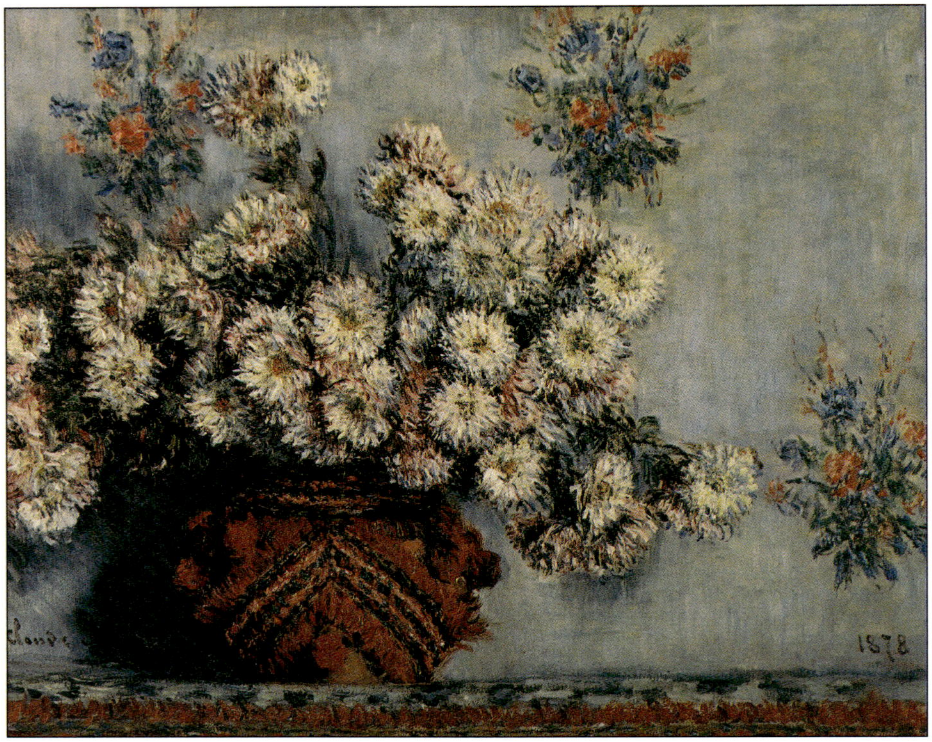

April at the Palais de l'Industrie. The most important section of the notice read: 'The impressionist school has the honour to inform you of the grievous loss it has suffered in the person of M. Claude Monet, one of its revered masters. M. Monet's funeral will take place on 1 May, at ten o'clock in the morning, the day after the opening, at the Church of the Palais de l'Industrie.'

Even now, nobody knows who leaked the information to *Le Gaulois.* Monet – a betrayer betrayed – was outraged, but his angry letters failed to elicit any confessions. The affair added to the strained relationships between the Impressionists, and Monet complained in a letter to Théodore Duret that 'I am suddenly being treated as a deserter by the entire group'. He added, 'I believe it was in my own interests to decide as I did, since I'm almost certain to make some sales ... once I've broken into the Salon'. It seems not to have occurred to Monet that his self-interest might be insufficient justification for 'desertion' in the eyes of the other Impressionists.

The regulation two canvases that he submitted to the Salon jury were both views of the Seine near Vétheuil, but they were very different in technique and intensity of feeling. Monet himself described *The Seine at Lavacourt* (pages 144-5) as 'bourgeois', meaning that it was relatively conventional and therefore calculated to appeal to the Salon public. Everything in it is clean, clear-cut and harmonious, with a smooth treatment and none of the blurs of striking sunlight or rapid movement that the critics and the public found so puzzling and offensive. It is, in fact, a charming painting, even though it lacks the energized surface and sense of excitement found in many of Monet's Vétheuil-Seine canvases. He submitted one of these with *The Seine at Lavacourt*, presumably to test whether there had been any significant alteration in Salon attitudes. As he probably expected, only the more conventional picture was accepted, and even then it was badly hung and made little impact. Despite sporadic liberal impulses, the general outlook of the Salon jury remained such that Emile Zola was still able to claim that Monet's canvas brought 'a rare note of light and the open air to a dark corner'. Zola had been championing Monet ever since 1865 and was still predicting a great future for him. 'Within ten years he will be accepted, exhibited and rewarded; he will sell his pictures for huge prices and will stand at the head of the present movement.'

This proved to be a remarkably accurate prediction, although Monet, hard-pressed at the time, probably took scant comfort from it. He had failed to conquer the official art world of Salons, state patronage, medals and prizes, and he appeared to have achieved no more than a certain notoriety as an Impressionist rebel. However, after the Salon a one-man exhibition at *La Vie Moderne* held out new hopes of advance. *La Vie Moderne* was an avant-garde magazine published by Georges Charpentier; as well as supporting the Impressionists, it housed a gallery in its office building on the Boulevard des Italiens. Auguste Renoir was the Charpentiers' favourite artist, thanks to his ability to create delectable portraits of Madame Charpentier and her children. He had had a show at *La Vie Moderne* in 1879 and persuaded the Charpentiers to stage a similar event for Monet in June of the following year.

At this, Monet's first proper one-man show, 18 canvases were on view, with a catalogue introduced by Monet's friend Théodore Duret. The reviews – led, of course, by *La Vie Moderne* – were fairly friendly and Monet made a number of sales; the dramatic *Ice Breaking up at Vétheuil* (page 136) was bought for 1,500 francs by Madame Charpentier. By contrast, in August Monet took part in a local show at Le Havre, but his tepid reception suggested that, even as a home-grown artist, he could not yet rely on much indulgence from provincial spectators.

Interviewed in connection with the *Vie Moderne* show, Monet took the opportunity to justify his recent activities. While asserting that he had always stuck to his principles, he effectively broke with his former associates. To the journalist Emile Taboureaux he complained that 'Our little church has become a banal academy whose doors are open to any tyro'. He was probably thinking of Pissarro's protégé, Paul Gauguin, a businessman and 'Sunday painter' whom Monet seems to have disliked personally and despised as an amateur. Obviously talented (although not in Monet's eyes), Gauguin was far from being the legendary figure he became in the 1890s who found – and painted – a savage paradise in the South Seas. Anxious to cast himself in a favourable light, Monet was unfair to Gauguin in his remarks and also guilty of rewriting history, since the 'Impressionist' exhibitions had never in fact housed a 'little church' of true believers, but had always admitted a very mixed company.

In the same interview Monet declared roundly, 'I am still an Impressionist and always will be'. In the sense that he remained faithful to immediate visual sensations, this was fundamentally correct. In the 1880s some other Impressionists began to try new formulas; Renoir, for example, attempted to forge a more monumental, classical style. Monet, however, continued to respond primarily to the motif in front of him (although, as we have seen, he had no compunction about doing some of his work in the studio). As it actually developed, Impressionism combined more than one strand, notably a preoccupation with modern-life subjects and a cult of open-air painting, along with the specific techniques that evolved from that way of working. The different Impressionist strands intertwined at various points, but were never indistinguishable from one another. In Monet's case the ambition to be a 'painter of modern life' was connected with ambition and an interest in new pictorial possibilities, rather than any profound commitment to modernity for its own sake. Only in the more limited *plein-air* sense of the term can Monet be called the ultimate or quintessential Impressionist, but, in that sense, he certainly deserved the title.

Better Times

Even though the immediate results were often disappointing, new ventures such as the *Vie Moderne* gallery were signs that the grip of the Salon was loosening. Alternative outlets for artists increased as small galleries and even cafés became prepared to show works outside the mainstream, while dealers such as Paul Durand-Ruel and Georges Petit took an independent line at home and found markets overseas that undermined the activity of the Salon as an arbiter of

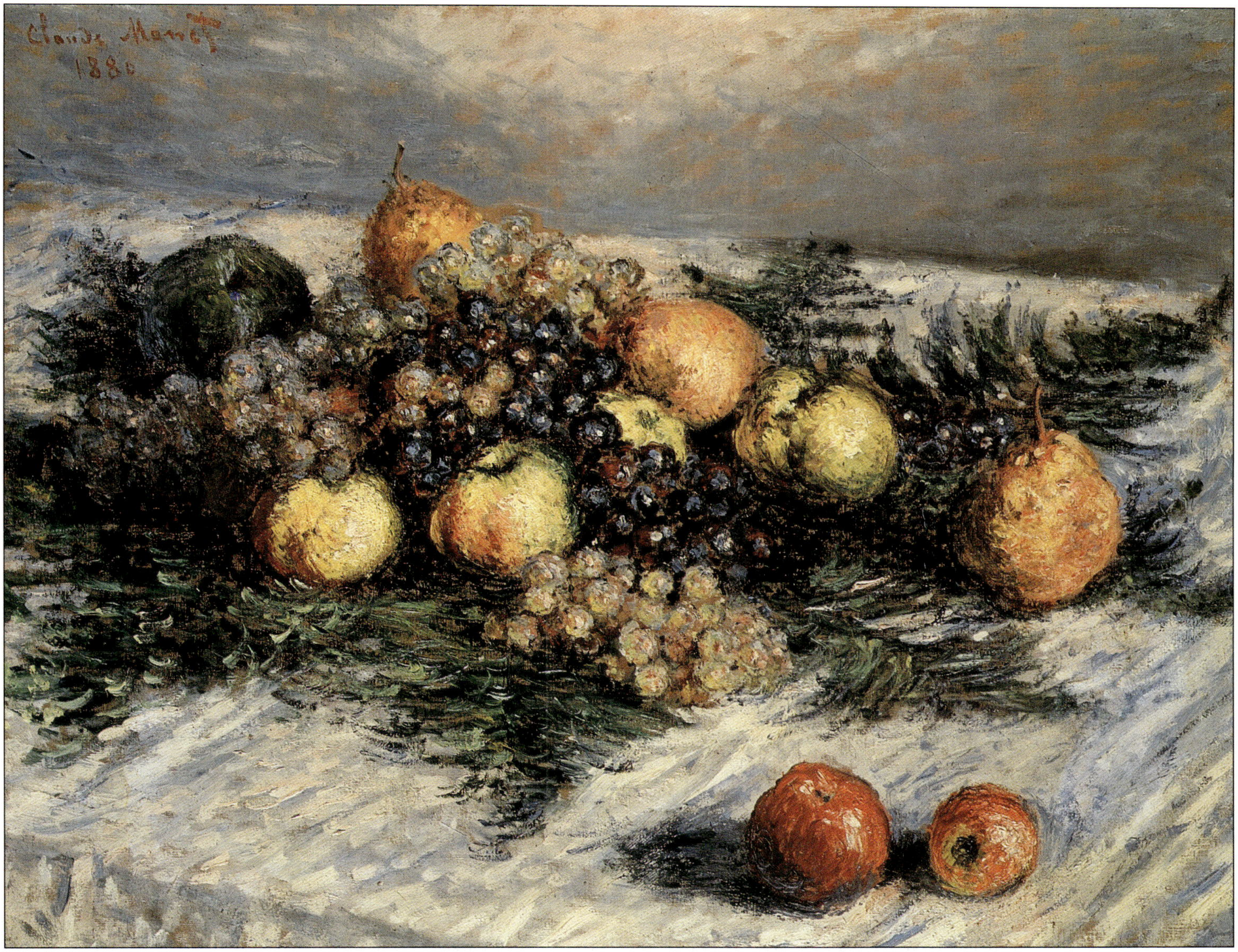

ABOVE:
Pears and Grapes
(1880)
KUNSTHALLE, HAMBURG

good taste. Durand-Ruel's role in Monet's life was a vital but unpredictable one, as the low points in the dealer's career – when he was forced to stop buying – influenced the artist's activities just as much as its phases of expansion. In the early 1880s Durand-Ruel was flourishing again, thanks to the backing of the Banque de l'Union Générale, and by the beginning of 1881 he was ready to sign a contract guaranteeing regular purchases of the artist's works; in practice, Durand-Ruel also paid the bills for painting materials and even clothing which Monet was unable to meet. This relieved the worst of Monet's anxieties, and in the event it proved to be the long-awaited turning point in his career. However, Durand-Ruel's fortunes were still apt to fluctuate and Monet was careful not to become too dependent on him, selling canvases to patrons on his own behalf and frequently doing business with other dealers.

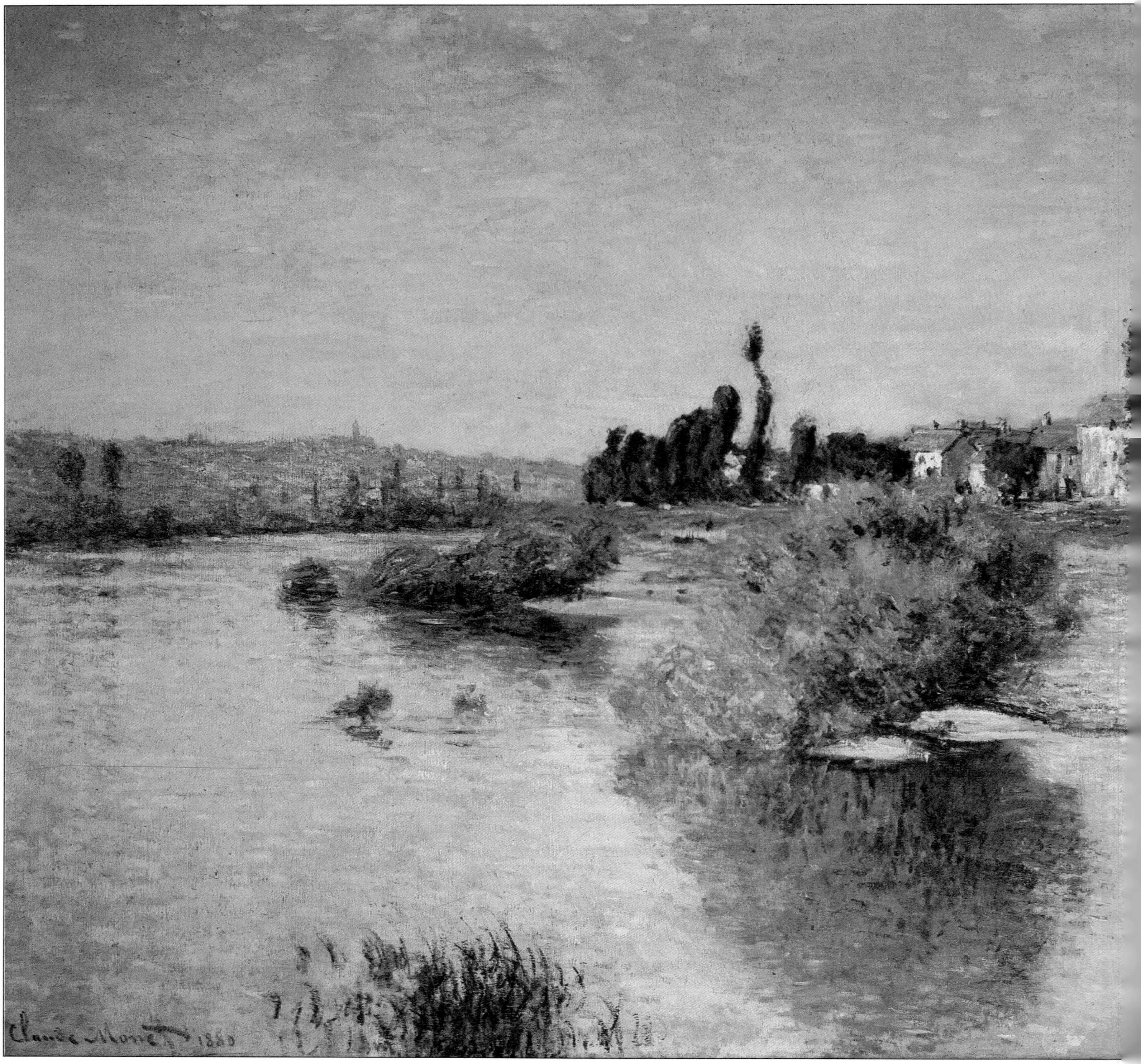

As if by design, he almost immediately found subjects, a technique and a mood that at last pleased the public. Shortly after signing the contract, he left for Fécamp, where he painted dramatic views of the Normandy coast and the wild sea that battered against it, subjects to which he would return again and again in the 1880s.

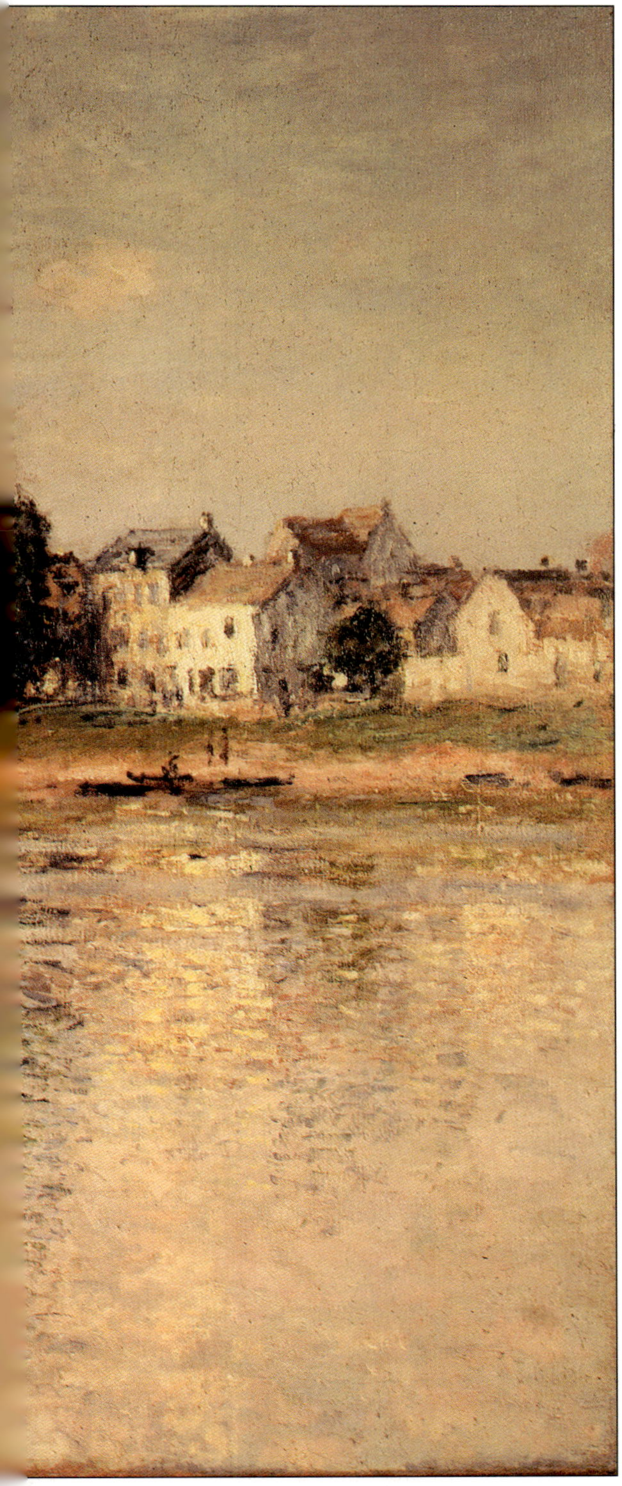

ABOVE:
The Seine at Lavacourt
(1880)
DALLAS MUSEUM OF FINE ARTS, TEXAS

Long painting trips away from home now became a feature of Monet's lifestyle in middle age, financially justifiable but perhaps also undertaken to procure periods of relief from the stresses of a large household.

By the time he returned to Vétheuil, Monet, encouraged by Durand-Ruel's support, decided against submitting any of his canvases to the Salon and, as it turned out, he would never do so again. Nor did he take part in the sixth Impressionist Exhibition; it had returned to the original venue, 35 Boulevard des Capucines, but out of the old leadership, Degas, Pissarro and Berthe Morisot were the only survivors.

By now Monet had decided that it was time to move on again. The lease on his house was about to expire, but that is not likely to have been the main motive. The overriding consideration was probably the need to end the difficulties caused by his equivocal situation, sharing a house with another man's wife. As the house had originally consisted of two separate partnerships, the facts were well known and, in a rural village atmosphere, had become a source of scandal and suspicion. Nor could the children be educated in the peasant milieu of Vétheuil. Consequently Monet asked his friend and supporter Zola to investigate the town of Poissy, not far from the novelist's own home at Médan. A much larger place than Vétheuil, it was still on the Seine, some 17 kilometres from Paris. Zola's report was satisfactory, but the move was not made until December – and, despite the improvement in Monet's prospects, it had to be paid for with money advanced by Durand-Ruel.

Meanwhile, Monet created glorious views of his garden at Vétheuil, notably the work shown on page 133 (dated 1880 by Monet, but in fact painted in 1881). It is tempting to interpret a picture of this kind as reflecting his improved circumstances or perhaps, now that his days in the village were approaching their end, he could again see it as a kind of paradise.

The presence of the two children – the younger Monet, Michel, and the youngest Hoschedé, Jean-Pierre – is also reassuring, suggesting that the house was inhabited by a united family. In fact the situation at home was clarified in the course of 1881. Ernest Hoschedé rather belatedly pressed Alice to join him in Paris, but she refused. And when the time arrived for Monet to leave, it became impossible to maintain any longer the pretence that Alice had merely been looking after the children in a household where circumstances had temporarily placed her. When Monet moved to Poissy, she and her children went with him.

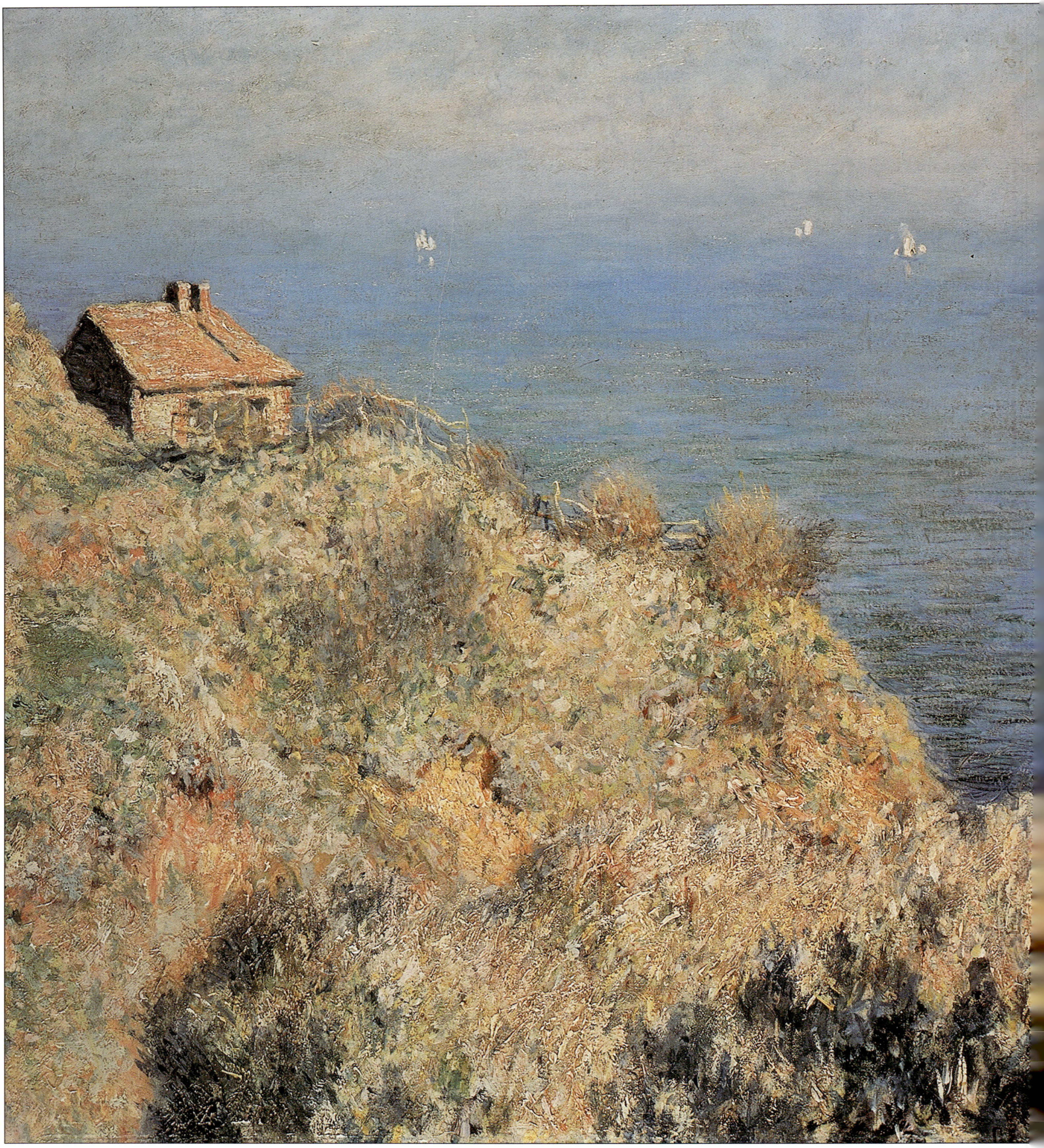

CHAPTER SEVEN

Poissy and Etretat

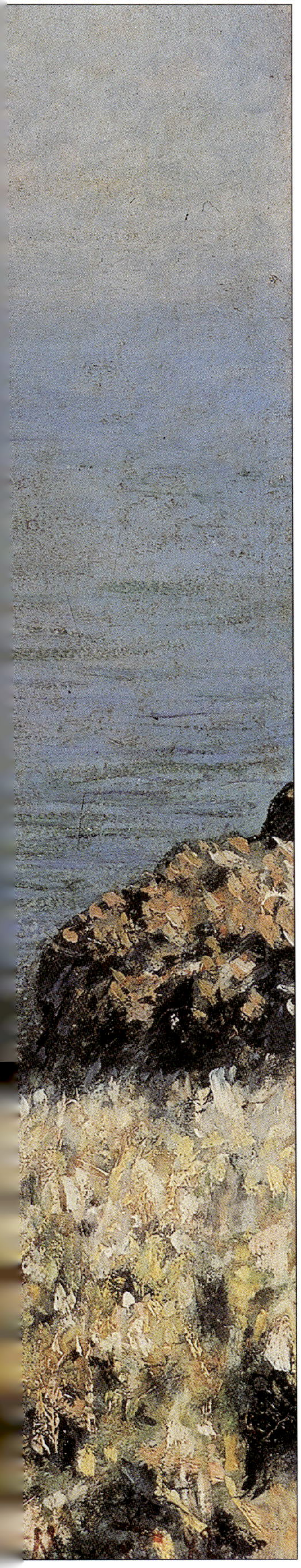

LEFT:
The Coastguard's House, Varengeville (1882)
MUSEUM BOYMANS-VAN BEUNINGEN, ROTTERDAM

THE MONET-HOSCHEDÉ FAMILY moved into the Villa Louis at Poissy, within sight of the river; but from the very beginning something about the town irritated Monet. He found almost nothing in it to inspire him and most of his work at home was devoted to finishing or touching up the canvases he had painted elsewhere. By February 1882 he had already returned to Normandy, this time using Dieppe as his base. Soon he had discovered Pourville, a little place further west along the coast where the hotels were cheaper and there were exciting seascapes closer to hand. Monet stayed in the area for most of the year, 'working like a madman', and when his family began to feel neglected he brought them to Pourville for the summer.

The Coastguard's House

The beach and sea at Pourville appear in some of his canvases, but the majority were inspired by a tiny nearby settlement, Varengeville, where a great gorge carved through the chalk cliffs giving the area its distinctively spectacular quality. Monet was even more excited by discovering a stone house close to the cliff edge.

Its origin was pedestrian enough: a lookout from which to spot smugglers, built during the period when the French Emperor Napoleon I was trying to destroy British trade by closing all the ports of Europe to her merchandise. Monet seized upon the pictorial possibilities of a small, solitary house set against a background of high, rugged cliffs, endless water and vast skies. He painted the 'coastguard's house' 20 times in 1882 alone (as well as returning to Varengeville 14 years later), achieving an extraordinary range of effects, from the spring-like to the vertiginous (pages 146-7 and 151), an effect created by the asymmetrical arrangement of the picture and the cropped 'close-up' effect which he had taken over from the masters of the Japanese print. As in the 1877 canvases of the Gare Saint-Lazare, he had created a series based on a single motif, not unlike variations upon a theme in music.

Meanwhile another Impressionist Exhibition had been held, in March 1882, at the Rue Saint-Honoré. In spite of all the bad feeling of the previous two years, Monet was represented by no fewer than 35 canvases. The exhibition was the last in which most of the founding Impressionists showed their work together: Degas was not there, but Monet, Renoir, Pissarro, Sisley, Morisot and Caillebotte all sent in exhibits. The apparent reconciliation had been brought about mainly by Durand-Ruel, who was temporarily embarrassed because of the collapse of the Banque de l'Union Générale, which had entailed the abrupt calling-in of the loans he had received from the bank. He now hoped to use the exhibition as a showcase for 'his' artists, and many of the canvases on display actually came from his stock. In reality, there was no united front and negotiations, recriminations and objections had continued until almost the final moment. Even the usually benevolent Pissarro had been belligerent, complaining that it was wrong to have admitted Monet, since he had not suffered 'just punishment' for his 'mistake' in defecting. Monet was again incensed by the admission of Pissarro's protégé, Paul Gauguin. Ironically, at the point where the Impressionist school was breaking up, the critics had become inclined to indulge these impertinent 'intransigents', who had by now become a regular feature of the Parisian scene. However, Monet did manage to infuriate a reviewer with *Sunset on the Seine, Winter Effect,* one of his Vétheuil canvases. Perhaps its superficial resemblance to the notorious *Impression: Sunrise* was to blame for his ire; at any rate, the writer fulminated against the low sun in the picture as 'a slice of tomato stuck onto the sky'. Ironically, he published his piece in a magazine entitled *Le Soleil* ('The Sun').

With characteristic energy, Durand-Ruel continued his campaign to win international recognition for the Impressionists, holding an exhibition of works by Monet and others at White's Gallery in London. However, he had been struck by the bitter in-fighting between the Impressionists, which made the prospect of future group exhibitions unappealing. He came up with a new proposition: that the group shows should be replaced by a series of comprehensive one-man exhibitions. In November 1882, when Sisley and Monet discussed the idea, it was Monet who was most resistant to it, perhaps fearing that such an arrangement would give Durand-Ruel too much control over the artists concerned. However, the dealer got his way and Monet actually became the first of the group to be shown at Durand's new Parisian gallery on the Boulevard de la Madeleine. From 1 March, 1883, 56 of his paintings were on display, but the general reaction was unsatisfactory – indifferent rather than hostile, largely, Monet believed, because the lighting was inadequate and Durand-Ruel had failed to prepare and advertise the event properly. His grumbles were probably unjustified, for when Durand-Ruel went ahead with shows for Renoir, Pissarro and Sisley, none of them were remarkably successful.

However, unconsoling though it may have been for the artists, an important precedent had been established. Although not entirely unknown, one-man shows were still not common. As well as providing the Impressionists with useful publicity, Durand's ambitious scheme helped to establish a practice that eventually benefited all artists. At the same time, Durand was promoting the Impressionists as a group in Europe and America. In 1883 he organized a show in London's New Bond Street, at Dowdeswell's Galleries and sent in pictures to the American Exhibition of Foreign Products in Boston. Impressionist works were also seen for the first time in Germany. Even more significant was the fact that American collectors were prepared to come forward and show their Impressionist holdings in public, as happened at the exhibition to raise funds to build a pedestal for the Statue of Liberty, France's gift to the United States, which would soon cross the Atlantic. Although he was too much the good Frenchman to feel very grateful about it, Monet owed a great deal to the boldness of American artists who championed his work and pioneer American collectors who bought it while his reputation was still uncertain in his own country.

Despite an occasional bad-tempered intervention by letter, Monet increasingly held aloof from the Parisian art world. He had at last given up his studio in the capital and was able to claim that 'I am a countryman again', although he still took good care to live within visiting distance of Paris. His family life was settled, despite Ernest Hoschedé's occasional appearances at Poissy when the artist was away; and even these would soon cease. The seascapes were proving remarkably popular and Monet's income was larger than in any previous year – which is not to say that it was yet enough to enable the family of ten to live in quite the style to which Monet and his ex-château-owning mistress aspired.

More or less free to concentrate on his work, Monet discovered that it, too, was a source of anxiety. He had often experienced difficulties before, but had understandably tended to blame them on fears of being unable to feed his family or pay the rent. In 1868 he wrote to Bazille, lamenting that 'my painting isn't beginning to come together' and in 1879 he told Ernest Hoschedé that he was incapable of finishing his canvases. In September 1882, at the end of months spent painting superb pictures of Pourville and Varengeville that now have the status of national treasures, he sent Durand-Ruel a letter in which he claimed to be overwhelmed by doubt, so that 'I think I'm finished and can do nothing more'. There was often a strong element of calculation in Monet's cries for help, but his letters to Alice confirm that he did indeed experience violently fluctuating emotions during his painting trips, alternating between intoxication at the splendours before him and despair at the impossibility of doing justice to them.

Many artists have had the same feelings, but they were peculiarly acute in Monet's case, probably because his approach to painting was so intuitive and dependent on the keenness of his perceptions. Unlike academic artists – and, for that matter, most of the 'Old Masters' – Monet had no 'formula' or set of conventions within which he could deploy his skills. In a sense, every work involved a series of decisions, based on the artist's judgement and sensibility, which might turn out to be irreparable mistakes. It was part of Monet's genius that he usually solved his pictorial problems triumphantly, but at the time he was making decisions and putting paint on his canvas he was not always convinced that this would be so. Moreover, an artist who produces something new – especially something that arouses the hostility of the reviewers and the public – is likely to experience serious doubts about its value and validity; one of the blessings of being associated with a group such as the Impressionists is the reassurance provided by companionship in dissent. Of course, since the advent of the Impressionists, the

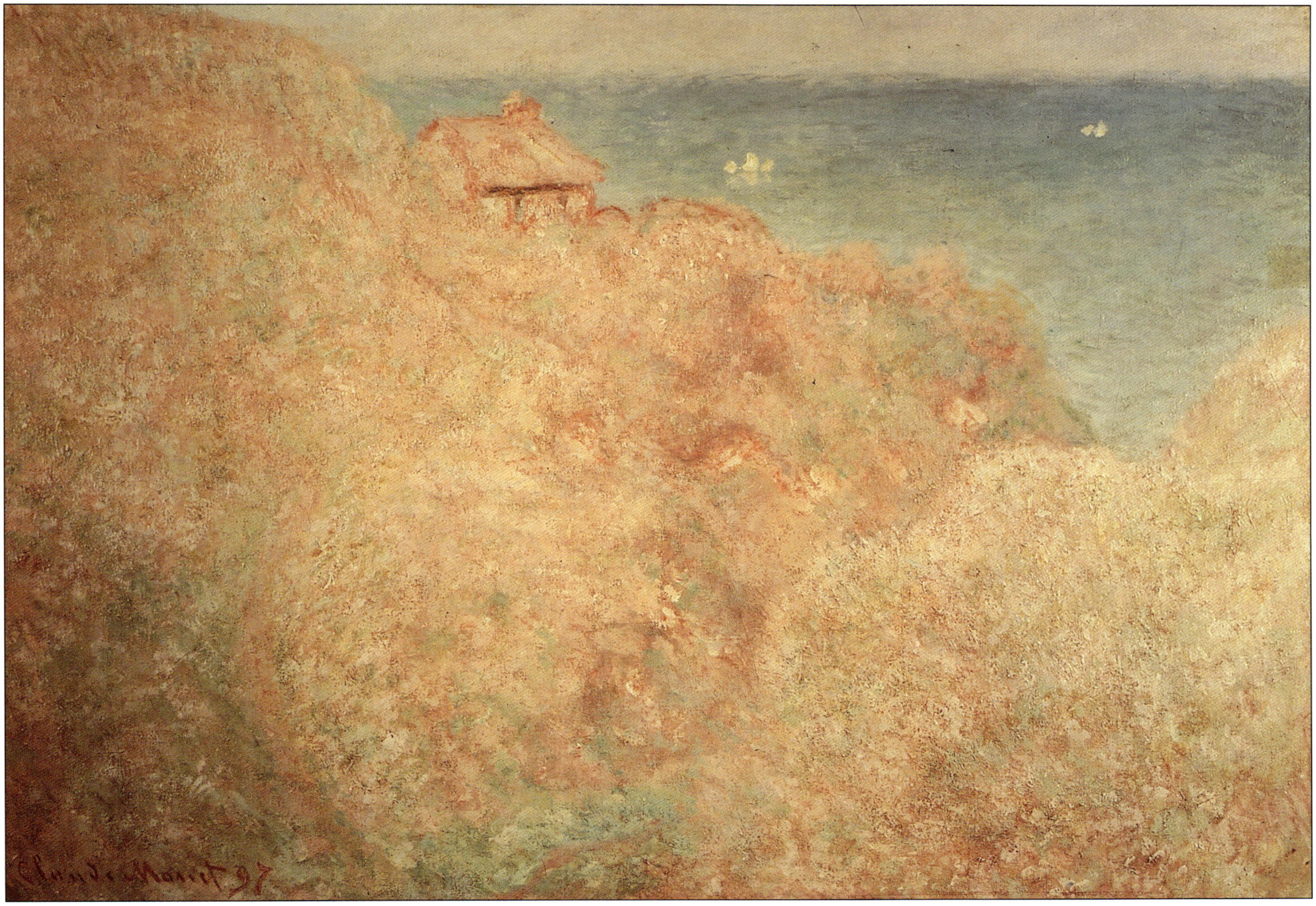

ABOVE:
The Coastguard's House, Varengeville (1897)
MUSÉE DES BEAUX-ARTS, LE HAVRE

practice of art has become increasingly experimental and innovative, so the kind of doubts and fears that Monet experienced have become part of being an artist and have even, in some instances, been made the subject of art.

The Arches of Etretat

Early in 1883 Monet encountered another fearful challenge. After a brief visit to Le Havre in January, he went to Etretat, a resort on the Normandy coast; it was further south than Pourville and Varengeville, just a few kilometres below Fécamp. Etretat was celebrated for its cliffs and, above all, for the great arches created by erosion, which pierce the cliffs so that great arms of rock curve out from the cliff-tops to anchor themselves in the sea. The effect is all the more dramatic because the arches immediately suggest other splendidly man-made structures – the flying buttresses that rear up to support the upper walls of a Gothic cathedral.

Although Etretat is only 25 kilometres from Monet's home

town, Le Havre, he had been there only once before, in the late 1860s, bringing back a single painting. This time, perhaps because he was painting in a more emotive vein and responding to the drama in nature, he was obsessed with what he saw and felt. He may also have believed that he was ready to take on the competition, for Etretat had long been popular with artists, including one of Monet's youthful heroes, Gustave Courbet. In a letter to Alice, he indicated that, even after so many years, he felt a certain risk in courting comparison with his dead friend. Etretat brought Monet back three years running (1883–5), providing him with a wealth of motifs to choose from or combine: the beach, the sea in all its moods and the fishermen's boats, including the worn-out craft which the men beached, roofed over and used to store their tackle. Above all, there were the cliffs and their astonishing arches – the Porte d'Amont, the Porte d'Aval with the high 'Needle' rising out of the sea nearby, and the giant among the arches, the Manneporte.

These natural wonders were spectacular when seen from a distance – from the cliffs or out at sea – but had an even greater impact at ground level, when they loomed over the visitor like the vast remains of some drowned prehistoric culture. The experience was perilous as well as awe-inspiring, since the tide changed rapidly and could easily trap the unwary on a flooding beach. Monet himself experienced such dangers while he was painting near the Manneporte on 27 November, 1885. An enormous wave broke over the shore and swept the painter and his equipment into the sea. 'I instantly believed myself lost,' he wrote to Alice, and went on to describe how he had barely managed to climb from the water on all fours, completely waterlogged and with blue and yellow paint daubed all over his beard.

Monet painted the cliffs and the great arches as they appeared in all kinds of weather and from many points of view, close up and, more conventionally framed, from a distance. Even so, his vision of Etretat was a highly selective one which admitted only the fisher-folk and their boats as representations of humanity. The spectator could be forgiven for believing that Monet's out-of-season pictures show a little fishing port, but although that is what it had once been, by the 1880s tourism had relegated the traditional occupation to a picturesque survival.

No doubt this had something to do with Monet's rejection of the city and modern-life subjects after 1877, but it was also not so very different from the way he had pictured Argenteuil a few years earlier. For all his interest in Argenteuil's railway bridge, the

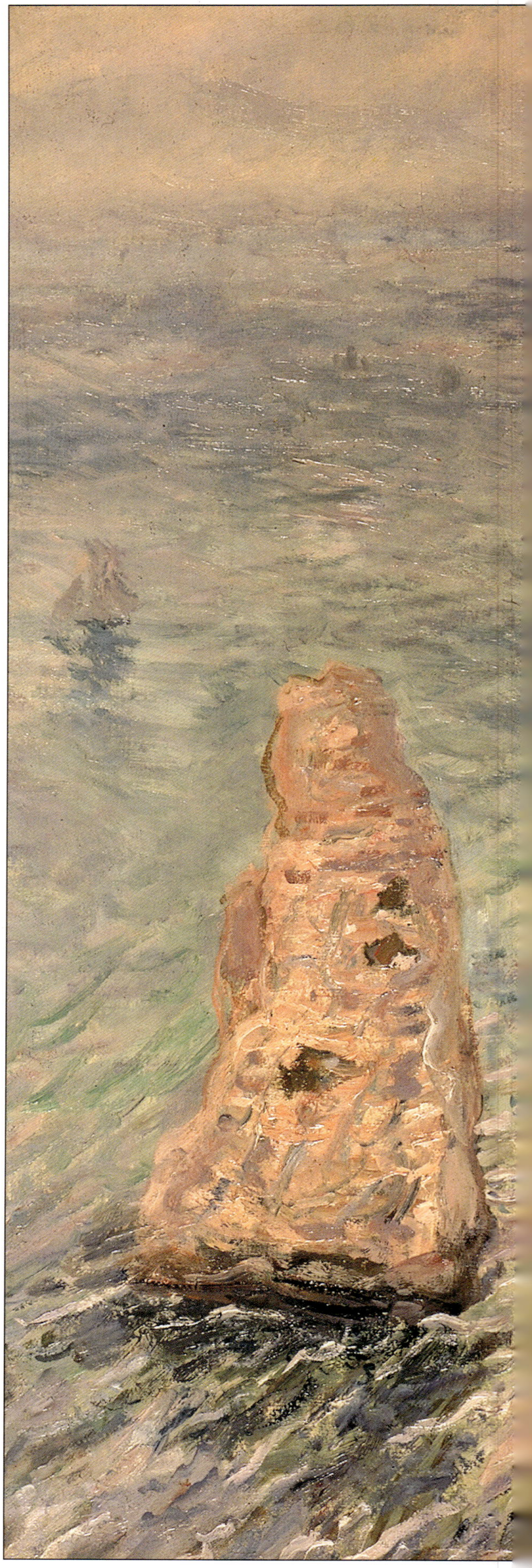

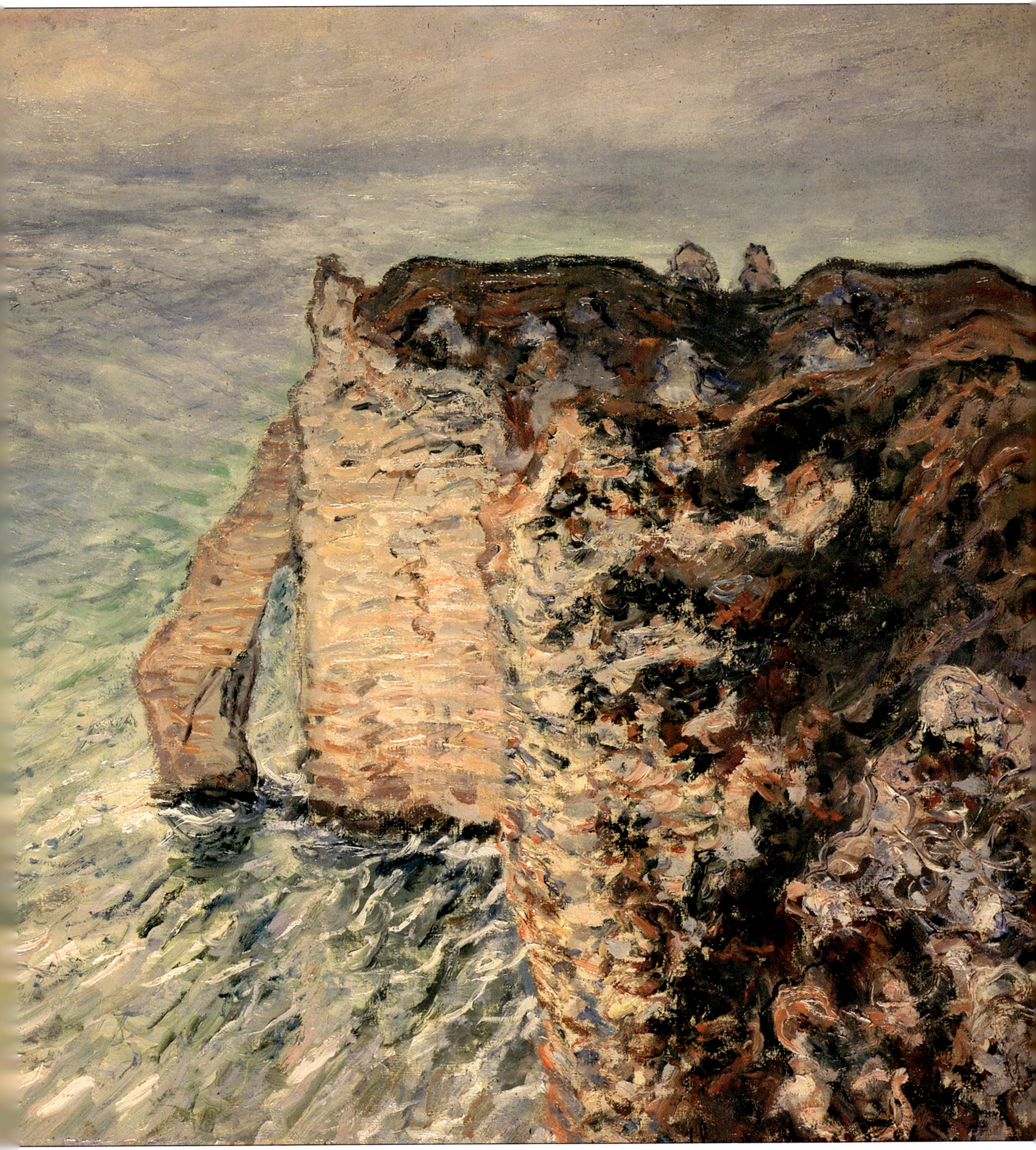

PREVIOUS PAGES 152-3: **The Needle and the Porte d'Aval, Etretat** (1885) PRIVATE COLLECTION

speeding trains and the new pastime of pleasure boating, human figures are only occasionally to be seen, and then only from a distance. Most of the boats contesting the regattas could well be directedby remote control, for there is little sign of a crew on them and the crowds that thronged the streets and river banks are nowhere in evidence.

A Meeting with Maupassant

Coincidentally, Etretat brought Monet into contact with the man who has best preserved the atmosphere of places such as Argenteuil. The novelist and short-story writer Guy de Maupassant (1850–93) was himself a passionate oarsman, and a number of his tales feature riverside settings and outings from the capital in which more or less boisterous young men have interesting encounters with girls whose responsiveness varies according to class, character and opportunity. (A similar atmosphere prevails in some paintings by Auguste Renoir, notably *The Boating Party,* and, appropriately, in *Une Partie de Campagne,* a film made by his son, the director Jean Renoir.) Maupassant, like Monet, was a Norman, born near Dieppe, and from time to time returned to his native haunts. He met the painter late in 1885, when Monet was staying at Etretat in a house owned by the opera-singer Faure, and the two men became friendly.

However, everything is grist to the writer's mill and the following year Maupassant wove his recollections of Monet into an article which appeared in the Magazine *Gil-Blas* on 28 September, 1886. In 'The Life of a Landscapist' Maupassant wrote, in the first person, what purported to be a letter to an unnamed friend, casting himself in the role of a landscape painter. The early part of the 'letter' is devoted to raptures in which the artist avows an unbridled desire to devour all the natural wonders he sees – sentiments so characteristic of Monet that Maupassant seems likely to have taken them over from his conversations with the painter. The fictional landscapist also makes pointed Impressionist-style remarks about the artist's delight in the true colours of things, as opposed to the academy-taught conventions. This is interesting evidence that, whether or not Maupassant learned it from Monet, this approach to colour was becoming sufficiently familiar to appear without incongruity in a popular, fairly light-hearted magazine article.

In his character as a painter, Maupassant went on to recall, quite truthfully, that 'Last year, in this very place, I often followed

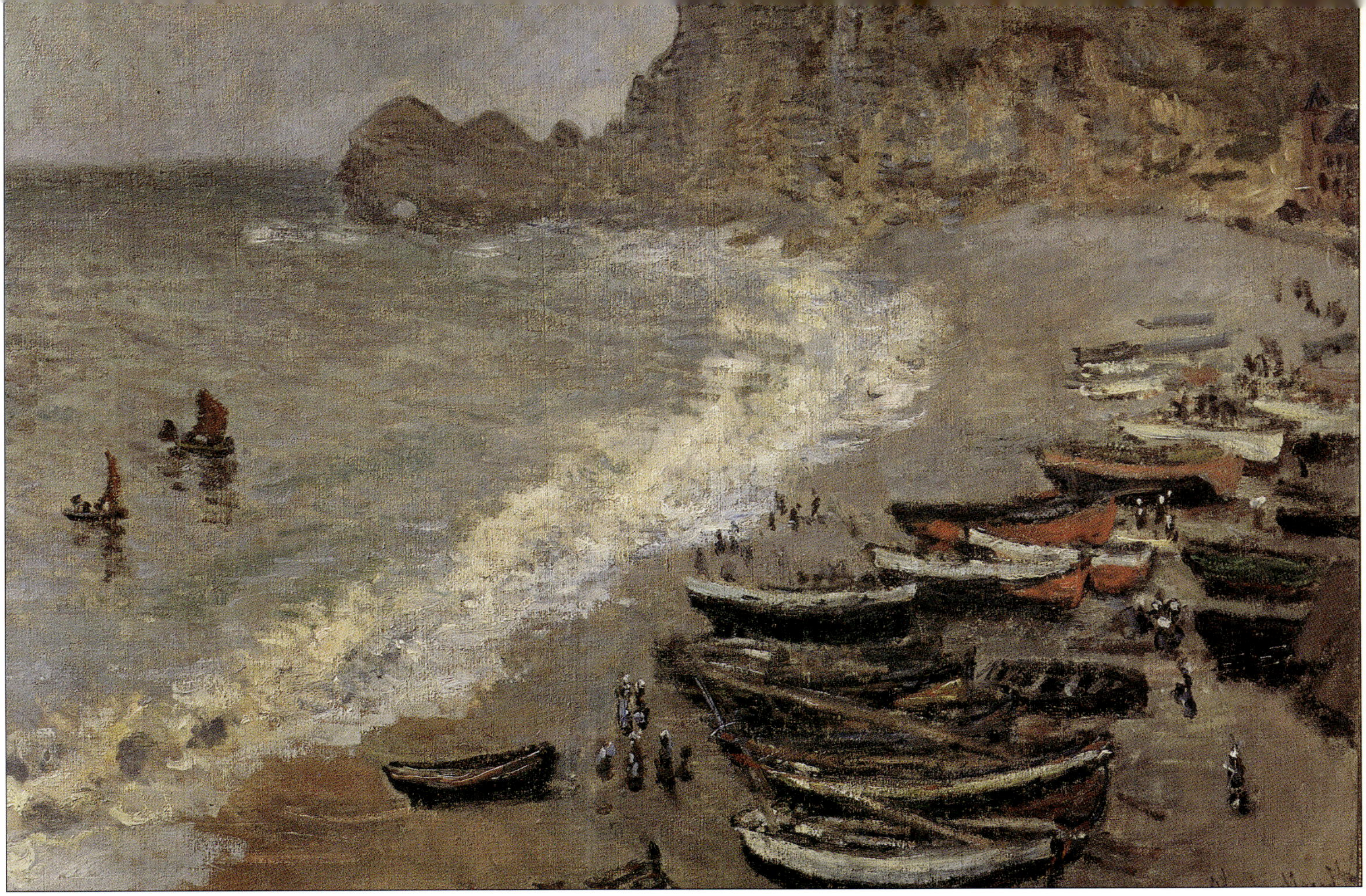

ABOVE:
Etretat (1883)
MUSÉE D'ORSAY, PARIS

Claude Monet, who was searching for impressions'. Monet in fact behaved more like a hunter than a painter, skilfully tracking his prey and closing in on it. Giving us an endearing sidelight on Monet's professional habits, Maupassant describes him employing a gang of children to carry five or six canvases, all representing the same subject at different times of day and in different atmospheric conditions. He worked on them in turn, according to the way the light changed, waiting for the appearance of a fleeting effect and then capturing it with a few strokes of a brush. The speed with which Monet could do this obviously astonished the writer, who slipped into hyperbole, claiming that the painter 'caught a burst of rain on the sea in both hands [!] and flung it onto the canvas'. Maupassant's article went on to record real or imaginary meetings with Corot and Courbet, ending with a description of the painter's torment at his inability to record what he sees. Although attributed to the 'I' writing the letter, the sentiments, lamenting the gap between vision and execution, were artistic commonplaces which might or might not have come directly from Monet. Even allowing for novelistic streamlining and exaggeration, Maupassant's piece evokes the central place that face-to-face confrontation with nature always held for Monet.

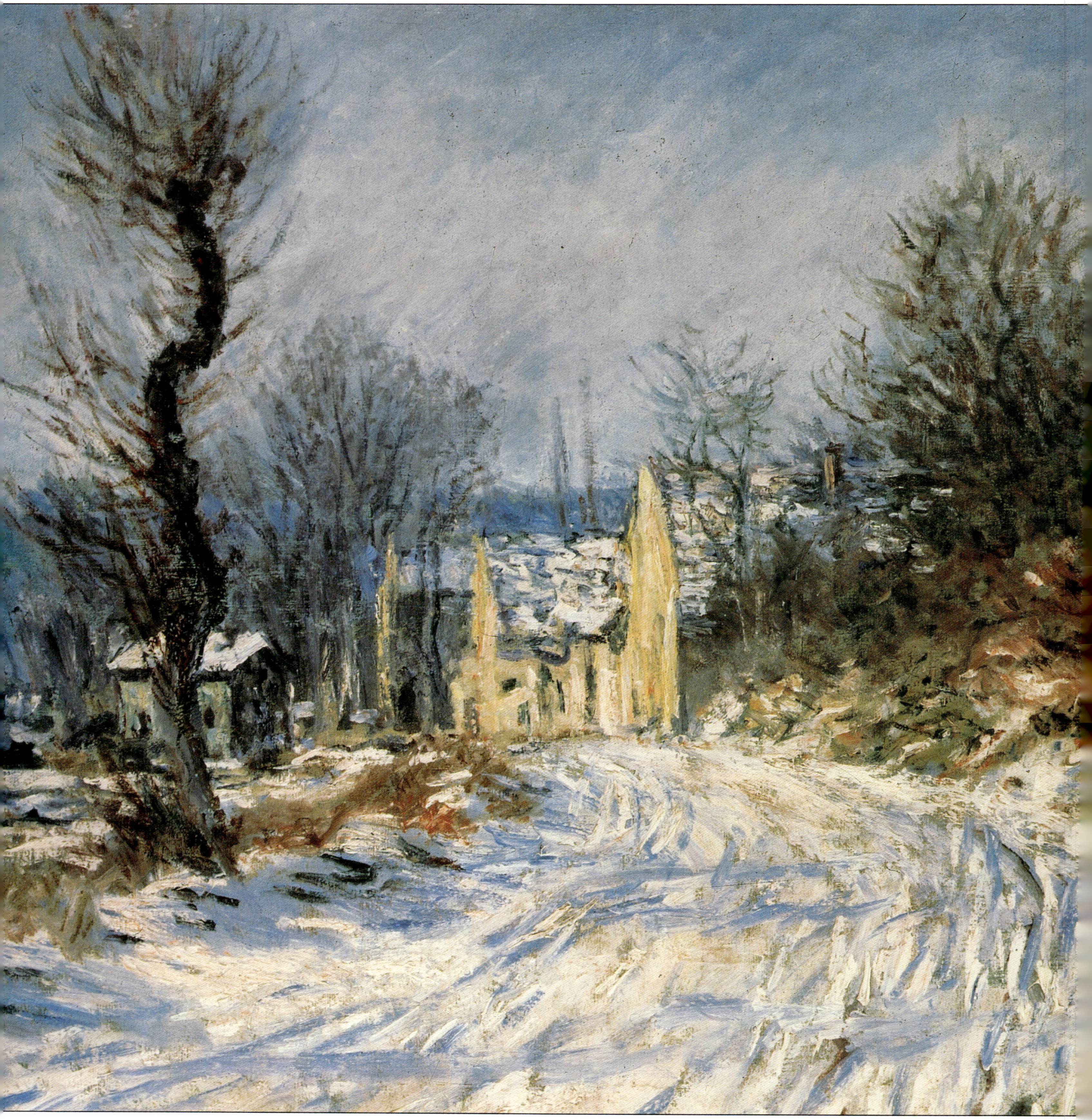

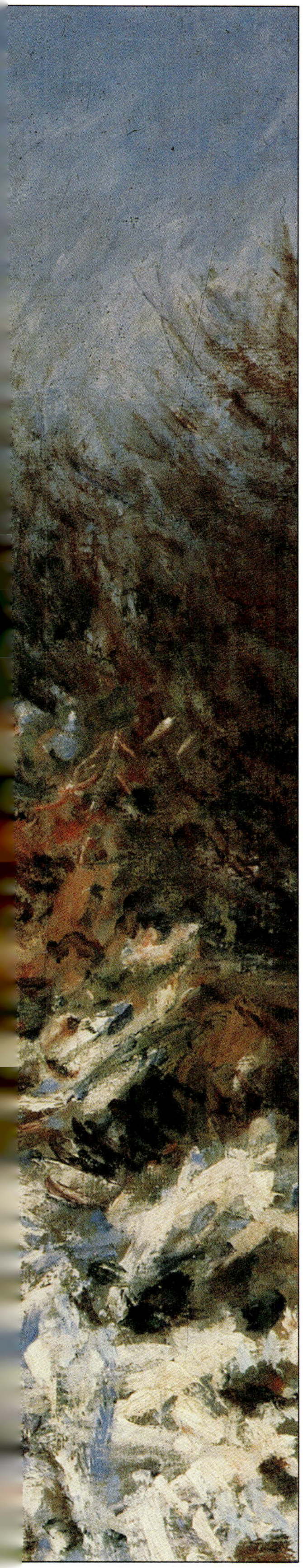

CHAPTER EIGHT

Giverny and Success

DESPITE HIS DISLIKE OF POISSY, Monet stayed there until the usual money troubles made the town an uncomfortable place to live in. Eventually it was Durand-Ruel (as so often the genie in Monet's bottle) who made possible one of the most important departures in the painter's life – his move to Giverny. In April 1883, when Monet finally left Poissy, it was the dealer who financed the move. Monet did not go far, since the valley of the Seine was still full of lovely places in which to stay, while being conveniently situated for his indispensable contacts with Paris. He was now determined to find a place where he could settle permanently with his companion and their eight children.

LEFT:
The Road to Giverny, Winter
(1885)
PRIVATE COLLECTION

Home at Last

The place he chose was Giverny, a little community of 279 inhabitants on the right bank of the Seine, some 80 kilometres from Paris. It had its own railway station, and the nearest town, Vernon, only five kilometres away, also stood on the familiar railway line from the

RIGHT:
Bordighera
(1884)
ART INSTITUTE
OF CHICAGO:
COURTESY OF MR.
AND MRS. POTTER
PALMER
COLLECTION

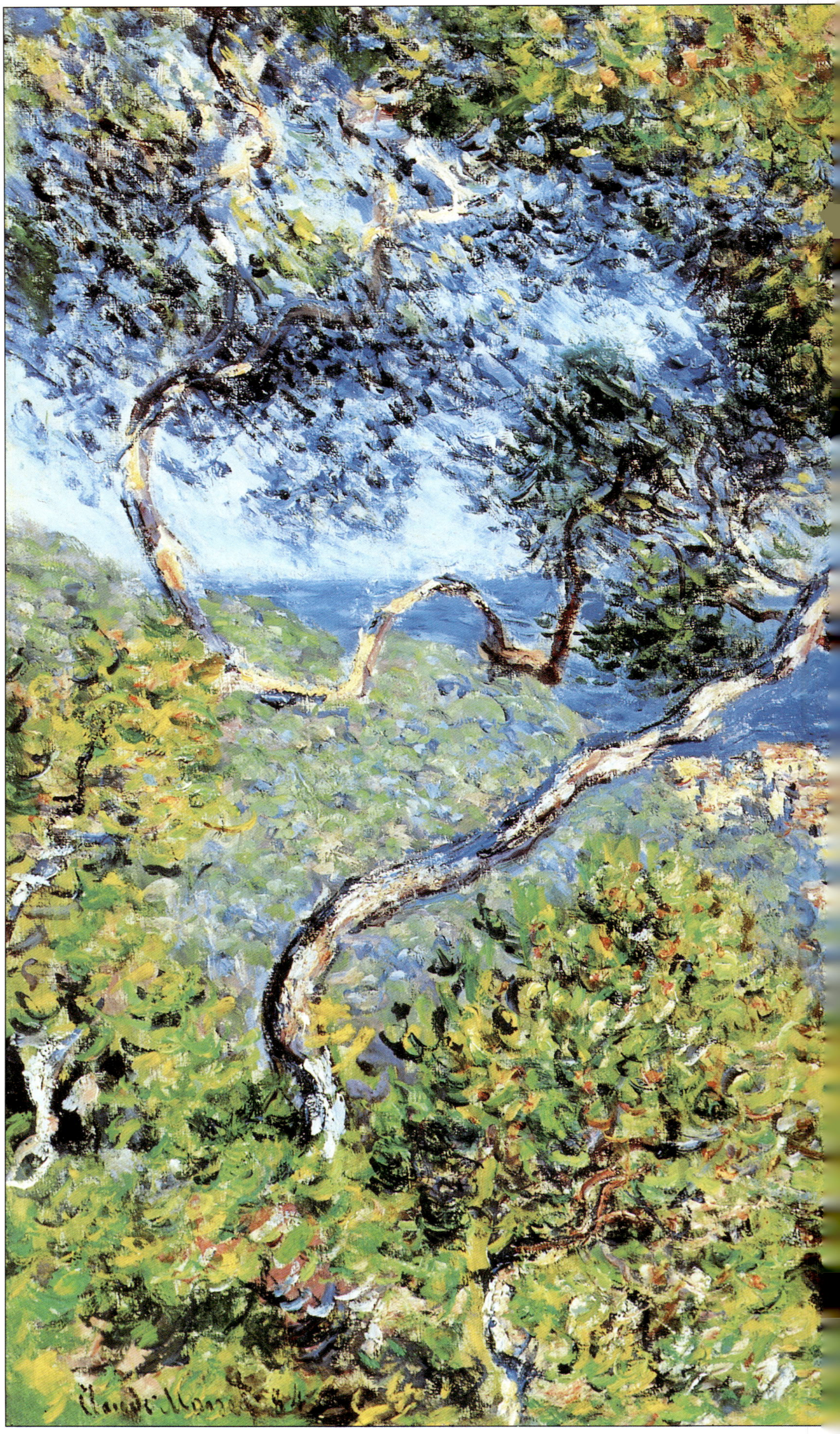

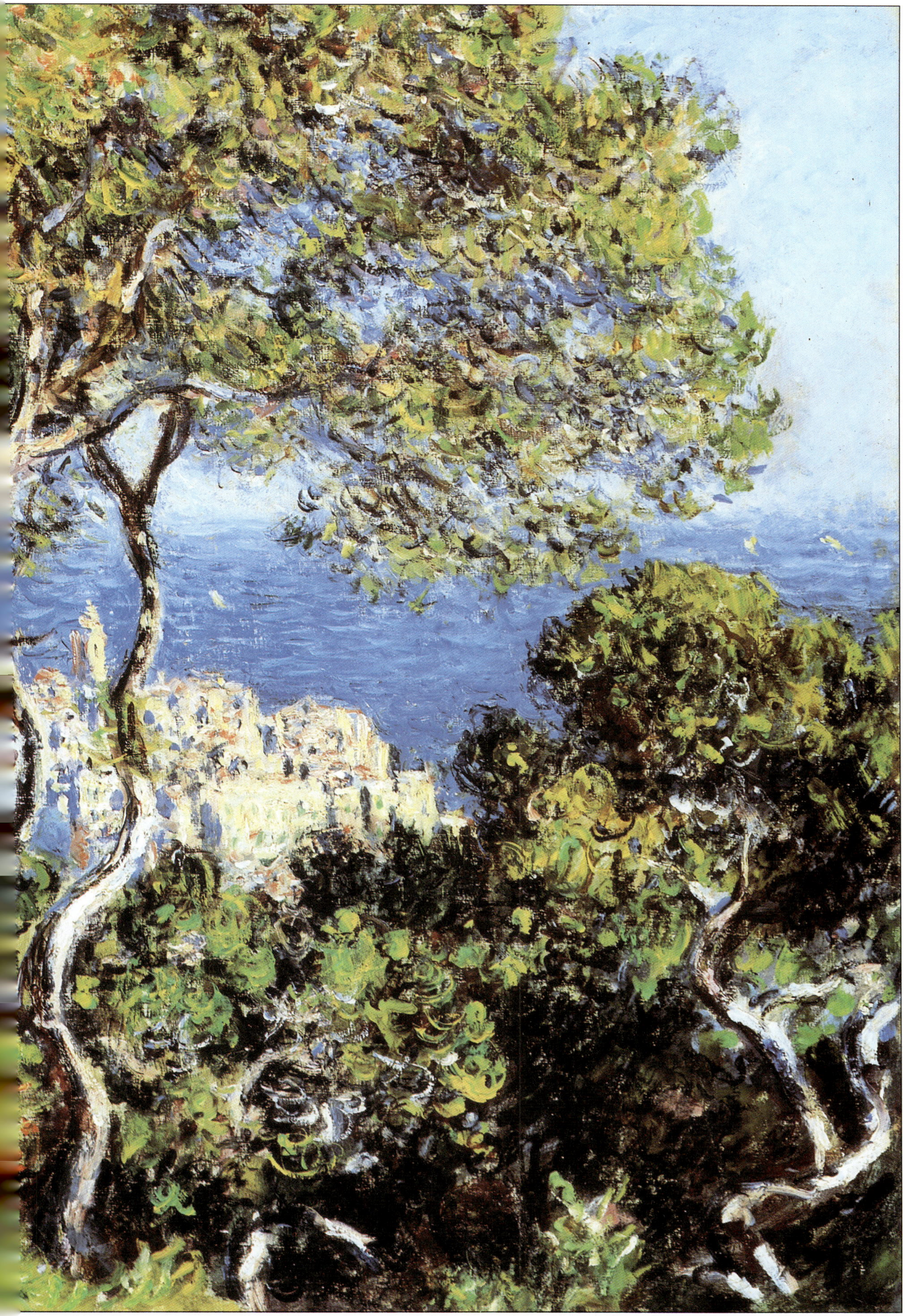

OVERLEAF PAGES
160-1:
Menton, seen from Cap Martin
(1884)
Museum of Fine Arts, Boston

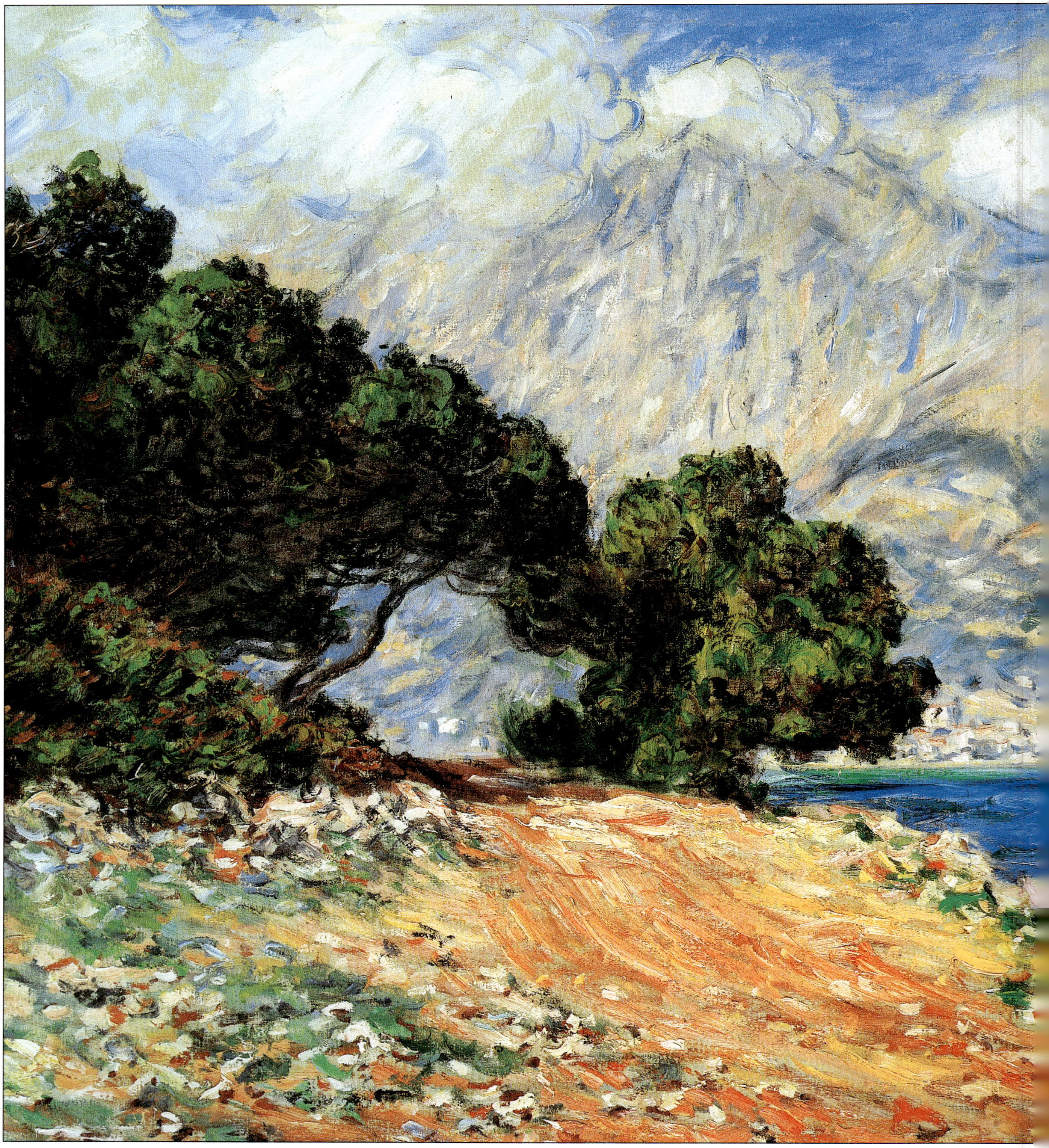

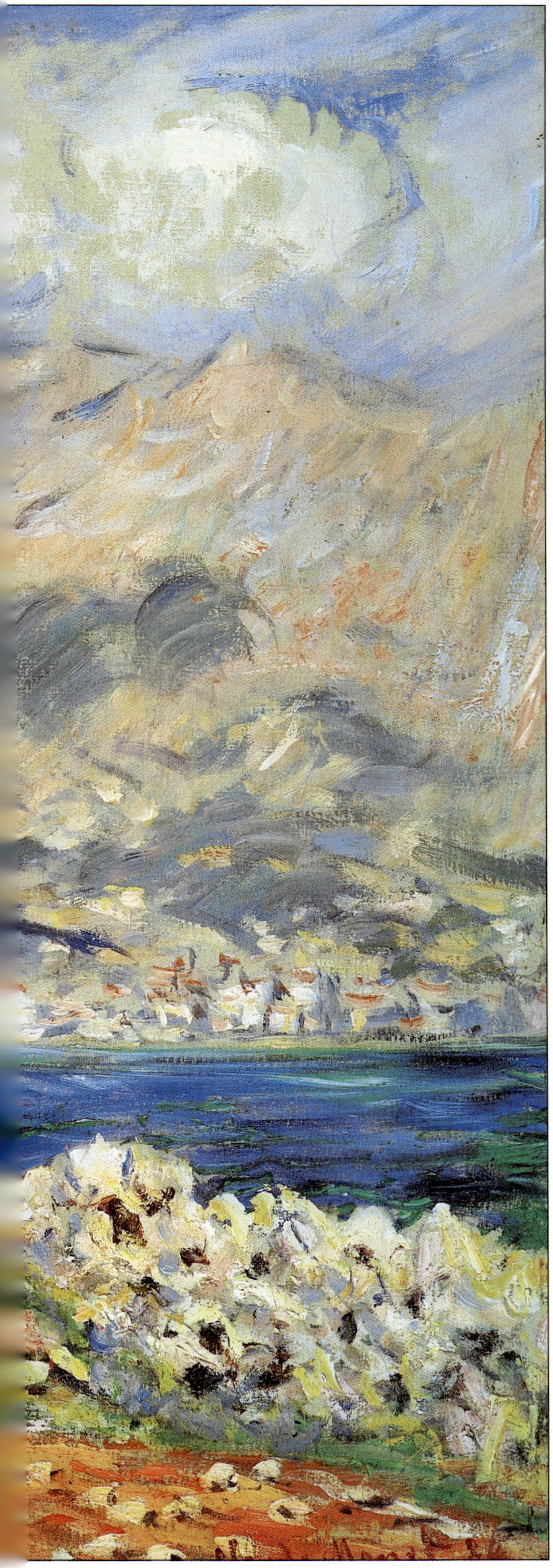

capital to Le Havre. Initially an orchard in the village, alive with blossoms, is said to have caught Monet's eye and made a favourable impression on him. He and his family put up at an inn until they found a house to let – a large, lovely, foursquare house with pink walls, green shutters and its own walled orchard. Monet took it and Le Pressoir (The Cider Press) became his home for the rest of his life.

While Monet and his family were settling in at Giverny, the news arrived that Manet had died after an excruciating struggle against the ravages of locomotor ataxia. Monet attended the funeral at Passy, serving as one of the pall-bearers. In the public mind, Manet had always figured as the leader of the rebellious moderns, and even his refusal to participate in the Impressionist shows had not shaken the general conviction that Monet and his friends belonged to *la bande à Manet* – Manet's gang. Naturally ambitious, Monet had set out early in his career to rival the older artist, but his competitive feelings seem to have faded away during the 1870s as his painting developed along its own distinctive lines. Moreover, Manet had shown himself ready to learn from the younger man by experimenting with *plein-air* painting; and above all, he had proved himself a generous friend, frequently rescuing the improvident Monet when he was in financial straits. Nevertheless, one effect of Manet's death was to leave open the 'leadership' of the moderns; in this sense, his passing opened the way for the rapid growth of Monet's reputation in the later 1880s. Appropriately, one use to which Monet would put that reputation was to champion Manet's own work and hasten public and official recognition of its greatness.

Back at Giverny after the funeral, Monet supervised the conversions required to accommodate his family of ten and provide the space he needed to work in. He also took over the garden, which became one of the great passions of his life; to begin with, the utilitarian vegetable plots were soon dug up and replaced by the multi-coloured masses of flowers that he loved.

The call of the river was as strong as ever. The village stood at the confluence of the Seine and one of its tributaries, the Epte, where Monet had a large shed built to hold a floating studio and other boats. The villagers charged the family a toll every time they walked across their meadows to reach the shed, evidently pleased to make some money out of people they regarded as a highly suspect gang of bohemians, led by a middle-aged man without a proper job. However, at Giverny the veiled hostility of the locals somehow

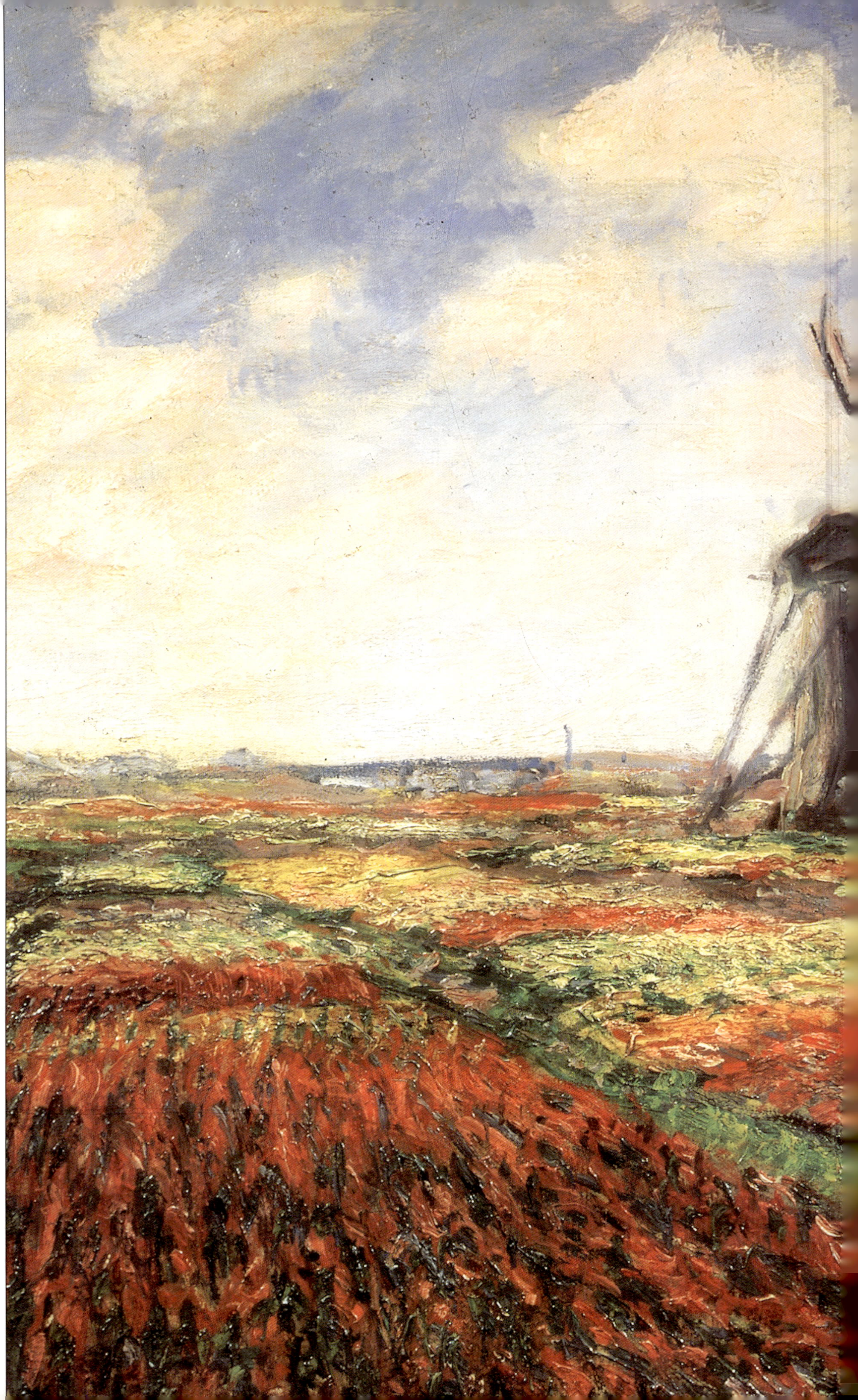

RIGHT:
Tulip Fields with Rijnsberg Windmill (1886)
MUSÉE D'ORSAY, PARIS

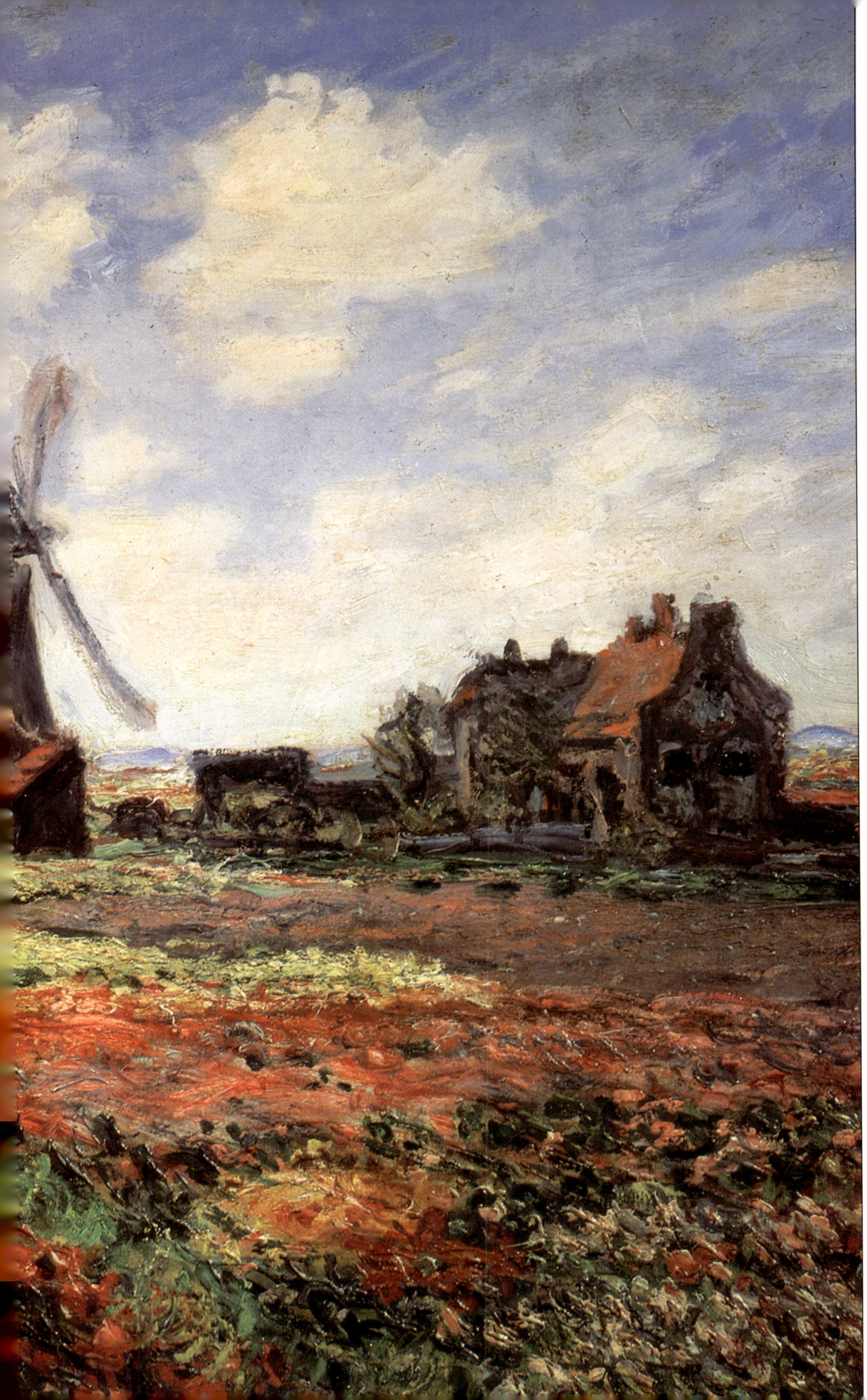

seemed not to matter. Monet paid up and by summer he was making trips in his boat along the river up to Jeufosse and Port-Villez on the opposite bank; later he would venture downstream to Vernon.

'I am delirious with joy: this Giverny is a splendid place for me,' he wrote to his friend Théodore Duret, and he never had cause to change his mind. Over the years he found the attractions of the area inexhaustible, whether he went on the river, tramped around the village or stayed at home painting subjects from his garden and orchard. Thanking Durand-Ruel for his financial help, Monet forecast that his new home would inspire him to paint masterpieces. His first Giverny paintings were ready by the autumn and he was also working on rather different subjects, directly commissioned by Durand-Ruel: a set of 36 still-life paintings of flowers and fruits, intended to decorate the doors of the dealer's Paris apartment in the Rue de Rome. In these, Monet again demonstrated an almost casual mastery of the genre, producing vividly sensuous off-centre paintings combining 'Japanese' cropping with rich, light-modulated colouring and textures.

On the Riviera

Happy though he was at Giverny, Monet remained eager to travel in search of new subjects. At the end of 1883 he accepted an invitation from Renoir, who had just discovered the Mediterranean, to take a trip to the Côte d'Azur. The friends set off in mid-December, travelling in the course of a fortnight from Marseilles via Monte Carlo and into Italy as far as Genoa. They also managed to visit the eccentric Paul Cézanne at L'Estaque, where the relatively minor Impressionist was living in obscurity while making himself into a great master with his own distinctive 'Post-Impressionist' style.

Like so many northern artists and writers before him, Monet was dazzled by his first experience of brilliant southern colour and winter warmth. For him they represented not only a feast for the senses, but also a challenge: could the technique of Impressionism, developed in front of northern landscapes with muted colours and enveloping atmospheres, be adapted to the vividness and hard clarity of the South? Almost immediately he wrote to Durand-Ruel, asking for an advance to pay for a working return trip and warning the dealer to say nothing about it to anyone. If Renoir learned of his plans, he would ask to go along too, but 'I want to go there alone. I have always worked better in solitude, in the light of my own impressions.' This became his fixed conviction

RIGHT:
Lady with a Parasol (facing left)
(1886)
MUSÉE D'ORSAY, PARIS

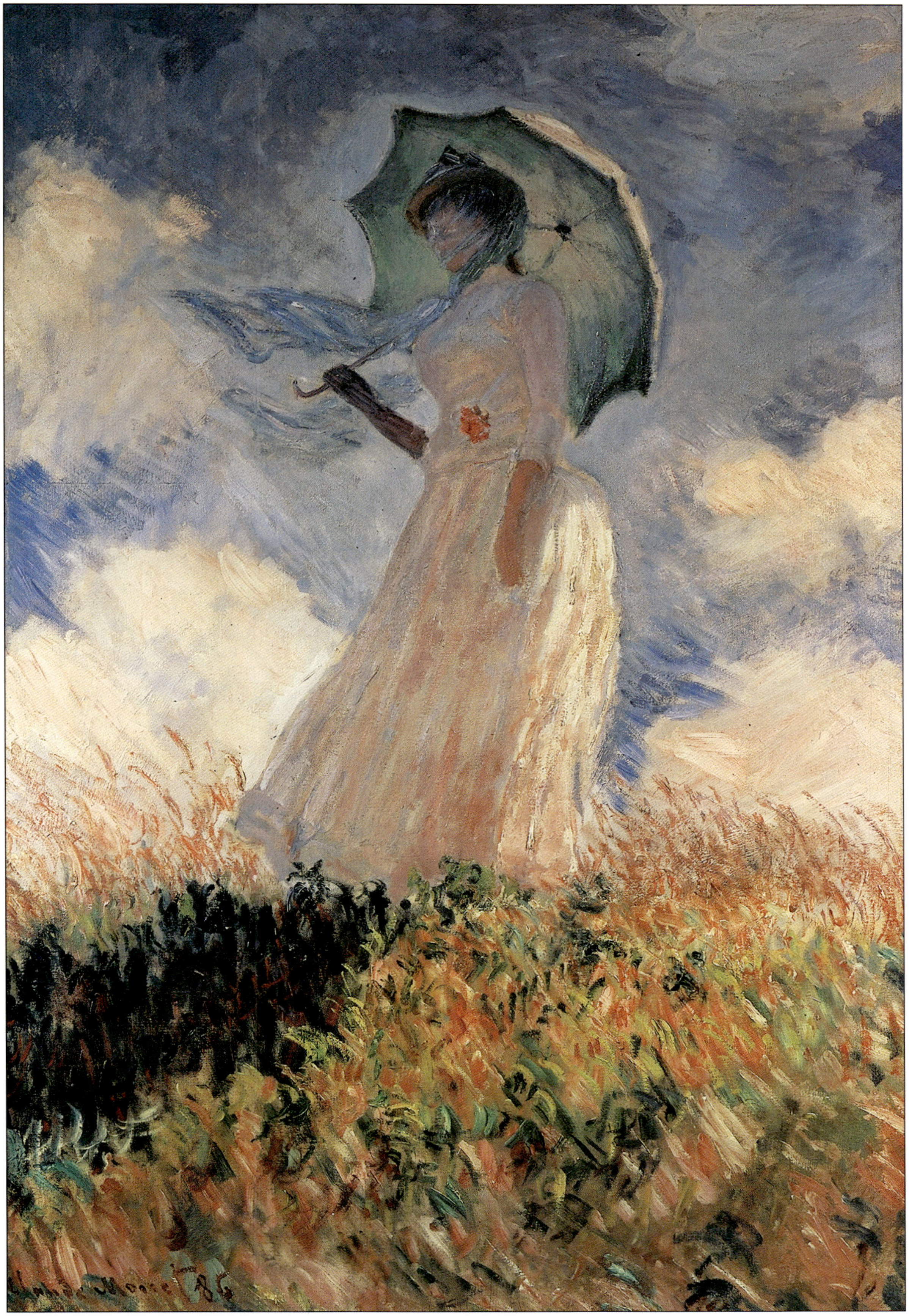

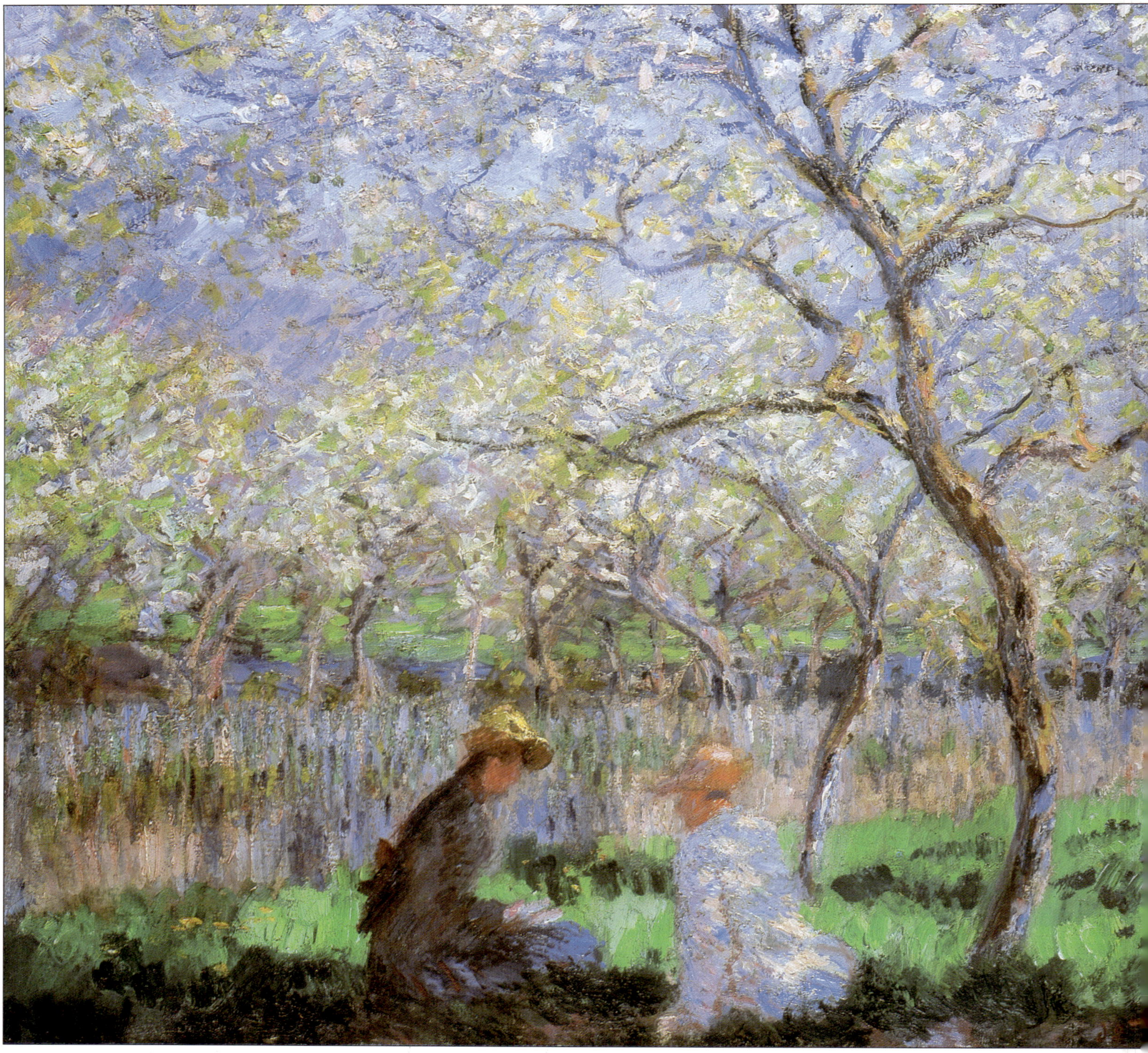

ABOVE:
Springtime
(1886)
FITZWILLIAM
MUSEUM,
CAMBRIDGE

('it is always bad to work *à deux*'), although rather an ironic, forgetful one in view of his partnerships with Renoir in Paris and at La Grenouillère, from which he had derived artistic benefit and, on occasion, welcome titbits from Renoir's parents' larder!

Monet decided to base himself at Bordighera, a delightful resort just across France's border with Italy. A revealing incident occurred on his first day, when he discovered that his hotel was full of Germans and immediately moved out. Although not much

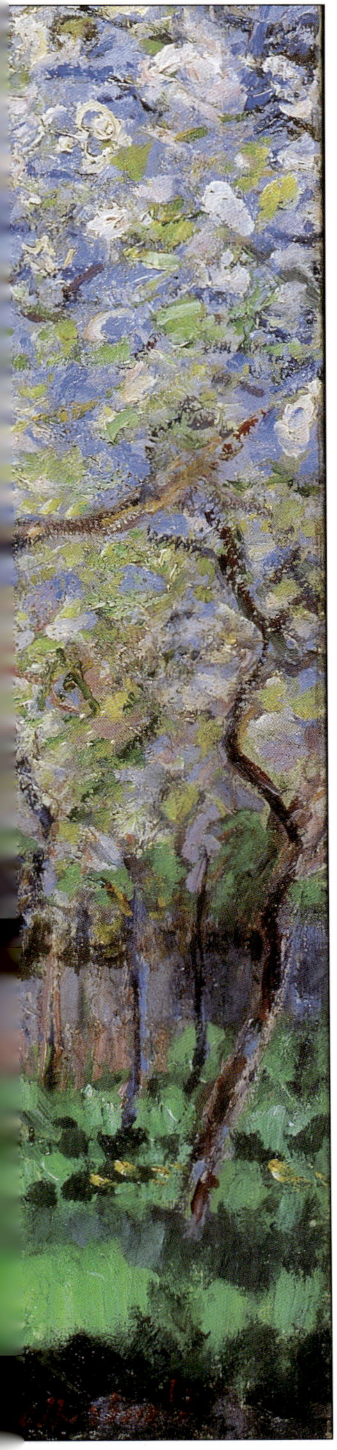

interested in politics and a non-combatant in 1870–1, Monet was patriotic enough to share the French resentment of their former conquerors and perhaps to dream of a future day of reckoning. He found a hotel where most of the guests were English and happily moved in. Although there was as yet no Anglo-French Entente Cordiale, Monet seems to have cherished an affection for England as a result of his 1870 stay in London; in any case, France was entering a period of Anglomania in which everything English was considered the last word in smartness. More surprising, given the general French opinion of English cooking, is one of his notes to Alice: 'I eat well – I'm so pleased to have chosen an English hotel'!

Bordighera thrilled Monet all over again, and he wrote ecstatic letters to Alice, praising the orange and lemon trees, the palms, the olives and the intense blues of the sea and sky. One of his great strengths was that he did not shy away from beauties that had come to seem clichéd, but proved able to approach every experience with a fresh eye. However, at first he found it difficult to isolate suitable subjects and get a grip on the unfamiliar tones and colour combinations in the southern landscape. To do it justice, he told Théodore Duret, one would need a jewelled palette. However, after his initial uncertainties he underwent an extraordinary burst of creativity, painting a great variety of subjects at Bordighera, Ventimiglia, Menton and other sites. His intended stay of a month lengthened into three, and he had to write in a loving, reassuring vein to Alice, who feared that the lure of the South might include some forms of temptation that went beyond the purely aesthetic. Monet insisted that he was leading a strenuous working life. Climbing about looking for subjects was hard on the legs, he told her. His routine was to work until evening and then eat a hearty meal. 'Afterwards I write a few lines to you, climb into bed, think with joy of Giverny, look over my canvases hanging on the wall, read for a while and finally fall into deep sleep until the morning.' In an interesting sidelight on the practicalities of a landscapist's life, he lamented that after only six or seven weeks he had used up his canvases and colours and worn out his shoes, socks and clothing.

Monet's letters make it clear that, with lovely things all round him, he still needed to find them in the right setting so that he could paint what he saw in front of him. Whatever final touches may have taken place in the studio back in Giverny, his claim that he worked directly from nature remained essentially true. In the past, landscapes had often been composites, merging elements from more than one scene. Even painters who set up their easels and painted the view in front of them made no bones about the synthetic nature of their art. This is nicely illustrated by a story about an older master of landscape, Corot, who was discovered painting a scene in the countryside by an inquisitive stranger, who compared the scene and the canvas and then asked, 'But where is the pool?' 'Behind me', answered Corot.

After a tussle with Italian customs officials over his lack of official certificates allowing the export of works of art, Monet returned to Giverny in April 1884 with a grand total of about 50 canvases; he had completed an average of one every two days. These pictures were so startlingly different from anything he had done before that he felt obliged to prepare Durand-Ruel for what he was to see. 'There may be protests from the enemies of blue and pink, since what I am trying to capture is precisely a brilliant, magical light. People who have never been here or have never looked at the place properly will no doubt dismiss my work as fantasy, whereas it is actually in a lower key than the reality. Everything is breast-of-pigeon or flambé, wonderful and still more wonderful every day, keeping me spellbound.'

Everything Monet said about the Italian Riviera was true, and accounts for the extraordinary change in the appearance of his work there. *Villas at Bordighera*, painted in a garden filled with palms, captures the intense colours and the combination of blinding heat and lushness so characteristic of the area. Even the undulating rhythms in many of the paintings are true to reality in that they reflect the gnarled, eccentric growth of olives and other southern trees, for example in *Bordighera* (pages 158-9). Yet, taken as a group, these canvases are more than the literal or understated impressions that Monet claimed them to be. They do tend to be higher in key than reality, and emphatic rhythms can be picked out in more areas of the surface than those occupied by olive trees. In a work such as *Menton, seen from Cap Martin* (pages 160-1) the moving forms and wild patterns of the brushstrokes are highly expressive and establish unexpected connections between Monet and Post-Impressionist artists such as Van Gogh and Cézanne, both of whom realized their full potential in the South. This points up the close relationship between landscape and style, suggesting that Monet's Impressionism, like Van Gogh's and Cézanne's, could not have survived prolonged exposure to the South without changing into something else. However, for Monet such a trip was, for all its intensity, only a strange and beautiful interlude.

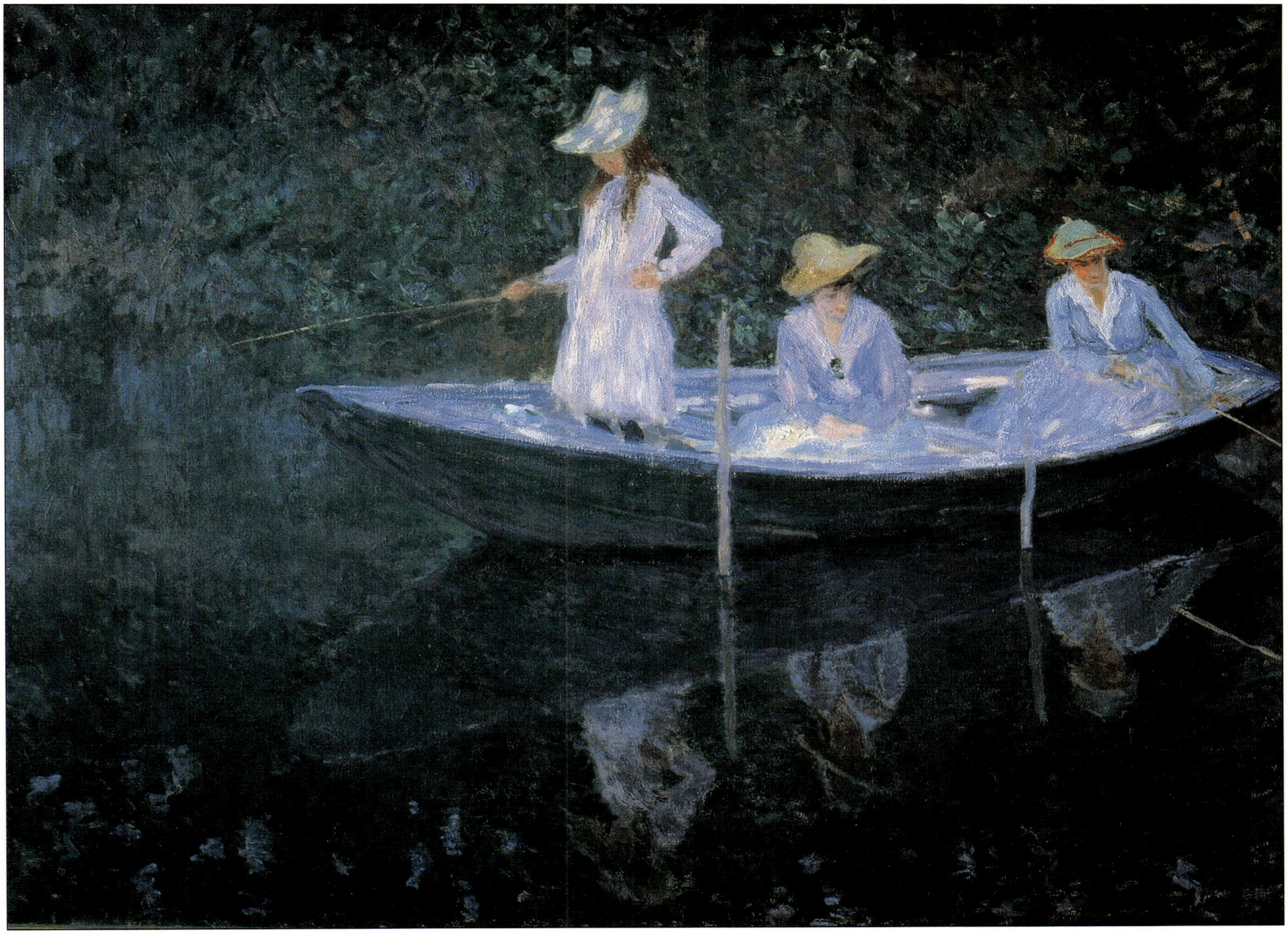

ABOVE:
The Boat at Giverny (1887)
MUSÉE D'ORSAY, PARIS

Dealing with the Dealers

Monet spent a few months at Giverny before setting out in August 1884 for a second visit to Etretat, where he became friendly with the famous opera singer Jean-Baptiste Faure, who was already a generous patron of the Impressionists and owned works by Monet. Meanwhile in Paris, after riotous goings-on, a new Society of Independent Artists had been formed and had put on its first exhibition. The members of the Society were united only by their opposition to the Salon and its jury system, but the very existence of such a group represented a new breach in the monopoly previously held by the Salon. Monet, although not directly involved, was bound to benefit indirectly from anything that undermined the academies and the Salon. Slowly but surely the system was becoming discredited and the public was beginning to reappraise the works of the Impressionists. However, the drift of events was less obvious to those who lived through them, and Durand-Ruel's renewed

OVERLEAF PAGES 170-171:
Boating on the Epte (1890)
MUSEU DE ARTE, SÃO PAULO, BRAZIL

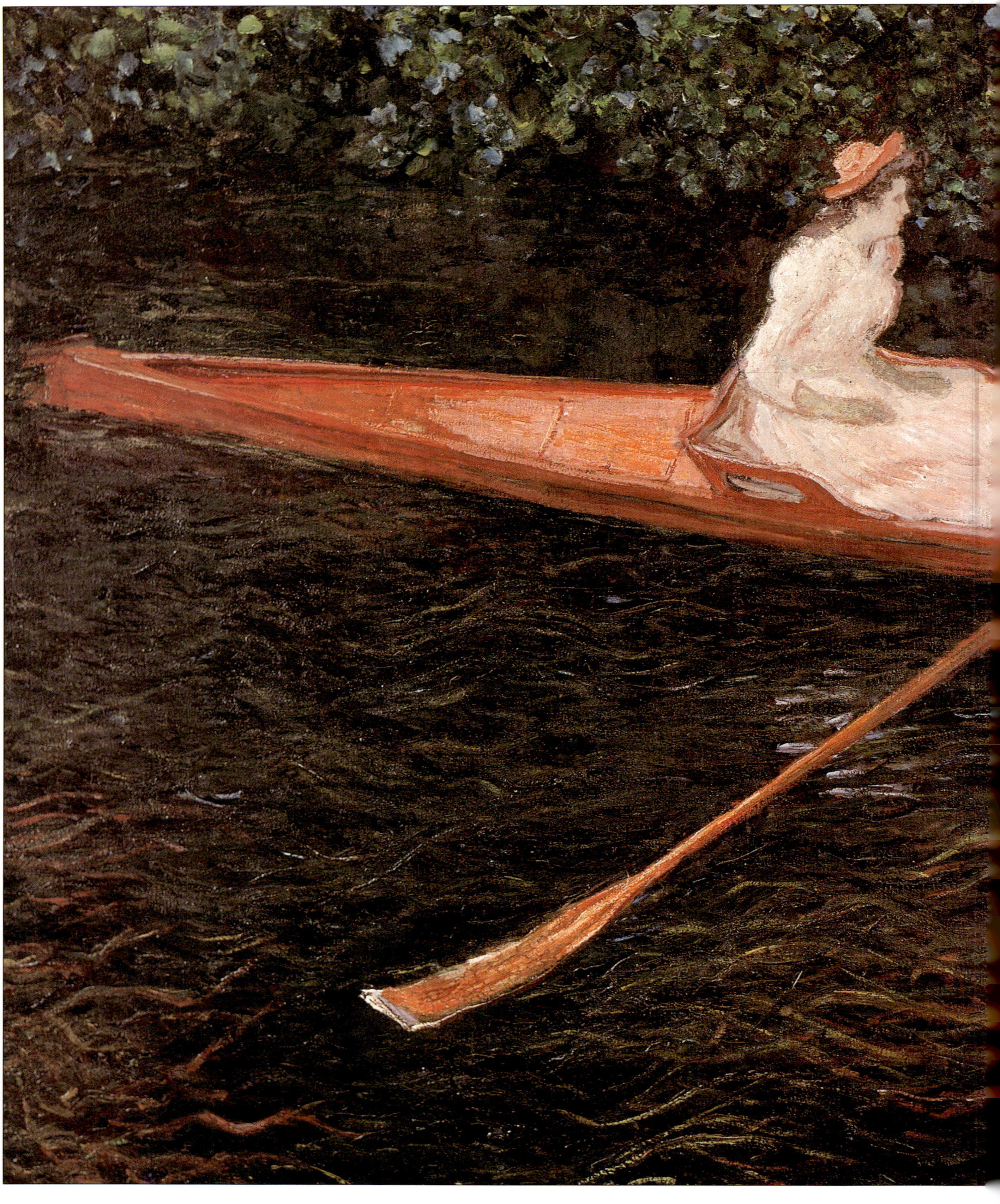

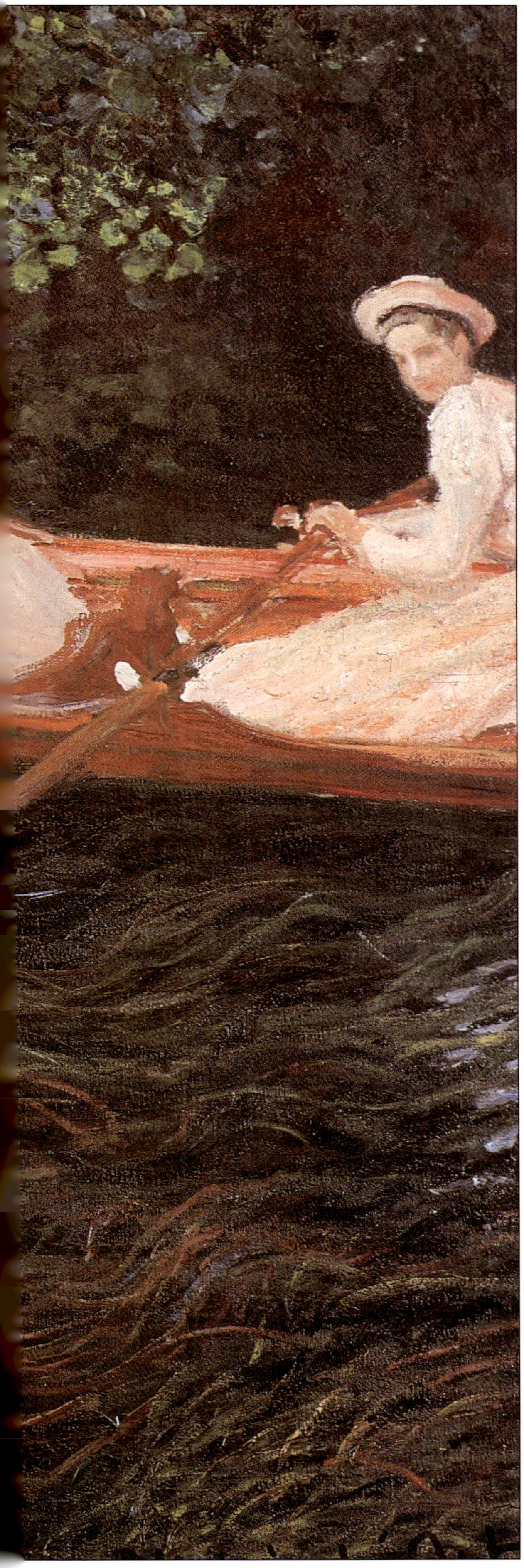

financial difficulties probably seemed more significant at the time. Doubts concerning Durand's reliability certainly encouraged Monet to maintain and strengthen his contacts with other dealers such as Adolphe Portier and Georges Petit.

For a self-proclaimed 'countryman', Monet was remarkably efficient in keeping his communications with Paris open, and especially in recruiting potential patrons and literary champions. In November he was introduced to the writer Octave Mirbeau, a fellow Norman who had already praised his work in the periodical *La France* and who would become a close friend and ally. Shortly afterwards Monet put forward the first tentative suggestion of a monthly dinner to be attended by him, his fellow painters and their friends and supporters. Doubtless he relished the idea of bringing together old friends who were now scattered, although it was ironic that the suggestion should come at a time when the Impressionist movement was effectively defunct. Nevertheless, although it took a couple of years to get off the ground, the idea led to the celebrated 'Impressionist dinners', held at the Café Riche until the mid-1890s.

In May 1885, ten of Monet's canvases were shown as part of the Fourth Exhibition of Painting at Georges Petit's gallery in Paris. Although there was no break between Monet and Durand-Ruel, who was still energetically publicizing the Impressionists' works, the dealer did resent what he saw as Monet's ingratitude. Monet could reasonably have replied that, apart from his need to support his family irrespective of Durand's circumstances, Durand himself operated as a businessman, buying when it suited him and with the ultimate intention of making money from the works of the artists he pushed. However, during this period Monet was more diplomatic, acknowledging his debt to Durand-Ruel and bemoaning the necessity of doing business with others. Monet's invitation to exhibit at the Galerie Georges Petit was actually another sign of changing times, since Petit normally dealt in the more fashionable type of academic art. If he was prepared to take on Monet, it meant that the painter's work was rapidly becoming acceptable to a wider public.

If Durand-Ruel was feeling unappreciated, part of the reason lay in the insular mentality of Monet and most of his colleagues, to whom only France – and, within France, Paris – seemed of the slightest importance in the world of art. The no-longer-New World across the Atlantic hardly existed for them, and Durand's plans for a major American show were generally met with indifference by the Impressionists. Monet told him bluntly that he would much prefer his work to be known and bought in France, as though there was a danger that it might disappear for ever if bought by Americans. Durand-Ruel went ahead all the same, crating and shipping over 200 works to New York, where the exhibition finally opened in April 1886. Monet was represented by 48 canvases, more than any of the other contributors. Like an old joke that is repeated every time a new audience appears, the confusion between the names Manet and Monet occurred yet again, this time in the instructive pages of the exhibition catalogue. Despite its ambition, the show was received without very much enthusiasm or understanding, but it proved to be one of those failures that remain in the memory and are perceived with hindsight as turning-points.Meanwhile, Monet had spent the last three months of 1884 at Etretat, where he stayed in a villa owned by Faure and had his first meeting with Maupassant. He returned for a final brief visit in the early spring, after which he would not work in the area again until the late 1890s. On this occasion, he seems to have left Giverny in some distress, at odds with Alice, who was still embarrassed by their irregular union and appears to have wanted to occupy a separate bedroom. A certain tension existed in their relationship for some years, although Alice's pious scruples did not prevent her from berating Monet when he stayed away from home too long on his painting trips!

In April 1886 he was less concerned with the Impressionist show in New York than with the publication of Emile Zola's novel *L'Œuvre* (The Masterpiece). Zola was now at the height of his fame as the author of a linked series of panoramic novels portraying every aspect of French life. *L'Œuvre* vividly pictured the Impressionist milieu, and its central character, Claude Lantier, is a great artist – but one whose obsessive work on his masterpiece-to-be ends with his madness and suicide; 'the masterpiece' he leaves behind him is unfinished and unfinishable. Long the champion of the moderns, Zola had noticeably cooled towards the Impressionists by the late 1870s, failing to understand their landscape technique and convinced that if they were truly great artists, they would be tackling big modern subjects – that is, producing pictorial equivalents of his own novels.

Zola's fiction was more widely read and immediate in impact than his art criticism, and the apparent association of Impressionism with delusion, failure and self-destruction alarmed Monet. 'Have you read Zola's book?' he asked Pissarro in a letter,

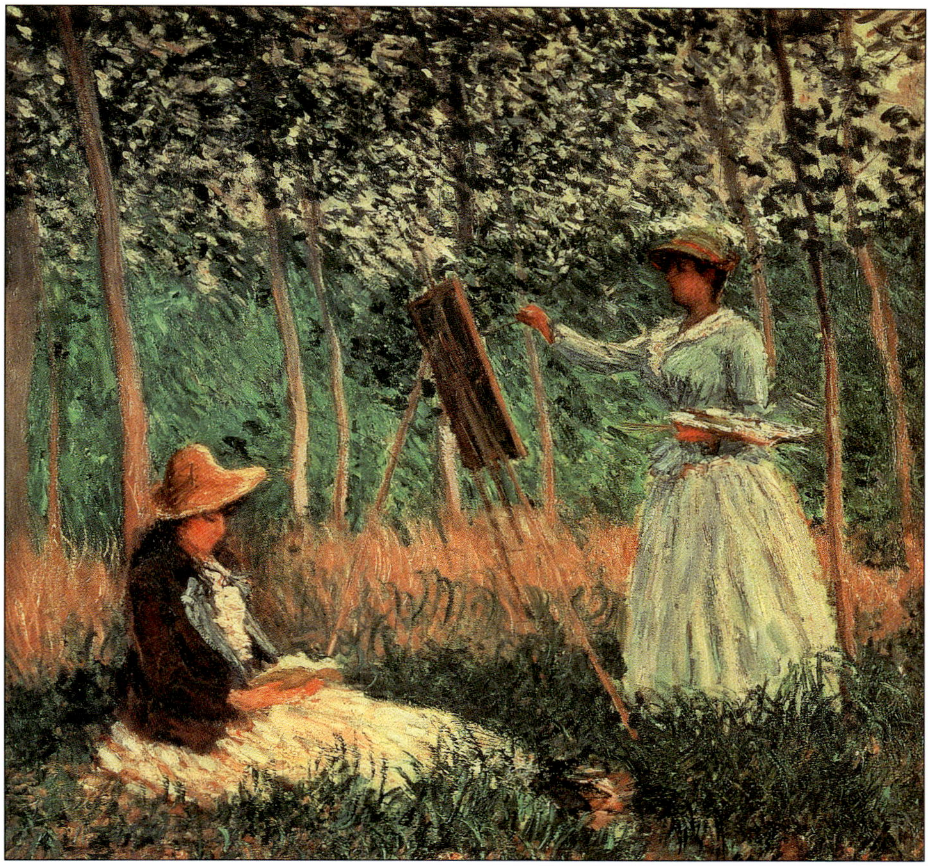

LEFT:
Blanche Hoschedé Painting (1887)
LOS ANGELES COUNTY MUSEUM OF ART

'I'm afraid it will do us a lot of damage'. Paul Cézanne, Zola's friend since their schooldays, recognized that he was the main model for Claude Lantier and, after briefly acknowledging receipt of the book, broke off all communication with the novelist. Zola also sent Monet a copy of *L'Œuvre*, to which the painter responded with surprising mildness. He praised the novel and observed that Zola had carefully avoided making any of his characters resemble one of the real Impressionists (a remark which shows that Monet knew much less about Cézanne's life than Zola did). Nevertheless, he made it very clear that he was deeply troubled by the conclusions that readers were likely to draw from Lantier's failure, although he protested that he 'refused to believe' that that represented Zola's view of Impressionism. Evidently Monet felt that it was better to have Zola as a tepid friend than an enemy. Fortunately Monet's fears of the power of literature proved exaggerated and, *L'Œuvre* had no discernible influence on the public response to Impressionism.

Soon afterwards Monet received an invitation to go to Holland, issued by the Secretary to the French Embassy at The Hague. His love of tulips was undiminished and he spent a pleasant fortnight painting the great expanses of the flowers cultivated by the Dutch. A picture such as *Tulip Fields with Rijnsberg Windmill* (pages 162-3) expresses his delight, turning a subject usually perceived as neat and orderly into a riot of colour.

Monet refused to show anything at the eighth Impressionist exhibition, which was held in mid-May on the premises of the Maison Dorée, at the junction of the Rue Lafitte and the Boulevard des Italiens. Renoir and Sisley also held off,t and other developments made it clear that Impressionism as a movement was dead. Pissarro had taken up the pointillist technique, which involved building up a picture with tiny, regular dots of colour, and the exhibitors included the greatest pointillist master, the youthful Georges Seurat (1859–91), who showed his huge *Sunday Afternoon on the Grande Jatte*, as well as works by two of his followers. Seurat's technique represented a 'scientific' elaboration of Impressionism, and the new movement was known as Neo-Impressionism; but the final result, cool and monumental, was very different from anything painted by Manet, Monet or Renoir. Other newcomers, such as Gauguin, were also developing alternative, decorative approaches to painting, while Renoir, like Pissarro, had become dissatisfied with Impressionism and was attempting to forge a more 'classical' style. Unsurprisingly, the eighth exhibition was the last ever held.

Paradoxically, although Monet had remained faithful to Impressionism, his canvases were now seen in the up-market galleries of Georges Petit, to whose fifth International Exhibition he contributed in June. In a letter to Berthe Morisot he noted with satisfaction that everything had been sold for good prices and to the right sort of client. However, Monet was still keeping several irons in the fire, having sent a number of paintings in January to a new avant-garde show, Les Vingt (The Twenty), in Brussels.

Figures in the Landscape

Like Pissarro and Renoir, Monet seems to have felt a certain staleness and dissatisfaction in the later 1880s, although his response involved a change in subject-matter rather than style. With the exception of one or two small-scale portraits, mainly of the Monet-Hoschedé children, he had virtually abandoned figure painting in the later 1870s. In the summer of 1886 he entered a new phase in which figures intermittently appeared in his canvases, especially when he was working at home in Giverny.

A possible explanation for this development is that Monet was spurred on by a sense of competition with Seurat and Renoir, feeling the need to assert the continuing validity and versatility of the

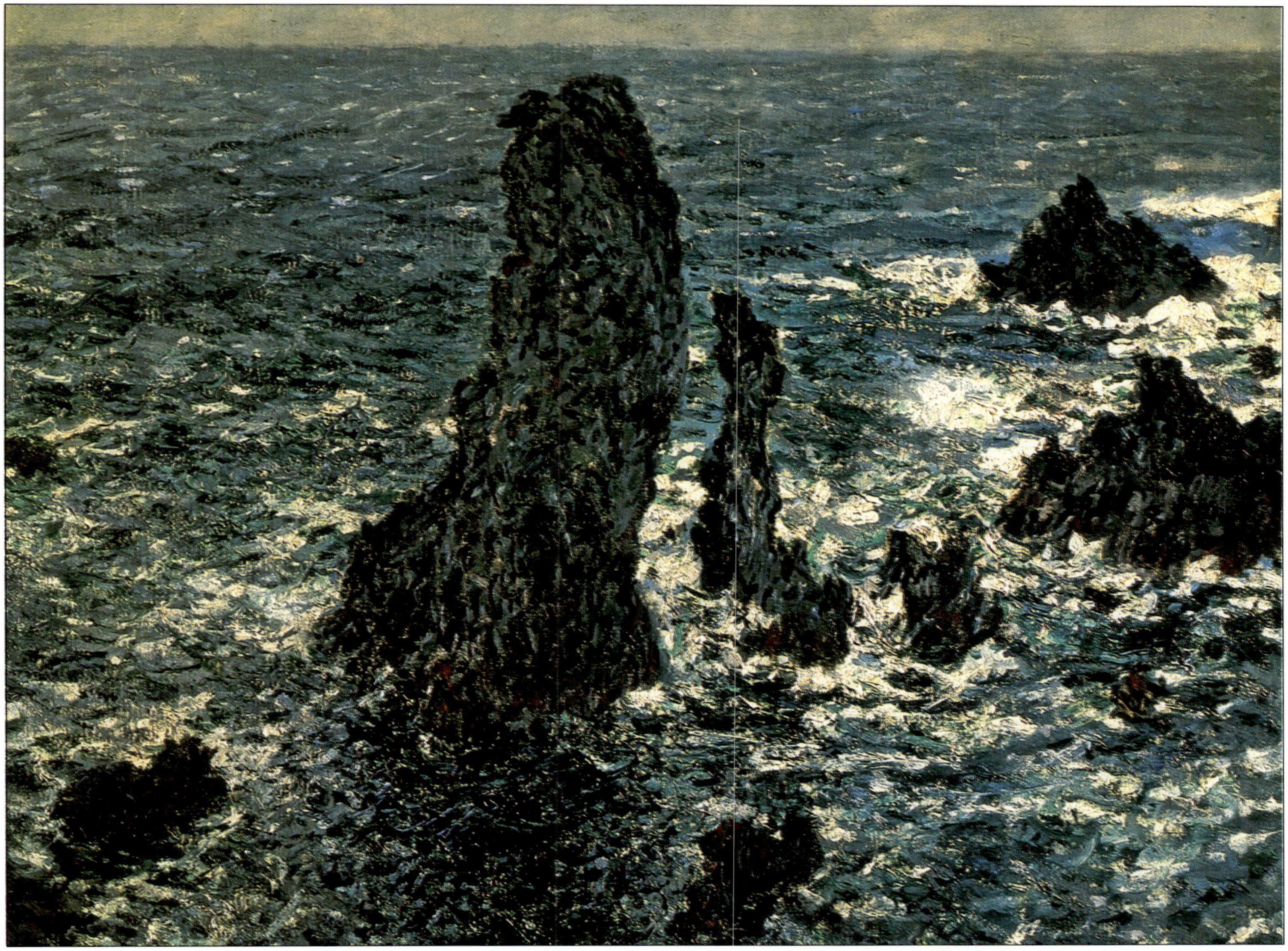

ABOVE:
Rocks at Belle-Ile (1886)
PUSHKIN MUSEUM, MOSCOW

Impressionist technique. An alternative, more prosaic view of the reappearance of human figures is that the children were growing up and the summer prettiness of the girls in particular reminded Monet of past pictures and past summers, in which Camille and one of her boys promenaded by a riverside or along the top of a cliff.

There is certainly a striking resemblance between a gusty *Promenade* of 1875, in which Camille and Jean are seen from below, standing on a cliff top, and two large canvases painted by Monet in 1886. Suzanne Hoschedé posed on the river bank for these works, both known as *Lady with a Parasol*, in which she faces right in one and left in the other; they are not mirror images of each other, however, although a 'family likeness' undoubtedly links them, along with the earlier *Promenade*. *Lady with a Parasol (facing left)* (page 165) has a slightly more pronounced sense of movement, with Suzanne leaning backwards to brace herself against the strong following breeze that is whipping away her veil, pressing her skirts forward and thrusting through the grass and flowers. The trailing scarf is an important element in the composition, carrying the clouds along with it and so setting the entire sky in motion.

Unlike *The Promenade*, in which Monet portrays Camille with a sad or anxious expression, Suzanne is virtually faceless; despite her prominence in the pictures, she is another of Monet's figures in a landscape. He offered an unusually explicit statement of his aims at this time in a letter to Duret: he was working on a new project, painting 'figures in the open air ... treated like landscapes'. This was 'an old dream of mine', he explained, and we have seen that almost all of Monet's figure painting can be viewed in this way. In the lovely *Springtime* (pages 166-7), also painted in 1886, the human element is very much a part of the landscape, and the white jacket of the figure on the left, barred with blue shadows, seems almost to be melting into the background. The colour harmonies and fascinating web of trees are reminiscent of Pissarro's orchard paintings – perhaps an ironic reminder of what Monet's old friend had turned his back on when he took up (temporarily, as it turned out) the pointillist technique of Seurat and his followers.

In 1886 Monet also painted a self-portrait. As far as we know, this was the first he had ever done; and there was not to be a second for another 30 years (page 222). Monet's lack of interest in his own features – at least as an artistic motif – was in fact typical of the outward-looking Impressionists. By contrast, Post-Impressionist masters, such as Cézanne, Gauguin and Van Gogh, were introspective to the point of self-obsession; Monet's canvas could, no doubt, be interpreted as a momentary response to the changing artistic weather. However, although the artist has shown himself with a somewhat self-questioning expression, this can hardly be reckoned a deeply introspective painting. Dressed in a blue working coat and a stylishly worn beret, Monet is evidently a man in the prime of life (still only 45), self-portrayed with a freshness that points up his keenness and vigour. The painting makes a kind of sunburst effect, thanks to the fact that the areas around the edge of the canvas have been left bare. This may be a happy accident, since Monet's stepson, Jean-Pierre Hoschedé, has recorded the fact that the artist never bothered about the edges while a canvas was in his possession, filling them in as a chore when a work was to be exhibited or sold – and that was never the case with the *Self-Portrait*, which Monet always kept by him.

He continued to produce figure works in the later 1880s, between trips away from Giverny which were made for a very different kind of painting, until about 1890, when he gave up for good. His models were always members of his extended family, although on one occasion he did plan to hire a professional, only to be told by Alice that if he did, she would leave the house at once. Monet capitulated, but probably without much regret, since he had made a lifelong habit of taking his models from his immediate circle of family and friends. In 1887 he painted several very large canvases of the Hoschedé daughters on the river, which certainly do go beyond his usual practice of producing 'figures in a landscape'. In *The Boat at Giverny* (page 169), also known as *In the Norvégienne*, the dappled light and reflections focus attention on the girls in a way that is rather unusual in Monet's work, and the absence of sky, the idiosyncratic stance of the youngest girl, Germaine, and the careful observation of Suzanne and Blanche's costumes all work in the same direction. This canvas and *Boating on the Epte* (pages 170-1) are among the most 'personal' that Monet created, with models whose identity is not in question and painted with an eye to their individual appearance. *Boating on the Epte* nonetheless has a rich, tapestry-like feeling, created by the close, skyless greenery and the mass of trailing underwater grasses enclosing the pinks and reds of the boat and the girls. The composition is audaciously asymmetrical, with both girls on the right-hand side of the picture and radical cropping that has eliminated almost half the canoe. These arresting pictures, being 'untypical' of Monet's output, have tended to receive less attention than they deserve. In 1890, when Monet's family feeling as an artist seems to have reached a climax, he painted one of his few portraits, of a deeply reflective *Suzanne with Sunflowers*.

At the very heart of the extended family, tensions continued to exist between Monet and Alice because of the irregular nature of their union. Ironically, Alice's strong religious faith made it impossible for her to seek a divorce from Ernest Hoschedé and rectify the situation, and she made rather unconvincing attempts to conceal the nature of her relations with Monet from the children and keep up a respectable front. Despite this, the Monet-Hoschedé household was a close-knit one, so much so that Blanche Hoschedé eventually (1897) married Monet's son Jean. By the mid-1880s Blanche had taken up painting and often accompanied her stepfather on his trips around Giverny; on one of these he painted her at work in front of her easel (page 173). She modelled her style on Monet's and during the twentieth century dishonest dealers have sometimes tried to pass off her work as his.

Wave-battered Belle-Ile

Although he insisted that his heart remained behind at Giverny, Monet continued to take long, solitary trips away from the family. In the autumn of 1886, as though reacting against human figures and domesticated landscapes, Monet returned to the sea. Metaphorically speaking, he plunged into it deeper than ever, travelling to Belle-Ile, a bleak little island off the south coast of Brittany. Unlike the cliffs and beaches of his familiar haunts in Normandy, the dark Breton rocks looked straight out into the Bay of Biscay and the Atlantic, which pounded them relentlessly.

Monet was soon caught up by the titanic struggle between the mighty rocks and the ferocious ocean. In his Belle-Ile seascapes all traces of humanity are notably absent; they are not needed to convey a sense of scale, as the wild grandeur of the setting makes its magnitude unmistakable. By contrast with even the dramatic Etretat canvases, there is no room in these elemental scenes for the softening, trivializing presence of human beings, their boats or habitations. Even the sky is an intruder, and Monet's paintings either have very high horizons or are seen from above so that everything but rock and water is entirely excluded.

In reality the struggle is an unequal one, since the seemingly powerful shapes of the rocks have themselves been created by the action of the waves. Monet exaggerated the spikiness of the 'Needles' or 'Pyramids' of Port-Coton in *Rocks at Belle-Ile* (page 175), as if anticipating their future shapes; and deluge in *Storm: Rocks at Belle-Ile* (page 179) might well be taken to foreshadow the eventual victory of the watery element.

The intensity of Monet's colours and the boldness of the contrasts accentuate the sense of a drama played out in these non-human land- and sea-scapes. (Indeed, they might almost be pre- or post-human.) This is not a merely fanciful interpretation of Monet's work: he himself described the scenes he wished to paint as 'sinister', 'fearful' and 'sombre'. He was aware that he had tackled nothing quite like them before and, with a typical mixture of motives, told both Durand-Ruel and Alice that extending his range was an artistic duty and would also, in the long run, be good for sales.

Monet's struggles to paint these canvases were appropriately heroic, in a physical as well as an artistic sense. At the inn where he had his meals, he encountered a young radical journalist and art critic, Gustave Geffroy; the two had never met before, although three years earlier Geffroy had devoted an admiring article to the

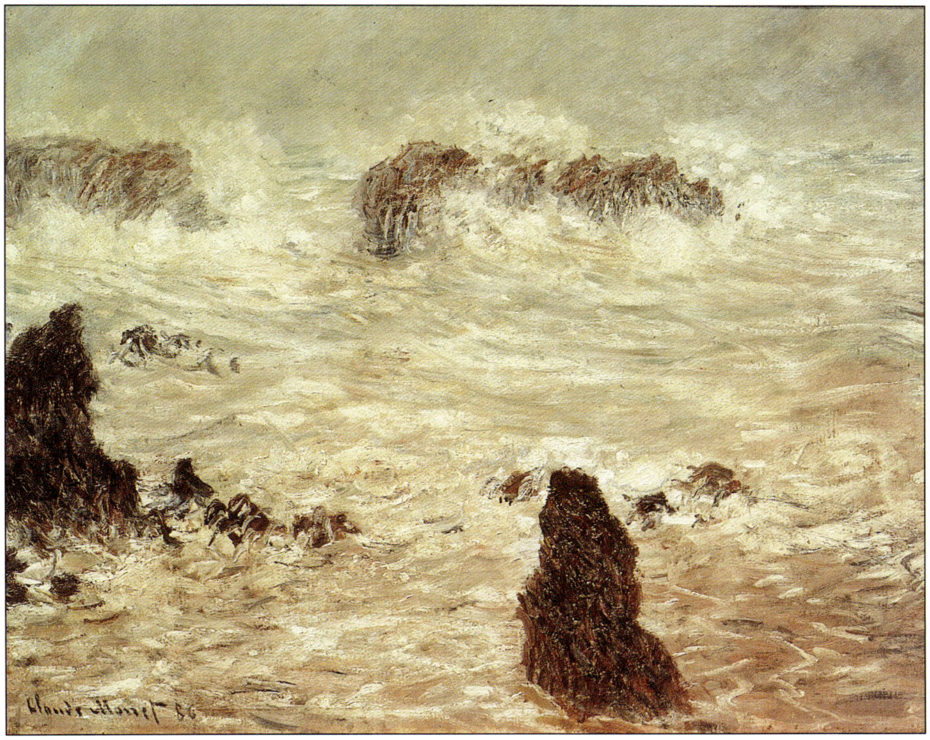

LEFT:
Storm: Rocks at Belle-Ile (1886)
MUSÉE D'ORSAY, PARIS

painter in the newspaper *La Justice* and had even corresponded with him. Writing to a friend at this time, Geffroy claimed that the meeting occurred because he had inadvertently occupied Monet's reserved table. However, it seems unlikely that there were more than two middle-class men staying at the tiny hamlet of Kervilhaouen and patronizing a fisherman's hostelry in winter on a remote little island, so the idea that they can have been unaware of each other's presence is not very plausible! No doubt Geffroy was indulging in a little harmless myth-making, for in a later account he stated more soberly that 'a meeting was easily arranged'. There may also have been an element of exaggeration in his description of Monet as 'a tanned and bearded tough' with a pipe stuck in his mouth, dressed in heavy clothes and big boots. They struck up a friendship at once and Geffroy accompanied Monet on some of his expeditions. His eye-witness reports confirm that Monet really did start several pictures in the course of a single afternoon, working with extraordinary speed to establish the basic colour relationships on each canvas. He could then go on with whichever of them suited the prevailing light, taking the entire group to the point at which they could be given the finishing touches in the studio at Giverny.

Geffroy also describes the unremitting hostility of the elements on Belle-Ile. Monet worked on in the wind and rain, his easel tied into place with ropes and weighted down with stones, but on occasion a gust of wind would seize on the brushes and palette and tear

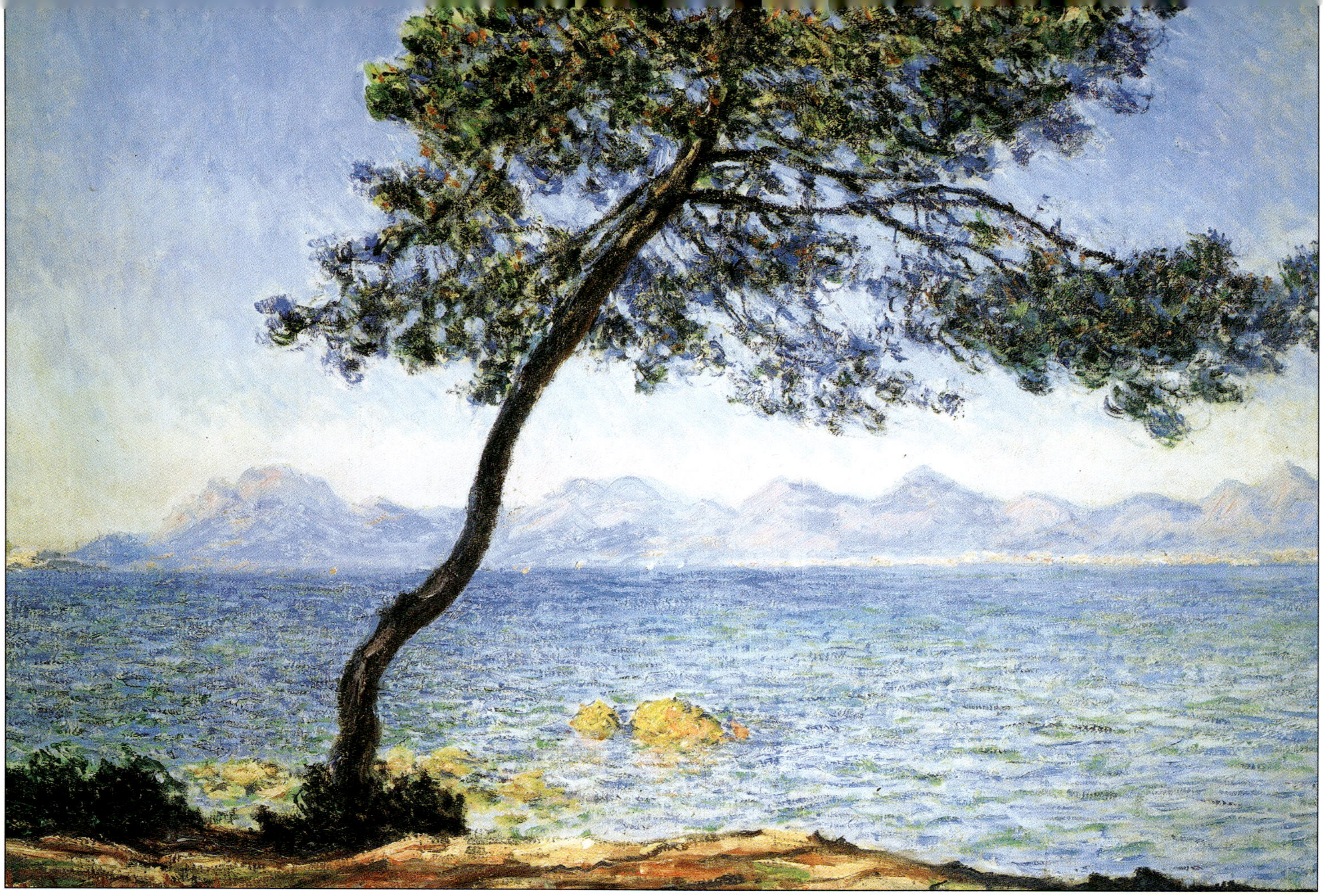

ABOVE:
Antibes (1888)
COURTAULD INSTITUTE GALLERIES, LONDON

them out of his hands. Just as he had toiled up and down slopes under the Mediterranean sun at Bordighera, he now withstood the ocean blasts at Belle-Ile. Obviously Monet could not have been Monet without the ox-like strength and stamina that are apparent even in the many photographs of his stocky, foursquare figure that were taken in his old age.

For most of his stay Monet must have lived a fairly solitary life, although Octave Mirbeau visited him for a week in November and provoked some amused exasperation by the extravagance of his praise for Monet's canvases. Despite his isolation and the harshness of Belle-Ile's aptly-named 'savage coast', Monet was as wildly enthusiastic about the place as he had been about the brilliant hues of the South. His letters to Alice are filled with comparable superlatives and the outcome was the same: he stayed for three months instead of one, writing regularly to pacify and reassure Alice. When he returned at last in November, he brought back with him 39 canvases which represent the culmination of his emotional and dramatic phase. However, not being cut all to a pattern, Monet had also taken time out to paint an unusual portrait of a weather-beaten fisherman, Poly, whom he employed to carry his painting gear; he kept it all his life as a souvenir of his wild and strange stay at Belle-Ile.

The Belle-Ile canvases had the kind of dramatic impact that was easy for spectators and critics to appreciate, and the notices were excellent when they were shown in May 1887 at Petit's sixth International Exhibition. After painting some memorable river pictures during the summer, Monet decided to return to the South, where he could produce works in the greatest possible contrast to the raging seas at Belle-Ile. In January 1888 he began a three-month stay at the Château de la Pinede, a kind of artist's hotel at Antibes. Once more his letters were full of delight in the luminous blues, pinks and golds of the area (this time Antibes and the neighbouring Juan-les-Pins about 30 kilometres west of Menton). However, there are hints that Monet found the weather just a little too perfect and was sometimes afraid that there was not enough variety in the scenes he was painting. At any rate, the works executed on this trip were sweeter and more serene than the Bordighera paintings of 1884, although the South still brought out in him an unexpected taste for flowing curves, seen in the well-known *Antibes* (page 180).

On Monet's return, ten of his new paintings were bought by Theo van Gogh, who was in charge of the Paris branch of Boussod and Valadon, dealers with premises in the Boulevard Montmartre. Theo is a character of considerable interest, both as the supportive, long-suffering brother of Vincent van Gogh and as a perceptive buyer whose taste for Impressionist paintings was not always shared by his employers. He had been acquiring canvases by Monet for some time, and in 1888 he made an arrangement by which Boussod's was to have the first offer of the painter's works, pay him 1,000 francs down and go halves on any profits on sales. Before showing at Boussod's, Monet snubbed an offer to take part in a mixed exhibition put on by Durand-Ruel. His relations with his old dealer did eventually recover from the shock of this new alliance, but henceforth Monet was in a position to play the Parisian firms off against one another, hypocritically writing letters in which he would take credit for his efforts to 'save' canvases from one in order to satisfy a supposedly preferred client such as Durand-Ruel. The fact that Boussod's sold so much of its stock to the United States gave Monet's games-playing an extra piquancy, since these 'savings' took on the air of patriotic gestures!

The show at Boussod's was a success with both the public and the critics, who increasingly took their cues from Monet allies such as Geffroy, Mirbeau and Duret. Monet's fellow Impressionists

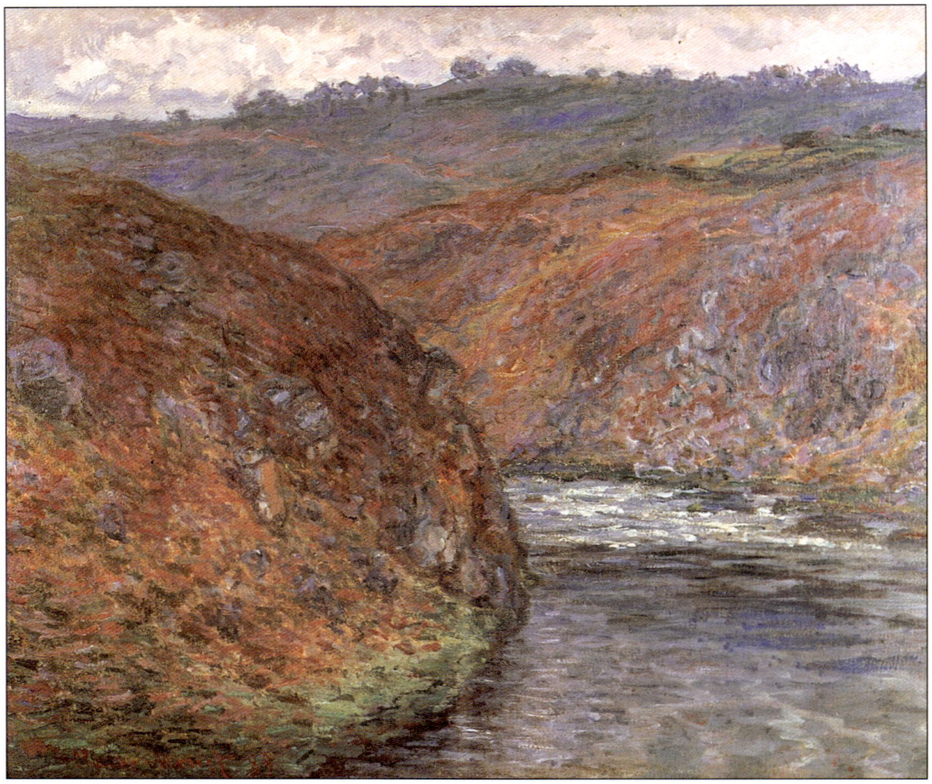

RIGHT:
Valley of the Creuse, Cloudy Day (1889)
HEYDT MUSEUM, WUPPERTAL

were less admiring; Pissarro thought that the Antibes paintings were beautiful as far as they went, but it was beauty 'of a low order', while Degas dismissed them as simply 'done to make a sale'. No doubt there was more than a handful of sour grapes in their remarks, but they were perceptive in noticing a shift in Monet's works towards a rather more decorative approach. Only Berthe Morisot was more generous, letting Monet know that 'You have really won over the public, despite its obstinacy. The visitors at Goupil's [the old name for Boussod and Valadon] are all full of admiration for your work.'

In July Monet took a short trip to London, staying with the American-born painter James McNeill Whistler, whose work had affinities with that of the Impressionists. Despite his modernity and devastatingly offensive wit, Whistler had by this time overcome the worst opposition and had made a successful career in Britain. Later in the year, as President of the Royal Society of British Artists, he ensured that four paintings by Monet were shown at the Society's exhibition.

A New Series

On his return, Monet went to Giverny and started work on a group of paintings of *Haystacks* which must have sown the seeds of the later series (pages 186-91). The five canvases dating from this summer proved to be the first of many, but work on them was interrupted by exhibition plans and another new painting experience. In February 1889 Monet was one of a party that accompanied Gustave Geffroy on a visit to his friend, the poet-composer Maurice Rollinat at La Pouge, his home in the remote little town of Fresselines; Geffroy later claimed that he had invited Monet in order to interest him in the local landscape.

In the event, the bleak, rugged countryside of this part of central France seized Monet's imagination at once. At the end of his stay he hurried back to Giverny to collect his painting gear and head right back to Fresselines. His three-month campaign in the valley of the Creuse was hindered by bad weather, and Monet's letters are as full of fears and laments as usual. He had come in order to confront a stern, wintry landscape, but he was soon worrying that his views of 'this terrible wilderness' would be intolerably gloomy. The coming of spring posed even greater problems, since every time he returned to a subject he found it changed. Everything was growing and blossoming, and the river was rising and falling, making it impossible for him to keep in step: 'I am just running after nature without being able to catch her up.' On one occasion Monet, less concerned with absolute authenticity than some of his admirers, hired men to cut off the burgeoning leaves that had appeared on an oak tree since he had begun to paint it! Despite all the difficulties, he finally managed to complete over 20 paintings, including a number of near-identical views of the valley at the point where the Great and Little Creuse rivers met. Painted with an extraordinary variety of colour schemes, corresponding to different weather and times of day, *The Valley of the Creuse, Cloudy Day* (page 182) and its companions take the concept of a series a step further.

The climate of public opinion had also changed, and at last for the better. One important indicator was the great International Exhibition of 1889 which opened in Paris. Such exhibitions were showpieces of industrial and cultural progress, and the host nation inevitably chose only exhibits of which it was unquestionably proud. In this instance, the Exhibition also celebrated the centenary of the French Revolution, and its high point – literally – was the opening of the Eiffel Tower. Consequently the inclusion of works by Monet in the concurrent Centennial Exhibition of French Art, along with Manet, Pissarro and a host of more conventional artists, was a real sign that Impressionism had quietly become part of the French tradition.

A fortnight later, on 21 June, 1889, Monet can be said finally to have 'arrived'. The doors of the Galerie Georges Petit opened on a great joint exhibition of work by Monet and the sculptor Auguste Rodin; curiously enough, the two men had been born on the very same day. More clearly than Monet had ever been in painting Rodin was the head of the modern school in sculpture. His greatness was no longer in question, yet his works continued to scandalize; *The Burghers of Calais*, on show for the first time at this exhibition, had appalled the municipal authorities of Calais who had commissioned it, and later projects such as Rodin's *Balzac* (1898) caused uproar and outrage. For Monet to partner Rodin, unaccompanied, was an event that put the painter's stature beyond question, and he had devoted a good deal of effort making sure there would be no third party.

The importance of the occasion was all the more apparent in view of its scale. The catalogue, complete with prefaces by Mirbeau and Geffroy, listed 145 works by Monet and 36 by Rodin. The exhibition was, in effect, a 25-year Monet retrospective, beginning with canvases painted as far back as 1864 and culminating in a group of the Creuse Valley paintings which themselves anticipated the work of the following quarter-century and beyond. There was a good deal of ill feeling between Monet and Rodin when Monet discovered that some of the arrangements had been changed without anyone consulting him, and he convinced himself that his works had become near-invisible behind quantities of stone and bronze. However, the critics had no difficulty in seeing them and, faced with the efforts of half a lifetime, their response was friendly and favourable.

Almost immediately after the joint exhibition, as though filled with a new sense of his eminence and responsibilities, Monet launched a public campaign to save Manet's great nude, *Olympia* (page 185), for the nation. Berthe Morisot encouraged him, writing 'You alone, with your name and reputation, can break down the doors – if they can be broken down'. Monet was spurred on by rumours that Manet's widow, who was in financial difficulties, might sell the painting to an American. There were, in fact, two campaigns that had to be carried on: to organize a subscription fund to raise 20,000 francs in order to buy the picture; and to persuade the French state to accept it as a gift. In some respects the second task was the more difficult, as the official art world was still hostile

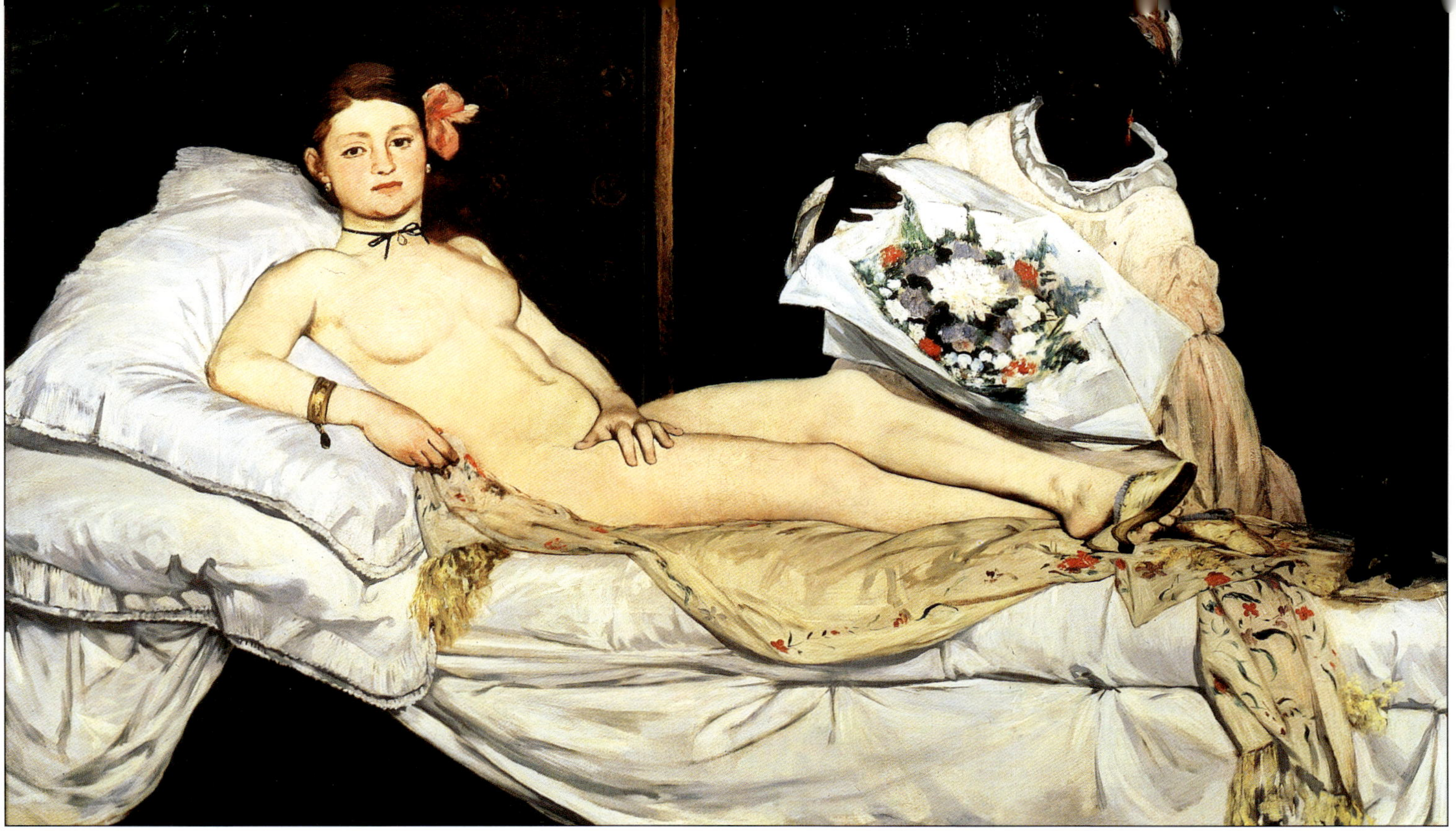

ABOVE:
Olympia (1863)
Edouard Manet
Musée d'Orsay,
Paris

and the government of the day inevitably took its views very seriously. At times the argument grew heated, and Monet was almost involved in a duel with the Commissioner for Fine Arts, Antonin Proust. Finally *Olympia* was accepted, as Monet had tactfully suggested, for the collections of the Musée du Luxembourg – not the Louvre, but a national museum that was recognized as a kind of antechamber to the Louvre; and, as expected, the painting was transferred to the premier museum in 1907.

The *Olympia* had always been a controversial painting, and even in 1890 there were grumbles and sniggers at the idea of admitting such a shamelessly modern piece of womanhood into the company of smoothly graceful classical nudes. Alive to the ludicrousness of this viewpoint, Monet treasured a cartoon in which Olympia entered the hall of sculpture on the arm of a frock-coated gentlemen, like a cockney flower-girl led before a party of duchesses. Here and elsewhere, the portrayal of the self-possessed Olympia as a cheeky slattern says a good deal about nineteenth-century ideals of womanhood. By securing her place in the Louvre, Monet posthumously cleared off his debt to Manet, but he also enhanced his own reputation and prospects. Although he had never painted anything remotely resembling *Olympia*, in the public mind he had always been one of 'Manet's gang' and was now behaving like a dutiful heir. If Manet went through the door into the Luxembourg and Louvre, Monet would be sure to follow in time.

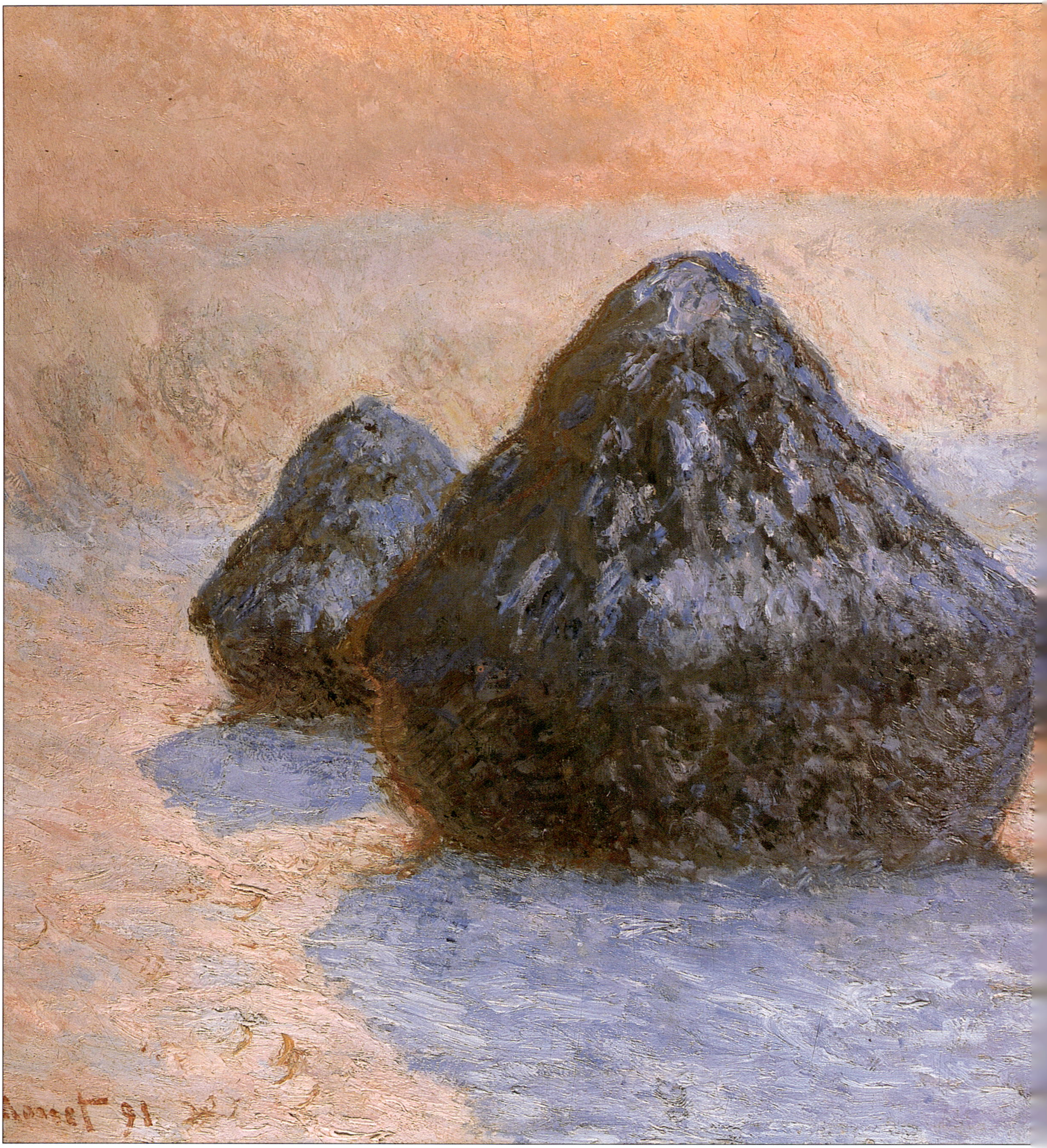

CHAPTER NINE

The Series Paintings

MONET'S ORGANIZATION of the *Olympia* campaign also served to obscure the fact that he had stopped working; for almost a year he seems not to have painted anything. However, if this interruption in his normally prolific productivity represented some sort of artistic crisis, Monet kept the fact to himself; and when the pause was over he entered yet another phase of intense creativity.

Once he had carried the Olympia project to a successful conclusion, Monet took up his brushes again. His urge to travel was temporarily spent and over the next two years the landscape of Giverny would inspire important new developments in his work.

Initially, in the spring of 1890, Monet painted the fields, rich with cereals or his brilliant, beloved poppies. The human element once more disappeared, creating the illusion of a happy, empty land. The paintings formed a kind of loose set or series, a concept that had clearly always attracted Monet. From now on, individual paintings without links to a larger group would become increasingly rare in his output.

LEFT:
Haystacks, Snow Effect (1891)
NATIONAL GALLERY OF SCOTLAND

The Haystacks

Towards the end of summer the sight of haystacks being built up in the fields distracted and attracted Monet. He left a number of his current works half done, not even putting finishing touches to canvases already promised to Durand-Ruel, and returned to the thatched houses of hay he had begun painting in 1888. But he tackled the new canvases as a more rigorously related group than he had done before. His own explanation was ingenuously simple; he painted what he saw. One day the light changed so rapidly that he sent his stepdaughter running back to the house for one canvas after another; and that was how the *Haystacks* series was born. 'It isn't difficult to understand,' he added.

Monet's easy-to-understand explanation was a not untypical example of simplification and myth-making after the event, although it is, of course, possible that some such incident played a part in the development of the series concept. In fact, Monet's description is not unlike those given a few years earlier by friends such as Maupassant and Geffroy. The painter often had several canvases in progress at one time, carrying them about, when there were no small boys available, in a special multi-compartment case. But except in the Creuse Valley, a change of light or weather had generally meant a change of subject, whereas it was precisely the identical nature of the subjects that made the *Haystacks* so distinctive. In this series of nearly 30 paintings, there were variations in the number of haystacks (but only a difference between one and two), as also in the size of the canvases and the angle from which the stacks were viewed. Nevertheless, their homogeneity is more striking than these differences, and what distinguishes them most in the eyes of the spectator is, as Monet intended, the light and atmosphere which envelop them.

In fact, it is often asserted that the real subject of these paintings is light; and time and distance make it easy to interpret them in this way. But contemporaries were far from indifferent to the rural quality of the views painted by Monet, and responded increasingly to the notion, which he carefully promoted, that they were the product of work done exclusively and somehow naturally in the open air, without a single second thought to prompt the addition of a few brushstrokes in the studio. Urban and industrial development was already advanced enough to generate nostalgia for the simple certainties of rural life, and something of a cult of 'blood and the soil' was already apparent in literary circles, for

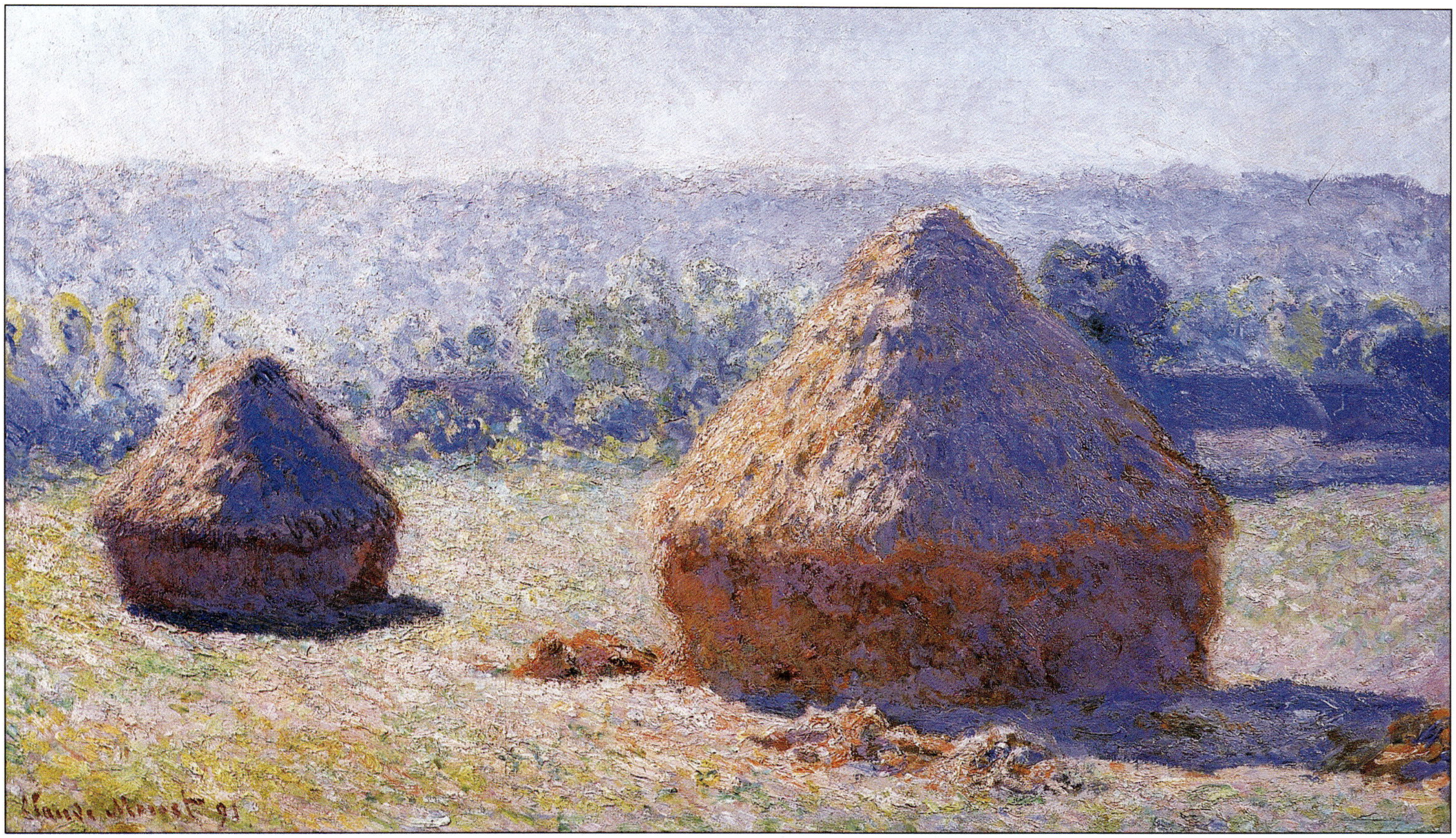

ABOVE:
Haystacks at the End of Summer, Morning (1891)
MUSÉE D'ORSAY, PARIS

example in the writings of Maurice Barrès. Coincidentally, among the great sensations of 1889–90 were the sale to an American of Millet's *The Angelus* (to this day still the most celebrated image of country simplicity and peasant piety), the national outcry that followed and the set of events that culminated in its return to a jubilant France. Whether relevant or not to the *Haystacks* as works of art, this mood certainly made its popular success more likely.

In retrospect, the significance of the series was rather different. It marked an important step away from the tradition of painting subjects that were informative, affecting or entertaining in their own right. To put it crudely, the spectator who passed from one of Monet's canvases to the next was not anticipating the pleasure of looking at another (let alone the same) haystack, but preparing to contemplate a different effect of the light. Moreover, the shift away from an emphasis on the subject had further implications, promoting awareness of the picture as an object in its own right rather than a mirror held up to nature. It is appropriate that the young Wassily Kandinsky had a first glimpse of his future as the founder of abstract painting when he saw one of the *Haystacks* in Moscow; according to his own account, he failed to grasp what it was supposed to represent and as a consequence, experienced a sudden revelation of the emotional charge released by unadulterated colour.

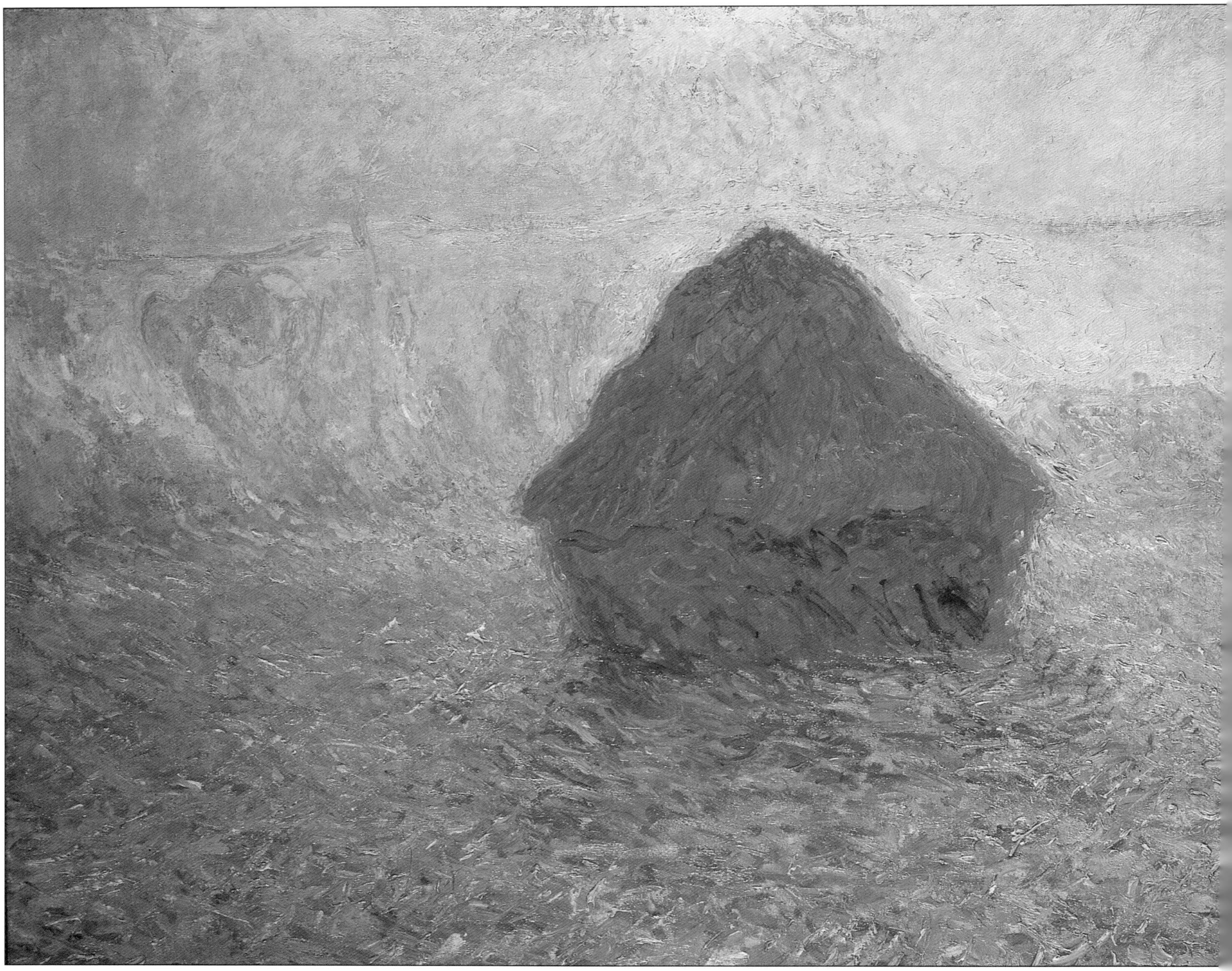

ABOVE:
Haystacks, Hazy Sunshine
(1891)
PRIVATE COLLECTION

The splendours of light and colour are what reach out to the modern viewer of the *Haystacks*, often following a period of puzzlement in the face of the seemingly banal subject matter. On closer examination, it becomes obvious that Monet has carefully selected his viewpoint and simplified the scene so that nothing distracts the attention from his harmonies of colour and atmosphere, which are not all to be found in nature. In other words, although originating as responses to nature, the *Haystacks* are, like so many of Monet's achievements, more deeply premeditated, worked on and carefully finished than he usually admitted.

Monet painted all through the helpfully mild winter of 1890–1, breaking off at last in February. In May, when 15 of the *Haystacks* were shown with other works by Monet at Durand-Ruel's

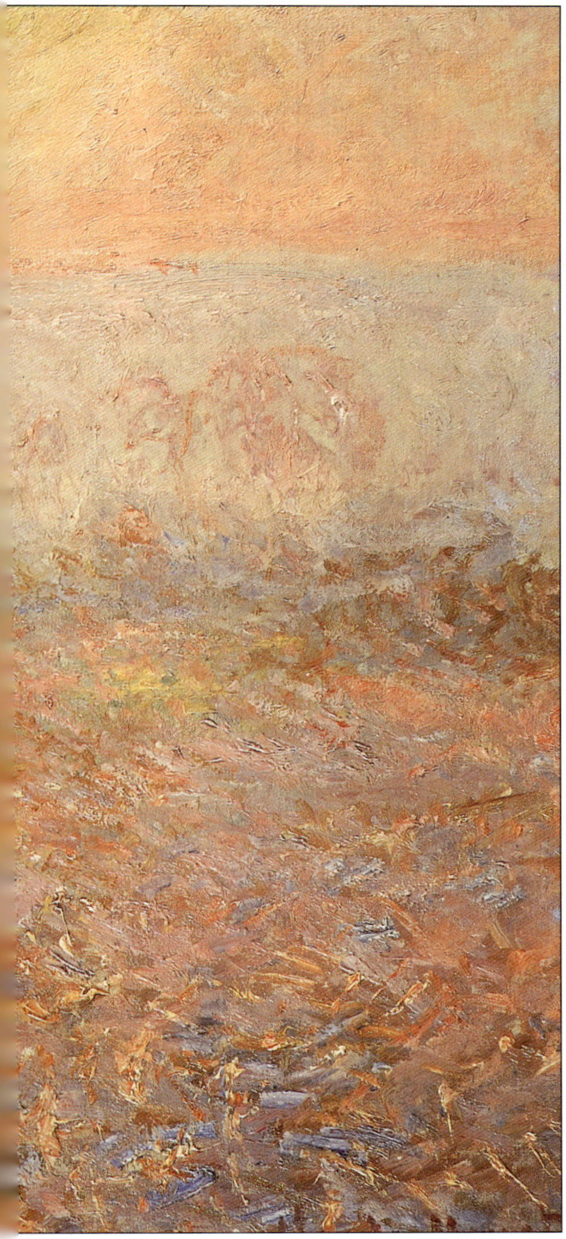

gallery, critics and public alike were wild with enthusiasm and the canvases were sold within days. Even some of his old comrades began to come round. Pissarro's comments were ambiguous but finally admiring: 'These paintings seem to me very luminous and are certainly the work of a master. The colours are pretty rather than strong, the draughtsmanship is fine but drifting, especially in the backgrounds. But all the same he's a very good artist!'

Despite his preoccupation with *Haystacks*, Monet took the important step of settling for good at Giverny: in October 1890 he bought 'Le Pressoir'. In spite of the fact that he was now earning a very large income – his pictures selling for several thousand francs each – the sound of a single echo from his indigent past was still heard: the 20,000 francs he needed were advanced by Durand-Ruel. However, this now seemed less like an act of generosity on Durand's part than a bid to retain some kind of priority over the rival dealers and eager collectors who were descending upon Monet. He and Durand were back on excellent terms, but Monet made it very clear that he had no intention of being tied to a single dealer. Having bought the house, Monet had finally come into his kingdom, making numerous improvements, buying more land and beginning a really thorough transformation of the garden, which was to become a work of art in its own right.

The Poplars

Even before the *Haystacks* went on show at Durand-Ruel's, Monet had begun a new series of paintings. As he had so often done before, he selected motifs that were as unlike the previous ones as possible – in this instance, vertical, slender, leafy and water-lapped in contrast with the broad, sturdy, packed forms of the landlocked haystacks. The new series consisted of views of the poplars that lined the river Epte, not far from his home. He painted most or all of them from his studio-boat, usually emphasizing the low viewpoint so that (again in contrast to the haystacks) they seem to soar into the sky.

The *Poplars* are rendered in wonderfully fresh colours that sometimes go beyond anything found in nature. With the slender parallels of the trees forming grids that often stretch right across the canvas, these paintings are obviously more patterned than the haystacks, signalling a decorative tendency that would become stronger in Monet's work with the years. It had long been implicit in the way that he usually avoided conventional perspective effects, preferring to indicate spatial relationships through the simple overlapping of objects (the near partly obscuring the more distant), and adopting viewpoints and treatments that allowed him to bring as many elements of the scene as possible to the front plane of the picture. On page 193, for example, the sky has been 'brought up' and appears to lie in the same plane as the poplars, to wonderful decorative effect. This technique was typical of the Japanese prints that Monet loved so much – he filled the walls of Giverny with them – as was also the concept of a series, expressed in albums such as Hokusai's *Thirty-Six Views of Mount Fuji.* However, while the influence of Japanese art on Monet seems beyond question, his actual painting technique, with its worked or textured surfaces, produced effects quite distinct from those of the Japanese masters. Both his handling of paint and the way in which he developed the concept of a series were feats of unquestionable originality, with no significant parallels in any artistic tradition.

RIGHT:
Poplars on the Epte
(1891)
TATE GALLERY, LONDON

Monet's paintings were now clearly both pre and post-meditated and yet he remained as committed as ever to working outdoors in order to capture fugitive impressions from which his imagination might take flight. This was highlighted by a telling incident that occurred during one of his poplar-painting sessions. While he was still working on a particular group, its owner, the town council of Limetz, voted to sell it for timber. The trees had been grown for that purpose and the decision was reasonable enough. But when Monet, equally reasonably, asked for a delay while he finished his work, the council refused to alter its decision. Monet thought of an ingenious, if expensive solution to the problem. He approached a local timber merchant, found out how much he was prepared to pay for the poplars when they came up at auction, and offered to make up any difference between the price the merchant could pay and the price needed to acquire the poplars. The merchant could keep the goods, provided that he was willing to delay the logging. The deal was struck, the auction went off successfully and Monet was able to finish his pictures in peace.

In March 1892, 15 of the *Poplars* paintings were put on show at Durand-Ruel's gallery. This was the first time that a series had been the sole subject of an exhibition, but the outcome justified Durand's audacity. Sales were again brisk and even previously hostile critics began to come round. The struggle was over and some of the drama vanished from Monet's public life. Until the 1890s, exhibitions were highly significant, fraught occasions in the history of his fluctuating fortunes; from this time onwards they became no

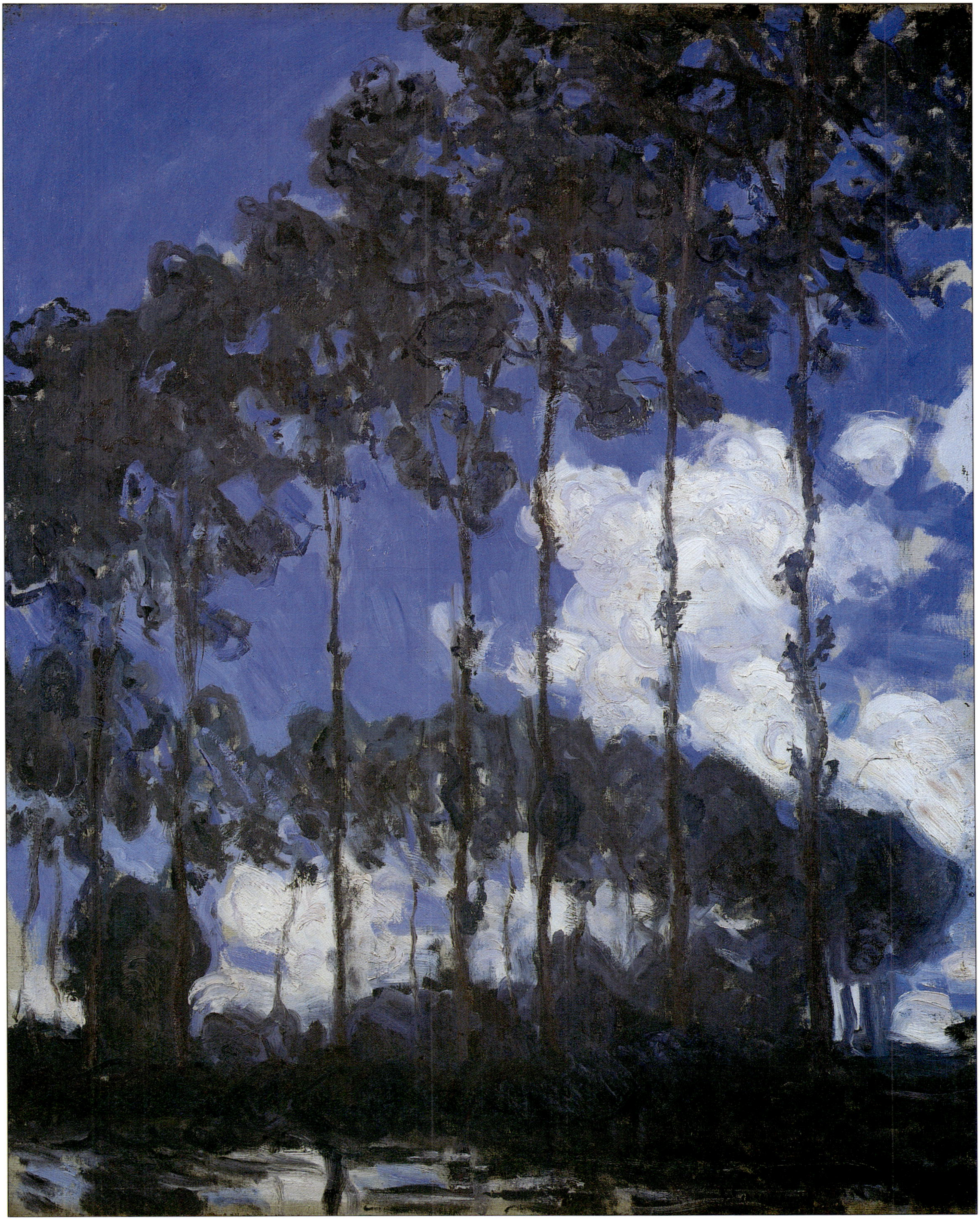

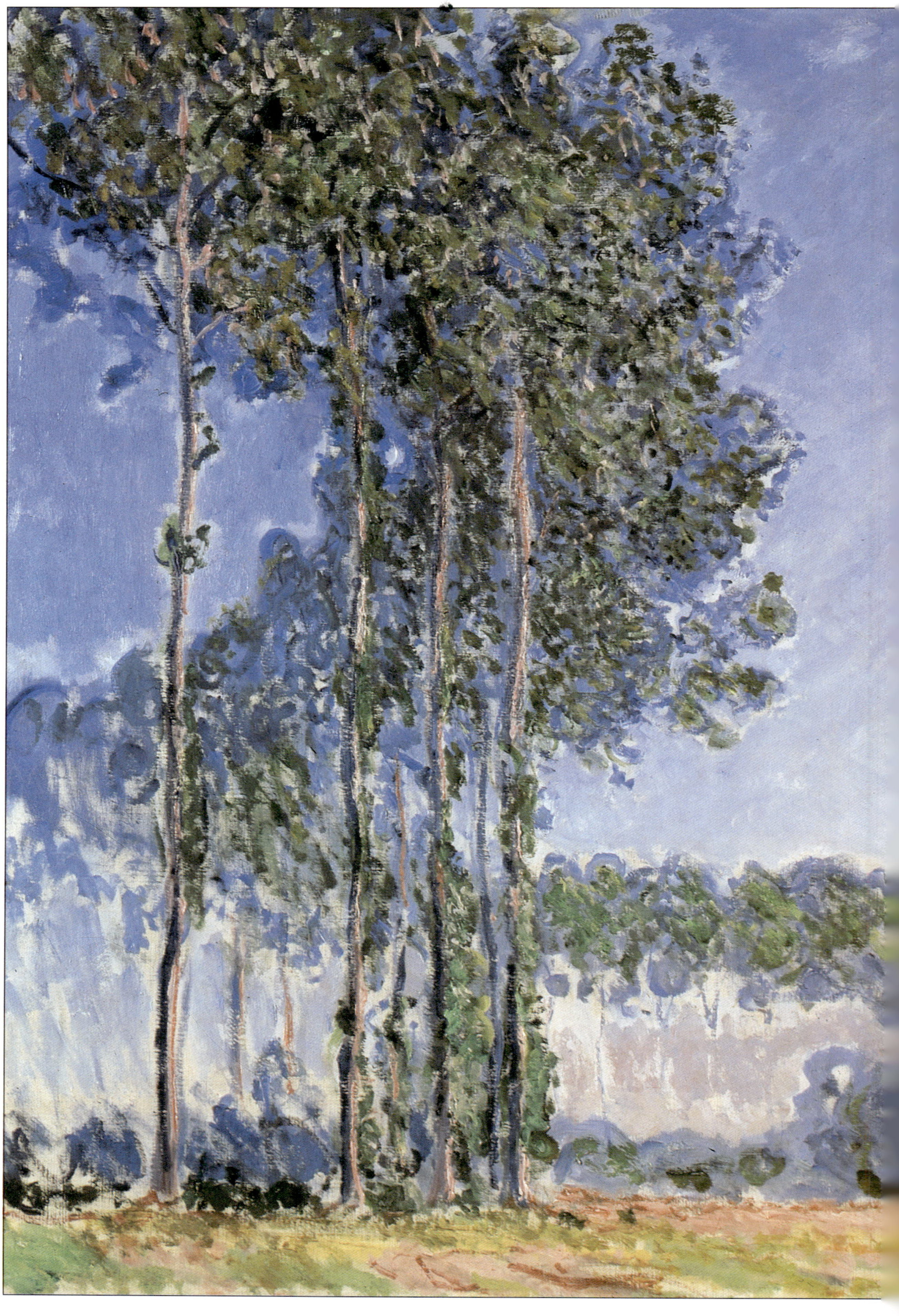

RIGHT:
Poplars on the Epte (1891)
FITZWILLIAM MUSEUM,

more than occasionally interesting events in the career of an acknowledged master.

Abroad, the effect of the 1886 show had been to consolidate the Impressionists' reputation in the United States, where collectors, less inhibited by tradition than their European counterparts, were already buying on a generous scale. By September 1892 the mainline *Century* magazine made no difficulty about publishing an appreciation of Monet by Theodore Robinson which boldly asserted that the Impressionists had definitely arrived: 'When the group of painters known as impressionists exhibited together for the first time twelve or fifteen years ago, they were greeted with much derision. In fact they were hardly taken seriously, being regarded either as mountebanks or as poseurs who served the purpose of furnishing the quick-witted but not infallible Parisians with something to laugh at once a year. But they have seen their influence increase steadily in a remarkable manner, first, as is always the case, with the painters, and latterly with the public.' Robinson, an American painter who had moved to Giverny to be close to Monet, was understandably in no doubt about the leadership of the Impressionists: 'Of them all M. Claude Monet is the most aggressive, forceful painter, the one whose work is influencing the epoch most'. Giving a familiar description of Monet's working methods, Robinson emphasized the extent to which the master's paintings conveyed the joy of living and predicted that his work would be the greatest single influence on the landscape art of the future.

Rouen Cathedral

'Nature never stands still' was, according to Robinson, one of Monet's favourite sayings; it might well have been applied to the artist himself. With careless confidence he again began a new series before the public had been permitted a glimpse of the one he had just completed. After a brief trip to London in December 1891, the start of the following February found him back in Normandy, in a room on the cathedral square in Rouen, painting views of the great Gothic edifice opposite his window. He later stated that the idea of the *Cathedrals* series came to him while he was painting the church at Vernon, just down river from Giverny, but even if this was the literal truth, it hardly explains the way in which Monet put it into practice. The open-air painter retired to a room in order to work, the countryman shut himself up in the city, the landscapist selected a motif that was entirely man-made and non-natural. Moreover, the choice of a cathedral was all the stranger because Monet had only a limited feeling for tradition and was an outspoken agnostic; it is said that during his time in Rouen he never even entered the cathedral until he was given a free ticket to a choral recital. As the completed paintings would show, the series had no meaningful relationship with religious symbols or beliefs.

For the first fortnight of his stay in Rouen, Monet rented an apartment directly opposite the cathedral, which he used as his studio. Then he fell ill and went back to Giverny for ten days to recover. When he returned on 24 February he hired a new set of rooms above a draper's, set at an angle so that he viewed the cathedral façade from slightly to the right. He packed up and left for Giverny in April, only to come back at exactly the same time the following year (1893), evidently determined to exhaust all the effects that the February-to-April period had to offer. This time the draper's rooms were taken and Monet had to be content with an apartment a few doors to the right. It says a good deal for the literalness of his transcriptions from the motif in front of him that the three different vantage points can be deduced from the paintings themselves. When he came to date them, Monet attributed them all to 1894, which probably means that he put the finishing touches to them at Giverny that year; but he may also have wanted to enhance his image by giving the impression that the entire series had been painted in a single, magical burst of creativity.

In reality, the *Cathedrals* took longer and used up more of Monet's psychic energy than any of his previous projects. The intensity of the struggle can be gauged by the fact that he completed 30 canvases in about six months' work – not a large haul for an artist of Monet's fecundity. His letters to Alice are, even more than usual, emotional roller-coasters in which the lows are far more pronounced than the highs. Fluctuations in the weather played their part, but the main cause of his frequent bouts of misery was the intensity of his desire to capture every nuance of the changing light conditions, a passion which seems to have reached a pitch that threatened his sanity: 'each day I discover something that I failed to notice the day before... In the end, I am trying to do the impossible'. The limits of the possible were reached on a day in March 1893 when Monet's 'running after nature' led him to work on 14 separate canvases between dawn and dusk. Understandably, for a time he suffered from nightmares and on one occasion, like some ancient prophet, dreamed that the

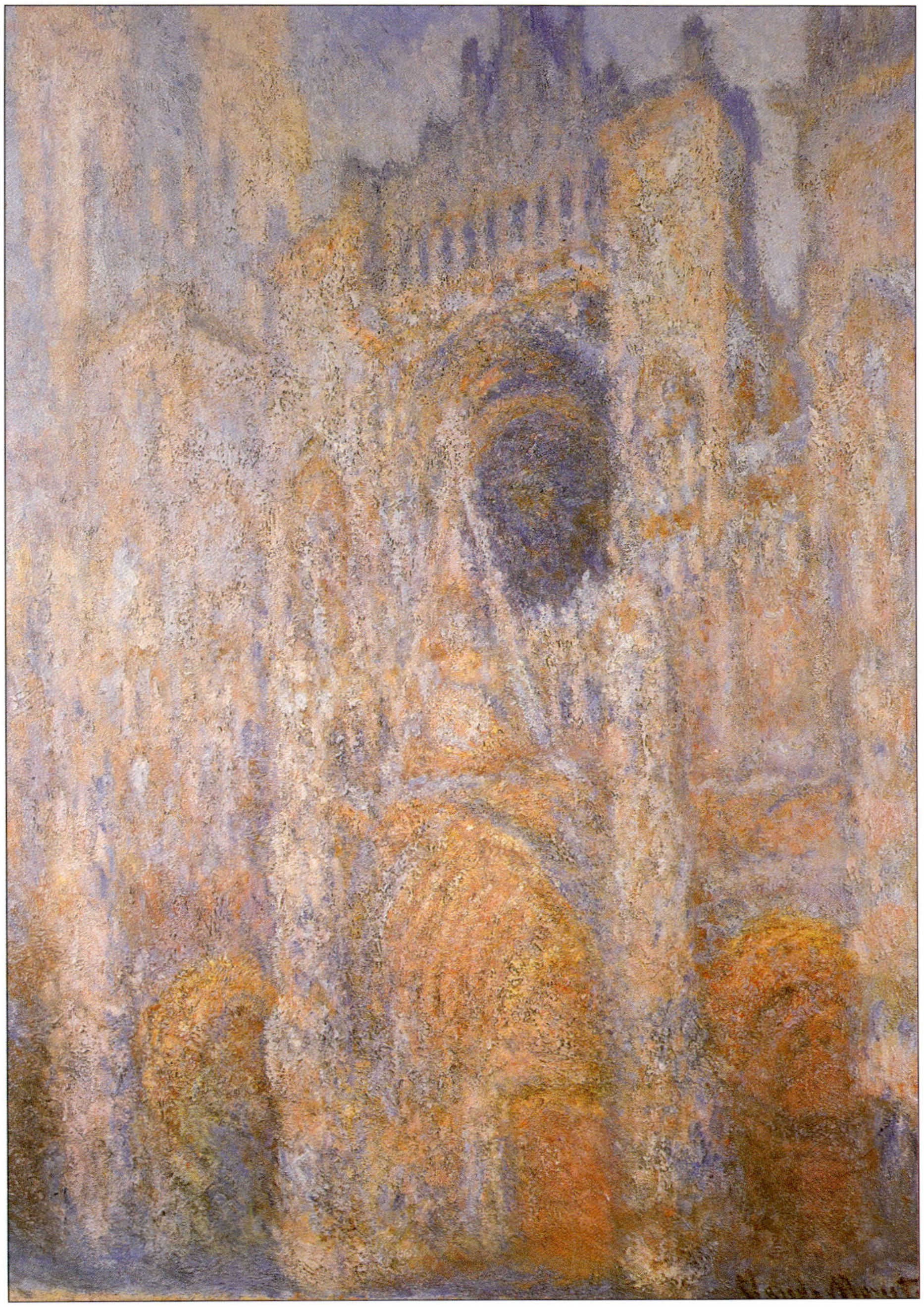

LEFT:
Rouen Cathedral: Morning Sun, Harmony in Blue (1894)
MUSÉE D'ORSAY, PARIS

cathedral was falling on him; interestingly, it was a Mediterranean cathedral that seemed to be coloured 'blue or pink or yellow'.

Monet returned from his first trip to Rouen deeply discouraged, although the subsequent reactions of visitors to Giverny were on the whole heartening. Even when he had finished his second three-month stint he was doubtful of the value of his work, and it is easy to see why. Canvases like these had never been painted before. Beside them, the much derided *Impression: Sunrise* looked conventional and there was little in the *Haystacks* or *Poplars* series to prepare spectators for the innovations to come. Although there may have been other considerations, Monet's fear of renewed pop-

RIGHT:
Rouen Cathedral: Midday (1894)
PUSHKIN MUSEUM, MOSCOW

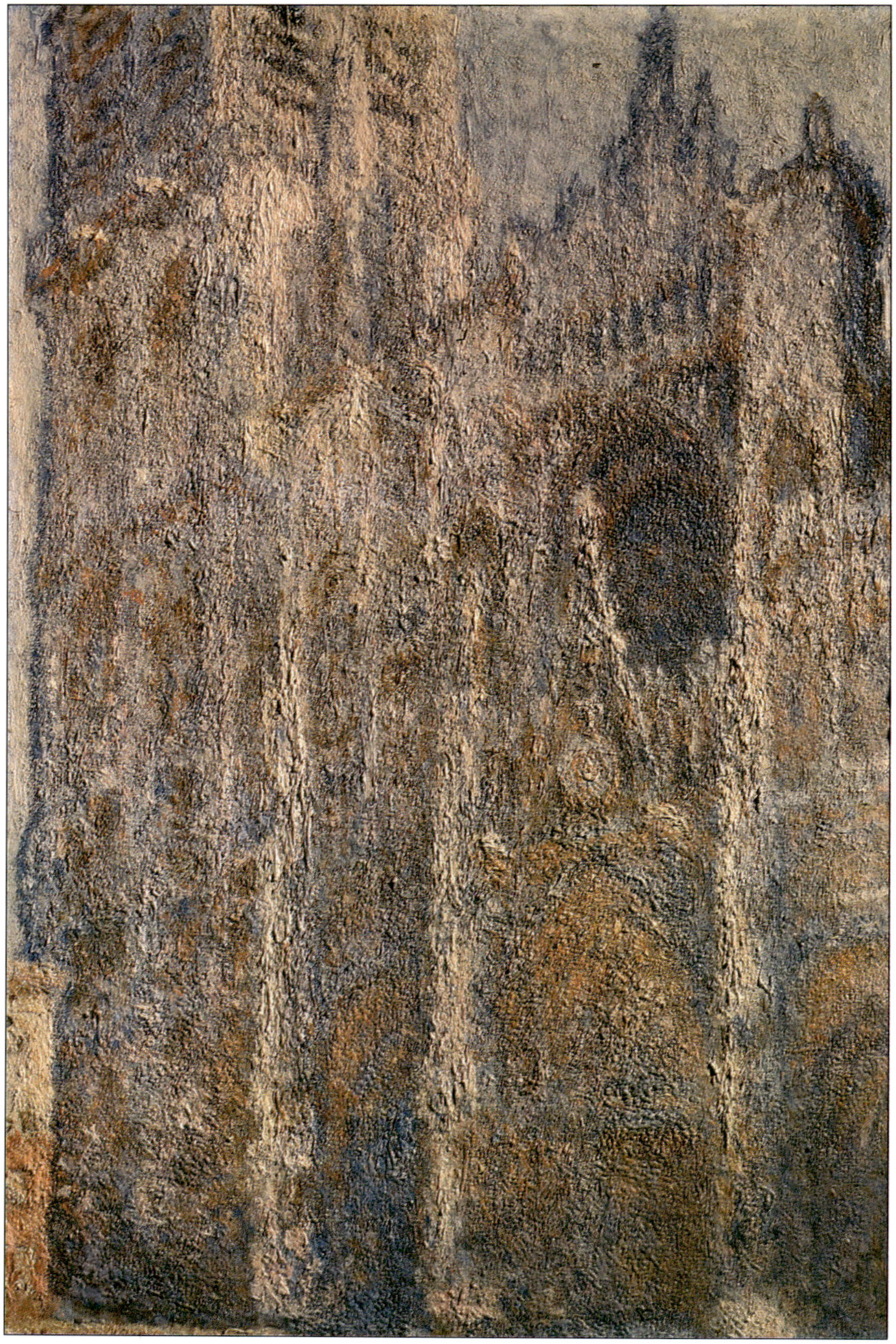

ular misunderstanding of his work was probably the main reason why the *Cathedrals* were not exhibited until 1895, by which time he had probably collected enough favourable private opinions to bolster his self-confidence.

One way of realizing the originality of the *Cathedrals* series is to consider what it does *not* attempt to achieve. In the first place, none of Monet's canvases begin to do justice to the great Gothic cathedral as such – its majestic form, its architectural details, its historic aura or its religious ethos. Although cathedrals and churches had appeared before as merely picturesque elements in view paintings, Monet's pictures were not views in any recognized meaning of the term. In all of them, drastic cropping makes it impossible to see the outline of the entire cathedral, which is shown close up and with no sense of a distance between the artist/spectator and the building; the intervening square is reduced, at best, to a narrow strip which, like the meagre patch of sky, serves only to emphasize the mass of the cathedral. The magnification of motifs by close-ups, already apparent in some of the *Haystacks* (pages 186-91), became one of the most significant features of Monet's later work.

The effect of all this was to minimize the importance of the motif and to focus the attention on light and atmosphere, or, to put it another way, on the actual paint and the colours. Having largely achieved this in the *Haystacks*, Monet now took the next logical step by virtually eliminating variety of scene; 28 of the 30 canvases are closely similar, although still not quite identical, views of the façade. Where it matters, however, they are stunningly, brilliantly different – in the manipulation of colours and the extent to which the forms are dissolved by sunlight, mist and overcast skies. The paint is heaped up on the canvas in a way that has often been described as mimicking the stone of the cathedral; if so, it is stone that responds to light and atmosphere more like an organism than solid inanimate matter. In effect, Monet's *Cathedrals* are a visual equivalent to variations on a theme in music, creating a marvellous diversity out of sameness. It is now possible to see that the elaborate Gothic detail and the patterns of solids and voids on the façade were important elements in Monet's project – not because of their intrinsic artistic or historical value, but because they enabled him to achieve more complex and dramatic effects (patterns of sun-touched ribs of stone, great shadowy ovals, melting stalagmites) than would have been possible with some simpler motif.

Between his two trips to Rouen Monet painted relatively little, especially during the remaining months of 1892. But this was a period of some importance in the affairs of his extended family. After a good deal of grumbling, he allowed the American painter Theodore Butler to marry Suzanne Hoschedé. Rather oddly to our way of thinking, Monet had taken on the role of the stern, conventional Victorian father, frowning on the suitor because he had not followed the proper procedure by first introducing himself to the girl's 'parents' and even objecting to the fact that the young man was a painter (and, therefore, presumably, likely to be an unreliable bohemian). Like many men of a certain age, Monet had evidently forgotten his own early indiscretions, but it is difficult to imagine how he squared his increasingly bourgeois attitudes with the nature of his relations with Alice. He was eventually won round, and on 20 July, 1892, he finally led Suzanne down the aisle. He was able to do so with an aura of complete respectability, since he and Alice were married – an event that had occurred exactly four days before Suzanne's wedding. Although Ernest Hoschedé had died over a year earlier, in March 1891, Monet and Alice had made no preparations to marry (curious, in view of Alice's supposed religious scruples), so it seems likely that they went through the ceremony specifically for Suzanne's sake.

During the winter of 1892–3 Monet painted views of the frozen Seine at Giverny, rendered like somewhat less dramatic reminiscences of Vétheuil in 1880, when Camille had still been alive. By February he was back in Rouen, where the Herculean task of painting the *Cathedrals* left him with relatively little creative energy for the rest of the year.

Julie's Diary

Interesting evidence survives from the autumn of 1893, when Giverny had a visitor who kept a diary. Julie Manet was the daughter of the artist Berthe Morisot, who had always been an ardent supporter of Monet. Her father was Eugène Manet, the brother of the painter of *Olympia*. On 30 October mother and daughter spent the day at Giverny and were shown the *Cathedrals*; Julie believed she had seen 26. Predictably she thought them 'magnificent' and was astonished by the range of colours, but – reading between the lines of her conventional praise – she was not quite sure what to think about the treatment of detail in the pictures.

During their visit Berthe Morisot and Julie were shown over the house and Julie's diary records the decorative scheme adopted by Monet once he had become the owner of Le Pressoir. His white bedroom, with its pitch-pine floor, was hung with works by Renoir, Manet and Pissarro. Alice's bedroom was panelled in blue, Blanche's and Germaine's in mauve. The drawing room, hung with Japanese prints, was panelled in violet. The dining room was entirely yellow (actually two different yellows). In many respects the interior was an example of typically 'advanced' late-nineteenth-century

RIGHT:
Rouen Cathedral: Harmony in Blue and Gold, Full Sunlight
(1894)
MUSÉE D'ORSAY, PARIS

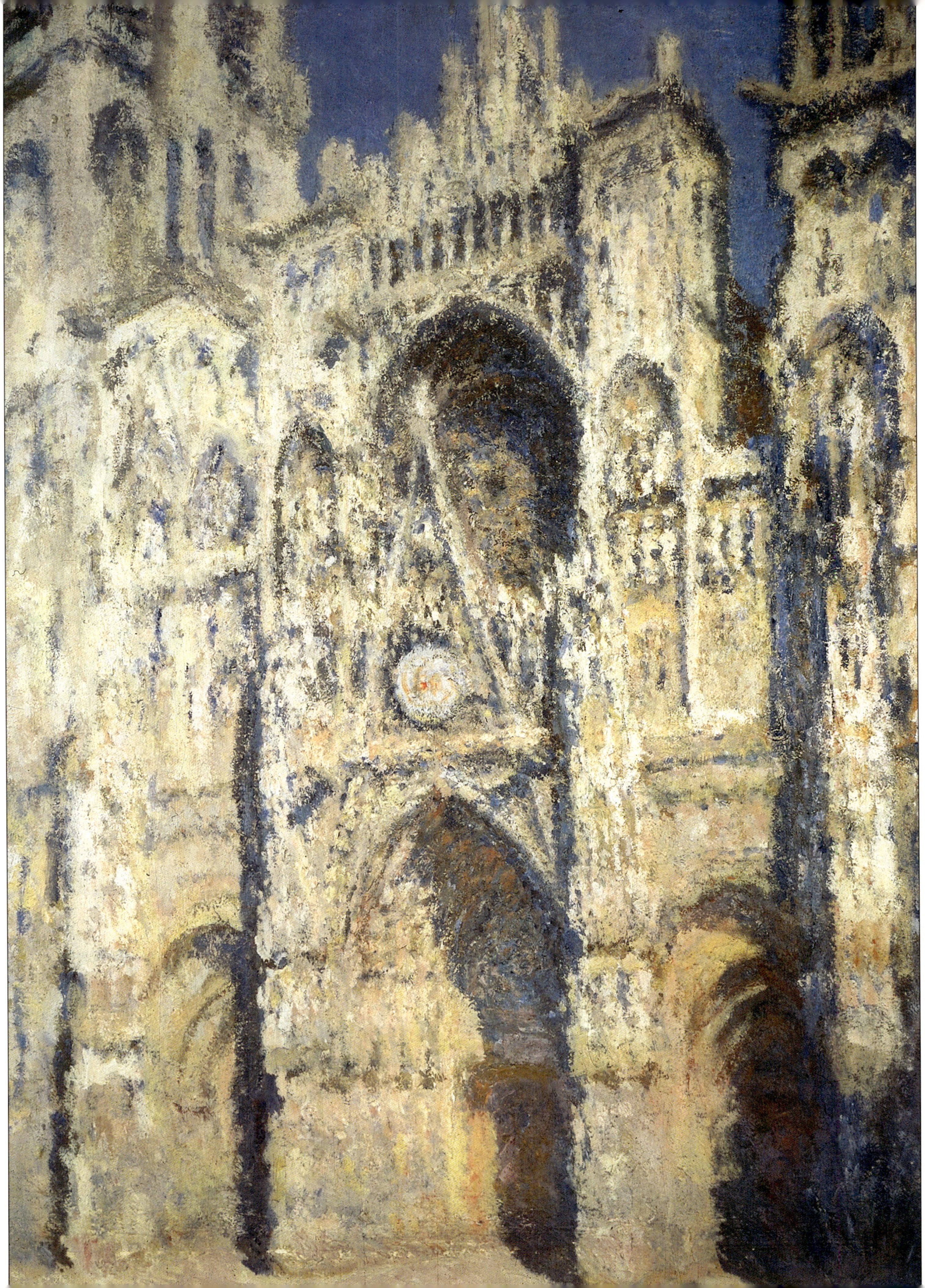

decor, with the *japonaiserie* and bold simplicity associated with the Aesthetic Movement and Monet's friend Whistler.

Julie Manet also commented on Monet's poplars, the chrysanthemums in his greenhouse, and the green bridge across the pond. This last item was brand new, representing the beginning of a personal paradise that Monet elaborated and enlarged over the decades to come. Earlier in the year he had bought a meadow on the other side of the road and railway tracks that ran beside his property. There was already a pond in the meadow, but Monet immediately began a campaign to transform it by diverting the river Epte and planting on a large scale – plans that testified to just how wealthy he had become. The hardest part of the project was to convince the local community that it would not be starved of water or poisoned by foreign plants. Over the next few months his persistence was rewarded and the celebrated water garden was created, surrounded by flowers and shrubs, filled with water lilies and spanned by the 'Japanese' bridge that later featured in so many canvases. Aside from painting, this became his most absorbing occupation, and in the final quarter-century of Monet's life, his art and his water garden would fuse into a single ruling passion.

Much of 1894 was passed at Giverny, painting the Seine, the meadows, and a series of views of the church at Vernon from the river which are like muted echoes of the *Cathedrals* series. One significant event followed the early death in 1894 of Gustave Caillebotte, whose own paintings were long undervalued because of his importance as a patron. Fine judgement, along with a desire to help impecunious friends, had enabled Caillebotte to accumulate a superb collection of Impressionist paintings, which he left to the nation, cannily specifying that they must not be relegated to a provincial museum but must hang in the Luxembourg.

The Caillebotte Bequest illustrated the deep divisions between sections of the public. Despite Monet's soaring reputation and the much improved position of the other Impressionists, the Academy of Fine Arts and the newspaper-reading public were as vociferously hostile as ever. Renoir, as Caillebotte's executor, conducted the long and difficult negotiations; Monet remained on the sidelines but wrote to his friend urging him not to compromise by allowing the bequest to be distributed (or 'lost') among provincial museums. Eventually a compromise was reached whereby the museum accepted 37 of the proffered 67 works. Eight out of Caillebotte's 16 Monets were taken and shown for the first time as part of the bequest in 1896; they included *Regatta at Argenteuil* (pages 92-3) and

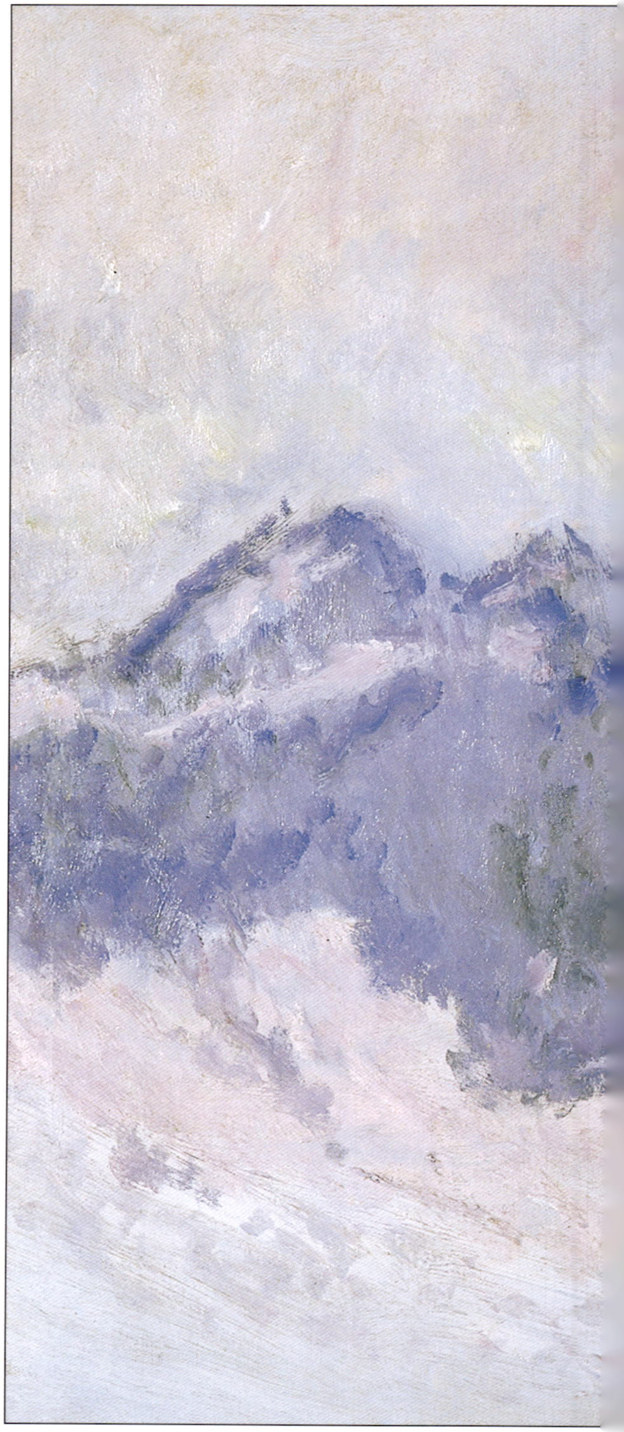

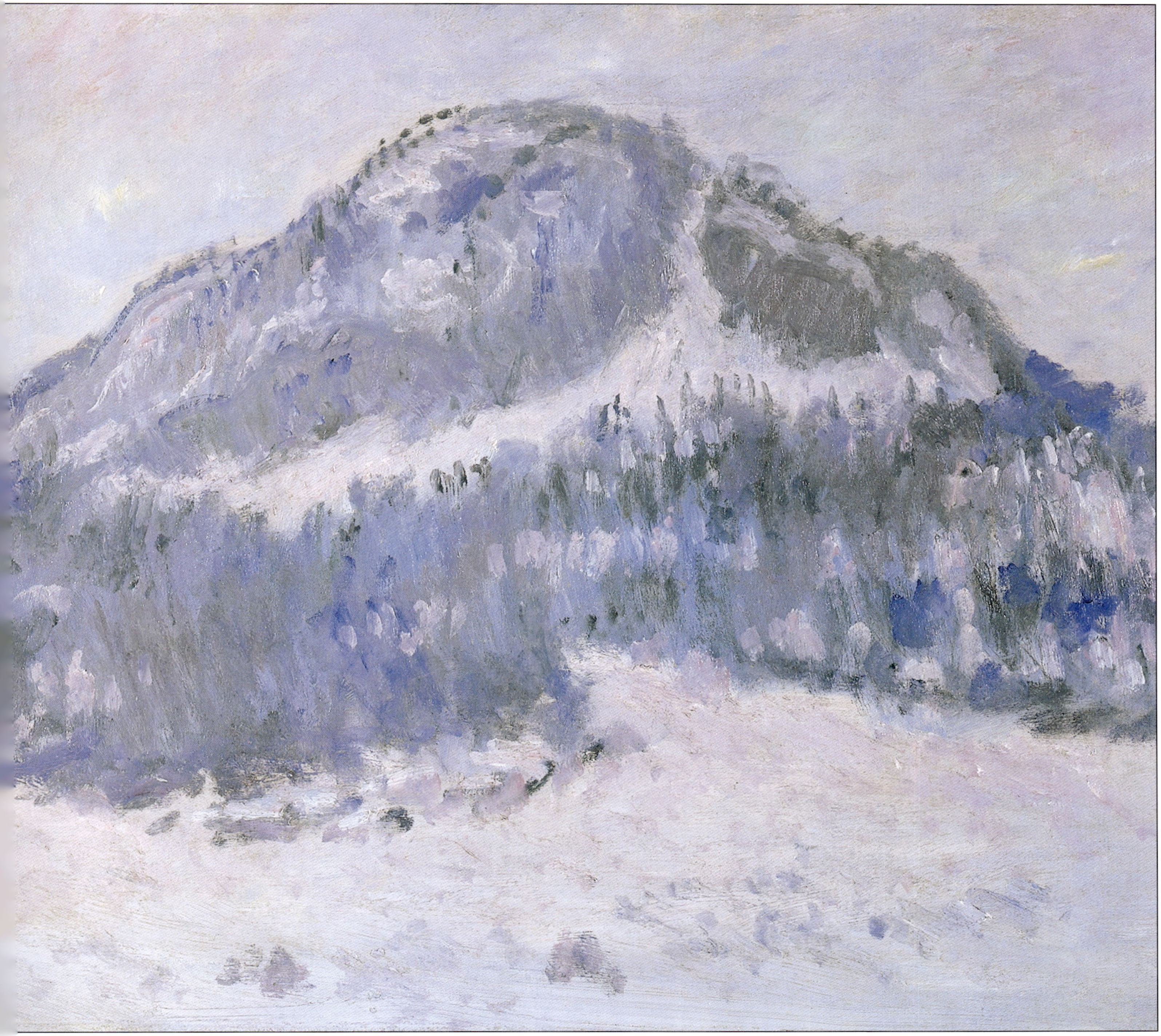

ABOVE:
Mount Kolsaas
(1895)
MUSÉE D'ORSAY,
PARIS

The Gare Saint-Lazare (pages 122-3). They were not moved from the Luxembourg to the Louvre until 1929, even though the French state had bought one of the *Cathedrals* as early as 1907 and had accepted four others in the series as part of the Camondo Bequest of 1908. Like all the state-owned Impressionist masterpieces in Paris, these and other Monets no longer hang in the Louvre, but in a relatively new museum dedicated to nineteenth-century French art, the Musée d'Orsay, or else in the Orangerie.

Meanwhile life at Giverny was diverted by visitors, notably Paul Cézanne, now living in almost complete obscurity in his native South. In September 1894 Cézanne, Rodin and the American painter Mary Cassatt put up at a local inn. Early in the proceedings at Monet's, Cézanne was apparently overwhelmed that Rodin had condescended to shake his hand. 'A man with a decoration [that is, the Legion of Honour]!' marvelled Cézanne, who went down on his knees in front of the great man. Some kind of intense nervous irritability and inverted timidity made him prone to such strange outbursts (this one rather more clownish than most) and it is not even possible to be sure whether he was being sincere at that moment or making a half-mocking demonstration towards an artist whose achievement, unlike his own, had been generally recognized. On this same visit Mary Cassatt was both appalled by Cézanne's table manners and greatly taken by his underlying thoughtfulness and his tolerance in matters concerned with art. However, Cézanne's stay was cut short when Monet gave a dinner in his honour and, believing he was being made fun of, Cézanne rushed away from Giverny in a huff. Monet understood and pitied Cézanne's mental difficulties, while continuing to recognize his greatness as an artist. Although their contacts dwindled, the two men never ceased to admire each other.

Monet in Norway

In January 1895 Monet embarked on a trip to Norway. In part, he was travelling on behalf of Alice to report on his stepson, Jacques Hoschedé, who had married a Norwegian widow and settled in Christiana (now Oslo). He also seems to have been hankering for some winter scenery to paint; the long mild spell at Giverny had been a disappointment. Coming to terms with a foreign country and an unfamiliar landscape proved more difficult than Monet had anticipated, and much as he admired its spectacular mountains, fjords and frozen lakes, he found it hard to settle down and harder

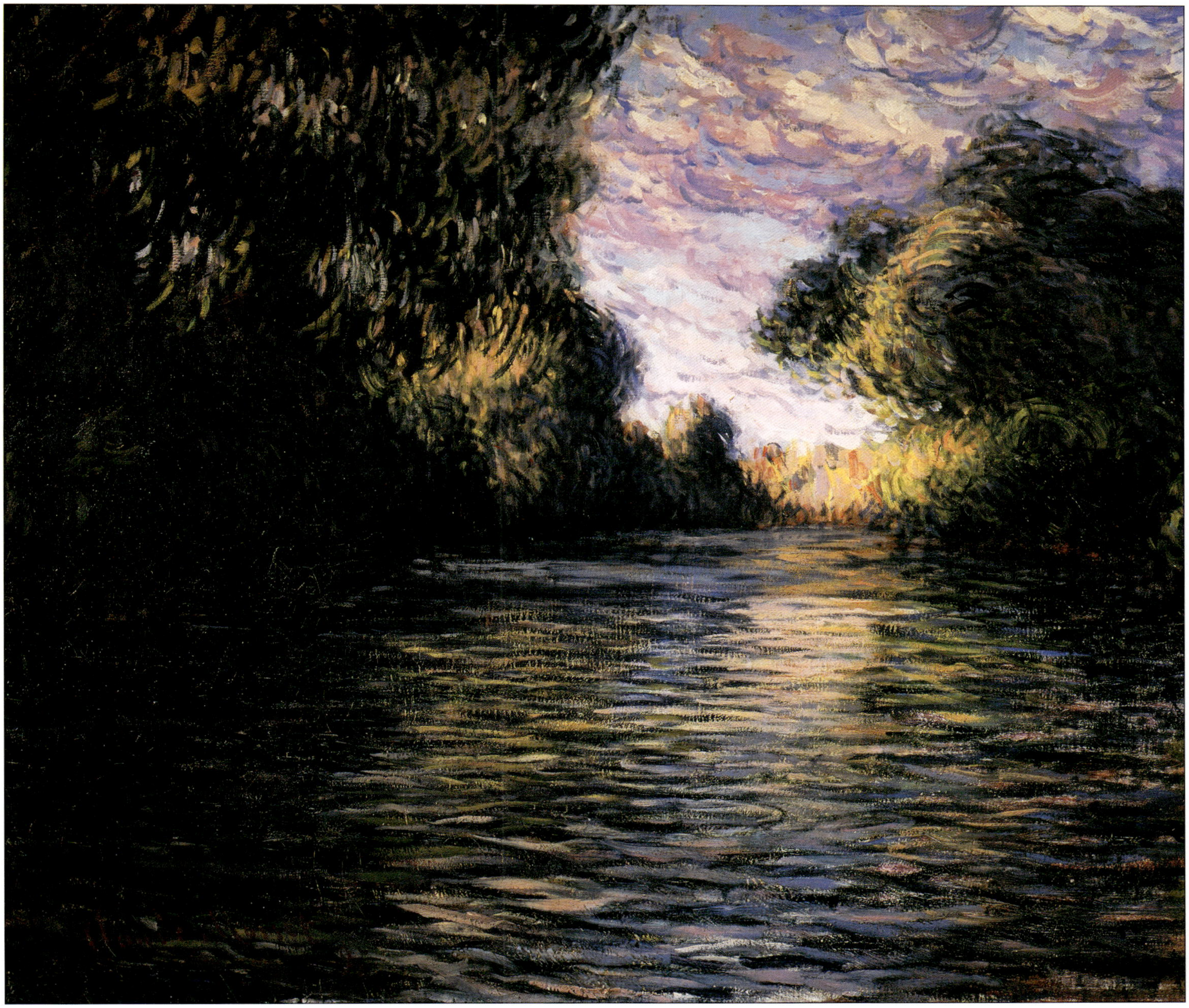

still to fix on a specific motif. He was also alternately irritated and touched by the discovery that in Norway he was a celebrity, frequently subjected to newspaper interviews and honoured by banquets. For all his driving ambition, Monet had a marked distaste for official occasions. (He had not even attended the ceremony in which *Olympia* was accepted by the state, an event largely brought about through his efforts.) Now he was compelled to put up with a good deal in his unsought role as an ambassador for French culture.

He found refuge outside Christiana, in the little town of Sandviken. This provided the romantically 'primitive' setting for which

ABOVE:
Morning on the Seine (1897)
PRIVATE COLLECTION

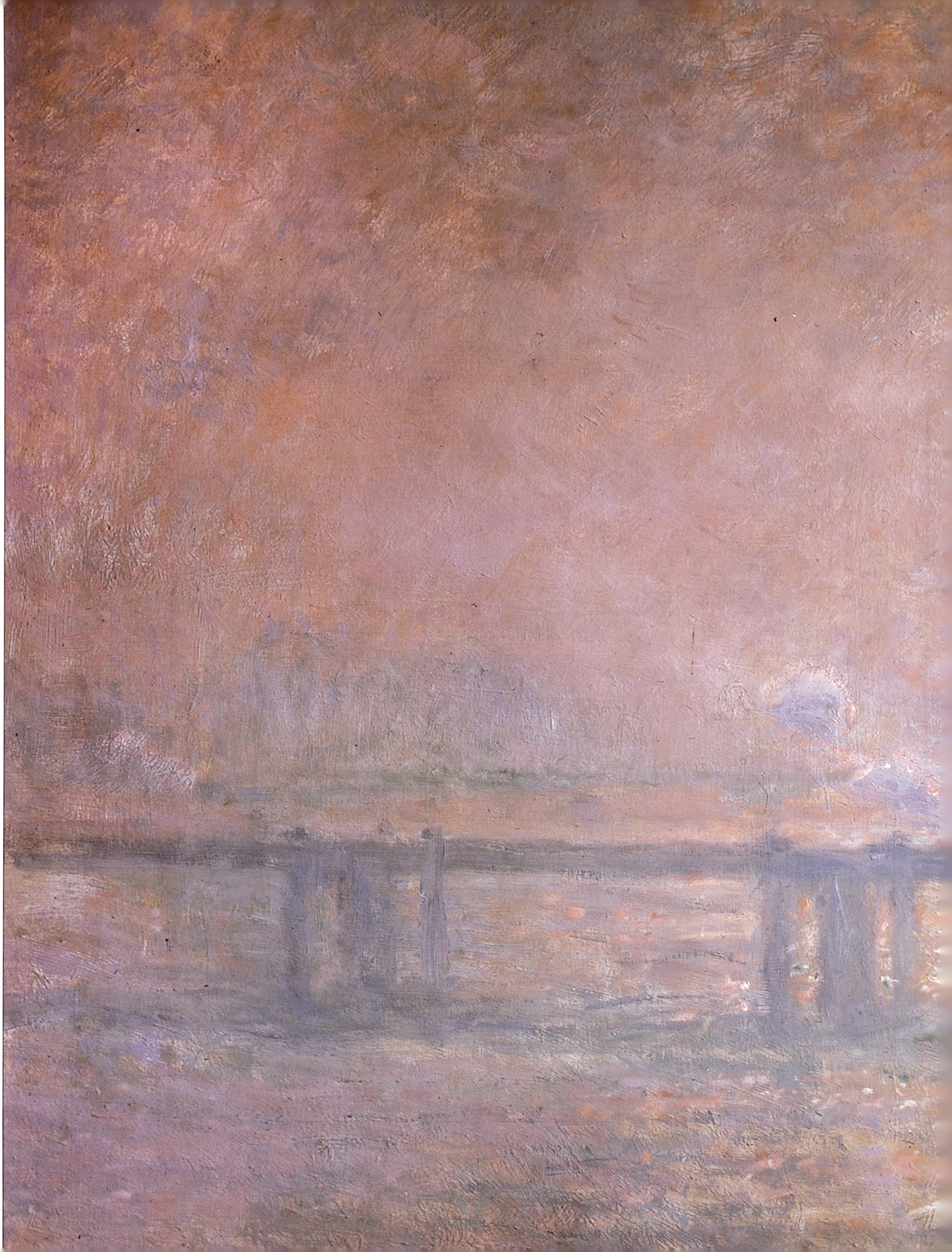

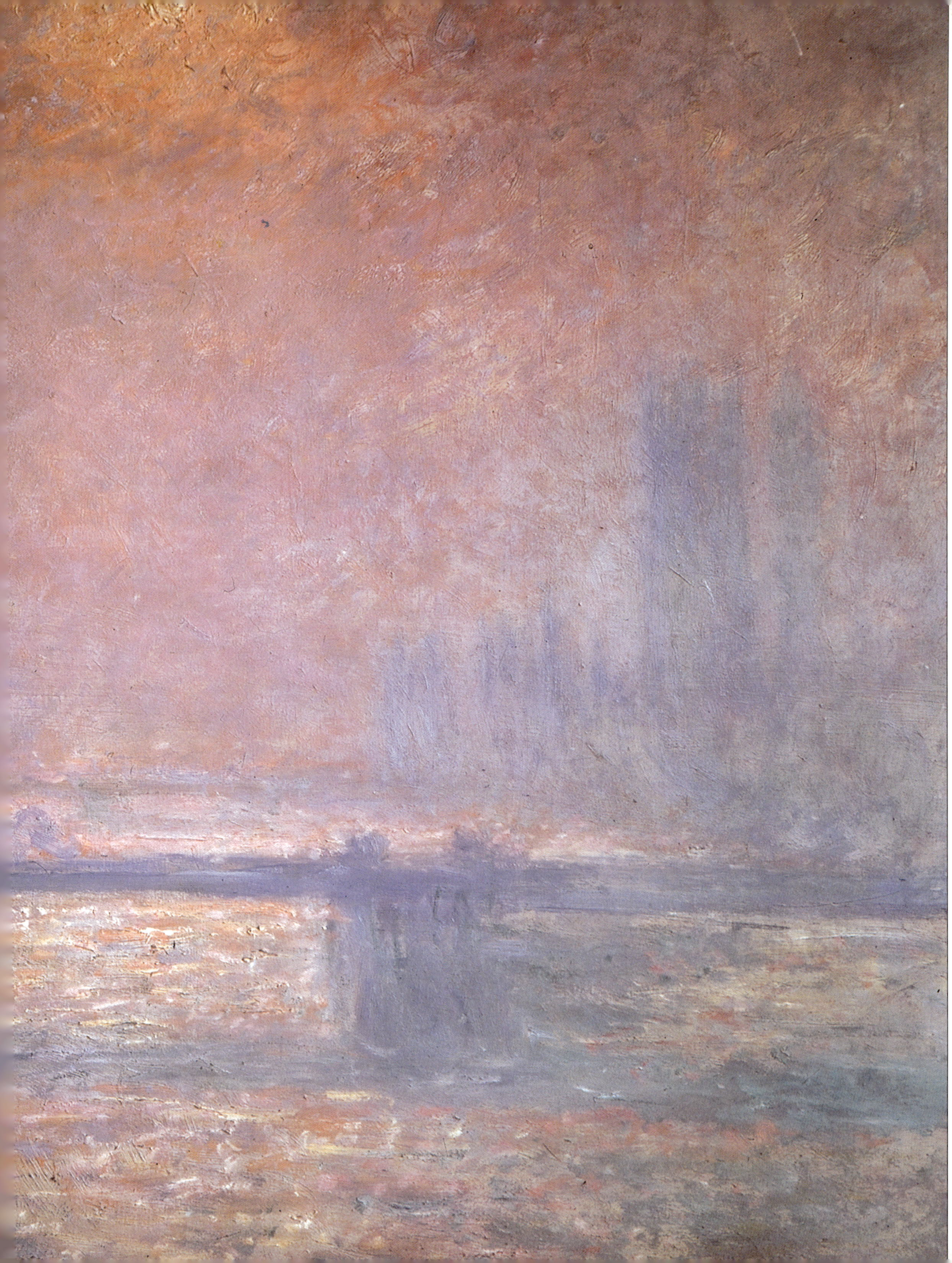

PREVIOUS PAGES 206-7:
The Thames at Charing Cross Bridge (1903)
MUSÉE DES BEAUX-ARTS, LYONS

he had come to Norway, and his work began to make some progress. He found an entirely new subject for his art in the snow-capped majesty of Mount Kolsaas, which inspired a series of 13 canvases. Monet himself recognized the affinity between this subject and the views of Mount Fuji among the Japanese prints that he owned, and he seems to have believed that a similarity existed between the Norwegians and the Japanese, both of whom he saw as simple, nature-loving peoples. The artistic affinity, unlike the ethnic one, was genuine, although only up to a point, given the important differences in intention and treatment between Monet and Japanese masters such as Hokusai and Hiroshige. All the *Kolsaas* canvases are painted from absolutely the same vantage point, so that they are truly variations on a theme, distinguished by startlingly different colour schemes and atmospheric effects. In one of his most incisive comments on his current work, Monet told an interviewer that he no longer thought of the motif as important in itself, but sought to convey his response to it. In effect, he was voicing a rejection of naturalism in favour of a subjective (expressive or decorative) response. By contrast with the *Cathedrals*, the *Kolsaas* paintings are rapidly, almost sketchily executed, partly, no doubt, owing to the extreme cold which made protracted outdoor working impractical; even so, Monet's Norwegian friends were astonished at his determination and powers of endurance. He returned to Giverny in April 1895 with a portfolio of 26 Norwegian paintings.

The Triumph of the Cathedrals

For almost two years Monet had kept Durand-Ruel dangling, at one moment swearing that he would never exhibit the *Cathedrals* series, at another naming a date and then cancelling. Although the delays had originated with his own self-doubts, he certainly became aware that holding off would encourage dealers to pursue him and bid against one another. He may also have wanted to exhibit a wider range of canvases in order to spread the risk of an unfavourable public reaction to the *Cathedrals,* and creating another group of new works had taken time. Now, at last given a go-ahead, Durand-Ruel mounted a show in May 1895 featuring almost 50 Monets, including 20 of the *Cathedrals*, paintings of the Seine, Giverny and Vernon, and a set of *Mount Kolsaas* canvases. In the event, public attention was concentrated on the *Cathedrals*, with the weight of opinion distinctly favourable; only the very conservative were offended by what they saw as an inappropriate treatment of a sacred national monument. Significantly, Monet's fellow Impressionists forgot their grievances and reservations; Pissarro declared that he was 'transported' by the *Cathedrals* and that Monet had achieved the unity of effect that Pissarro himself had sought for so long.

The most enthusiastic and perceptive review was written by the radical politician Georges Clemenceau (1841–1929), who had become a close friend of Monet's (he was one of those present at the Giverny dinner where Cézanne kow-towed to Rodin). Clemenceau's headline article in *La Justice*, his own newspaper, carried the title 'The Revolution of the Cathedrals'. Clemenceau shrewdly noted that Monet's project – to capture the effect of the moment – was one that could have been expanded infinitely, filling every second of the artist's life. Endlessly transformed by the light, the cathedrals were part of a constantly changing world, filled with a pleasure-giving vital pulse which human beings sought to grasp. In capturing this, Clemenceau wrote, art teaches us 'to look, to perceive, to feel'. Anticipating his own later role in Monet's career, he called upon the President of the Republic to ensure his own immortality by buying the entire series for the nation. Since the paintings have even greater impact when seen side by side, this would certainly have been a good deed, although only partly achievable: several had been sold before the show even opened. Instead, they all went to individual purchasers and, now scattered all over the world, can be seen together in any number only once in a lifetime, as in the great 1989 show, 'Monet in the '90s: The Series Paintings', seen in Boston, Chicago and London. There are,however, five on show in the Musée d'Orsay, Paris.)

Monet's delaying tactics and exploitation of the competition paid off handsomely. Durand-Ruel was outraged by his asking a price of 15,000 francs a picture for the *Cathedrals* and Monet eventually let some go for 12,000 francs (a price that would still have seemed outrageous if he had started with it). He did get amounts closer to the full 15,000 francs for what he considered to be the best canvases in the series. Among other things, the prices his works commanded show that the vagaries of the art market are not an exclusively twentieth-century phenomenon. Scarcely worth 200 francs in 1876, a canvas by Monet brought a more acceptable 3,000 francs or so in the early 1890s, had multiplied by five in value by 1895, and by 1921 had reached an incredible 200,000 francs.

Although Monet undoubtedly drove hard bargains, the higher prices he asked for were not, generally speaking, arbitrary.

They were usually based on the rapidly increasing amounts that were being paid for pictures he no longer possessed, as they sold at auction or changed hands at one or more remove from the original purchaser. When, for example, financial losses forced Théodore Duret to sell his collection in 1894, the top bid at the auction was 12,000 francs for Monet's *White Turkeys*. (The news of this must have stirred old memories in a bitter-sweet fashion, for Monet had gone to Alice's château for the first time to paint *White Turkeys* and its companion-pieces to decorate the dining room of the grand Madame Hoschedé.)

Monet was now an extremely wealthy man and at last a lender rather than a borrower. In 1892 he put up the 15,000 francs Pissarro needed to make the house he lived in at Eragny his permanent home. He was also able to afford the magical transformation at Giverny, taking to gardening as a worry-free substitute for painting during the unproductive periods that sometimes afflicted him during the second half of his career. Finally, wealth and fame generated more wealth and greater fame: Monet's independence of the dealers and the public meant that he could hold back the presentation of recent works while expectations mounted, releasing them every few years in major, headline-grabbing exhibitions which sent his stock soaring even higher.

After his return from Norway, the rest of 1895 proved to be one of Monet's unproductive periods. There were a number of difficulties and distractions that may partly account for his inactivity. The women of the family fell ill almost simultaneously and had to be looked after; and the proposal to build a starch factory at Giverny sent Monet into one of his rare flurries of letter writing and wire-pulling. Failing to persuade the Giverny council not to sell the land to the chemical company that planned to build the factory, he finally bribed them into compliance, handing over 5,500 francs in return for a guarantee that the property concerned would not be sold for 15 years. The significance of the time limit is obscure: perhaps Monet felt that, since he would by then have reached the biblical age of three score and ten, he would not much care what happened. If so, he greatly underestimated his own staying power: although already afflicted with severe rheumatism, he had over 30 years of life and artistic activity left in him.

Although Monet's cares in 1895 were genuine enough, family troubles and other worries had never seriously restricted his productivity in the past. His months of inactivity probably represent a period of doubt or self-renewal, or possibly, in view of the rigours

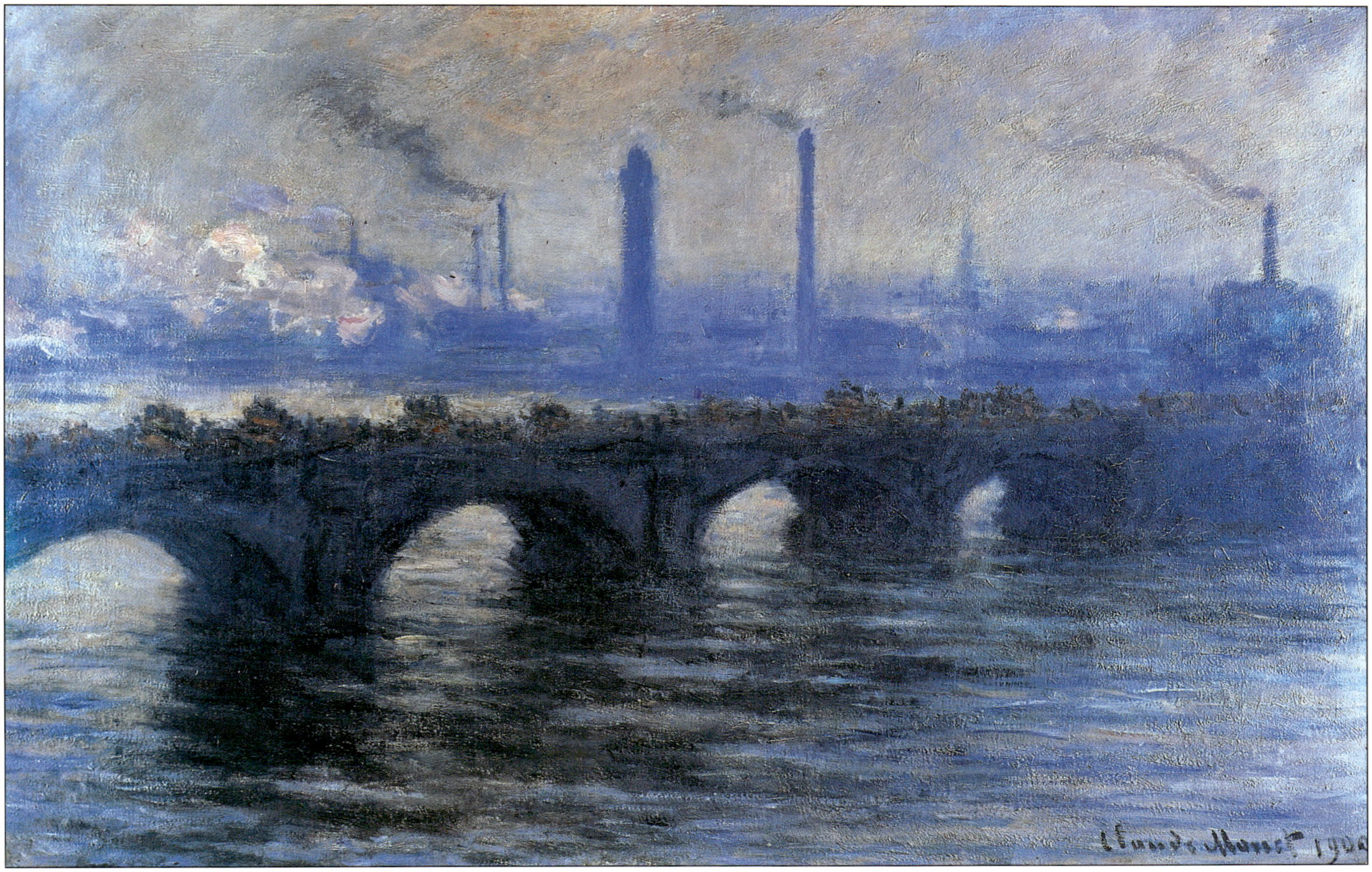

of Norway, of recuperation. If there were crises during such periods, they must have been silently overcome, for Monet remained extraordinarily creative and prolific to the end of his days. In this instance, he was ready for new endeavours by February 1896, setting off for the Channel coast, full of delight at the prospect of seeing the sea again and working in the old familiar places.

This has often been called a nostalgic trip, and with a certain amount of justice. But although Monet tackled a number of his former subjects, his intention was not to look back but to do better than before, particularly by applying his series approach to the coastguard's house at Varengeville (page 151) and the cliffs and sea at Pourville and Dieppe. These motifs are rendered with Monet's customary vigour, but are now swathed in the continuous, all-enveloping atmosphere that he had perfected in the earlier series paintings. This was an even more striking feature of some canvases he painted a few months later, the *Mornings on the Seine* series (page 205). In these, the water is no longer the rippling, sparkling element that we associate with Monet's earlier works, but a mirror of riverbank and sky which creates views of near-symmetry, pointed up by his choice of squarish canvases, very much in contrast to the horizontal

ABOVE:
Waterloo Bridge, Cloudy Weather (1900)
HUGH LANE MUNICIPAL GALLERY OF MODERN ART, DUBLIN

framing of the coastal paintings. In fact, the two series are so strikingly unalike that they were obviously intended to demonstrate the range of Monet's painterly resources. Whereas Normandy is boisterous, the mornings on the Seine are utterly peaceful; even the brushwork is smoother, eliminating any possibility of agitation. In some of these river paintings Monet's decorative impulse takes him to the verge of abstraction, where soft, indefinite areas representing earth, sky and water fuse into quasi-oriental patterns in which the forms seem to have spread out and met one another like coloured inks on blotting paper.

After another visit to Normandy in the winter of 1896–7, Monet went on with the *Mornings on the Seine* series. The journalist Maurice Guillemot visited Giverny in August 1897 and wrote a description of the master setting off to paint at 3.30 in the morning, warmly dressed, booted and with his habitual cigarette glowing like a spark in his big, bushy beard. Monet walked down the central path of his garden, crossed the empty road, slipped through the fence beside the railway track, skirted the water-lily pond and crossed the meadows to the river. A helper unpacked the 14 canvases on which he was working and Monet rowed over to the little island a few metres away where his studio-boat was moored. At which point he must have told Guillemot to fly back to bed, for the journalist's article moves on to other matters. Among them were the studies of water lilies painted on panels – the first we hear of what was to become Monet's greatest obsession.

In June 1898 Monet put on the first large-scale exhibition of his work since 1895. True to his principle of playing dealers off against one another, he allowed Durand-Ruel's rival, Georges Petit, to host the show in which paintings from the Normandy and Seine series were shown alongside seven of the *Cathedrals*. The event was his greatest triumph so far, and there were few dissenting voices to be heard. Newspapers of both main political persuasions ran supplements describing the exhibition, and the version put out on 16 June by *Le Gaulois* showed a photograph of a sturdy, much-bearded Monet, one hand on his hip and the other grasping his stick, staring defiantly out at the world. The exhibition, it declared, was 'an event too important for *Le Gaulois* to look on with indifference. We believed that our readers would be glad to have a souvenir of it and are pleased to include a portrait of the celebrated artist, reproductions of some of his works and appreciations of his magnificent talent by the most authoritative of contemporary critics.' Clearly, in the eyes of the media Monet was moving from

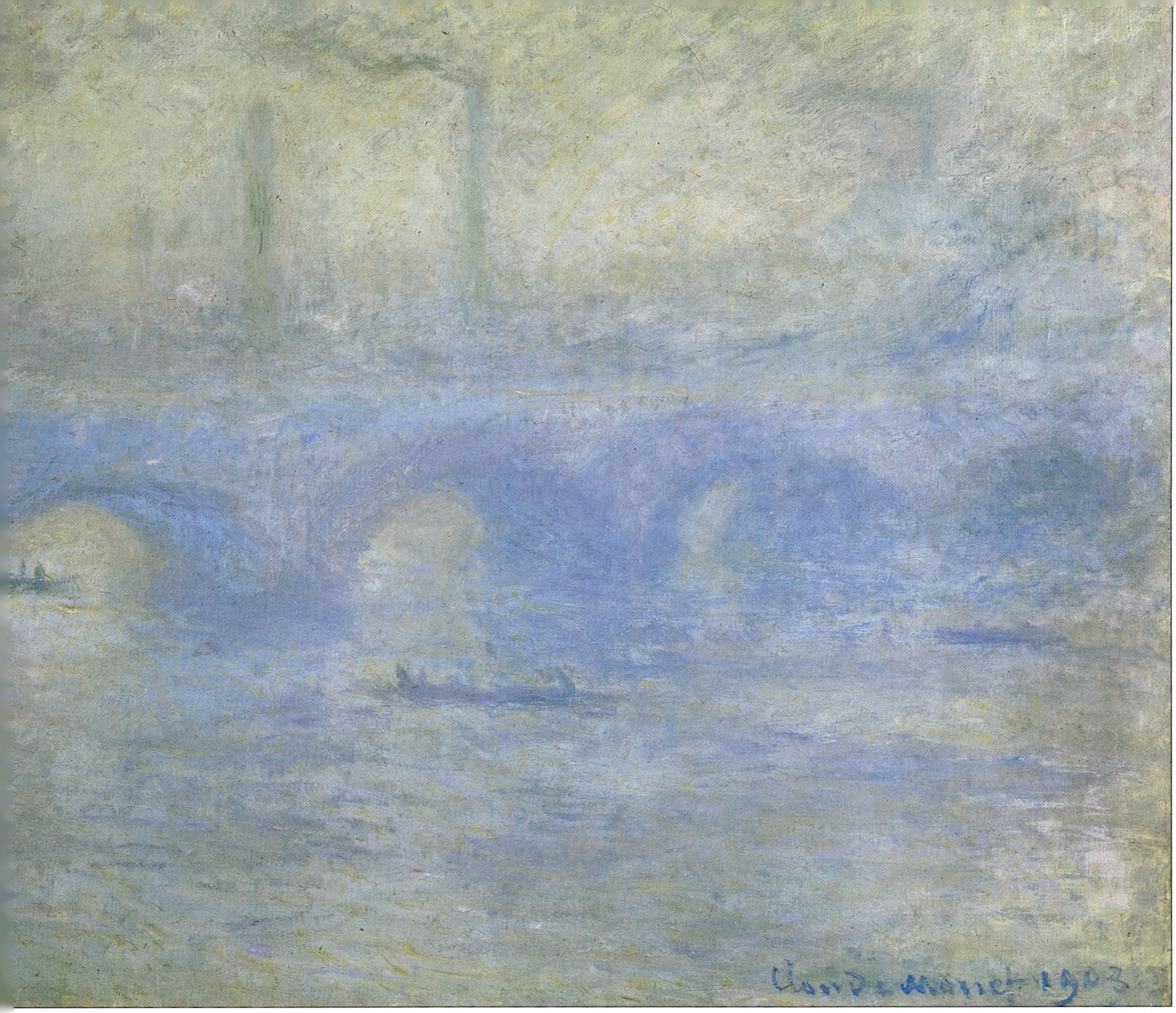

his position as the most admired and highly paid of the Impressionists towards his apotheosis as the Grand Old Man of French painting.

ABOVE:
Waterloo Bridge, Effect of Mist
(1903)
HERMITAGE MUSEUM, ST. PETERSBURG

Monet and the Dreyfus Affair

Meanwhile France had been shaken by the biggest political scandal of the century. It broke in 1897, when evidence began to come to light that Captain Alfred Dreyfus, convicted in 1894 of selling military secrets to Germany, had been sent to Devil's Island on the basis of forged documents and biased hearings. Dreyfus' Jewishness had probably been a factor in the original proceedings and anti-semitism certainly helped to sustain the opposition to any revision of the verdict. When the actual traitor, Count Esterhazy, was put on trial, he was acquitted. The turning point came immediately afterwards, on 13 January, 1898, when Clemenceau's newspaper *L'Aurore* published a front-page article, *J'Accuse*, in which Emile Zola forcefully indicted the politicians and the army for suppressing the truth. Zola, former art critic and ally of the Impressionists, was now a celebrated novelist and his intervention was too bold and public to ignore. The authorities were compelled to counter-attack by putting him on trial for libel and the affair became the famous 'Affair', bitterly dividing the nation. The army, the Church, royalists and anti-semites lined up against republicans, radicals and socialists in what became a test of the Third Republic's capacity for survival.

Even the artists were divided over the Affair: Degas, Renoir and Cézanne were against Dreyfus, while Monet and Pissarro were convinced of his innocence. Monet was sufficiently moved to forget any grudges he may have held against Zola. In December 1897 he had congratulated the novelist on his articles defending Dreyfus and the day after the publication of *J'Accuse* he wrote a second time, 'Bravo once again and accept all my heartfelt feelings for your gallantry and courage'. He also took a public stand by putting his signature to the Manifesto of the Intellectuals published a few days later in *L'Aurore* to support the demand for a full investigation. A month later, when Zola's trial began, Monet again wrote admiringly to the novelist, excusing himself from attending the proceedings because he and his family were ill. This may have been a pretext for avoiding the fray, since Monet usually steered clear of political involvement and the signature he had provided for *L'Aurore* marked the limit of his commitment. However, his letters to Zola and to his friend Geffroy make it clear that he did feel strongly about the Dreyfus case.

Whether it had any long-term effect on his outlook is less obvious. It has been argued that the Affair destroyed a positive image of France that had been in Monet's mind when he painted the *Haystacks*, *Cathedrals* and other great series, and that this accounts for his lack of productivity in 1898–9 and for the very different emphases in his later works, which are concerned only with a few places outside France and with Monet's personal and private world at Giverny. In the 1880s and 1890s, the argument runs, Monet had celebrated traditional images of France, but the traditional institutions were the very ones that had turned out to be corrupt and bigoted. Moreover the Affair went on and on,

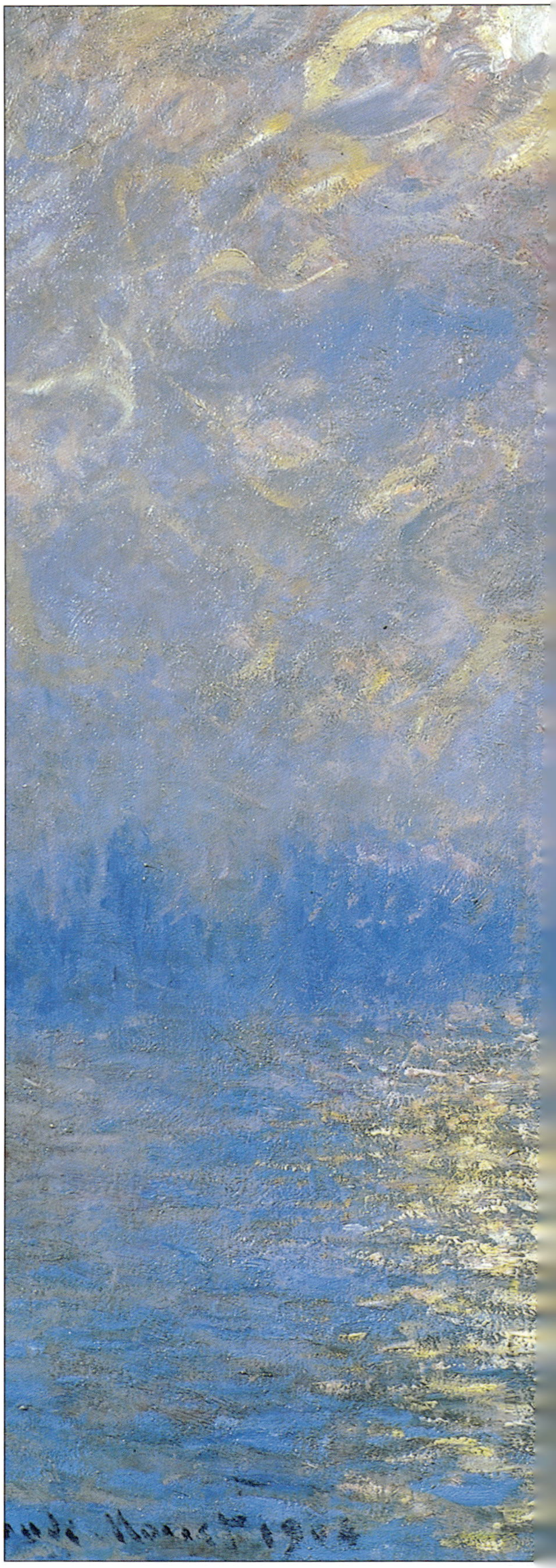

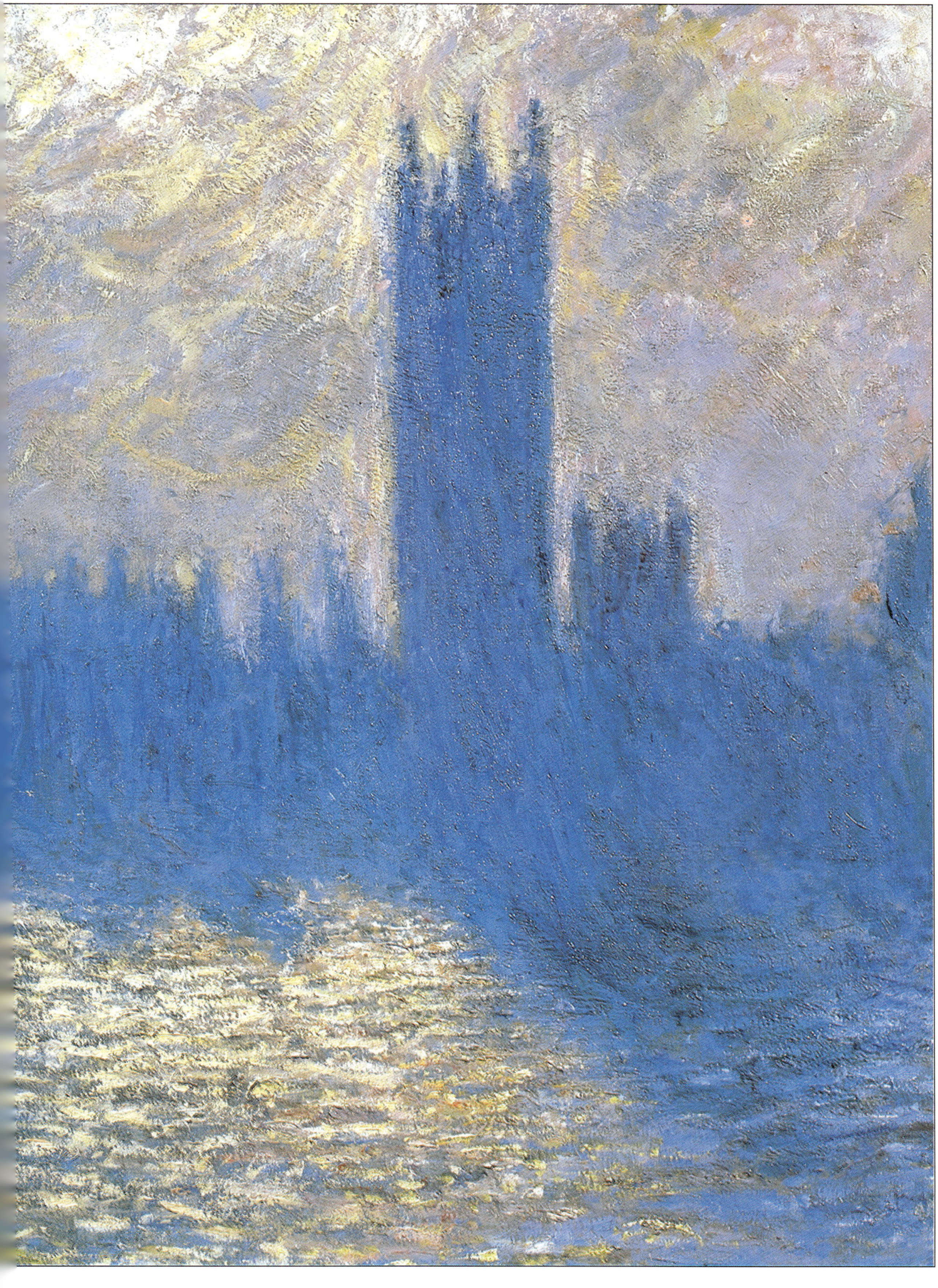

LEFT:
The Houses of Parliament, Stormy Sky
(1904)
MUSÉE DES BEAUX-ARTS, LILLE

dividing families and tainting the atmosphere. Zola was found guilty of libel and sentenced to a year in prison, although he remained free by slipping away to England while his appeal was being heard. After a year, a legal technicality enabled him to return to France without serving his sentence. A few months later, Colonel Henry, who had led the original investigation into the sale of the secrets, admitted that he had forged some of the evidence against Dreyfus and committed suicide. Yet when Dreyfus was finally granted a retrial in 1899, he was again found guilty, albeit 'with extenuating circumstances'. This peculiar, meaningless formula amounted to a virtual admission that a mistake had been made. The government made the best of a bad job by pardoning Dreyfus, but the guilty verdict was not overturned until 1906.

The Dreyfus Affair certainly damaged the good name of France and because it was so long-drawn-out must have influenced the outlook of the French themselves. However, there is no documentary evidence that Monet's vision of France was profoundly affected by it, and other explanations for his lack of productivity and change of direction seem more likely. The late 1890s were stressful for Monet and his family. Despite his disapproval, Monet's son Jean married Blanche Hoschedé in 1897; and following a long struggle against a paralytic illness, Suzanne died in 1899. (The close-knit nature of the family group is shown by the fact that, 18 months later, the widower married Suzanne's older sister Marthe, who had been looking after the Butler children ever since Suzanne had become ill in 1894.) Quite apart from such considerations, this was not the first of Monet's barren periods and it was not unnatural that he should need a break and follow it by setting a new course. He may well have felt that he – and his public – had had enough of northern French landscapes, although he did in fact conduct just one more 'nostalgic' campaign at Vétheuil in 1900–1.

The London Series

The first foreign place that Monet chose to visit was London in September 1899. He may have been following Zola's example in flying from a corrupt France to the land of liberty, but in the absence of any statementsby Monet to that effect, it seems simpler to suppose that he was motivated by the need for a change of scene, both personally and artistically. Besides, he knew London well and had found views of the Thames worth painting several times almost 30 years before.

Monet brought Alice with him to London, probably in an attempt to distract her after the shattering blow of Suzanne's death. He was now so wealthy that he checked in at the Savoy, London's new luxury hotel, for the full six weeks of his stay, putting up there again for three months at a time in 1900 and 1901. It was an ideal place for his purpose, standing right on the embankment and furnished with wide windows that gave wonderful views of the Thames. He had known the river, the bridges linking central London with the South Bank, and the Houses of Parliament since 1871 (page 80-1) and had returned several times over the years. Now he embarked on what would become a triple series: views of Charing Cross Bridge, of Waterloo Bridge to the north and of the Houses of Parliament just to the south.

The two bridges were quite different in appearance. Charing Cross was a relatively low, narrow railway bridge, whereas Waterloo Bridge was a broad, imposing structure serving horse-drawn vehicles, a few new-fangled automobiles and hosts of pedestrians. Both could be painted from Monet's sixth-floor suite at the Savoy, but he chose St Thomas's Hospital, on the south bank of the Thames across Westminster Bridge, as his viewpoint for the Houses of Parliament.

There was nothing particularly surprising about Monet's decision to spend some time painting in London, but no one could have predicted that the city (more precisely the Thames) would become the subject of three closely related series that eventually extended to almost 100 canvases. Monet shared the current French fad for things English and admired the liberal attitudes which had made the country a sanctuary for political refugees such as Karl Marx and Emile Zola. (It is unlikely, however, that he sympathized with the war that Britain began to wage, during his first stay, on the Boer farmers in South Africa.) These are hardly artistic motives. It is more plausible to suppose that he was consciously measuring up against the great English tradition of landscape painting, and in particular against J.M.W. Turner (1775–1851), whose works he and Pissarro had admired as exiles almost 30 years before. Interestingly, Turner's art had evolved in a way that was in certain respects comparable to Monet's, from painting views to painting light and atmosphere so intense and all-embracing that they seemed to melt and dissolve the forms they enveloped and saturated.

Monet may also have wished to emulate his friend Whistler, who had described his works as 'harmonies' some 20 years or

RIGHT:
The Houses of Parliament with the Sun Breaking Through (1904)
MUSÉE D'ORSAY. PARIS

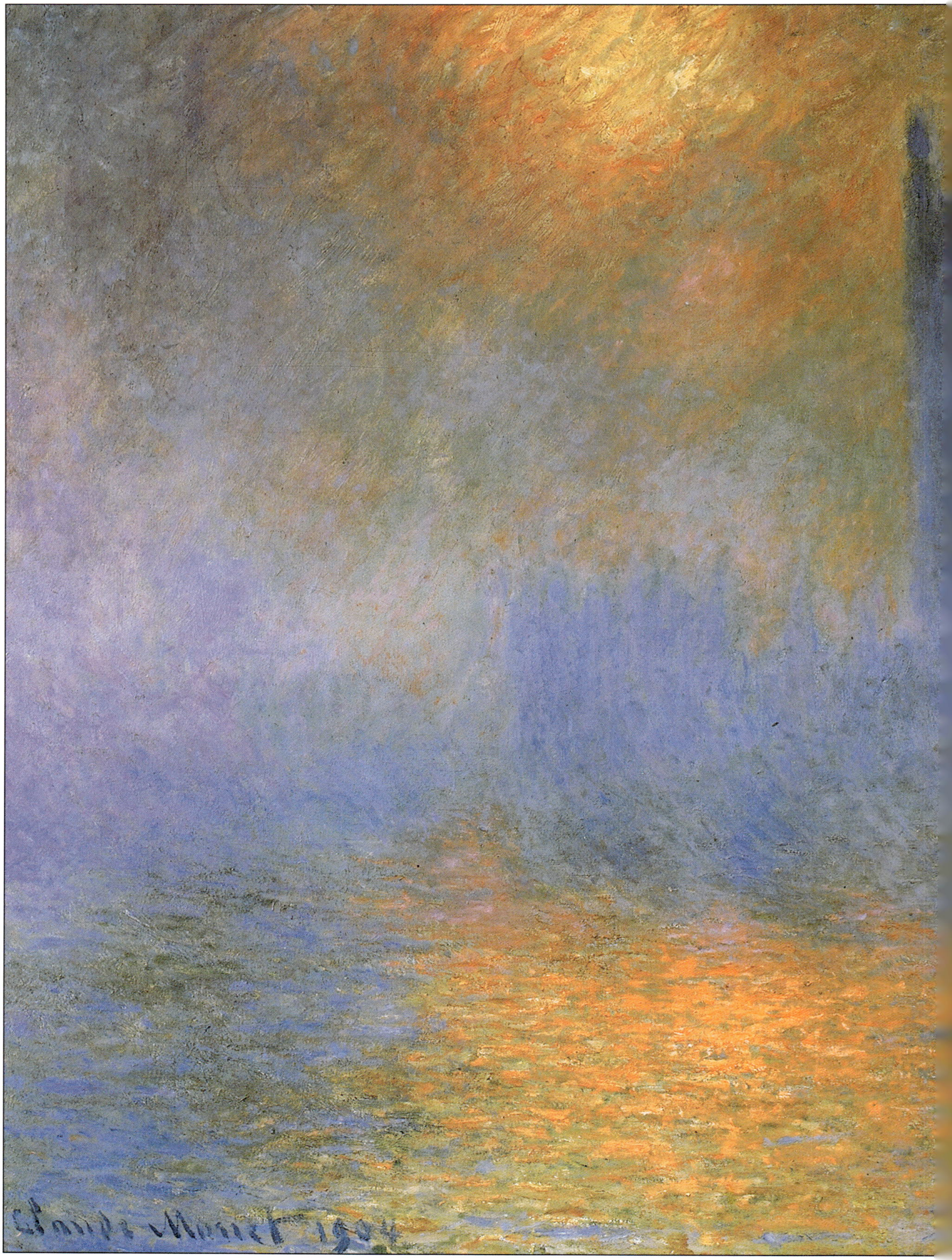

more before Monet began to use the term. More inclined than Monet to indulge in public pronouncements about art, Whistler had already identified the attitude of artistic autonomy that was implicit in Monet's series paintings. 'Art should be independent of all claptrap – should stand alone and appeal to the artistic sense of eye or ear, without confounding this with emotions entirely foreign to it, as devotion, pity, love, patriotism, and the like. All these have no kind of concern with it, and that is why I insist on calling my works "arrangements" and "harmonies".' In other words, art, like most music, should not be 'about' anything susceptible to literary description, although Whistler, like Monet, never entirely dispensed with a recognizable subject taken from the real world. Another musical title used by Whistler was 'Nocturnes', which he applied to night scenes of the Thames; these, too, must have been in Monet's mind as he began his own London paintings.

More than anything else, he seems to have been attracted by the murky atmosphere of London, which seemed distinctly romantic to generations not yet alerted to the hazards of pollution. This was, after all, the period when Sherlock Holmes and Dr Watson summoned hansom cabs and plunged into swirling fogs, as though into the criminal heart of darkness. In a similar spirit, Monet referred to the London fog as a 'mysterious mantle' and declared that he loved the city only in winter, the season when the smoke from millions of coal fires darkened the damp streets. Not all of Monet's London paintings are literally foggy, but their atmosphere is palpably thick, presumably creating visual effects that could not be found in France. Generally speaking, the sun struggles through the clouds with difficulty, diffusing a weak light throughout the scene, but on occasion it breaks through at some point, with spectacular, lightning-like consequences (page 218).

Monet finished a dozen Charing Cross and Waterloo paintings in 1899–1900, but all the other London pictures remained in various states of incompletion until 1904. This was, at least in part, because Monet felt them to be interrelated. The extent to which he thought of them as a series – or rather, as a single work of art – is revealed by a note to Durand-Ruel in which he told the dealer that he was unable to send off a single canvas, as he needed them all in front of him; ideally, no doubt, he should have added the finishing touches to every one of them in the same session. Most of this work was done in the studio and the pretence that Monet worked exclusively from nature was beginning to wear very thin. When he was accused of basing one of his views of the Houses of Parliament

RIGHT:

Seagulls over the Houses of Parliament

(1904)

PUSHKIN MUSEUM, MOSCOW

on a photograph, Monet simply retorted that it was nobody's business how he worked, for only the result signified and, for that matter, there were plenty of trashy paintings on the market that had been done directly from nature!

Taken as a whole, the London series is truly astonishing in its variety. No other painter has produced a comparable set of works without ever repeating himself. Monet constantly rings the changes on his restricted repertoire of motifs, which are rendered with widely different degrees of distinctness and vivified by small appropriate inclusions, such as the birds in *Seagulls over the Houses of Parliament* (pages 220-1), the smoke-belching trains that race over Charing Cross Bridge (pages 206-7), the factory chimneys rising up behind Waterloo Bridge (page 211) and occasional boats and barges on the river. Although it is true in a sense to say that light and atmosphere are the real subjects of these canvases, the pictured scene (the subject in the ordinary sense of the word) is far from irrelevant to the final effect. In fact, it is noticeable that Monet tends to strike a balance between the degree of atmospheric drama and the amount of activity visible in the picture: light and mist are rarely deployed more strikingly than in the paintings of the Houses of Parliament, whose brooding presence appears only in the form of a gigantic, mysterious silhouette.

Instead of returning to Britain, Monet spent part of 1903–4 working on the London paintings in his studio at Giverny. Although he had finished canvases in the studio before, he had never done so on quite this scale, making memory and imagination a highly significant element in the series. There were sound practical reasons for this. Monet was now in his sixties and in 1901 had suffered a collapse brought on by overwork, a result of making strenuous trips to London and also, two years running, to Vétheuil, while spending his time at Giverny painting water lilies and a Japanese Bridge series! In the event, London proved to be the last place outside his own home where Monet would labour long and hard (with the partial exception of Venice in 1908). Instead, during the final quarter-century of his career he created an artistic universe out of the little world of Giverny.

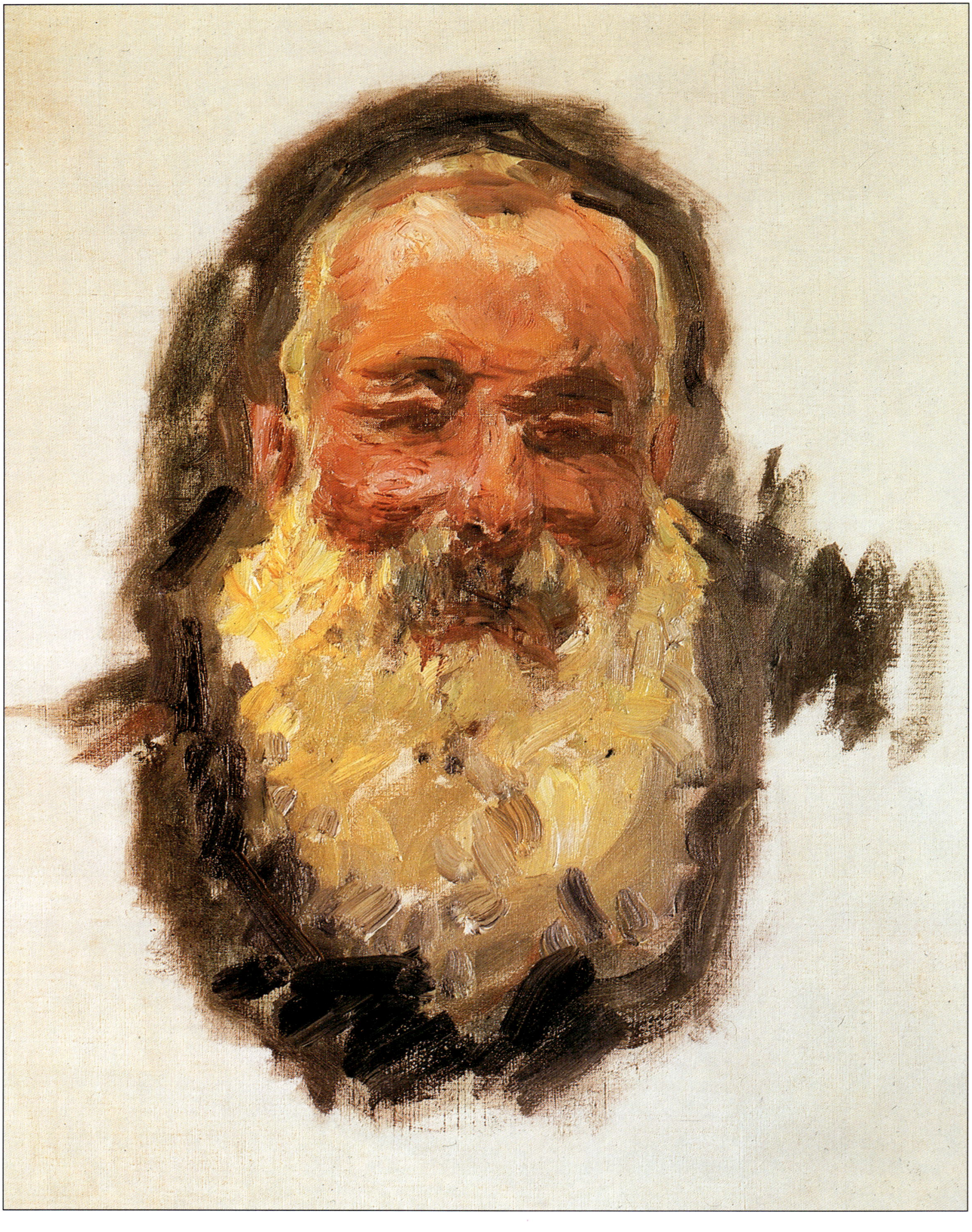

CHAPTER TEN

Painter in Paradise

THE EARLY YEARS of the twentieth century confirmed Monet's status in his own country as a great artist. Fourteen of his paintings were included in the Fine Art section of the 1900 International Exhibition held in Paris, and over the next few years his works continued to enter state museums. Finally, in 1914, Count Isaac de Camondo's collection of Impressionist paintings was hung in the Louvre, making the surviving members of the group – Monet, Renoir and Degas – the first living artists to be so honoured.

One phase of Monet's artistic activity culminated with the showing of 37 of his London paintings at Durand-Ruel's in May and June 1904. He was still career-minded enough to revisit the British capital in a vain effort to arrange a similar show there, but honour was evidently satisfied by the great exhibition organized by Durand-Ruel in January of the following year. Over 300 works were hung at London's Grafton Galleries, of which 55 were canvases by Monet. This still ranks as the most comprehensive display of Impressionist masterpieces ever mounted and can be seen as the group's moment of final triumph – appropriately so, since as outrage

LEFT:
Self-portrait
(1917)
MUSÉE D'ORSAY,
PARIS

and scandal were about to explode again, but this time in response to even more sensationally unorthodox movements such as Fauvism and Cubism, which served to confirm the respectability of Impressionism.

The Master at Giverny

Monet himself would become increasingly absorbed by Giverny, leaving it less and less often and more and more reluctantly. But there was nothing austere or hermit-like in his way of life. Over the years Le Pressoir became a bourgeois Versailles, with apartments for his stepdaughters, new studios, a darkroom for photography, domestic staff, a team of six gardeners, a greenhouse, new acreage and new plantings. By no means indifferent to useful innovations, Monet acquired two Panhard motor cars in which he was driven about in style; in the autumn of 1904 he and Alice went by road to Madrid, mainly to see the works of art in the city's Prado Museum. Nor had Monet lost his taste for fine clothes, although the flamboyance of his young manhood survived only in his lace-cuffed shirts. Otherwise he favoured woollen suits in the country-weekend English style, beautifully tailored to enclose his increasing bulk. His appetite had always been huge, but his discrimination gave the hospitality of Giverny an attraction rivalling that of the master himself, and visits by friends and admirers provided Monet and his family with all the company they needed.

Deaths had begun to thin the ranks of Monet's contemporaries: Berthe Morisot had died in 1895, the poet Stéphane Mallarmé, a staunch supporter, in 1898, Sisley in 1899, Pissarro in 1903 and Cézanne in 1906. But as well as survivors such as Clemenceau, Rodin, Mirbeau and Geffroy, there were more recent friends who came to Giverny, including the actor-playwright Sasha Guitry and his wife, the writer Paul Valéry, and American artists such as John Singer Sargent, Theodore Robinson and Lilla Cabot Perry. They found Monet good company, but their recollections suggest that he also enjoyed taking on the role of the temperamental man of genius who experienced moments of despair when he flung his equipment into the Epte and declared that he would never paint again. At other times he revealed that he had put his foot through one of his works in progress in an anguish of dissatisfaction, or had even procured older works of his own and destroyed them because they were not up to the standard he set himself. On one occasion, having told Lilla Cabot Perry that he

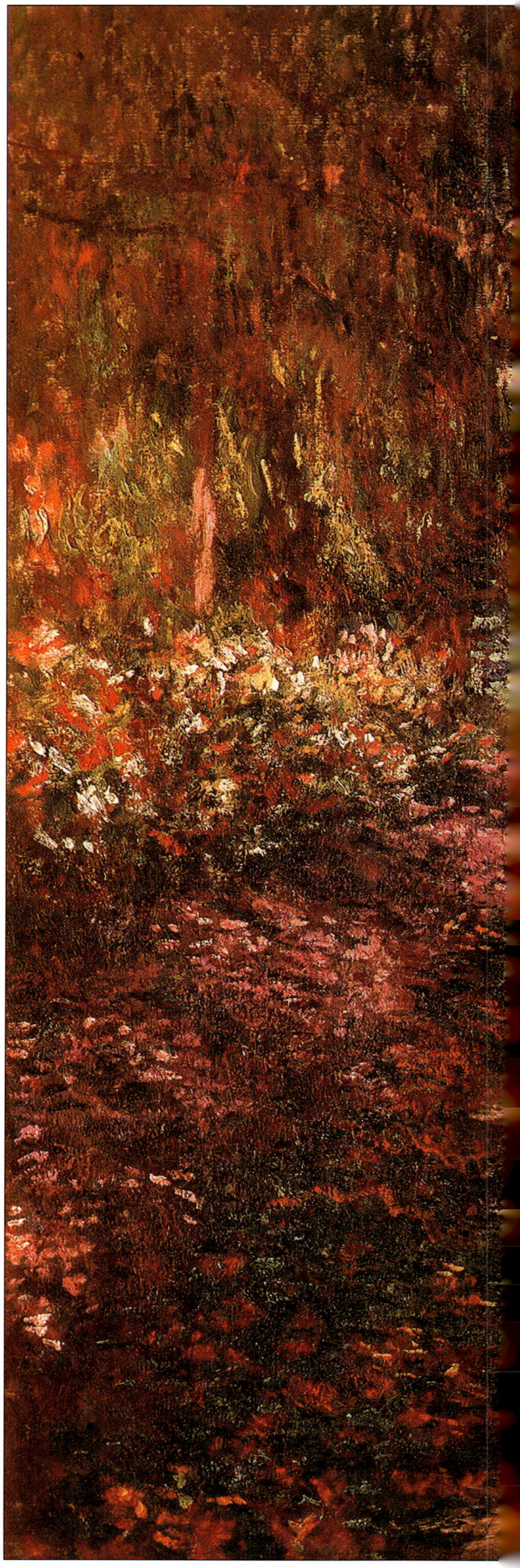

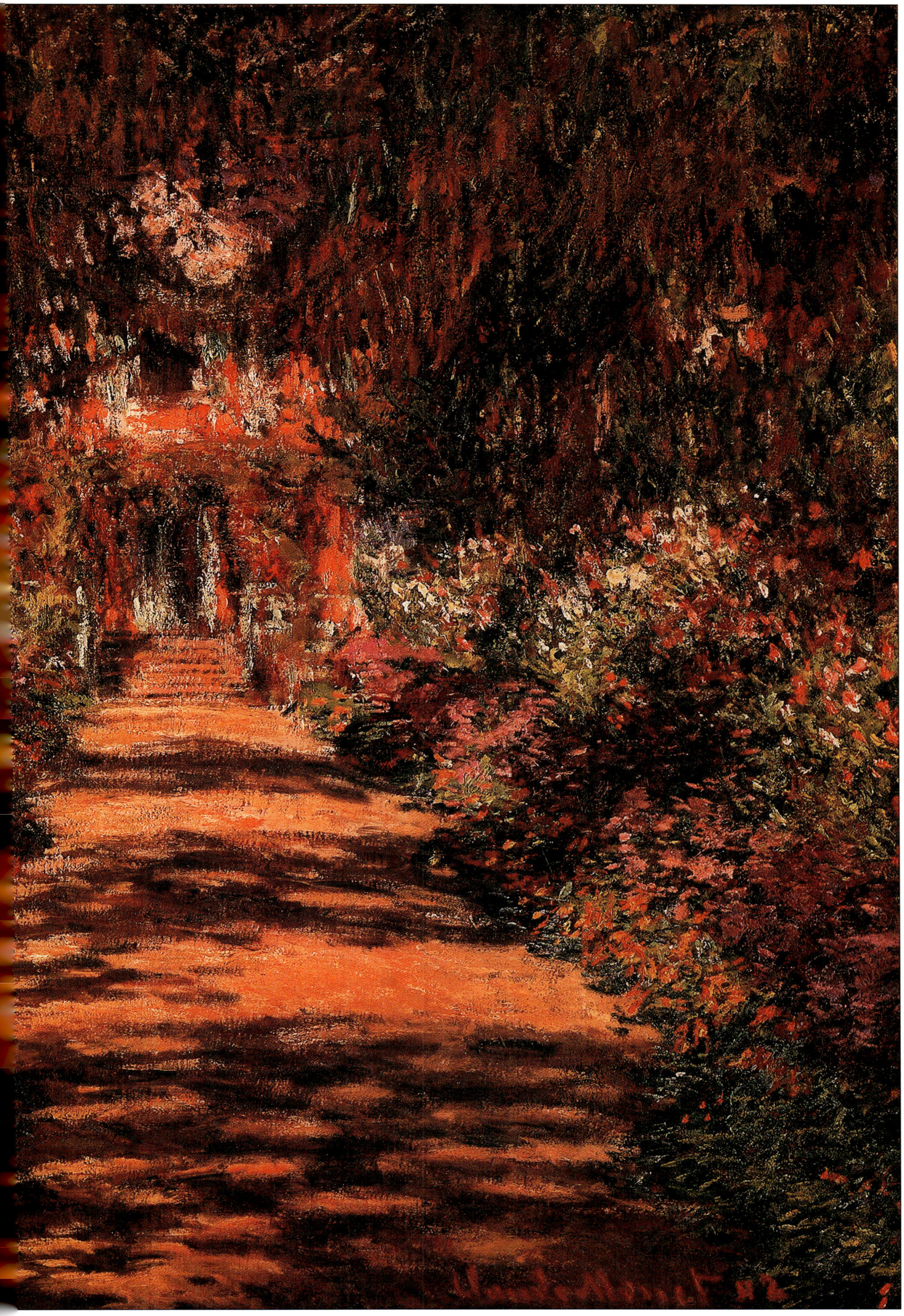

LEFT:
A Pathway in Monet's Garden at Giverny
(1902)
KUNSTHISTORISCHES-MUSEUM, VIENNA

RIGHT:

Waterlily Pond

(1899)

NATIONAL GALLERY, LONDON

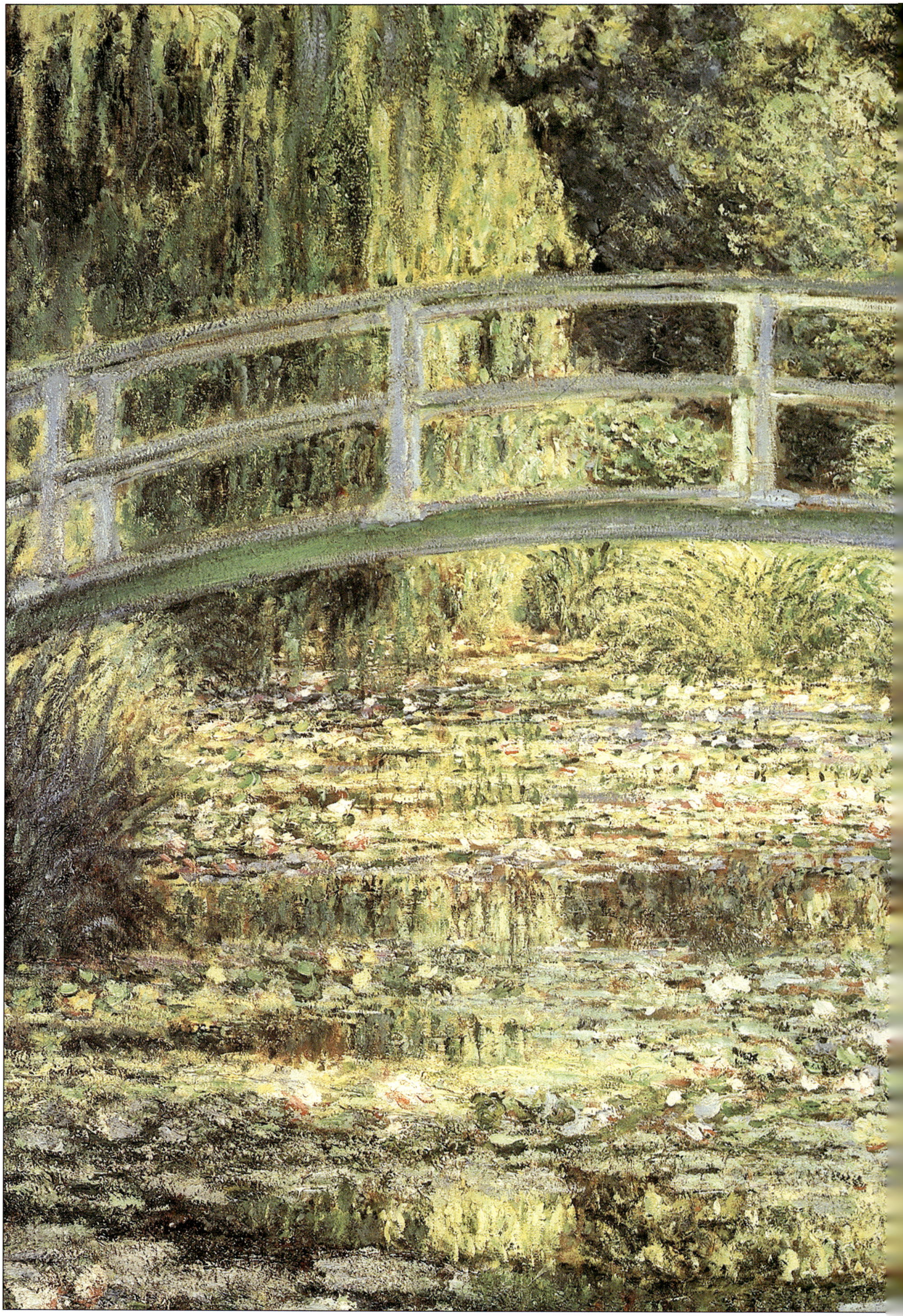

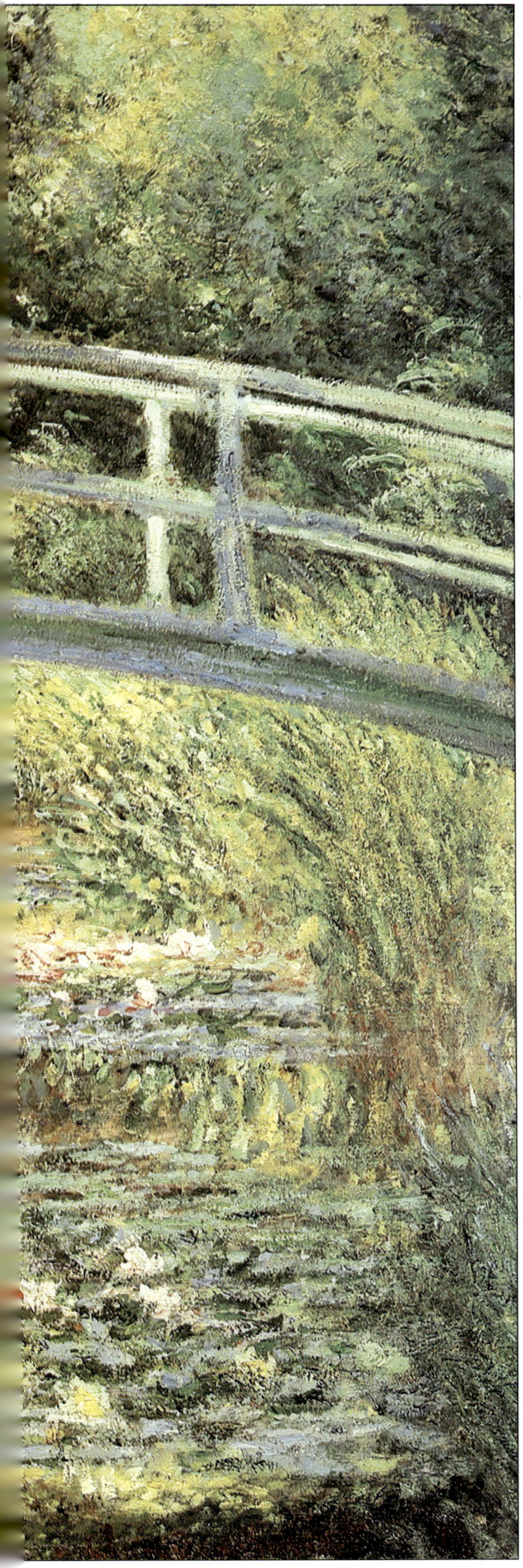

had just burned over 30 canvases, he remarked 'I must look after my artistic reputation while I can; once I am dead, no one will destroy any of my paintings, no matter how poor they may be.' It is difficult to believe there was no element of play-acting or myth-making in all this, although Monet's assertions can neither be verified nor disproved. Whether true, exaggerated or false, they succeeded in promoting an image of Monet that was rarely challenged until quite recent times.

By the turn of the century the gardens at Giverny were maturing and this, no doubt, made them increasingly attractive to Monet. The flower garden just outside the house and the water garden beyond the road and railway provided pleasant contrasts. The flower garden represented a compromise between the formal garden of French tradition, with straight gravel paths and geometric topiary, and the 'English garden', cunningly landscaped to look natural and only accidentally picturesque. At Giverny there were gravel paths, but the flowers were allowed to encroach on them, and the sheer colourful abundance of blossoms made an overwhelming impression that was anything but formal (pages 224-5). By contrast with the riot in the flower garden, the water-lily pool and its surrounding flowers, trees and shrubs breathed a stiller, more tranquil atmosphere, of a kind commonly associated by Monet and his contemporaries with the oriental sense of beauty and contemplative approach to nature.

Flowers and gardens had interested Monet as subjects almost throughout his career, and at Argenteuil, prompted by Caillebotte, he had taken up gardening on his own behalf. At Giverny, especially once the house and land became his own property, his hobby became something close to an obsession. He studied handbooks and catalogues with zeal, and his wealth enabled him to order shrubs and flowers from all over the world in order to create a unique private landscape. As we have seen, the creation of the water-lily pond was a minor feat of engineering; in order to bring it off Monet was roused to agitate and negotiate in his most hard-headed fashion – almost as though he divined that this site would eventually take precedence over the flower garden and everything else in his art.

The Japanese Bridge

Monet's earliest canvases of the water garden dated from the mid-1890s. His first series of *Water Lilies* was painted in 1899–1900 and consisted of views in which the 'Japanese' bridge across the pond was the central feature. All of these celebrated pictures show an uninhabited and all the more lovely for remaining inviolate. Everything is seen close up and the bridge is so near that not all of it will fit into the frame. In all the paintings the sky is barely glimpsed or entirely absent, eliminating any sense of a horizon or of a wider world outside. The geometry of the bridge anchors this private paradise to the real world, putting a certain restraint on the impression of an unbelievable, trailing, melting, floating luxuriance. As usual, Monet refused to stand still, moving from the lush, tightly rendered aquatic canvases of 1899 (pages 226-7) to more freely painted scenes, enlivened with fiery reds, oranges and mauves, in which the bridge is viewed off-centre so that the banks and vegetation are given more prominence (page 229).

A number of these paintings were shown at Durand-Ruel's gallery in November 1900, together with some earlier works by Monet. This double grouping may have been included to remind spectators of the artist's past achievements and to put the new canvases into a wider context. Monet was evidently conscious that he was moving away from familiar subjects and compositional devices and hoped to make the transition comprehensible to his public. If so, his strategy was successful, for the *Water Lily Pond* paintings were readily accepted, although their apparently introspective character muted the reception given to them by most critics. Japanese prints were by now widely known and the affinity between Monet's canvases and the many prints featuring bridges was widely commented on. The Japanese, too, exploited unusual viewpoints and celebrated nature, but in retrospect the differences between Monet and Hiroshige or Hokusai are more striking than the similarities; for example between the superb designs, strong outlines, flat colours and stylization of the prints and the painterly richness and more immediate sense of living nature that are characteristic of Monet. The artist was of course aware of the comparison, in particular between the bridge paintings and Hiroshige's celebrated *Tenjin Shrine at Kameido*, masked with wisteria. It seems likely that Monet deliberately avoided charges of plagiarism (in his garden design as well as in the painting) by leaving the bridge clear of plants until the series was finished. Almost immediately afterwards, in 1901, he added a trellis along which wisteria was soon climbing, Hiroshige-style!

During the next two-and-a-half years Monet worked in the studio on the canvases he had brought back from London. But he was

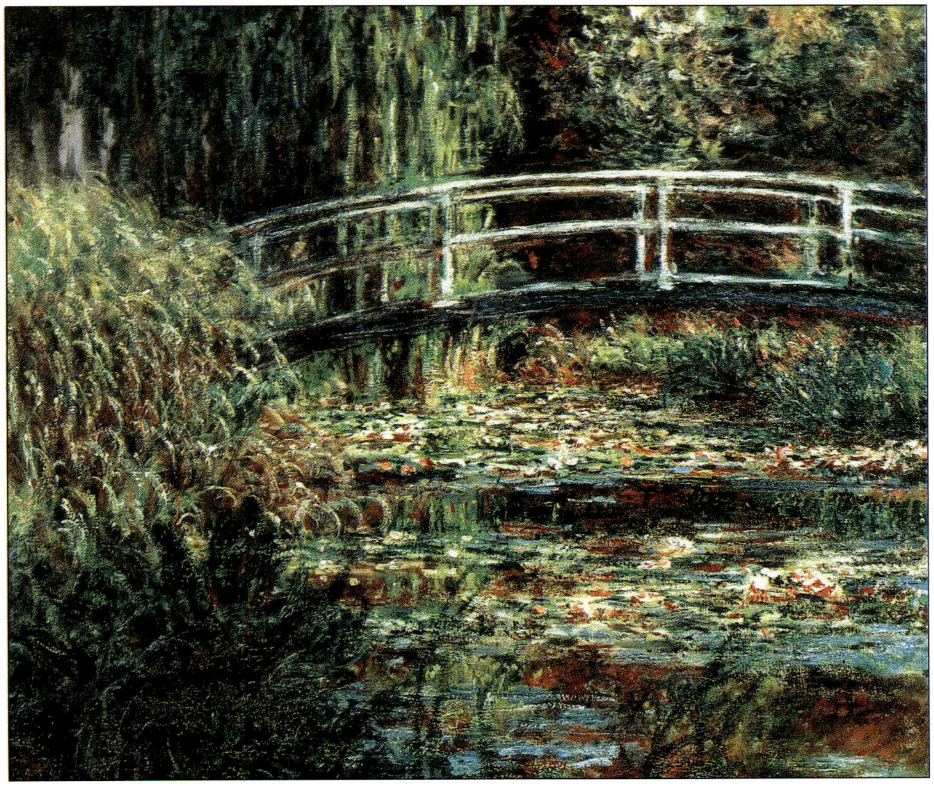

LEFT:
Waterlily Pond, Rose Harmony
(1900)
MUSÉE D'ORSAY, PARIS

also pushing forward with paintings of his flower garden (pages 224-5) and above all of his water-lily pond. In these the lure of water becomes even stronger and the area of solid ground on the surface shrinks until it is restricted to a strip of green bank along the top edge of the picture. As Monet continued, even this disappeared and the lily pads became the only objects of any substance. However, the sky reappeared, in the form of reflections in the water, frequently flooding down from the top of the canvas (page 235), but at other times forming part of a gentler harmony (page 237).

In the paintings of this period Monet displayed an extraordinary virtuosity in handling the transitions between a sense of the water's depth and the brilliant surface reflections of the sky or overhanging banks, both elements broken by pads and blossoms of varying size and number. Although their beauty now seems obvious and indisputable, these were paintings of unprecedented intangibility, apparently without substance, without indications of scale or depth, with no solid land in sight and only a topsy-turvy sky stretching down towards the bottom of the canvas.

Monet was uncertain about the direction he was taking and even more uncertain of the reception he was likely to get from the public. For several years he put off mounting an exhibition, despite the protests of Durand-Ruel, while he worked to satisfy himself. Finally, in May 1909, Durand was able to exhibit the largest number of Monet series paintings ever shown at a single time: 48 *Water Lilies* or *Nymphéas.* (Nymphéas was the type of native water lily grown by Monet at the time; later he added variety to the surface of the pond by introducing African lilies.) Even the subtitle of the show, *paysages d'eau* (water landscapes), could have been taken as a provocation, but there was no significant controversy and the exhibition was a great success. Monet was now such a revered master that he could do no wrong, in ironic contrast to his earlier career. Moreover, the disrepute of painting badly, improperly and tastelessly had been assumed by younger artists such as the Fauves, whose stridency made the essential harmony of the *Water Lilies* all the more obvious by contrast.

Venetian Interlude

A few months before the exhibition, in October 1908, Monet made the very last of his painting trips beyond the confines of Giverny. Driven by their chauffeur-servant, he and Alice made the long journey to Venice, where they stayed in style at the Palazzo Barbaro, owned by friends of Monet's friend, the American painter John Singer Sargent, and later at the Grand Hotel Britannia. They enjoyed themselves immensely and were photographed feeding the pigeons in St Mark's Square; indeed, after Alice's death their stay in Venice became one of Monet's most precious memories.

But he also took the working aspect of the trip seriously. Like so many earlier artists, he was enchanted by the mellow light falling on buildings that seemed to rise up straight out of the sea. He may well also have been tempted to continue his duel with Turner, who had painted dazzling, melting views of Venice from the early 1820s. However, although Monet seems to have come away with about 50 canvases, they were in a far less advanced condition than the fruits of earlier expeditions. Once he had left Venice, he was half-inclined to dismiss them as holiday souvenirs, evidently feeling impatient to get on with his water-lily studies. Although he promised the dealer Bernheim-Jeune that he would finish them and mount an exhibition of Venetian works, he neglected them for almost two years.

This was a period of worries, distractions and outright disasters. Monet's eyes were probably already troubling him. He had canvases that needed finishing for his *Water Lilies* exhibition at Durand-Ruel's. In 1910 floods threatened to destroy his beloved gardens, and when the danger was past he had to begin work on an official commission, a set of paintings from which tapestry designs could

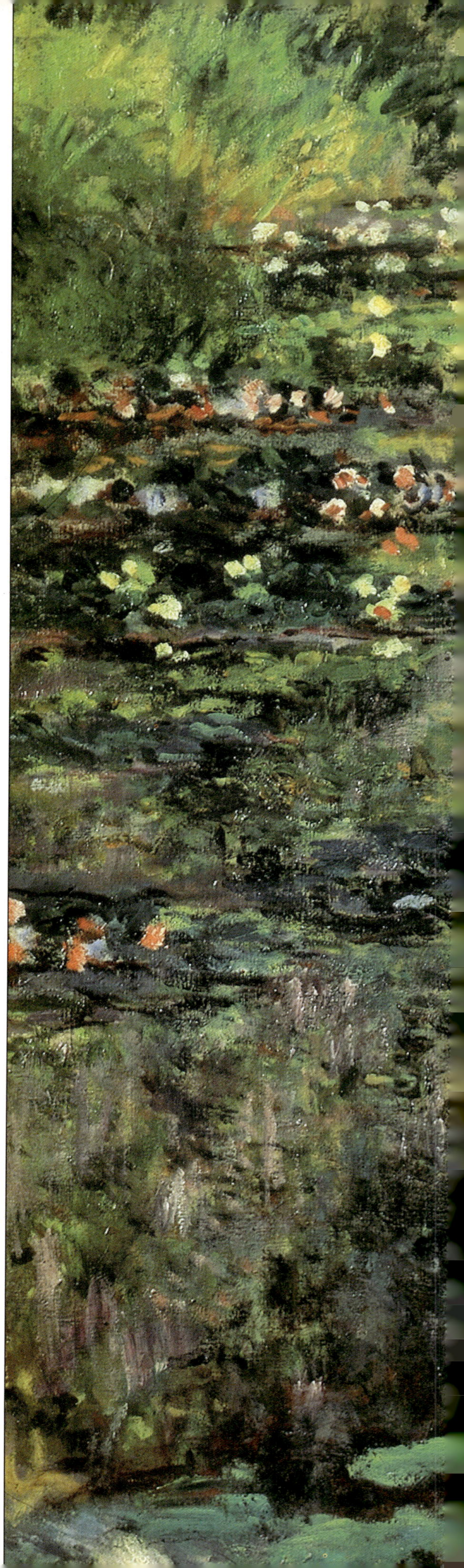

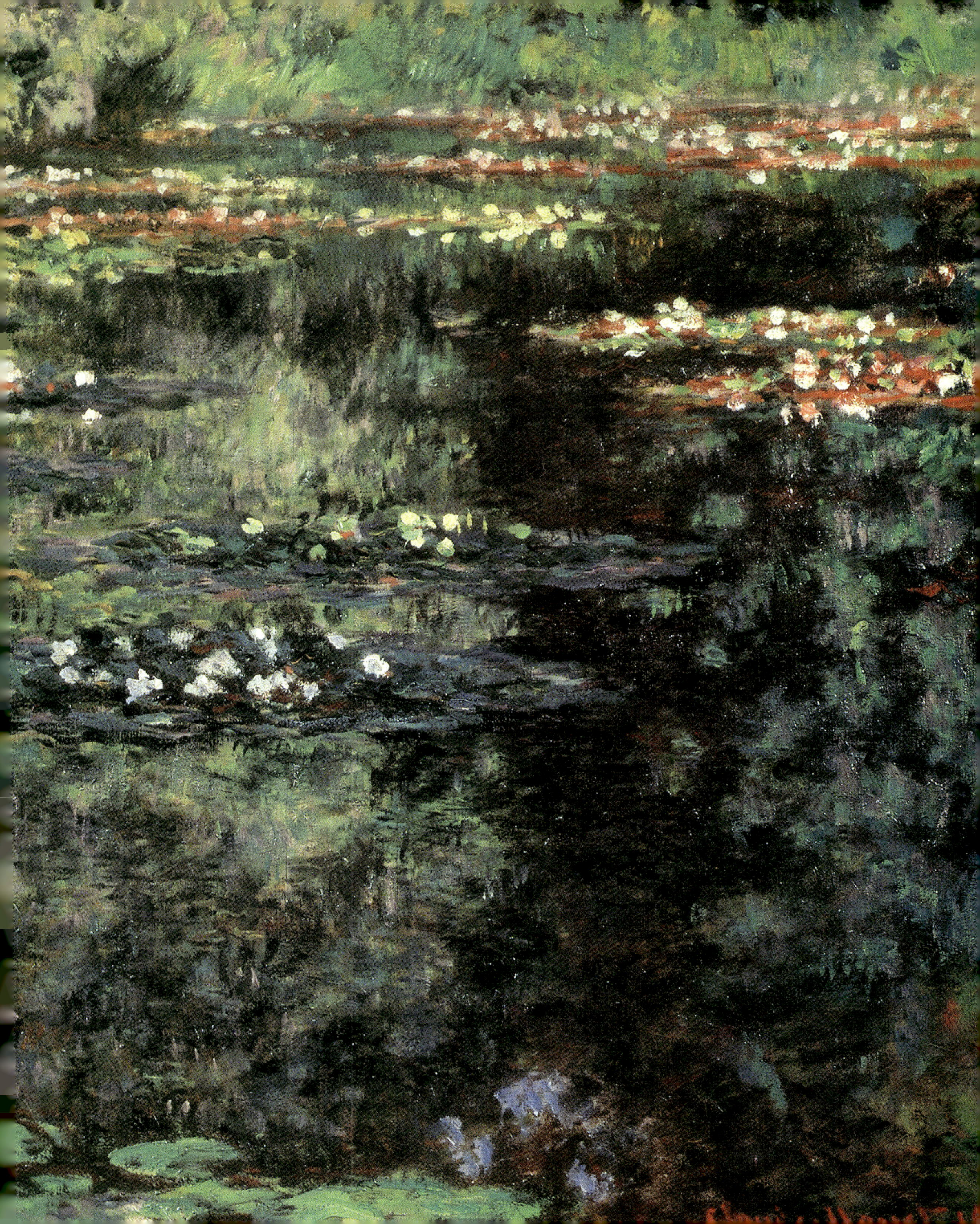

PREVIOUS PAGES 230-1:
Waterlillies
(1904)
Musée des Beaux-Arts, Caen

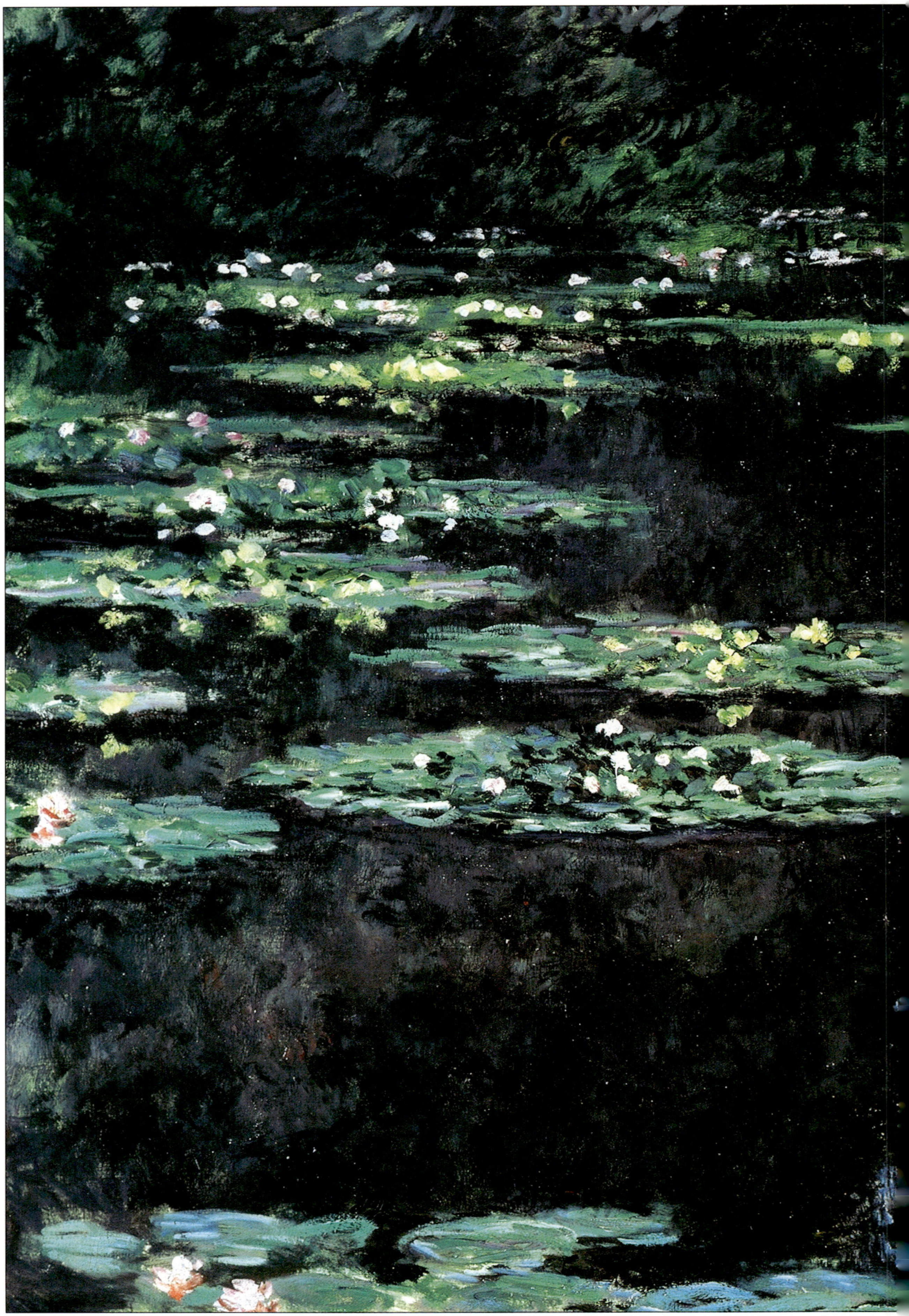

RIGHT:
Waterlillies
(1904)
Musée des Beaux-Arts, Le Havre

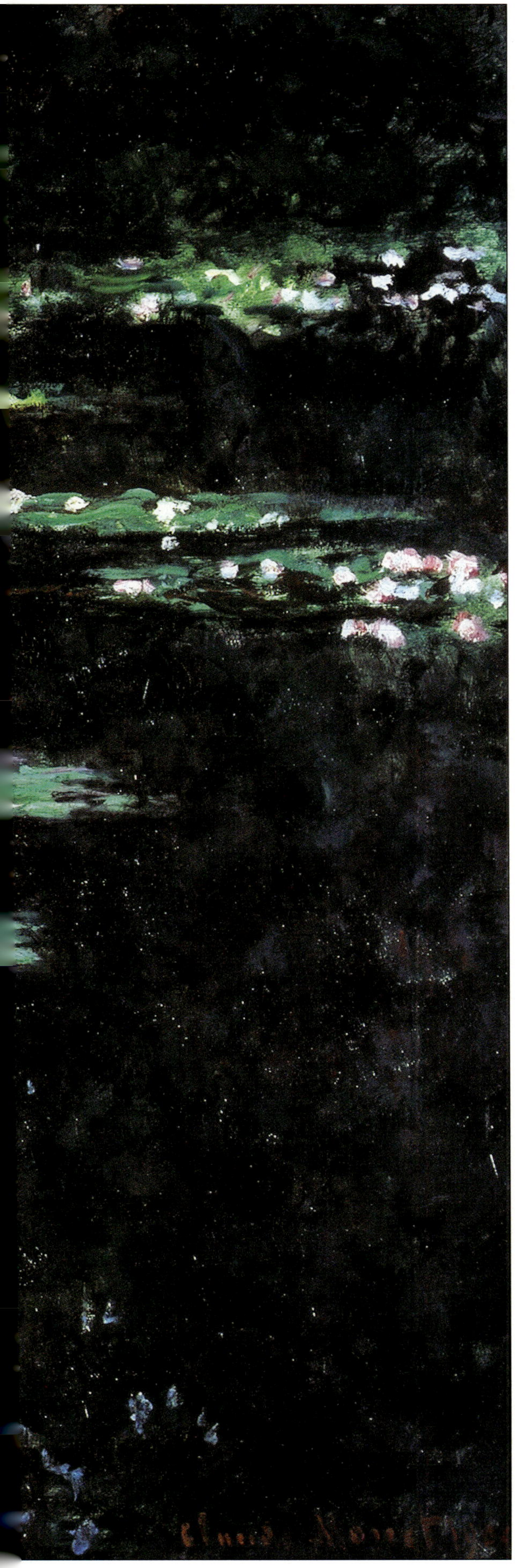

be made up at the famous Gobelins works. The idea originated with Monet's friend and future biographer, Gustave Geffroy, who had been appointed director of the Gobelins.

Trials and Tragedies

Then Alice became seriously ill. Diagnosed as suffering from leukaemia, she went into a rapid decline and died on 19 May, 1911. Faced with the end of more than 30 years of intimacy, Monet was devastated. For a time he was disorientated and helpless, feeling that he had lost interest in everything. He was even indifferent to the garden and to painting. When he did take up his brushes again, he was so depressed by the results that he declared – not, however, for the first time – that he would have to give up painting.

Inevitably, he came back to life again and finally completed 29 of the Venetian views, which went on show at the Bernheim-Jeune Gallery in May 1912. The favourable public response was by now predictable, although Monet felt that the paintings were not up to his normal standard. The Neo-Impressionist artist Paul Signac wrote to Monet perceptively, describing the paintings in terms which might have been applied to all of his mature works as 'expressions of your will in which no detail runs counter to your emotion'. The Venetian pictures have conventionally been grouped by subject (as they were at Bernheim's), notably studies of the Grand Canal (pages 238-9) and the Church of San Giorgio Maggiore (pages 240-1). These were the last buildings to appear in Monet's canvases and, as was usual by now, they were rendered as so atmospherically enclosed that they seemed like natural features in the landscape. Like cathedrals and factories and London's Houses of Parliament, the historic buildings of Venice were appropriated by Monet as purely visual motifs, divested of their historic meaning and function. In this sense Monet was a forerunner of the modern breed of autonomous artists, such as Picasso, self-authorized to make use of everything in the visible world without feeling any obligations towards it.

The completion of the Venetian pictures left Monet free to go on with his garden paintings, which became his sole subject for the rest of his life. However, the period between 1912 and early 1914 proved to be almost barren, as his work was undermined by personal and family afflictions. His sight had worried him intermittently for decades, but in July 1912 he was horrified to discover that he could not see at all with his right eye and that his left eye was also affected.

A specialist's diagnosis was that the lens was being obscured by a cataract and Monet was advised to have surgery. He resisted the idea and apparently did nothing, claiming a few months later that his right eye had begun to improve. There must have been some kind of remission, or at least a pause in the deterioration of Monet's vision, but just how serious the problem remained is impossible to assess. Monet evidently decided to dismiss the matter from his mind and coped in silence for a surprising number of years until the effects on his life and art could no longer be ignored.

Monet's elder son, Jean, underwent a more rapid and appalling deterioration. In July 1912, shortly before Monet became aware of his loss of vision, Jean suffered a savage mental attack which marked the onset of a brain disease. It almost certainly represented the tertiary phase of syphilis, a sexually transmitted infection that took a terrible toll until the development of modern antibiotics. Usually revealing itself years or decades after the original infection, tertiary syphilis took the form of locomotor ataxia, an agonizing complaint of the nervous system that had, for example, caused Edouard Manet's early death, or of brain disease culminating in general paralysis of the insane, which was to be Jean's fate. He made a partial recovery from his 1912 attack, but by early 1913 he was so ill that Monet bought a house at Giverny and brought Jean and Blanche to live there. One indication of the strain placed on Monet is the fact that he took a two-week holiday in Switzerland and that on this, the last trip he would ever take abroad, he seems to have made no effort to paint. Within a few months Jean's condition was deteriorating so fast that Monet had him moved to Le Pressoir, where he died, still only 46 years old, on 10 February, 1914.

The feelings of a man in his seventies, watching at his son's death-bed in his own house, are beyond imagining. The only positive feature of the tragedy was that Blanche, Jean's widow and Monet's old painting companion, decided to stay on at Giverny and look after him. Her care of him, and the order she introduced into the household, freed Monet from worries and undoubtedly helped to sustain the creative impulse of his final period.

That impulse was felt remarkably soon after Jean's death, which may finally have come as a relief. At any rate, by April 1914 Monet was 'feeling wonderful' and declaring himself, as always in his best days, 'obsessed with the desire to paint'. He threw himself into his work, painting his beloved water lilies on much larger canvases than he had used before. Never much interested in official occasions,

RIGHT:
Waterlilies
(1906)
PRIVATE
COLLECTION

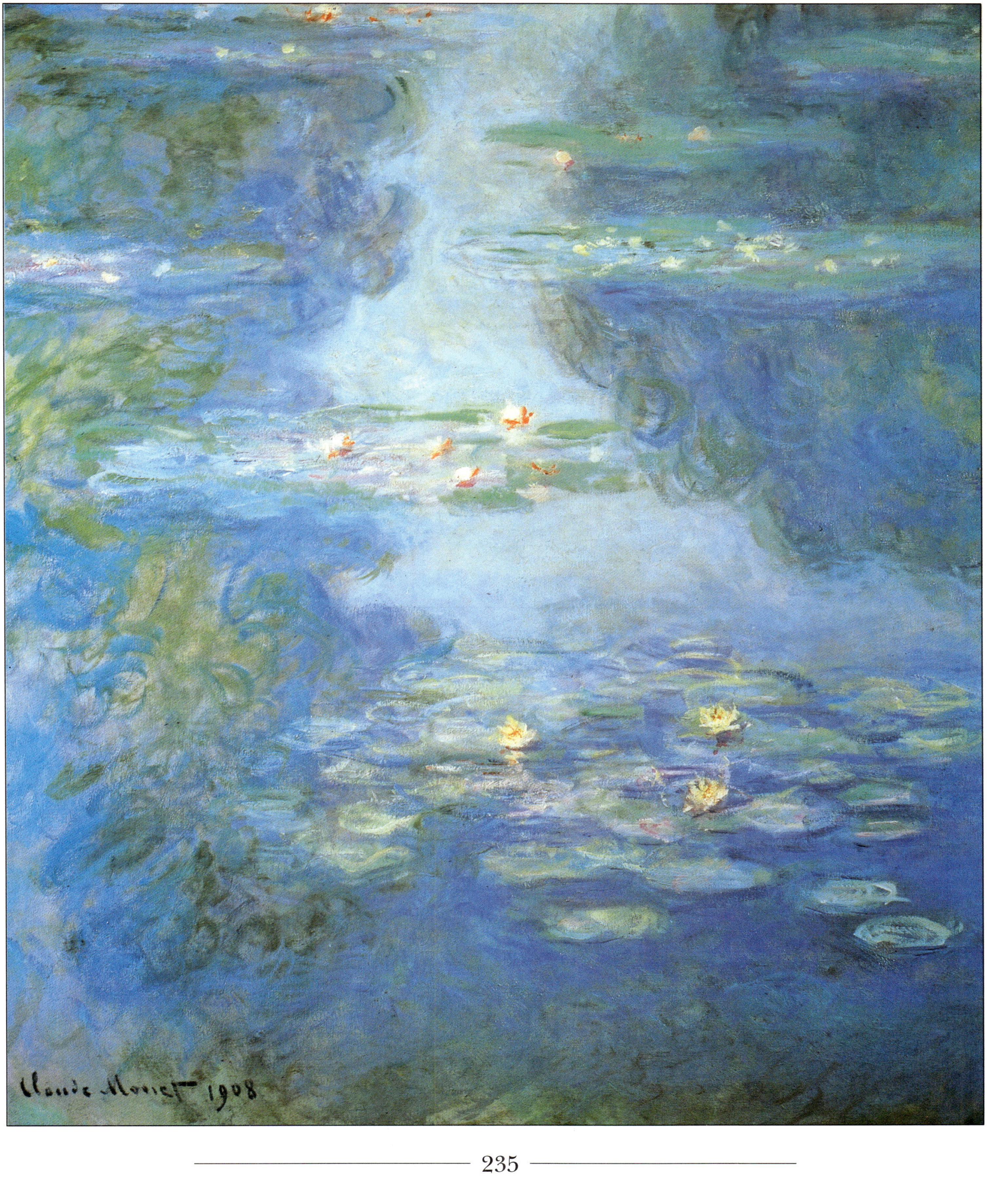
Claude Monet 1908

he even refused an invitation to see his own works installed in the Louvre as part of the Camondo Bequest.

Despite their size, the new canvases were often painted in a quite cursory fashion, as though Monet only explored as far as seemed necessary and useful to him and then left off without further ado. Understandably, it has been suggested that this large group of canvases, executed between 1914 and 1917, were essentially studies made in preparation for the *Grandes Décorations* with which his career culminated. However, such specific connections between the pictures and the *Grandes Décorations* are hard to establish and many of the individual 'studies' are fine works of art in their own right (pages 242-3).

Monet's euphoria was rapidly dissipated in August 1914 by the outbreak of World War I and the German invasion of Belgium and France. Like millions of others, he experienced the anxiety of seeing his son Michel and his Hoschedé stepsons join the colours. The huge numbers of wounded men who were assembled in the villages behind the front line soon made him aware that the conflict was infinitely more intense and bloodier than anything that had ever taken place before in European history. Moreover, Giverny was disturbingly close to the front, and at any time during the war it seemed possible that a successful German 'Big Push' would lead to the village being overrun, a prospect that Monet viewed with mingled apprehension and defiance.

At 74 years old he could contribute to the war effort only by means of his wealth and fame, and he was unusually active in the sales, subscriptions and exhibitions launched to help the military and civilian victims of the conflict. Only one serious effort was made to utilize Monet's now venerated name for propaganda purposes: in 1917 he was offered a state commission to paint Reims Cathedral, which had been shattered by a German bombardment that Frenchmen interpreted as an act of cultural barbarism. Influenced by the passions of war and perhaps by the inescapable implication of the offer that he was France's greatest living artist, Monet uncharacteristically accepted the commission, but for some reason the project went no further.

Monet's greatest contribution, of course, was to go on working to the advantage of the entire world and also as a distraction from the fears and hopes occasioned by the war. Despite his age, he often experienced the non-combatant's feeling that it was embarrassing and humiliating to be preoccupied with non-essentials – in his case, unworldly matters such as colour harmonies and composition.

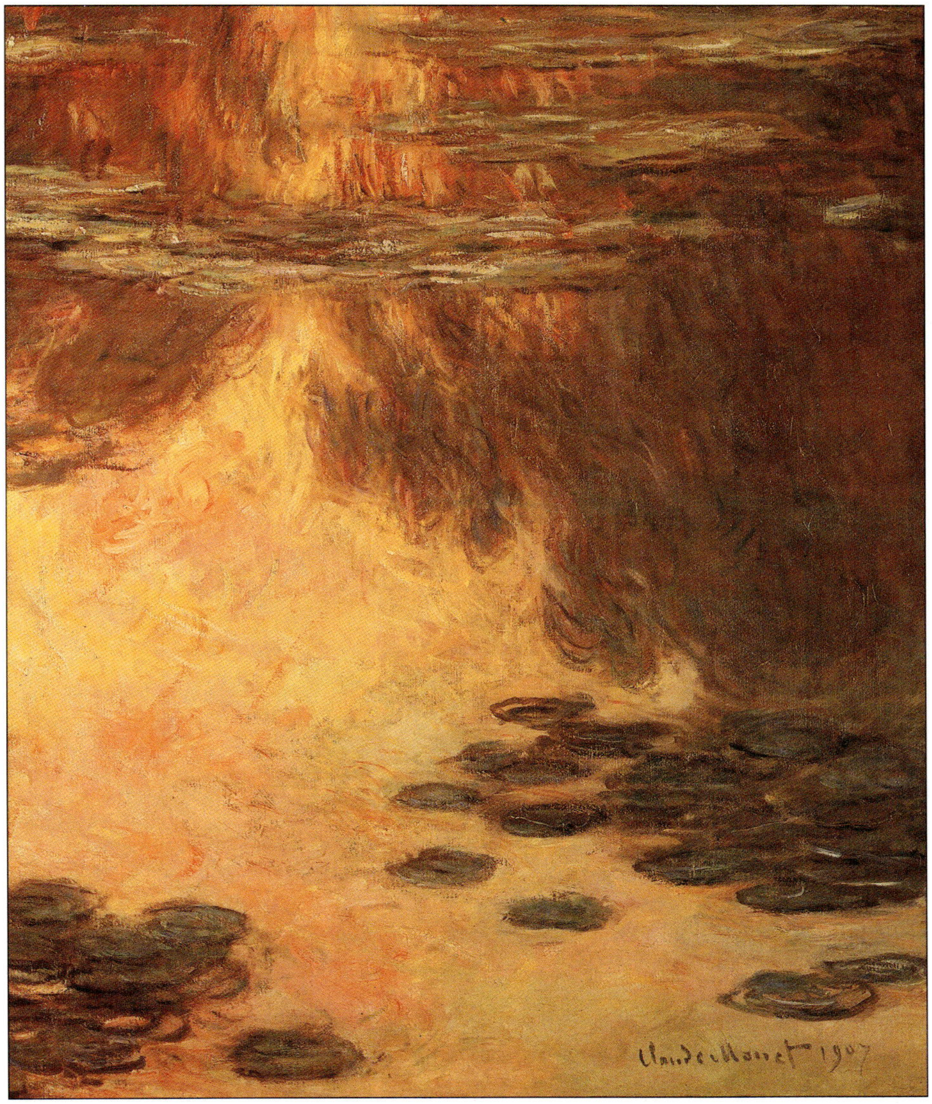

LEFT:
Waterlilies
(1907)
PRIVATE COLLECTION

But within a few months he was again absorbed in 'work, the great consolation', painting more large studies of water lilies and contemplating the even more ambitious undertaking that would crown his career.

The Grandes Décorations

OVERLEAF PAGES 238-9:
The Grand Canal, Venice
(1908)
PALACE OF THE LEGION OF HONOR, SAN FRANCISCO

The idea of the *Grandes Décorations* had been present in Monet's mind almost 20 years earlier, when it was mentioned in an article by a journalist, and it somehow lingered on in artistic circles even after Monet himself appeared to have forgotten it. The original article was by Maurice Guillemot, who in August 1897 had accompanied Monet on a dawn trip to his studio-boat. By his own account Guillemot was also successful in prompting the artist to reminisce

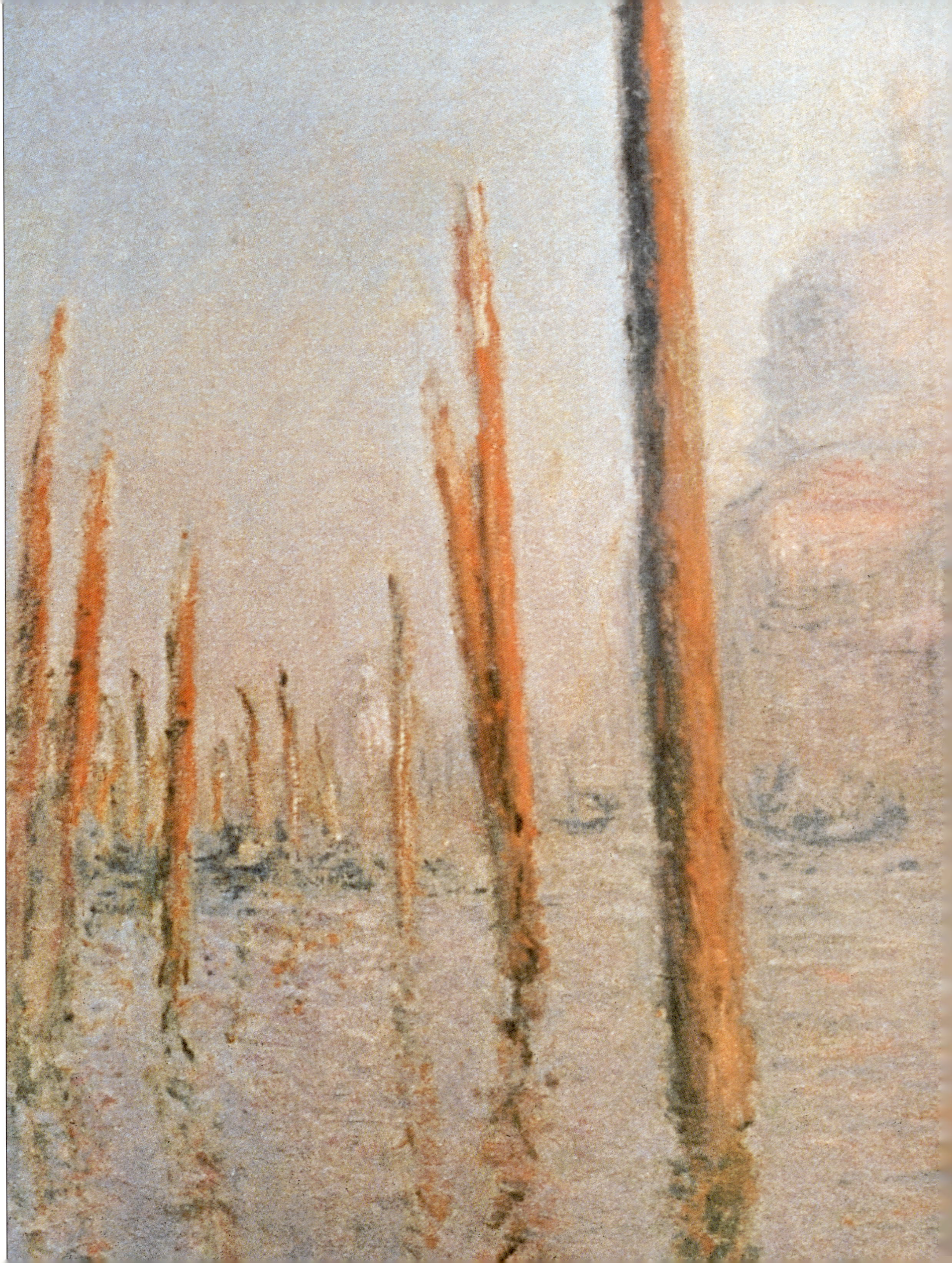

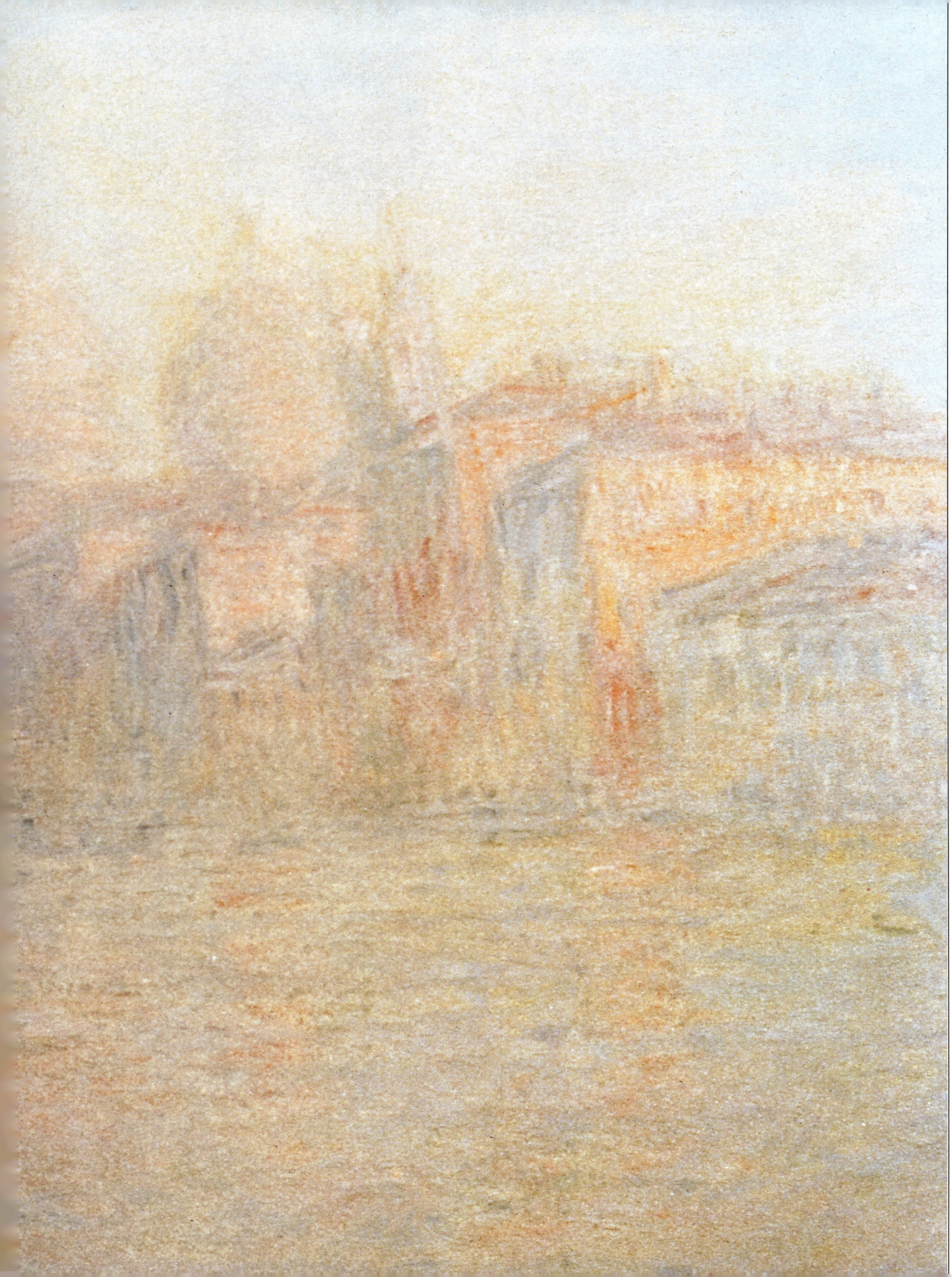

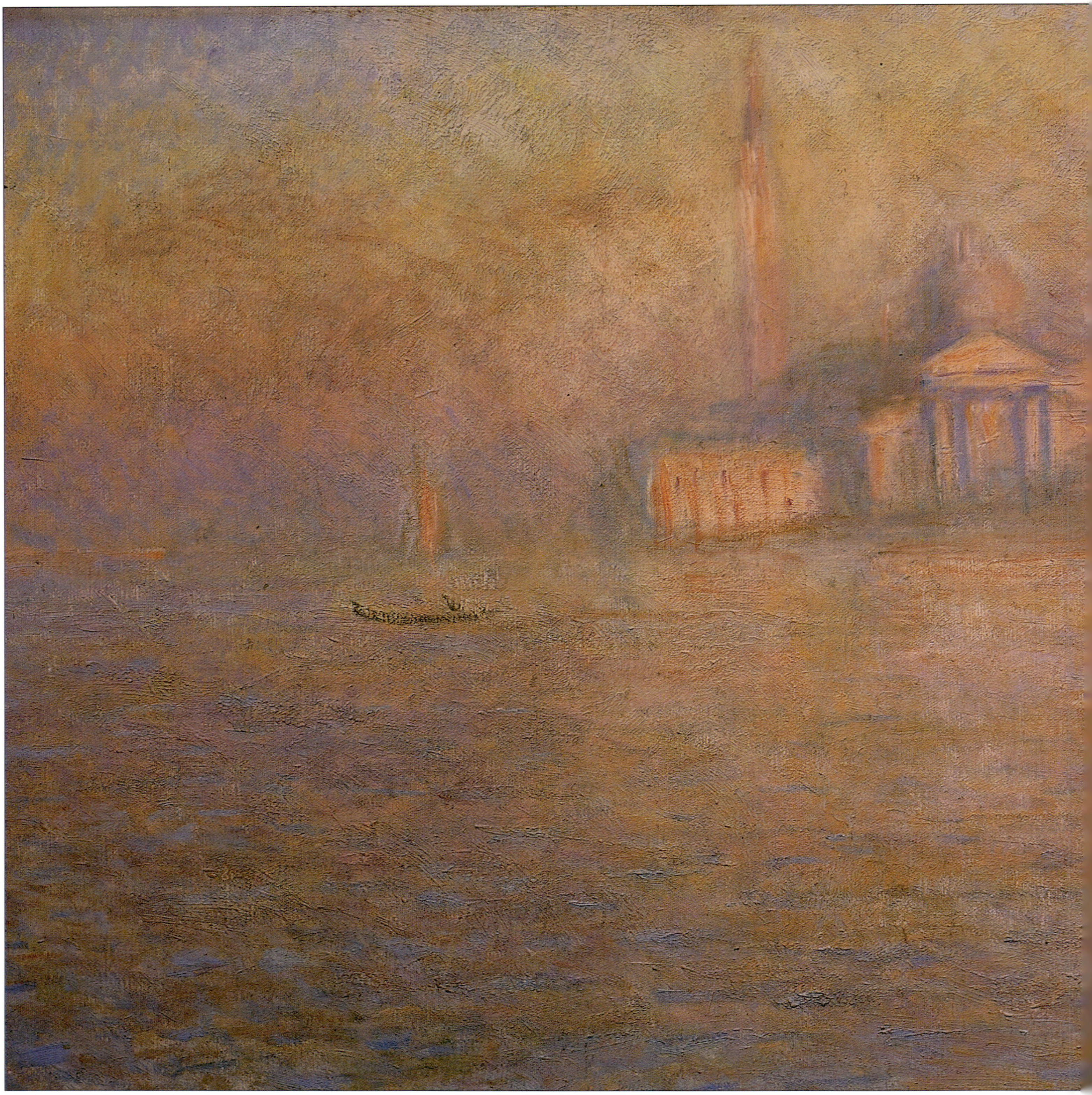

about his Impressionist past and was shown Monet's studio 'or sitting room, rather, since our open-air painter works only out of doors', wrote Guillemot, faithfully retailing the central Monet myth. Among the canvases Monet showed him were large panels which were intended to serve as studies for a great decorative work.

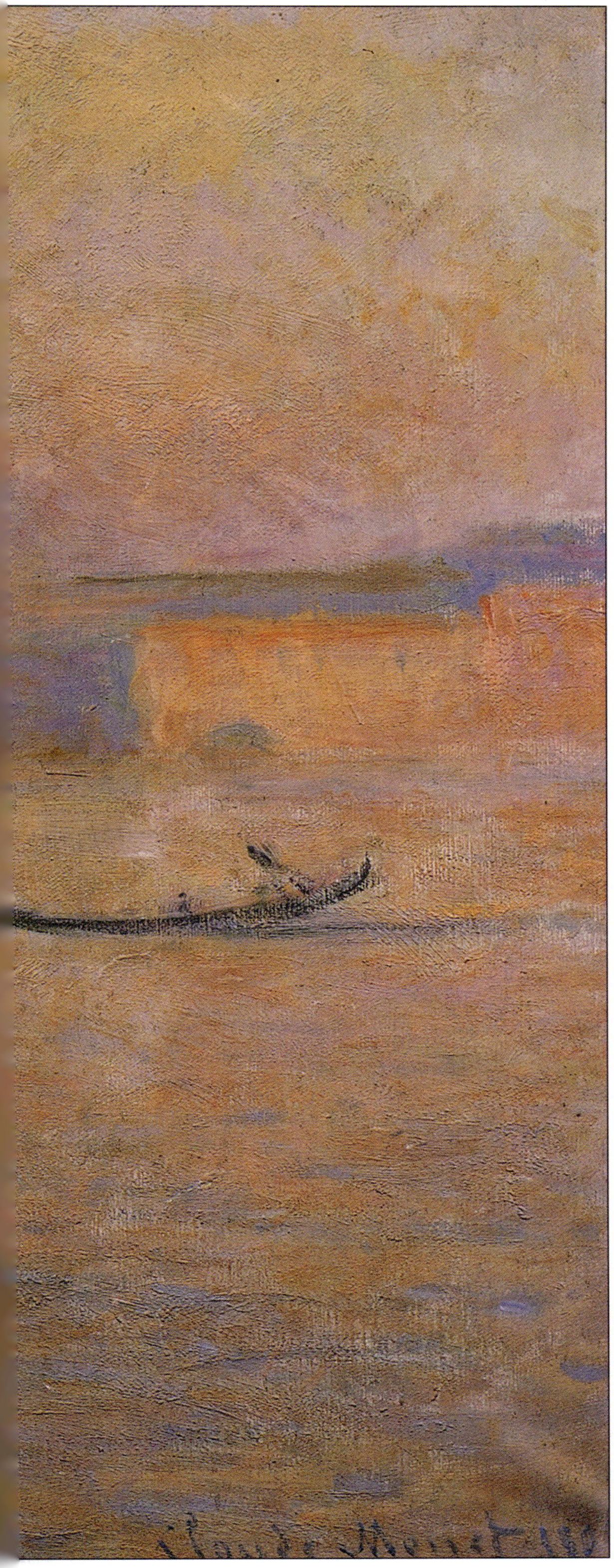

ABOVE:
San Giorgio Maggiore, Venice (1908)
NATIONAL MUSEUM OF WALES, CARDIFF

Monet evidently confided the nature of the projected decorations to Guillemot, since the journalist passed it on to his readers: 'Imagine a circular room in which the area beneath the moulding is covered with water and dotted with plants to the very horizon, walls of a transparency alternately green and mauve, the calm and silence of the still waters reflecting the opened blossoms. The tones are vague, deliciously nuanced, with a dreamlike delicacy.'

This is not bad as a description – or prophecy – of the great decorative panels that were installed in the Orangerie 30 years later. Although it has proved impossible to identify the panel-studies that Guillemot claimed to have seen, the fundamental accuracy of his account seems beyond dispute. Strangely, although Monet must have shelved the project, the idea remained in the air. Monet himself may have made a habit of mentioning it; if not, we can only suppose that other writers found Guillemot's description so memorable that it influenced their responses to what they saw some 11 years later, which is hard to believe. Reviewing the 1909 exhibition of water-lily paintings in the *Gazette des Beaux-Arts*, Roger Marx included a long diatribe, put into the mouth of Monet but probably mostly fictional, in which the painter is made to say 'I was once briefly tempted to use water lilies as the sole decorative theme in a room. Along the walls ... water without horizon or shore.' Even more remarkably, writing a little earlier in the periodical *Comoedia*, Arsène Alexandre put forward, as though it was his own and certainly with details not mentioned by Guillemot, the vision of a bare circular room with 'mysteriously seductive reflections' all the way round it.

As far as we know, it was only at some point in 1914 that Monet became interested in the project again. He was increasingly working in a broad style highly suitable for large-scale decorations and he could now contemplate the tempting prospect of creating a lasting memorial to his art in the form of a series that would never be dispersed. Still a little doubtful about embarking on such an ambitious task, Monet was encouraged by his friend Georges Clemenceau, who told him firmly, 'You can do it!' From this point onwards, Clemenceau took on the role of Monet's artistic conscience. The two men were almost the same age, and Clemenceau's undiminished activity as a politician and journalist gave him the authority to rally the artist when the fatigues and fears of old age took hold of him.

Monet's artistic eminence and political contacts stood him in good stead during the war. At a time of shortages, he was able to

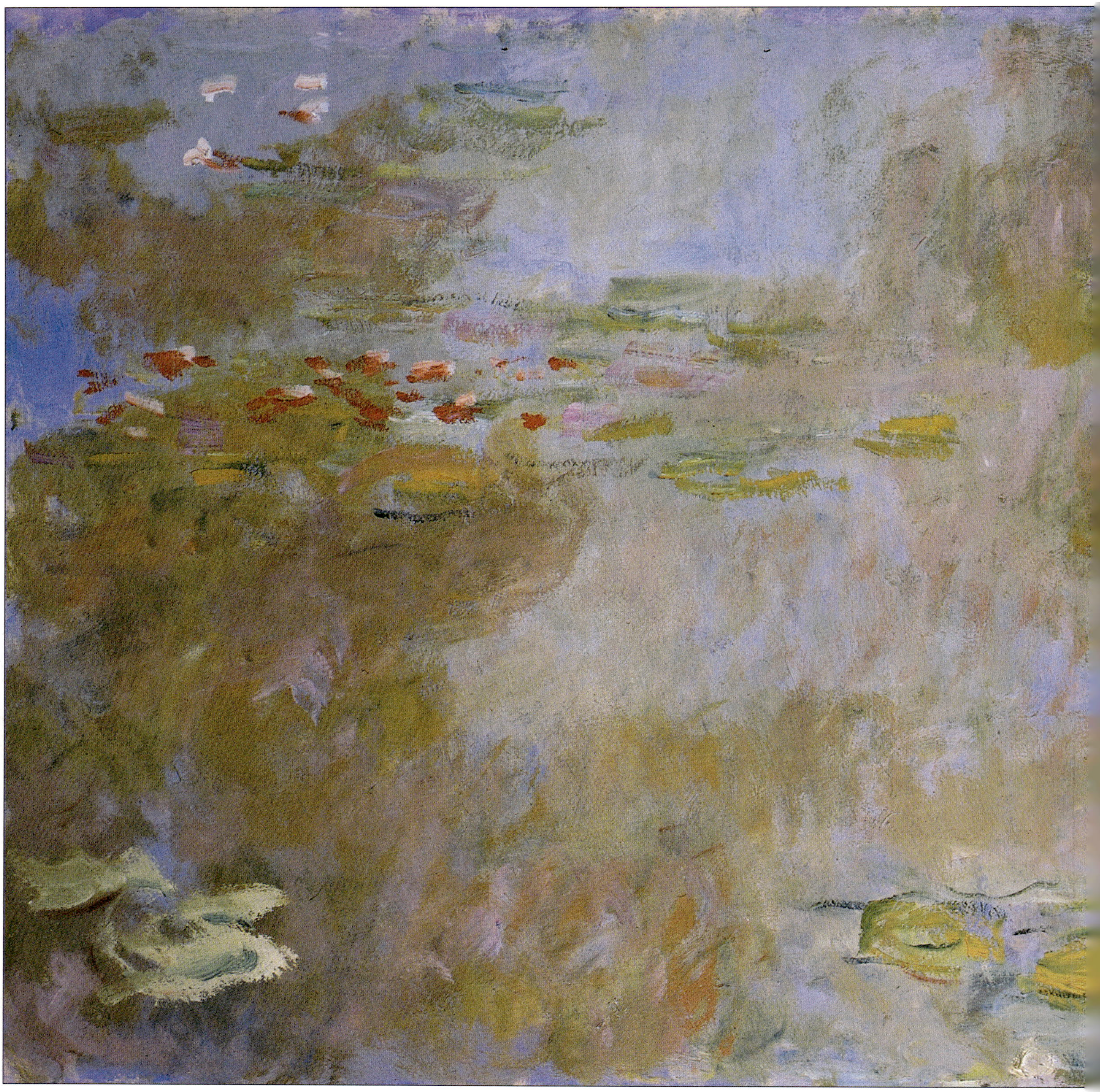

procure all the materials he needed to go on working, as well as petrol and, above all, the official permission, labour and materials which enabled him to build a third studio at Giverny. This huge, single-space, top-lit structure was effectively in place before the end of 1915. Monet was a little embarrassed by its ugliness, but it

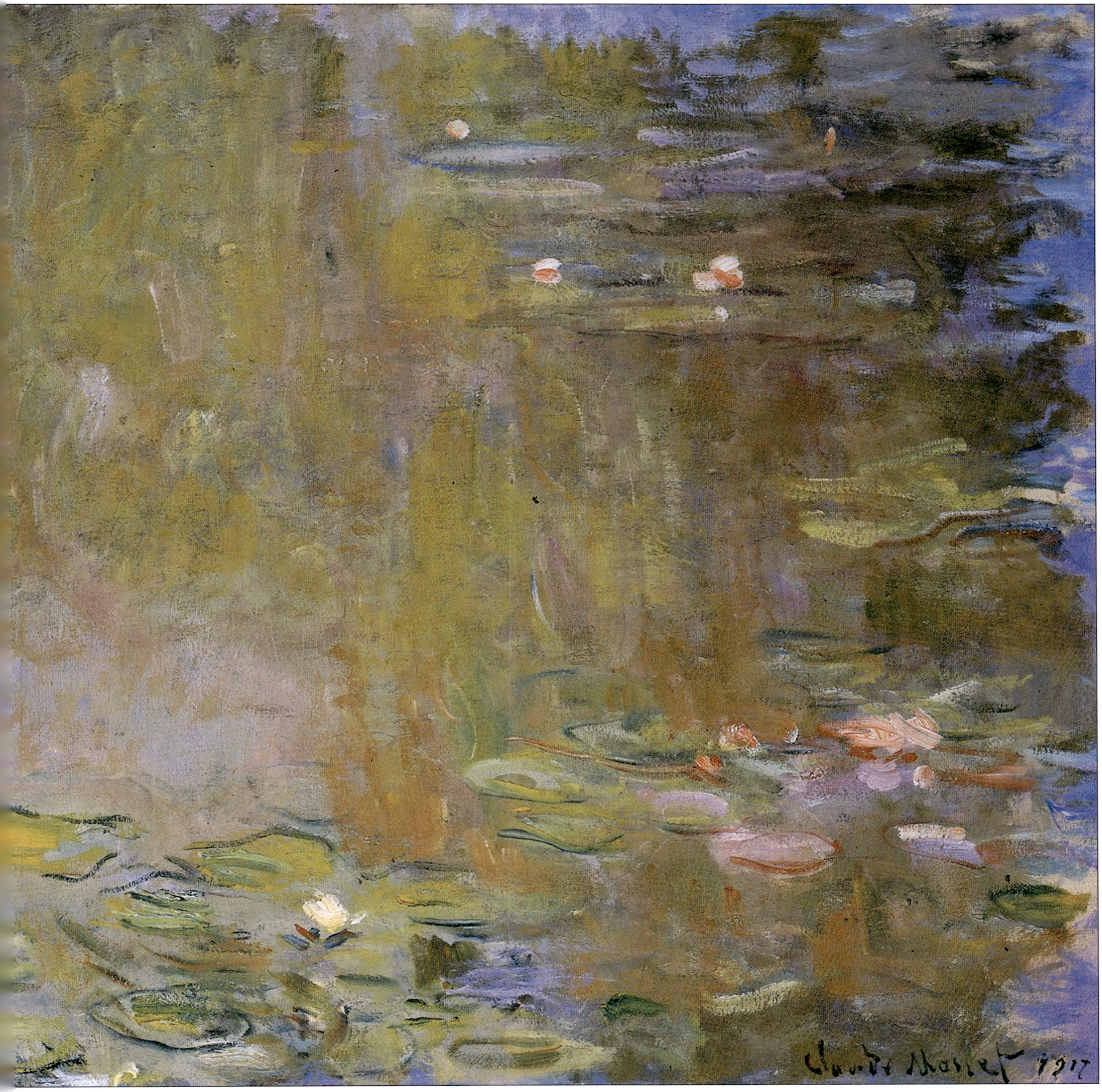

ABOVE:
Waterlillies (1917)
MUSÉE DES
BEAUX-ARTS,
NANTES

provided him with the indispensable setting for his work on a set of wide, high, curved panels that also had to be mobile so that they could be compared, arranged and finally integrated into a multi-section work of art. The panels were placed on special easels fitted with rollers, but to paint the upper halves of these two-metre-high

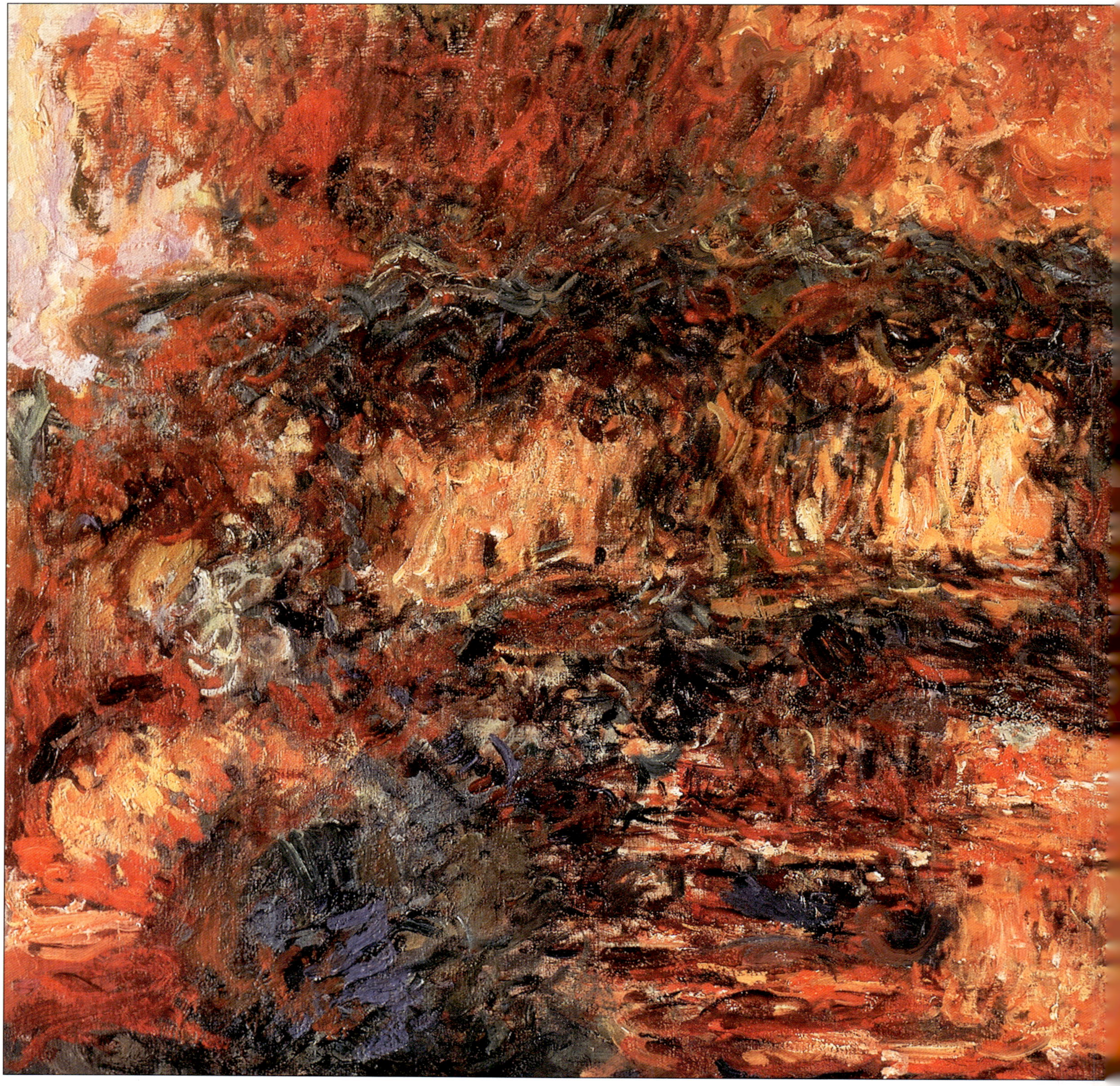

ABOVE:
Japanese Bridge
(1918-22)
SOCIETY OF FINE ARTS, MINNEAPOLIS

canvases Monet used the less high-tech device of a low table. Needless to say, these works were not painted in the open air but inside, from memory and imagination, assisted to some extent by studies.

During the war, Monet worked hard on his *Grandes Décorations*, as well as painting many other large canvases. At this stage, the

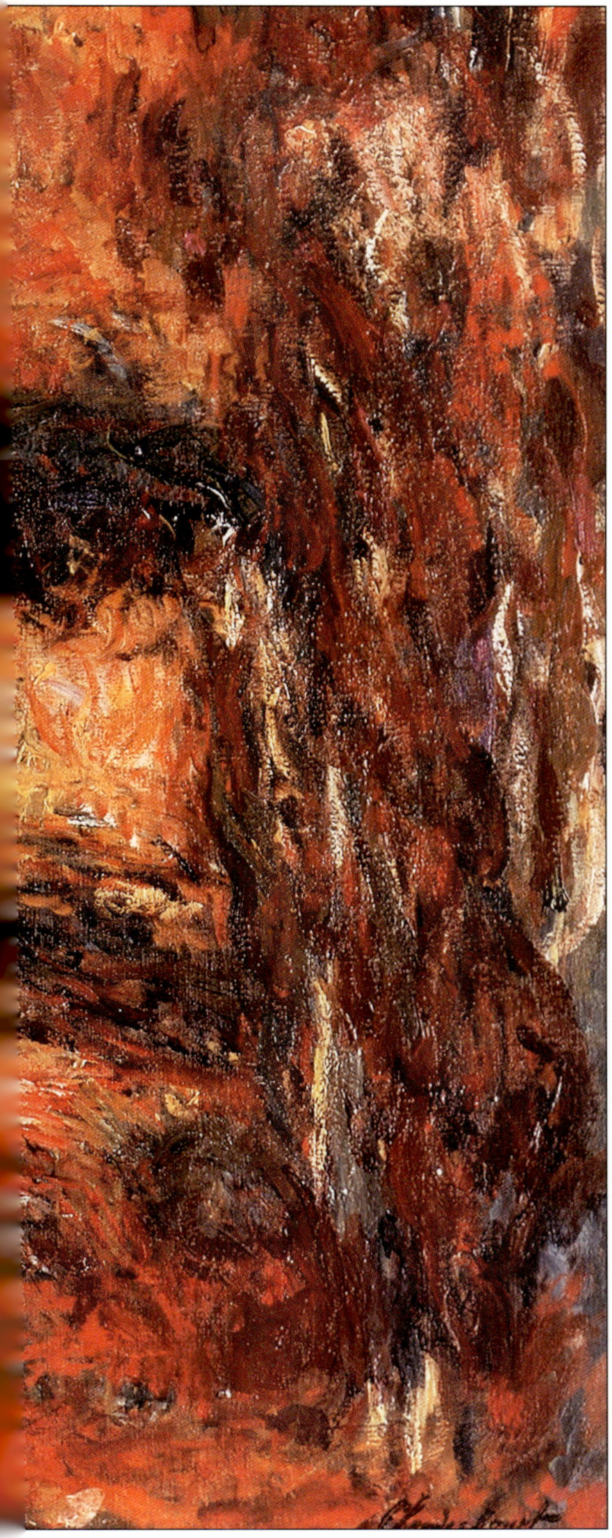

major project was intended to comprise a dozen panels, although Monet painted several more of the same size in order to widen his choice when it came to making the final arrangement. In November 1917, Durand-Ruel and his son visited Giverny and took a series of photographs which show the canvases in an apparently advanced state, although in view of Monet's working methods it would have been impossible to predict when he was likely to consider them finished.

A year later, with the victory of France and her allies assured at last, Monet wrote to Clemenceau, who had now become a hero to his fellow-countrymen and earned the nickname 'the Tiger': having become Prime Minister in November 1917, he had steered the

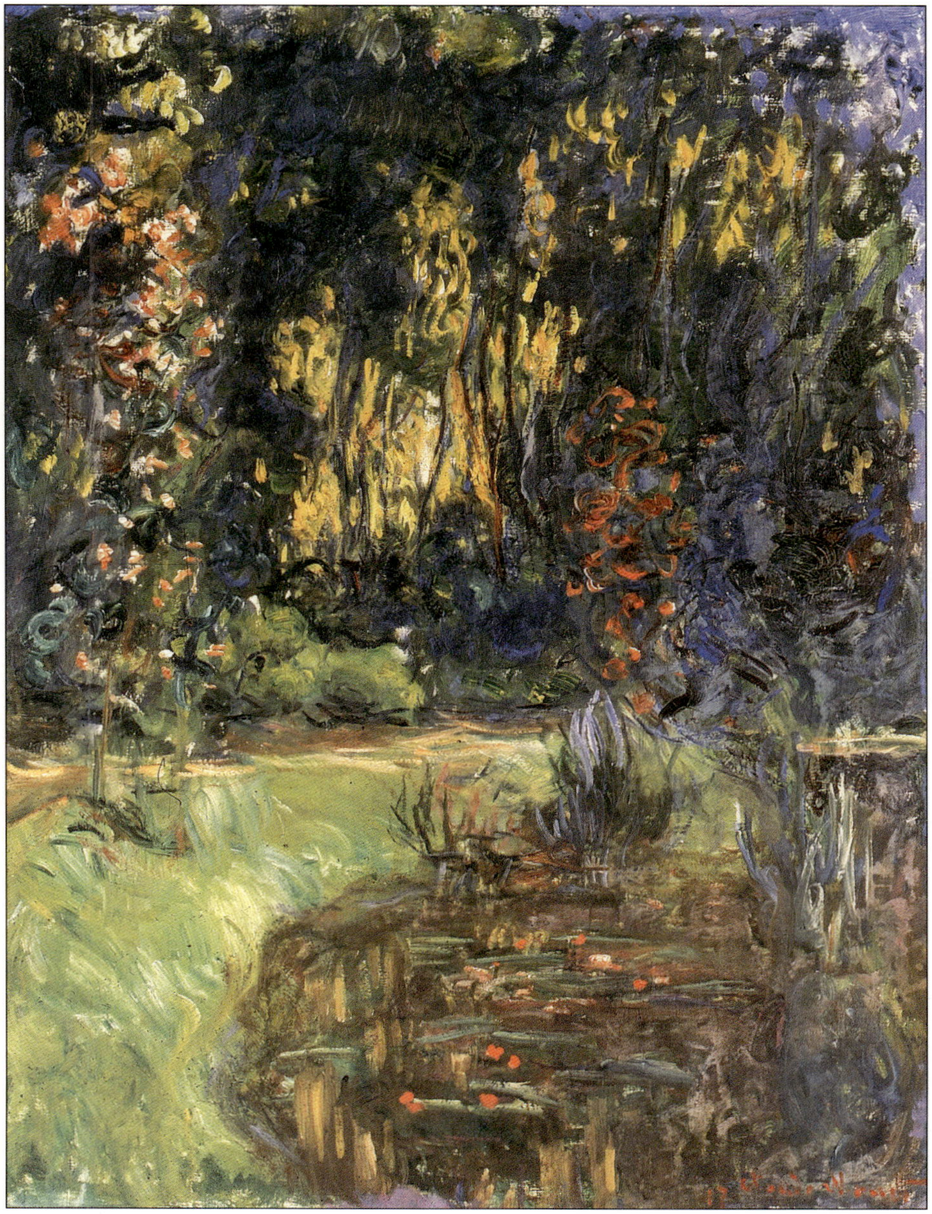

RIGHT:
The Garden at Giverny
(1923)
MUSÉE DE GRENOBLE

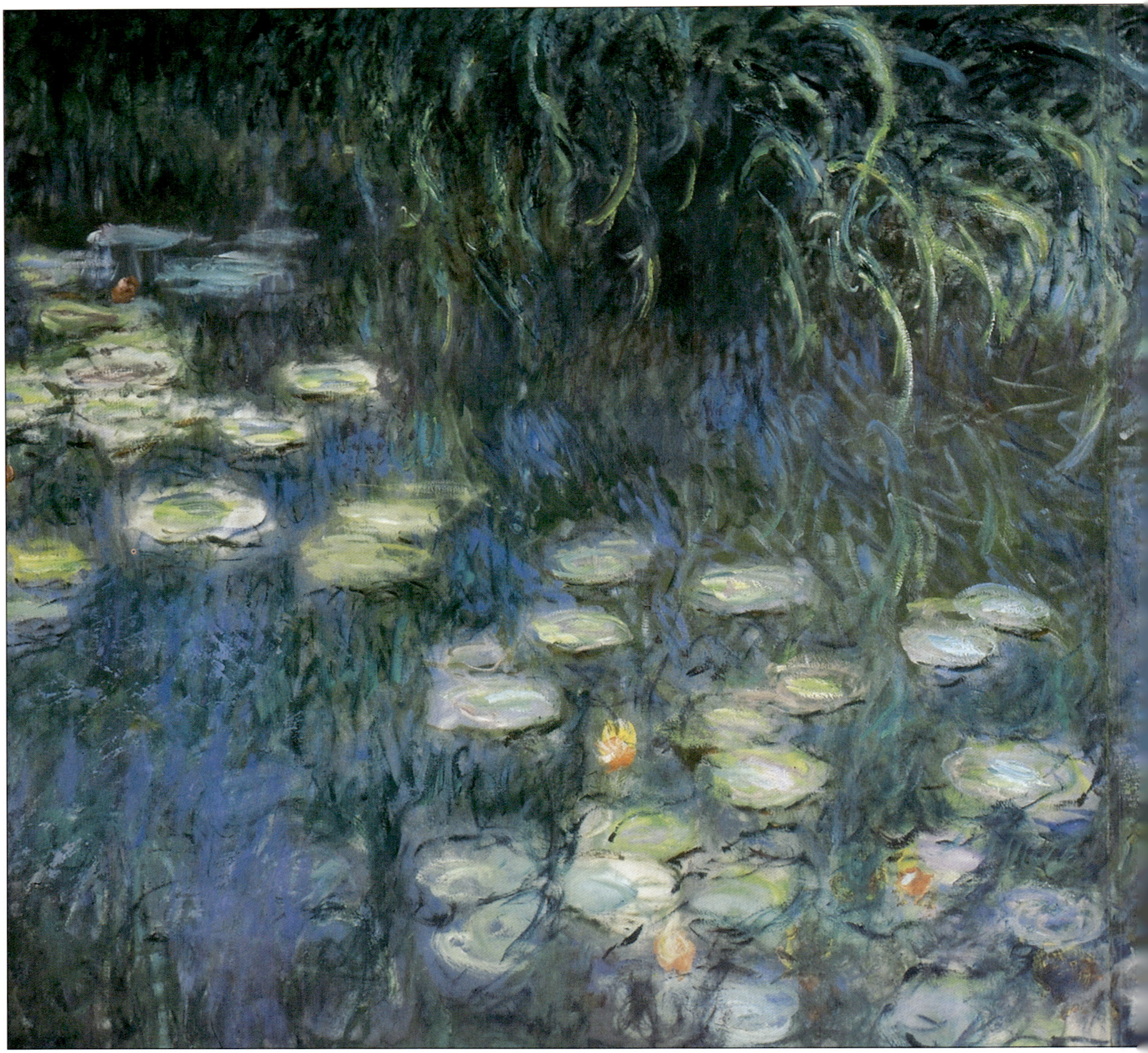

ABOVE:
The Grandes Décorations Waterlillies: Morning (left section)
MUSÉE DE L'ORANGERIE, PARIS

country through the final, tense phase of the war. Evidently rejoicing in the turn of events, Monet told his friend that he was about to finish two decorative panels which he intended to sign on the day Germany surrendered: would Clemenceau offer the panels on his behalf to the French state?

Monet's offer indicates that he had indeed been working on more than the intended 12 canvases and felt able to part with two panels that did not fit into the final scheme – if there was, as he

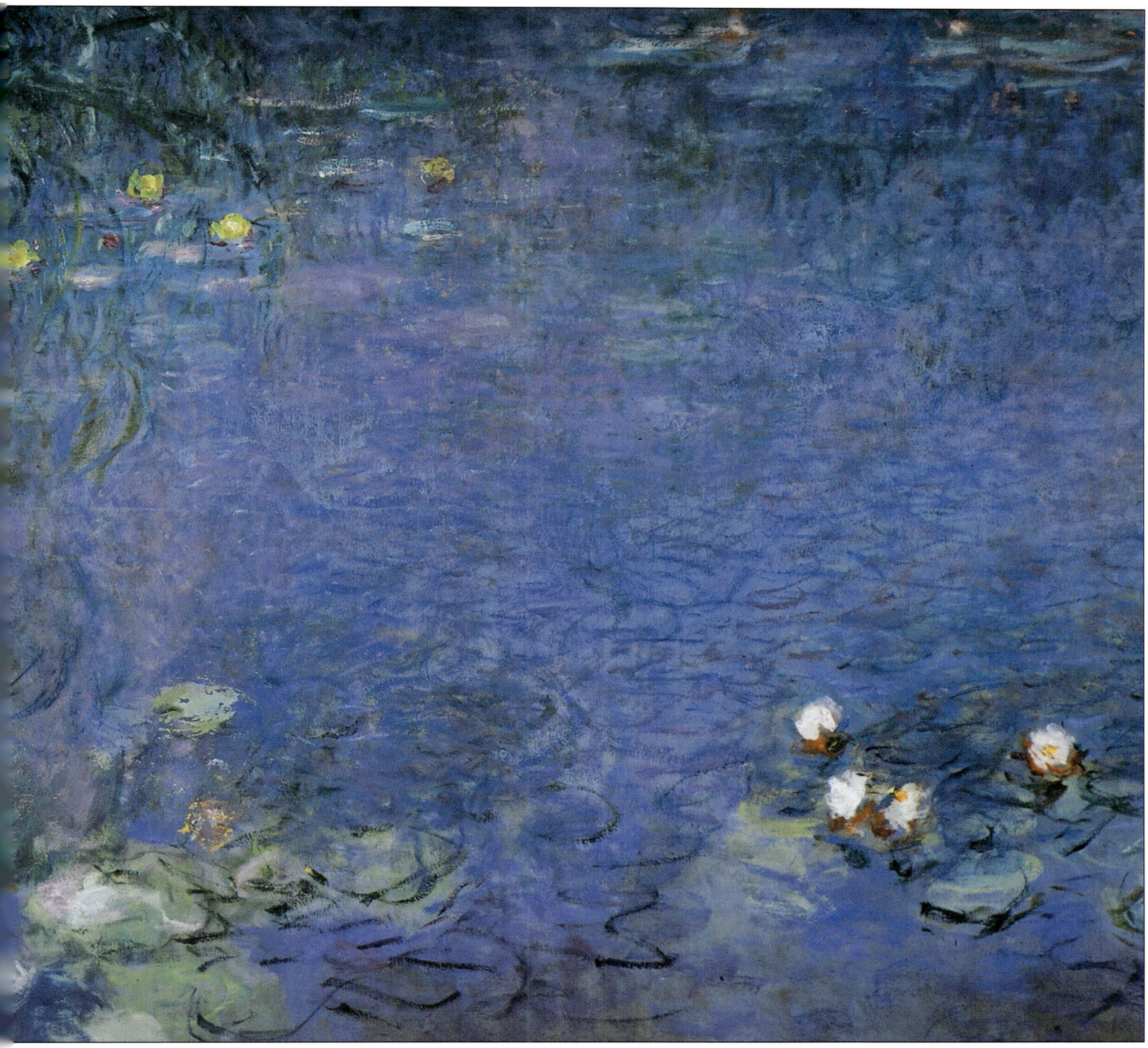

claimed at about the same time, a final scheme approaching completion. Such considerations rapidly became irrelevant when Monet's proposal was transformed into a much larger donation, probably suggested to him by Clemenceau: the artist would give the entire set of circular decorations to France and, in return, the French state would house it appropriately. In effect, there would be a national monument to Monet's art, raised in his own lifetime.

With Clemenceau's power and prestige behind it, the scheme

seemed bound to be realized and Monet went on confidently with his work. He had now become an almost symbolic figure, representing a generation of artists who were remembered with increasing nostalgia. The deaths of Degas (1917) and Renoir (1919) left him as the last of the great Impressionist masters. He referred to himself as 'the last survivor of the group', rather ungenerously forgetting the existence of Armand Guillaumin (1841–1927), an admittedly minor Impressionist who outlived even the master of Giverny.

Finalizing the details of the donation proved more difficult than anticipated, especially since Clemenceau unexpectedly fell from power. He had rashly allowed his name to be put forward for the presidency, but his candidature was defeated by a coalition of his enemies in the National Assembly and he felt obliged to resign the premiership. His influence remained strong, however, and he created a pressure group consisting of politicians and journalists to agitate for the completion of the *Grandes Décorations* project.

In the summer of 1920 a satisfactory arrangement appeared to have emerged. The Hôtel Biron in Paris, formerly the studio of Monet's friend Auguste Rodin, had passed to the state and had been transformed into a museum devoted to the great sculptor's memory. It was now proposed that a pavilion should be built in the grounds of the Hôtel to house Monet's *Grandes Décorations*, incidentally bringing together on a permanent basis the co-exhibitors of 1889. As Rodin had worked in a different medium and was not a direct competitor, Monet favoured the idea; moreover, the fact that he and Rodin had been born on the same day must have made their final interlinking seem laid down by a decree of fate. The building, with a single large circular room to hold the *Grandes Décorations*, was designed before the end of the year.

Monet was giving the canvases to France, but in February 1921 the state showed its appreciation by a generous *quid pro quo*, purchasing his 1866–7 *Women in the Garden* (page 39) for a staggering 200,000 francs. Possibly the politicians and officials concerned were unaware of the irony involved in the transaction, for this was the ambitious figure painting so humiliatingly rejected by the Salon jury of 1867. Consciously or otherwise, Monet had notched up a final victory in his long duel with the establishment.

If Monet's association with Rodin had been decreed by fate, the decree was swiftly cancelled. Murmurings began to be heard concerning the cost of a new, specially designed building, and the Hôtel Biron project was cancelled. Instead, Monet was offered an existing building, the Orangerie. The site was a fine one in the

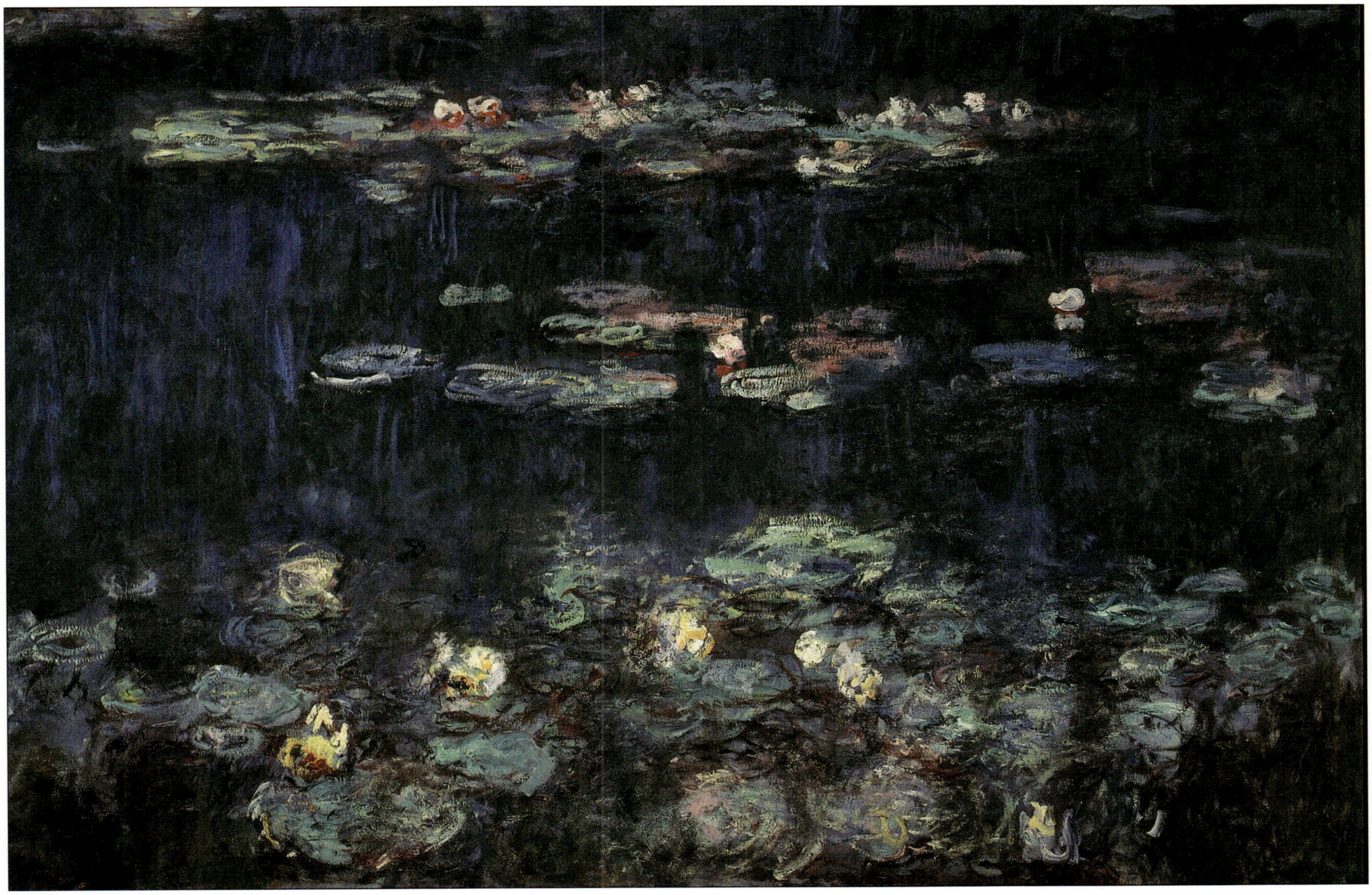

very heart of Paris, in one corner of the Tuilleries Gardens, with the Louvre itself standing at the other end of the gardens beyond the Arc du Carrousel. But the change of plan was bound to entail a daunting amount of extra work, since there were to be two rooms instead of one and their shape was to be oval instead of circular. Nevertheless, Monet agreed and in January 1922 signed a contract in which he undertook to deliver the stipulated works by April 1924. In retrospect, this contract between the state and an 81-year-old artist with bad eyesight seems rather rash from both points of view and the outcome might well have been a fiasco.

ABOVE:
The Grandes Décorations Waterlillies: Green Reflections (right section)
MUSÉE DE L'ORANGERIE, PARIS

The Final Struggle

By this time Monet was engrossed in other garden paintings, including a Japanese bridge series begun as early as 1918 (pages 244-5). These canvases are painted with a raw expressionist ferocity like nothing else in his life's work. The subject is only just discernible

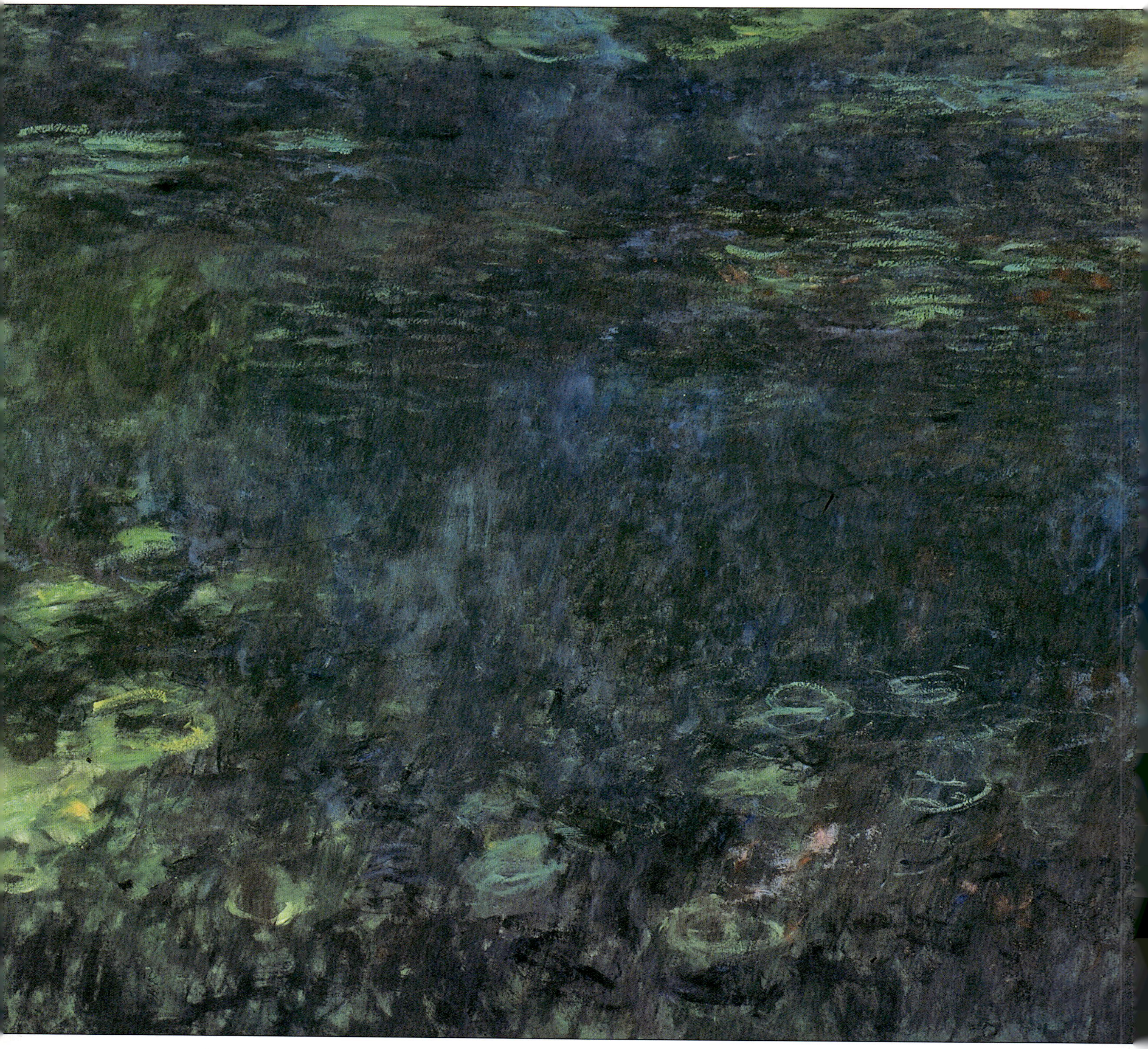

ABOVE:
The Grandes Décorations Waterlillies: The Clouds (left section)
MUSÉE DE L'ORANGERIE, PARIS

and the paint seems to have been laid on in a frenzy. It is hard not to read into this tumult Monet's rage and terror in the face of his physical decay and, above all, the near-blindness which must in part account for their appearance. Evidently his sight was deteriorating again and had reached a point at which the damage could no longer be ignored or denied. Monet recognized with reluctance

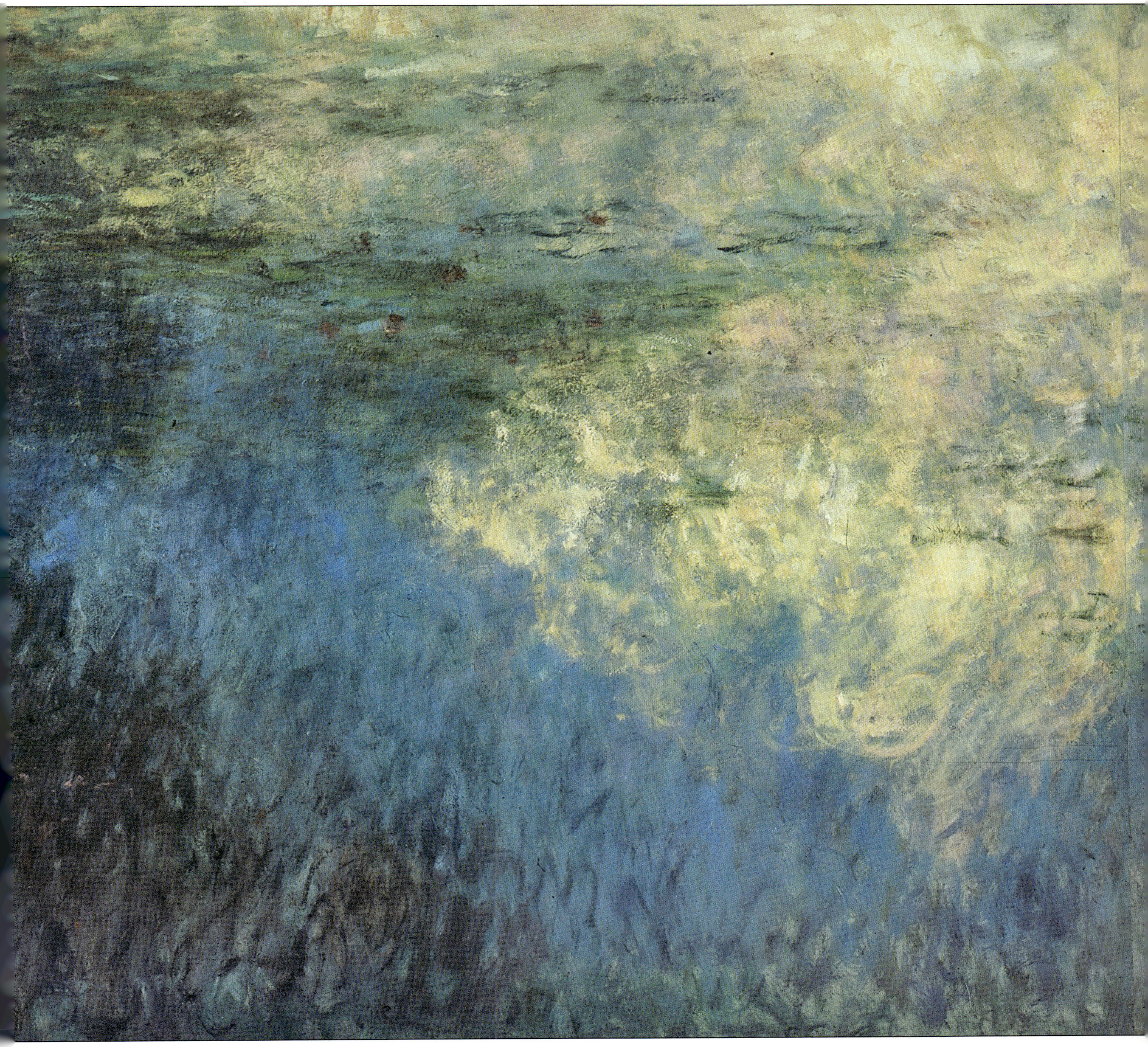

that something must be done, and early in 1923 nerved himself to undergo two sessions of surgery to remove his cataracts.

The immediate result was a marked improvement, but over the following two years Monet's ability to distinguish colours accurately and even to see at all fluctuated considerably. After a third operation in July 1923, he refused to have further surgery,

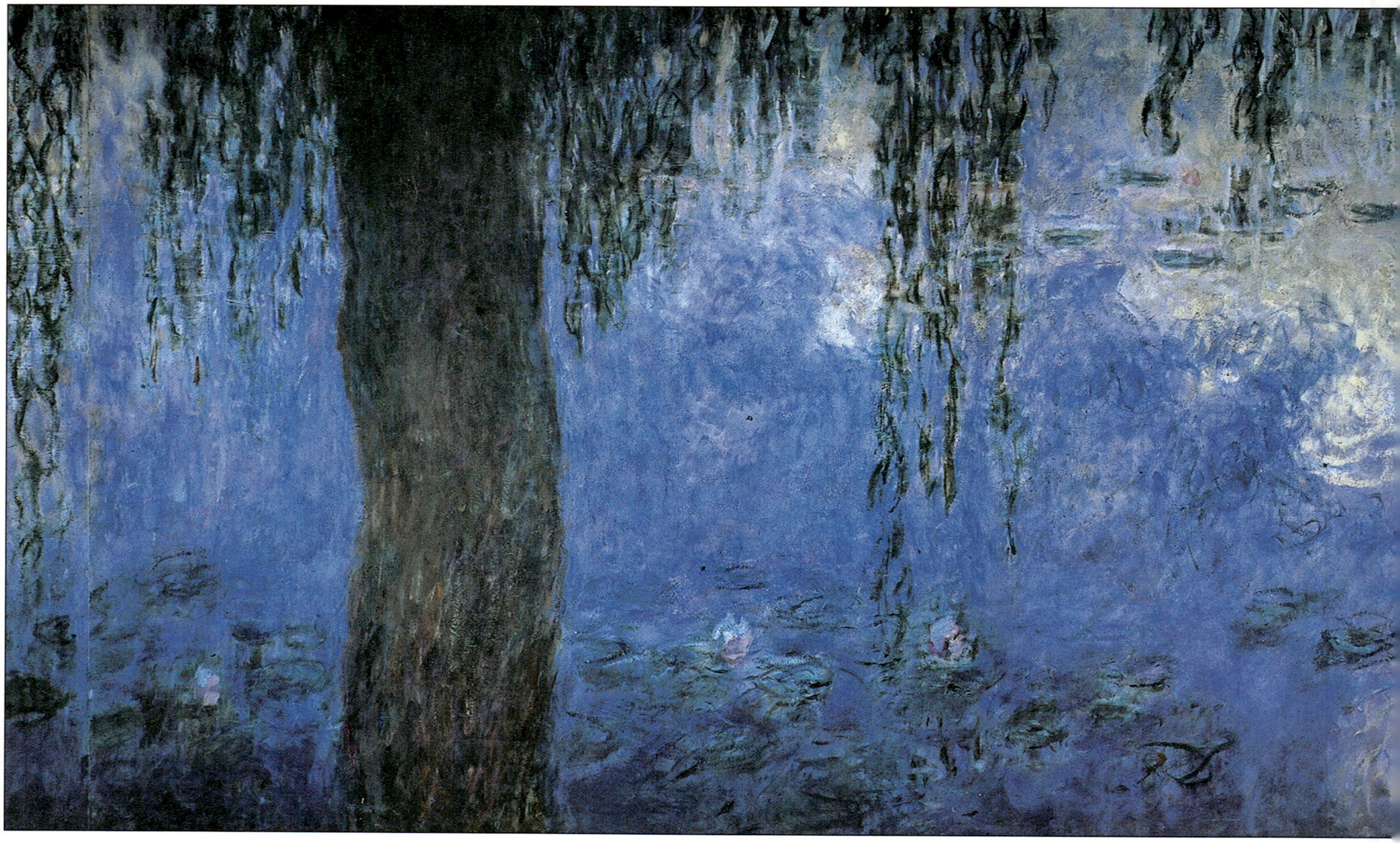

but on more than one occasion specially designed spectacles brought new hope and enabled him to go on working for a time. Understandably, these ups and downs affected Monet's spirits and he was often depressed and ready to give up everything, including painting. The most powerful counteragent was Clemenceau, who nagged and threatened and even accused Monet of using his eye problems to disguise a collapse of morale that made him ready to contemplate a shameful deed – the failure to honour his contractual obligations to the French nation. Whether this upset Monet or kept him up to the mark is difficult to assess, but in spite of strains, the friendship endured.

Suddenly, in April 1925, a new pair of Zeiss spectacles brought about a dramatic and lasting improvement. 'My sight is completely restored, I am working as never before and like what I'm doing. If the new spectacles are even better, my only desire will be to live to be a hundred.' Monet worked hard all year, and by the following spring had completed the panels for one of the Orangerie rooms. Probably, to all eyes but his own, the entire project was ready and

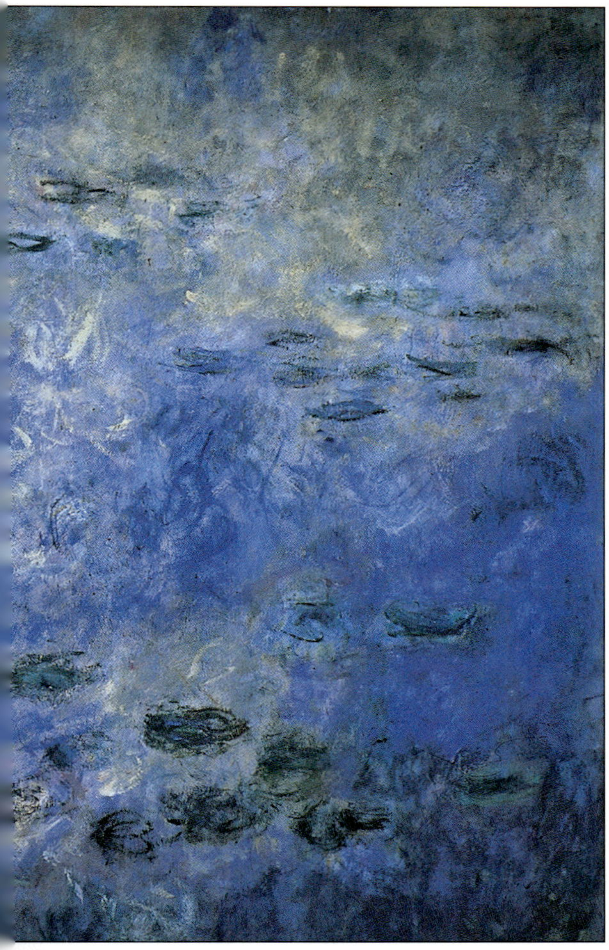

LEFT :
The Grandes Décorations
Waterlillies: Morning with Willows
(right section)
MUSÉE DE L'ORANGERIE, PARIS

it is possible that he was actually reluctant to deliver the canvases during his own lifetime. In fact, the end was closer than he or anyone realized. After falling seriously ill in spring, he rallied only briefly towards the end of 1926 before taking to his bed again. On 5 December, three weeks after his eighty-sixth birthday, a respiratory disease ended the life of Claude Monet. He was buried at Giverny, without religious ceremonial, alongside Alice, Jean and other members of his extended family. Prominent among the mourners were Michel Monet, Blanche and Georges Clemenceau, who was seen to break down in public for the only time in his life.

The Legacy

Early in 1927, the panels comprising the *Grandes Décorations* were shipped to the Orangerie and carefully glued, end to end, onto the oval walls, forming two continuous friezes broken only by the doorways. As Monet intended, they promote inner peace and fuse art and nature in a fashion wonderful to contemplate – but also none too easy to contemplate amid the crowds whose presence is a witness to Monet's wide appeal. His place among the masters has never been seriously challenged, and collectors and museums all over the world have vied with one another to acquire examples of his work. In his native France, Monet's paintings have made a triumphal progress through the great Parisian museums into the Louvre, the Musée Marmottan, the Jeu de Paume and, most recently, into the new Musée d'Orsay, a former railway station converted into a spacious treasure house, set up to celebrate nineteenth-century French art on the grand scale.

Finally, Monet has a memorial outside Paris: the house and gardens, lovingly restored in the 1980s after long neglect of Giverny, and the most enduring source of his inspiration.

Index to Illustrations

All pictures by Claude Monet unless otherwise credited

Acknowledgements

The Publisher would like to thank the following for their kind permission to reproduce the paintings in this book:

Bridgeman Art Library, London/Giraudon, Paris – 115: /**Musée d'Orsay, Paris** – 10-11, 14, 16-17, 22-3, 26-7, 34, 35, 38, 55, 58-9, 62-3, 68-9, 73, 82-83, 88-9, 90, 92-3, 94-5, 99, 106-7, 120, 122-3, 127, 138-9, 140, 155, 162-3, 165, 169, 185, 189, 197, 201, 218-9, 222, 229[also used on front cover]: /**Musée des Beaux Arts, Lille** – 137, 215: /**Musée des Beaux Arts, Le Havre** – 151, 232-3: /**Musée des Beaux Arts, Lyons** – 206-7: /**Musée des Beaux Arts, Nantes** – 242-3: /**Musée des Beaux Arts, Caen** – 230-1: /**Musée de L'Orangerie, Paris** – 246-7, 249, 250-1, 252-3: /**Museu de Arte, São Paulo, Brazil** – 170-1: /**Walters Art Gallery, Baltimore, Maryland** – 98-9: /**National Gallery of Art, Washington, DC** – 133: /**The Art Institute of Chicago** – 45:

Bridgeman Art Library, London/Private Collection – 101, 136, 156-7, 205, 235, 237: /**Noortman (London) Ltd** - 8-9: /**Musée d'Orsay, Paris** -28-9, 39, 74-5, 86, 93, 100, 179: /**Musée de Grenoble** – 245: /**Städelsches Kunstinstitut, Frankfurt** – 60: /**Wallraf-Richartz Museum, Cologne** – 13: /**Kunsthaus, Zurich** – 31: /**Kunsthalle, Hamburg** – 143: /**Kunsthalle, Bremen** – 37: /**Heydt Museum, Wuppertal** – 182: /**Kunsthistorisches Museum, Vienna** – 224-5: /**Bayerische Staatsgemaldesammlungen, Munich** – 96-7: /**Pushkin Museum, Moscow** – 33, 104-5, 128-9, 175, 198, 220-1: /**Hermitage, St Petersburg** – 50-1, 116-7, 119, 212-3: /**Museum Boymans-van Beuningen, Rotterdam** – 146-7: /**Courtauld Institute Galleries, University of London** – 91, 180: /**The National Gallery, London** – 67, 70-1, 80-1, 130-1, 226-7: /**Christie's, London** – 152-3: /**Agnew & Sons, London** – 190-1: /**Fitzwilliam Museum, University of Cambridge** – 166-7, 194-5: /**National Gallery of Scotland** – 186-7: /**National Museum of Wales, Cardiff** – 240-1: /**Hugh Lane Municipal Gallery of Modern Art, Dublin** – 211: /**Rhode Island School of Design, RI** – 76-7: /**Dallas Museum of Fine Arts, Texas** – 144-5: /**Los Angeles County Museum of Art** – 173: /**Palace of the Legion of Honor, San Francicso** – 238-9: /**Society of Fine Arts, Minneapolis** – 244-5:

Musée d'Orsay, Paris (Photographs © R.M.N.) – 18-19, 110-1, 134: / © Réunion des Musées Nationaux – 202-3
Musée Marmottan, Institut de France, Academie des Beaux Arts, Paris – 6, 109, 124-5:
The Tate gallery, London – 193:
The Metropolitan Museum of Art, New York [Copyright © 1996} – 42-3: /The bequest of William Church Osborn, 1951 [Copyright © 1951] – 46-7; /The bequest of Mrs. H. O. Havermeyer, 1929. The H.O. Havermeyer Collection [29.100.112] – 64-5:
The Art Institute of Chicago Claude Monet, French, 1840–1926 – *On the Bank of the Seine, Bennecourt* (*Au bord de l'eau, Bennecourt*), oil on canvas, 1868, 81.5 x 100.7cm. Mr. and Mrs. Potter Palmer Collection, 1922 [477]. Photograph Copyright © The Art Institute of Chicago, All Rights Reserved – 52-3: /*Bordighera*, oil on canvas, 1884, 64.8 x 81.3cm. Mr. and Mrs. Potter Palmer Collection, 1922 [426]. Photograph Copyright © The Art Institute of Chicago, All Rights Reserved. – 158-9:
The Museum of Fine Arts, Boston, Ma. Copyright © 1995 All Rights Reserved – 102-3 /Copyright © 1995 The Juliana Cheney Edwards Collection – 160-1:
Allen Memorial Art Museum, Oberlin College, Oberlin, Ohio – 41.

Every effort has been made to attribute the copyright holders of the paintings used in this publication and we apologise for any unintentional ommissions or errors. On notification we will be happy to insert an ammended credit in any subsequent edition.